Microsoft® Expression® Web 2 on Demand

D1417654

Steve Johnson

Perspection, Inc.

Que Publishing
800 East 96th Street
Indianapolis, IN 46240 USA

Microsoft® Expression® Web 2 on Demand

Library of Congress Cataloging-in-Publication Data

Johnson, Steve, 1961-
  Microsoft Expression Web 2 on demand / Steve Johnson.
      p. cm.
  ISBN 0-7897-3785-X
  1. Web sites—Authoring programs. 2. Microsoft Expression Web. I. Title.
  TK5105.8883.J66 2008
  006.7'86—dc22

2008006965

ISBN-13:   978-0-7897-3785-4
ISBN-10:   0-7897-3785-X

Printed and bound in the United States of America
First Printing: April 2008
11 10 09 08   4 3 2 1

Que Publishing offers excellent discounts on this book when ordered in quantity for bulk purchases or special sales.
For information, please contact: U.S. Corporate and Government Sales
    1-800-382-3419 or corpsales@pearsontechgroup.com
For sales outside the U.S., please contact: International Sales
    1-317-428-3341 or International@pearsontechgroup.com

Publisher
Paul Boger

Associate Publisher
Greg Wiegand

Acquisitions Editor
Loretta Yates

Managing Editor
Steve Johnson

Author
Steve Johnson

Technical Editor
Beth Teyler

Page Layout
James Teyler

Interior Designers
Steve Johnson
Marian Hartsough

Photographs
Tracy Teyler

Indexer
Katherine Stimson

Proofreader
Holly Johnson

Team Coordinator
Cindy Teeters

Acknowledgements

Perspection, Inc.

Microsoft Expression Web 2 On Demand has been created by the professional trainers and writers at Perspection, Inc. to the standards you've come to expect from Que publishing. Together, we are pleased to present this training book.

Perspection, Inc. is a software training company committed to providing information and training to help people use software more effectively in order to communicate, make decisions, and solve problems. Perspection writes and produces software training books, and develops multimedia and Web-based training. Since 1991, we have written more than 80 computer books, with several bestsellers to our credit, and sold over 5 million books.

This book incorporates Perspection's training expertise to ensure that you'll receive the maximum return on your time. You'll focus on the tasks and skills that increase productivity while working at your own pace and convenience.

We invite you to visit the Perspection Web site at:

www.perspection.com

Acknowledgements

The task of creating any book requires the talents of many hard-working people pulling together to meet impossible deadlines and untold stresses. We'd like to thank the outstanding team responsible for making this book possible: the writer, Steve Johnson; the technical editor, Beth Teyler; the production editor, James Teyler; proofreader, Holly Johnson; and the indexer, Katherine Stimson.

At Que publishing, we'd like to thank Greg Wiegand and Loretta Yates for the opportunity to undertake this project, Cindy Teeters for administrative support, and Sandra Schroeder for your production expertise and support.

Perspection

About The Author

Steve Johnson has written more than 45 books on a variety of computer software, including Microsoft Office 2007 and 2003, Microsoft Windows Vista and XP, Microsoft Expression Web, Apple Mac OS X Leopard, Adobe Photoshop CS3 and CS2, Adobe Flash CS3 and 8, and Adobe Dreamweaver CS3. In 1991, after working for Apple Computer and Microsoft, Steve founded Perspection, Inc., which writes and produces software training. When he is not staying up late writing, he enjoys playing golf, gardening, and spending time with his wife, Holly, and three children, JP, Brett, and Hannah. When time permits, he likes to travel to such places as New Hampshire in October, and Hawaii. Steve and his family live in Pleasanton, California, but can also be found visiting family all over the western United States.

We Want To Hear From You!

As the reader of this book, *you* are our most important critic and commentator. We value your opinion and want to know what we're doing right, what we could do better, what areas you'd like to see us publish in, and any other words of wisdom you're willing to pass our way.

As an associate publisher for Que, I welcome your comments. You can email or write me directly to let me know what you did or didn't like about this book—as well as what we can do to make our books better.

Please note that I cannot help you with technical problems related to the topic of this book. We do have a User Services group, however, where I will forward specific technical questions related to the book.

When you write, please be sure to include this book's title and author as well as your name, email address, and phone number. I will carefully review your comments and share them with the author and editors who worked on the book.

Email: feedback@quepublishing.com

Mail: Greg Wiegand
         Que Publishing
         800 East 96th Street
         Indianapolis, IN 46240 USA

For more information about this book or another Que title, visit our Web site at *informit.com/register*. Type the ISBN (excluding hyphens) or the title of a book in the Search field to find the page you're looking for.

This Book Is Safari Enabled

The Safari® Enabled icon on the cover of your favorite technology book means the book is available through Safari Bookshelf. When you buy this book, you get free access to the online edition for 45 days. Safari Bookshelf is an electronic reference library that lets you easily search thousands of technical books, find code samples, download chapters, and access technical information whenever and wherever you need it.

To gain 45-day Safari Enabled access to this book:

◆ Go to *http://informit.com/onlineedition*

◆ Complete the brief registration form

◆ Enter the coupon code **KKRW-XZLP-E1BC-SEPW-WZ1R**

If you have difficulty registering on Safari Bookshelf or accessing the online edition, please e-mail customer-service@safaribooksonline.com.

Contents

Introduction

Welcome to *Microsoft Expression Web 2 On Demand*, a visual quick reference book that shows you how to work efficiently with Expression Web 2. This book provides complete coverage of basic to advanced Expression Web 2 skills.

How This Book Works

You don't have to read this book in any particular order. We've designed the book so that you can jump in, get the information you need, and jump out. However, the book does follow a logical progression from simple tasks to more complex ones. Each task is presented on no more than two facing pages, which lets you focus on a single task without having to turn the page. To find the information that you need, just look up the task in the table of contents or index, and turn to the page listed. Read the task introduction, follow the step-by-step instructions in the left column along with screen illustrations in the right column, and you're done.

What's New

If you're searching for what's new in Expression Web 2, just look for the icon: **New!**. The new icon appears in the table of contents and through out this book so you can quickly and easily identify a new or improved feature in Expression Web. A complete description of each new feature appears in the New Features guide in the back of this book.

Keyboard Shortcuts

Most menu commands have a keyboard equivalent, such as Ctrl+P, as a quicker alternative to using the mouse. A complete list of keyboard shortcuts is available in the back of this book and on the Web at *www.perspection.com*.

Step-by-Step Instructions

This book provides concise step-by-step instructions that show you "how" to accomplish a task. Each set of instructions include illustrations that directly correspond to the easy-to-read steps. Also included in the text are time-savers, tables, and sidebars to help you work more efficiently or to teach you more in-depth information. A "Did You Know?" provides tips and techniques to help you work smarter, while a "See Also" leads you to other parts of the book containing related information about the task.

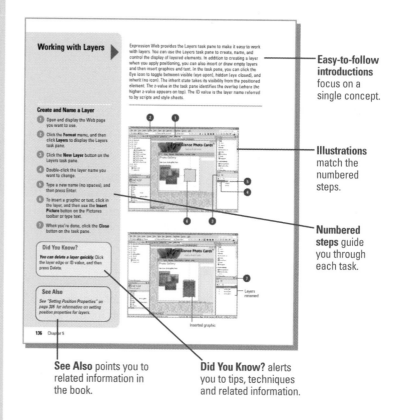

Easy-to-follow introductions focus on a single concept.

Illustrations match the numbered steps.

Numbered steps guide you through each task.

See Also points you to related information in the book.

Did You Know? alerts you to tips, techniques and related information.

Real World Examples

This book uses real world examples files to give you a context in which to use the task. By using the example files, you won't waste time looking for or creating sample files. You get a start file and a result file, so you can compare your work. Not every topic needs an example file, such as changing options, so we provide a complete list of the example files used through out the book. The example files that you need for project tasks along with a complete file list are available on the Web at *www.perspection.com*.

Real world examples help you apply what you've learned to other tasks.

Workshop

This book shows you how to put together the individual step-by-step tasks into indepth projects with the Workshop. You start each project with a sample file, work through the steps, and then compare your results with project results file at the end. The Workshop projects and associated files are available on the Web at *www.perspection.com*.

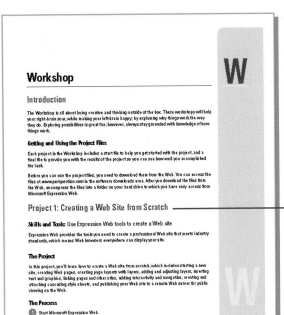

The **Workshop** walks you through indepth projects to help you put Expression Web to work.

Get More on the Web

In addition to the information in this book, you can also get more information on the Web to help you get up to speed faster with Expression Web. Some of the information includes:

More Content

◆ **Photographs.** Download photographs and other graphics to use in your Web pages.

◆ **More Content.** Download new content developed after publication.

You can access these additional resources on the Web at *www.perspection.com*.

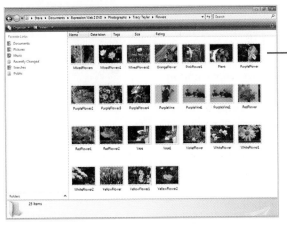

Additional content is available on the Web. You can download photographs for your own use.

Get Updates

Like any software, it continues to change and get better with updates and patches, so it's important to regularly check the Microsoft Expression Web site at *www.microsoft.com /expression*, and then click Expression Web under Products.

Check the Expression Web onlne site to **Get Updates**.

Expression Studio

Expression Web is part of the Microsoft Expression Studio, which includes Expression Design, Blend, and Media. Expression Design is a professional illustration and graphic design tool that lets you build compelling elements for both Web and desktop application user interfaces. Expression Blend is the professional design tool to create engaging, Web-connected, user experiences for Windows. Expression Media is a professional asset management tool to visually catalog and organize all your digital assets for effortless retrieval and presentation. See Chapter 16, "Working with Expression Studio" on page 385 for more information and step-by-step instructions for using individual Expression Studio programs.

Expression Studio combines Web tools to create an expanded Web development environment.

Getting Started with Expression Web 2

Introduction

Microsoft Expression Web 2 is a professional design tool to create Web sites that conform to modern, standards-based sites on the Web. Expression Web is part of the Microsoft Expression Studio, which includes Expression Design, Blend, and Media. Expression Design is a professional illustration and graphic design tool that lets you build compelling elements for both Web and desktop application user interfaces. Expression Blend is the professional design tool to create engaging, Web-connected, user experiences for Windows. Expression Media is a professional asset management tool to visually catalog and organize all your digital assets for effortless retrieval and presentation.

Before you install Expression Web 2, you need to check your computer hardware and software and make several setup decisions that relate to your computer. After installing Expression Web 2, you will find many of the same elements that you've come to know from other Microsoft programs.

There are four different Web site views in Expression Web that help you work more efficiently. The first one, Folders view displays a list of files in the Web site, organized by folder. Reports view displays a list of information and links to help manage the site. Another, Hyperlinks view shows the structure of the page links in the form of a flowchart. When you're ready to publish your Web site, Remote Web Site view displays a comparison of files in the current local Web site and the remote site.

Once you've familiarized yourself with the look and feel of Expression Web, you can begin using it by creating a simple Web page. You can insert, copy and paste text and get it ready to add more specific elements as your skills progress. After creating your page, you can save it to work on later.

What You'll Do

Prepare to Install Expression Web 2

Install Expression Web 2

Start Expression Web 2

View the Expression Web Window

Work with Toolbars

Use Task Panes

View the Folder List

Create a Simple Web Page

Save a Web Page

Open an Existing Web Page

Work with Views

Switch Between Pages and Views

Use Visual Aids

Get Help While You Work

Get Expression Web Updates on the Web

Close a Web Page

Exit Expression Web

Preparing to Install Expression Web 2

System Requirements

Before you can install Expression Web 2, you need to make sure your computer meets the minimum system requirements. You need to have a computer with the following minimum configuration:

- ◆ PC with Pentium 700 or faster processor.

- ◆ Windows XP Service Pack 2 or later or Microsoft Windows Server 2003 Service Pack 1 or later operating system.

- ◆ 512 MB of RAM or more.

- ◆ 1.5 GB of available hard disk space; a portion of this disk space will be freed after installation.

- ◆ CD-ROM or DVD-ROM drive.

- ◆ 1024 x 768 or higher resolution monitor.

- ◆ Broadband connection.

If you are not sure that your computer meets the minimum requirements, you can check your computer for the information. In Microsoft Windows XP or Vista, you can check system information on your computer using the System Information accessory. Click the Start button on the taskbar, point to All Programs, click Accessories, click System Tools, and then click System Information. You can also access the System Information accessory from within Expression Web. Click the Help menu, click About Microsoft Expression Web 2, and then click System Info. In the System Information window, click System Summary to find out the information you need about your computer.

Install Microsoft .NET Framework First

Before you can install Expression Web, you need to install Microsoft .NET Framework 2.0, 3.0, 3.5 (recommended) (**New!**), or later. The software is available at *www.microsoft.com/downloads*

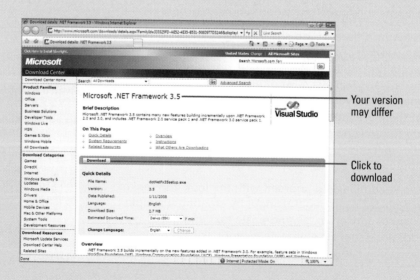

Your version may differ

Click to download

Installing Expression Web 2

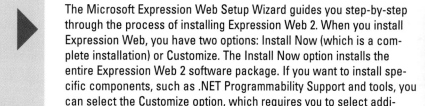

The Microsoft Expression Web Setup Wizard guides you step-by-step through the process of installing Expression Web 2. When you install Expression Web, you have two options: Install Now (which is a complete installation) or Customize. The Install Now option installs the entire Expression Web 2 software package. If you want to install specific components, such as .NET Programmability Support and tools, you can select the Customize option, which requires you to select additional options as you step through the Expression Web Setup Wizard.

Install Expression Web 2

1 Insert the Microsoft Expression Web 2 disc into your drive.

The Microsoft Expression Web Setup Wizard appears.

◆ If the Setup Wizard doesn't start, open the disc, and then locate and double-click the WebDesigner.exe icon. You can also download the software from the Microsoft Web site at *www.microsoft.com*.

◆ You can also purchase and download the software from the Microsoft Expression site at *www.microsoft.com/expression*, and then double-click the downloaded file.

2 Type the 25-character product key, type the optional code, and then click **Continue**.

3 Click **Install Now** or **Customize**.

4 If you selected a custom installation, select the options you want and follow the Setup Wizard.

The Installation Progress bar appears, displaying the progress of the installation.

5 When the installation is complete, click **Close**.

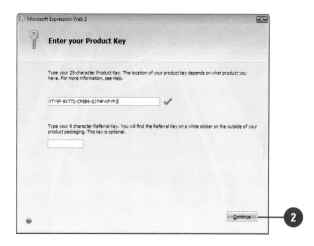

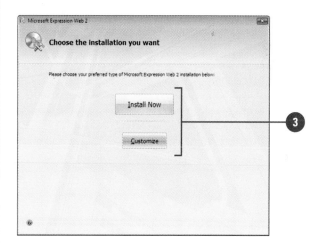

Starting Expression Web 2

When you first open Expression Web 2, the program window opens, displaying a blank new page, menus, a toolbar, task panes, and a status bar. The title bar across the top of the screen contains the program and Web site name, with the menu bar directly below it, and the Common toolbar below the menu bar. The task panes provide options that relate to the current task. The View tabs—which offer access to Design, Split, and Code modes—occupy a small area at the bottom of the screen. These tabs allow you to view pages from different perspectives; the program's default is Design view.

Start Expression Web 2 Using the Start Menu

1 Click the **Start** button on the taskbar.

2 Point to **All Programs**.

3 Click **Microsoft Expression**.

4 Click **Microsoft Expression Web 2**.

The Expression Web 2 program opens and a blank new page appears, ready for you to enter text. By default, this page is titled *Untitled_1.htm.*

5 If prompted to set Expression Web as your default HTML editor, click **Yes** or **No**.

◆ If you don't want to perform this check each time you start Expression Web, clear the **Always perform this check when starting Expression Web** check box.

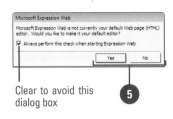

Clear to avoid this dialog box **5**

Did You Know?

You should close the blank page before creating a new site. Before you begin working on a new site, close the blank page that opens when you start Expression Web. If you don't, it will be added automatically as the first page of your Web site.

Viewing the Expression Web Window

Expression Web 2 appears with an updated gray color scheme for the program window (**New!**) that complements the look of other Microsoft Expression Studio programs. The gray color scheme is only applied to the program window, dialog boxes continue to use your Windows color scheme. If you prefer to view the Expression Web program window with your Windows color scheme instead of

the new gray color scheme, you can change it in the Application Options dialog box (**New!**). Simply, click the Tools menu, click Application Options, click the General tab, select the Use your current Windows color scheme check box, click OK, click OK to alert, exit Expression Web, and then restart it. For purposes of consistency, the screen shots in this book use the Windows color scheme.

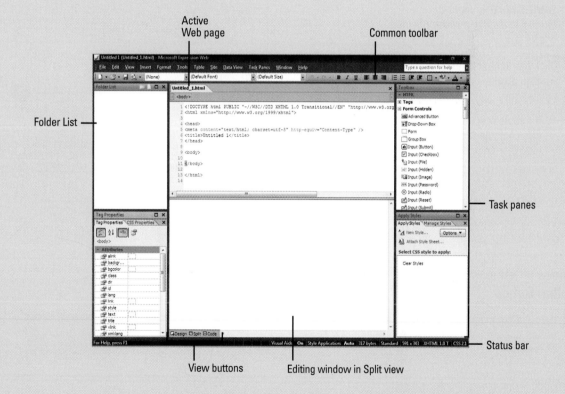

Active Web page

Common toolbar

Folder List

Task panes

Apply Styles

Tag Properties

View buttons

Editing window in Split view

Status bar

Working with Toolbars

Toolbars contain buttons you can click to carry out commands you use frequently. Expression Web provides 11 different toolbars for you to use to execute commands. The Common toolbar appears by default under the menu bar and provides the most commonly (as the name suggests) used commands. You can quickly show or hide the toolbars you need or no longer using to customize the way you use Expression Web. When you show a toolbar (except the Common toolbar), it displays in separate window by default, known as **undocked**. The Common toolbar under the menu bar appears as **docked**, or attached to a window. If you need to move or resized toolbar, you can make the changes using the mouse.

Show or Hide a Toolbar

1 Click the **View** menu, and then point to **Toolbars**.

> **TIMESAVER** *Right-click a toolbar to display a shortcut menu of toolbars.*

2 Click the unchecked toolbar you want to display or the checked toolbar you want to hide.

◆ If a toolbar is undocked, you can click the **Close** button to hide the toolbar.

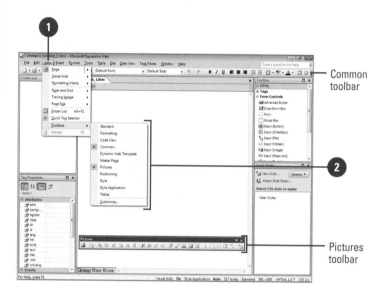

Common toolbar

Pictures toolbar

Choose a Command Using a Toolbar Button

1 If you're not sure what a toolbar button does, point to it to display a ScreenTip.

2 To choose a command, click a toolbar button or click the **Toolbar Options** list arrow, and then click a toolbar button.

When you select a button from the list arrow, the button appears on the toolbar, showing only the buttons you use most often.

Move or Resize a Toolbar

◆ **Move**. Point to the title bar of a undocked toolbar or the dotted lines on the left side of a docked toolbar, then click and drag (the cursor changes to a four-headed arrow) the toolbar to a new location.

◆ **Resize**. Point to the edge of a undocked toolbar, and then click and drag (the cursor changes to a two-headed arrow) to enlarge or reduce the toolbar.

◆ **Dock** or **Undock**. Move the toolbar towards or away from the toolbars under the menu bar. As an undocked toolbar approaches the other toolbars, it snaps in place (docked).

Did You Know?

You can use menus to execute commands. Instead of using toolbars to execute commands, you can also use the menu bar. An icon to the left on a menu means a toolbar button is available for that command. A keyboard combination to the right of a menu command indicates a shortcut key is available for the command.

Drag to move

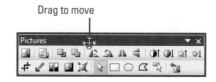

Drag to resize

Drag here to dock

Drag to undock

Using Task Panes

When you start Expression Web, four task panes appear by default: Folder List, Tag Properties, Apply Styles, and Toolbox. You can open any of the 18 task panes in the Expression Web window using the Task Panes menu. The task panes are grouped together in a window based on the sections displayed on the Task Panes menu and appear as tabs in the same task pane. Each task pane displays various options that relate to the title. When you open and close task panes or move them around, Expression Web saves the arrangement and uses it as the default the next time you start the program. When you no longer need a task pane or need more room, you can close a task pane.

Open and Close Task Panes

◆ **Open**. Click the **Task Panes** menu, then click the closed task pane you want to open. The task panes with a check mark next to the name are already open.

◆ **Close**. Click the **Task Panes** menu, then click the open task pane you want to close, or click the **Close** button in the upper-right corner of the task pane.

Click to open or close

Maximize and Minimize Task Panes

◆ **Maximize**. Click the **Maximize** button in the upper-right corner of a docked task pane. The task pane expands to show more elements.

◆ **Minimize**. Click the **Restore Window** button in the upper-right corner of a docked task pane. The task pane collapses to its original size.

Maximize

Restore window

Display Content in Task Panes

◆ **Switch Tabs**. Click a visible tab to display it in front.

   If there are to many tabs to display, click the left or right arrow below the title bar to scroll to the tab you want.

◆ **View Tools**. In the Toolbox, click the plus sign (+) to expand a single category or click the minus sign (-) to collapse a single category.

   TIMESAVER *Right-click the Toolbox pane title bar, then click a view command to Collapse All, Expand All, Icons Only, Names Only, or Icons and Names.*

Rearrange Task Panes

◆ **Dock**. Click the pane's title bar or tab name, and then drag it to either side of the Editing window. As an undocked task pane approaches the other task panes, it snaps in place (docked).

◆ **Undock**. Click the pane's title bar or tab name, and then drag it to a new location.

◆ **Move**. Click the pane's title bar or tab name, and then drag it within the pane area.

◆ **Restore Default Positions**. Click the **Task Panes** menu, and then click **Reset Workspace Layout**. Expression Web displays the four default task panes in their original position.

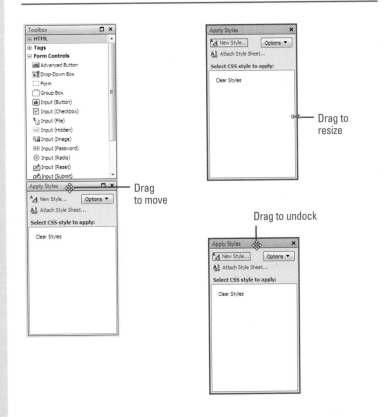

Switch Tabs

View tools

Drag to resize

Drag to move

Drag to undock

Viewing the Folder List

The **Folder List** is a useful task pane for managing files and folders. When you create or open a Web site, a tab for the site appears at the top of the Editing window, with all the site's file listed in the window and adjacent Folder List. The Folder List displays the file hierarchy of all the folders and files in your Web site, and the Editing window displays Web site files and folders, or individual Web pages. This arrangement enables you to view the file hierarchy of your Web site and the contents of a folder simultaneously, making it easy to copy, move, delete, and rename files and folders. Using the plus sign (+) and the minus sign (-) to the left of an icon in the Folder List allows you to display different levels of folders in your Web site without opening and displaying the contents of each folder. You can open folders and files by double-clicking them. When you open a Web page, the icon changes (adding a pencil) to make easier to identify.

View the Folder List

1. Open the Web site in which you want to view.

2. If necessary, click the **View** menu, and then click **Folder List** to display the Folder List.

3. Perform the commands you want to display folder structure and contents:

   ◆ To show the file and folder structure, click the plus sign (+).

   ◆ To hide the file and folder structure, click the minus sign (-).

   ◆ To display the contents of a folder, click the folder icon.

   ◆ To open a file, double-click the file.

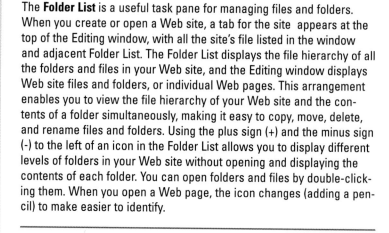
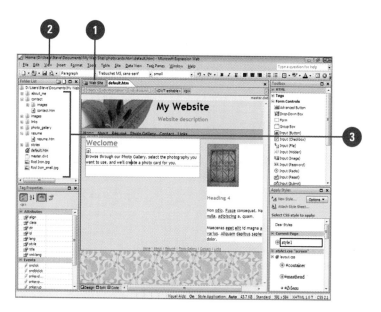

Did You Know?

You can quickly determine if a folder contains folders. When neither plus sign (+) nor minus sign (-) appears next to an icon in the Folder List, the item has no folders in it.

Creating a Simple Web Page

When you start Expression Web, a blank new page appears, ready for you to enter text. By default, this page is titled *Untitled_1.htm*. You can create new Web pages and sites in several ways: using the New Document button on the Common toolbar or the New command on the File menu. Expression Web numbers new pages consecutively. The insertion point (blinking cursor bar) appears in the page where text will appear when you type. As you type, text moves, or wraps, to a new line when the previous one is full. You can move the insertion point anywhere within the page so that you can insert new text and edit (or insert, revise, or delete) existing text. You can copy or move items (including blocks of text) from one place to another within a Web page, or from other programs.

Create a Web Page

1 Click the **New Document** button on the Common toolbar.

◆ You can also use the **File** menu, point to **New**, and select the page type you want. The default page type is HTML.

2 Click where you want to insert text, or select the text you want to edit.

3 Make the change you want:

◆ Type to insert new text.

◆ Press Enter to begin a new paragraph or insert a blank line.

◆ Press Backspace or Delete to erase text to the left or right of the insertion point.

◆ Use the Copy or Cut and Paste buttons on the Common toolbar to copy or move items around.

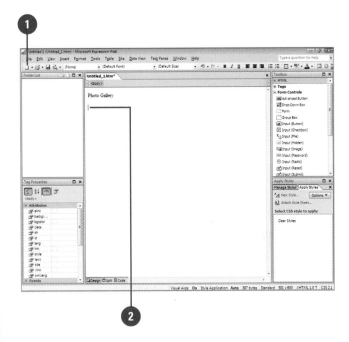

Saving a Web Page

Saving your files frequently ensures that you don't lose work during an unexpected power loss. The first time you save a Web page, specify a file name and folder in the Save As dialog box. The next time you save using the Save button on the toolbar or Save command on the File menu, Expression Web saves the file with the same name in the same folder. If you want to change a file's name or location, you can use the Save As dialog box again to create a copy of the original file.

Save a Web Page

1. Create or open the Web page you want to save.

2. Click the **File** menu, and then click **Save As**.

   TIMESAVER *Click the Save button on the Common toolbar to save a Web page or open the Save As dialog box for a new page.*

3. Click an icon on the Navigation pane (Vista) or Places bar (XP) to open a frequently used folder.

4. Navigate to the drive and folder location where you want to save the Web page.

5. Type a name for the page, or use the suggested name.

6. To edit the page title, click **Change title**, type a title for the page, and then click **OK**.

7. Click **Save**.

8. If the Save Embedded Files dialog box appears, click **OK**.

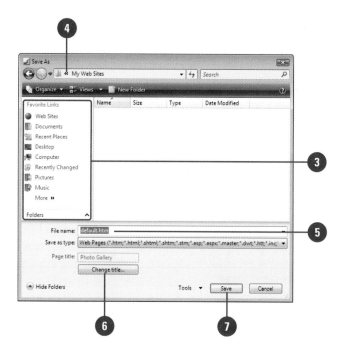

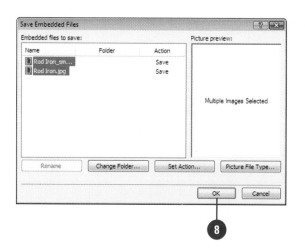

Did You Know?

You can delete, rename, move, or copy a file in a dialog box. In the Open or Save As dialog box, right-click the file, and then click Delete or Rename. To move or copy, right-click the file, click Cut or Copy, open a folder, right-click a blank area, and then click Paste.

Opening an Existing Web Page

Opening a Web page is a simple procedure and can be accomplished using the Open button list arrow on the Standard toolbar. You can open a Web page from your local hard drive, a network drive, or a Web server using an Uniform Resource Locator (URL). By default, Expression Web opens the last Web site you worked on every time you open the program. If you open a new page while another site is still open, the new page opens in a new Expression Web window. For Web pages you recently opened, you can quickly reopen them again by pointing to Recent Web Pages on the File menu, and then selecting the Web page you want to open.

Open a Web Page in Page View

1. Click the **Open** button list arrow on the Common toolbar, and then click **Open**.

2. Click an icon on the Navigation pane (Vista) or Places bar (XP) to open a frequently used folder.

3. Navigate to the drive and folder location where you want to open the Web page.

4. Select the page you want to open from the page list in the working folder, or type the URL of the page you want.

5. Click **Open**.

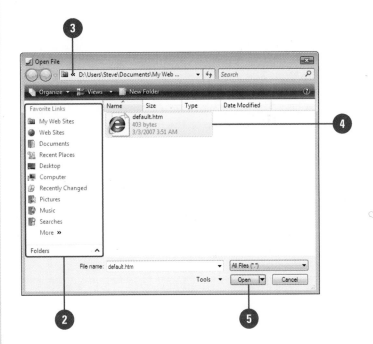

Did You Know?

You can open a recently opened Web page. If you've recently accessed a Web page, you can use the File menu to quickly open it again. Click the File menu, point to Recent Files, and then click the file you want.

See Also

See "Opening Web Pages from Within a Web" on page 46 for information on opening Web pages within a Web site.

Working with Views

Expression Web displays the contents of a Web site and Web page in different ways to help you work efficiently with your content. When you click a Web Site tab, Expression Web displays four views at the bottom of the window, which you can also access from the Site menu.

Folders view displays a list of files in the Web site, organized by folder. From this view, you can manage files and folders, and open files with the corresponding editor.

Remote Web Site view displays a comparison of files in the current local Web site and the remote site. From this view, you can copy a working version of a site to the live site on a service provider's Web server.

Reports view displays a list of information and links to help manage the site.

Hyperlinks view displays files in a site, organized by hyperlink reference.

When you click a Web page or document tab, Expression Web enters Page view and displays as many as three views at the bottom of the window.

Design view displays Web pages in WYSIWYG (What You See Is What You Get) view for editing.

Split view displays the screen in half horizontally. The top half displays the current page in Code view and the bottom half displays the current page in Design view.

Code view displays the HTML and any embedded code for a page.

Folders view

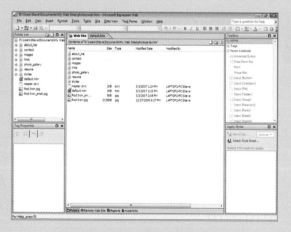

Remote Web Site view

Reports view

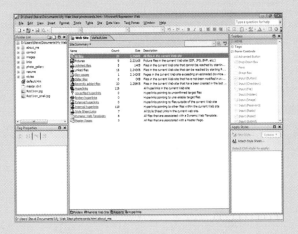

Hyperlinks view

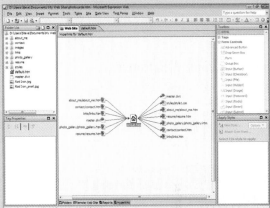

Page view

Design, Split, and Code views

Switching Between Pages and Views

The tabs across the top of the Editing window indicate the currently open Web pages and sites. You can click the tab to display the page or site you want. At the bottom of the Editing window, the view buttons—Design, Split, and Code—appear for the currently page tab. Design view displays the page or site as it appears on screen, while Code view displays the HTML code that makes up the page or site. Split view shows you Code view at the top and Design view at the bottom. This view is helpful for learning how the code and design elements work.

Switch Between Web Pages and Sites

◆ **Web Pages** or **Web Sites**. Click the tab with the name you want to display.

> **TIMESAVER** *Press Ctrl+Tab or Ctrl+Shift+Tab to cycle to the tab you want.*

Click tabs to switch pages or sites

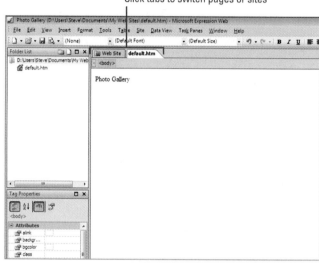

Switch Between Page Views

◆ **Switch Views**. Click the **Design**, **Split**, or **Code** button at the bottom of the Editing window, or click the **View** menu, point to **Page,** and then click the view you want.

> **TIMESAVER** *Press Ctrl+Pg Up or Ctrl+Pg Dn to cycle to the view you want.*

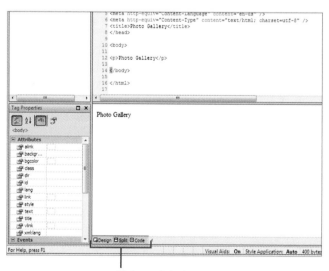

Click to switch views

Using Visual Aids

When you're working in Design or Split view, you can use Expression Web visual aids to make it easier to work with page elements, such as borders, margins and cell padding that are normally invisible. Sometimes it's hard to adjust elements without being able to see the edge. For example, the Margins and Padding command on the Visual Aids submenu makes it easier to view and change the margins and table cell padding on a page. You can show or hide all the visual aids at once or select each item individually. The Visual Aid menu highlights the menu icon or display a checkmark when a visual aid is turned on.

Show or Hide Visual Aids

◆ **All**. Click the **View** menu, point to **Visual Aids,** and then click **Show**.

> **TIMESAVER** *Press Ctrl+/ (forward slash) or double-click Visual Aids in the status bar to show or hide all visual aids.*

◆ **Individual**. Click the **View** menu, point to **Visual Aids,** and then click each item you want to show or hide.

The Visual Aids submenu remains open until you click away, so you can click multiple items.

Click to show/hide all

Click to show/hide individual items

Getting Help While You Work

At some time, everyone has a question or two about the program they are using. The Expression Web Help Viewer provides the answers and resources you need, including feature help and related information. The Web browser-like Help Viewer allows you to browse an extensive catalog of topics using a table of contents to locate information, or ask a question or enter phrases to search for specific information. When you use any of these help options, a list of possible answers is shown to you with the most likely answer or most frequently-used at the top of the list.

Use the Help Viewer to Get Answers

1 Click the **Help** menu, and then click **Microsoft Expression Web Help**.

TIMESAVER *Press F1.*

2 Locate the Help topic you want.

- ◆ Click a Help category on the home page, and then click a topic (? icon).

- ◆ Click the **Table of Contents** button on the toolbar, click a help category (book icon) and then click a topic (? icon).

3 Read the topic, and then click any links to get Help information.

4 Click the **Back**, **Forward**, **Stop**, **Refresh**, and **Home** buttons on the toolbar to move around in the Help Viewer.

5 If you want to print the topic, click the **Print** button on the toolbar.

6 To keep the Help Viewer window (not maximized) on top or behind, click to toggle the **Keep On Top** button (pin pushed in) and **Not On Top** button (pin not pushed in) on the toolbar.

7 When you're done, click the **Close** button.

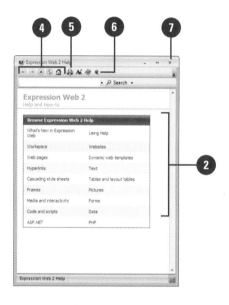

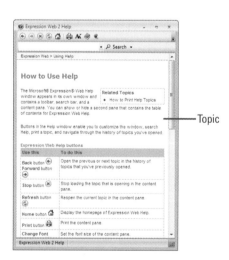

Topic

Search for Help

① Click the **Help** button on the Ribbon.

② Click the **Search** button list arrow below the toolbar, and then select the location and type of information you want.

③ Type one or more keywords in the Search For box, and then click the **Search** button.

④ Click a topic.

⑤ Read the topic, and then click any links to get information on related topics or definitions.

⑥ When you're done, click the **Close** button.

Get Help in a Dialog Box

① Display the dialog box in which you want to get help.

② Click the **Help** button (? icon).

The Expression Web Help window opens, displaying help related to the dialog box.

③ Read the topic, and then click any links to get information on related topics or definitions.

④ When you're done, click the **Close** button.

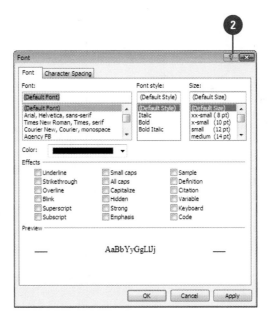

Getting Expression Web Updates on the Web

Expression Web offers a quick and easy way to get updates of any new software downloads that improve the stability and security of the program. From the Help menu, simply select the Check for Updates command to connect to the Microsoft Expression Web Online Web site, where you can have your computer scanned for necessary updates, and then choose which updates you want to download and install. You can use Microsoft Expression Web Online Web site to check out other options that are available. Using the links on the Expression Web site, you can check out Expression Web-related news, obtain the most up-to-date help from Microsoft, and locate training and assistance with any aspect of Expression Web.

Get Expression Web Updates on the Web

1 Click the **Help** menu.

2 Click **Check for Updates**.

The Microsoft Expression Web Online Web site opens, displaying the Downloads page.

3 Check the Web site to find out if you need Expression Web updates, and then choose the updates you want to download and install.

4 When you're done, click the **Close** button.

> ### Did You Know?
>
> **You can access other helpful resources from the Help menu.** The Help menu also includes commands to access other helpful resources, including Microsoft Expression Web Online, Extending Expression Web, Contact Us, Privacy Statement, Activate Product, Privacy Options, Community, and About Microsoft Expression Web.

3 Your screen may differ

Closing a Web Page

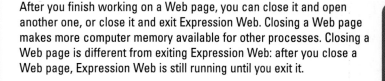

After you finish working on a Web page, you can close it and open another one, or close it and exit Expression Web. Closing a Web page makes more computer memory available for other processes. Closing a Web page is different from exiting Expression Web: after you close a Web page, Expression Web is still running until you exit it.

Close a Web Page

1. Click the **File** menu, and then click **Close**.

   TIMESAVER *Click the tab to display the Web page, and then click the Close button in the Editing window.*

2. Click **Yes** to save any Web changes; click **No** to close the Web without saving any changes; or click **Cancel** to return to the Web without closing it.

> ### Did You Know?
>
> *You can close all Web pages at one time.* Click the Window menu, and then click Close All Pages.

Click to close active Web page

Exiting Expression Web

After you finish working on a Web page or site, you can close it and exit Expression Web. If you haven't saved your changes, Expression Web asks you to save or ignore them. After you make a selection, Expression Web performs the command, closes the Web page or site, and exits the program.

Exit Expression Web

1. Click the **File** menu, and then click **Exit**, or click the **Close** button on the Expression Web program window title bar.

2. Click **Yes** to save any Web changes, or click **No** to ignore any changes.

Click to exit Expression Web

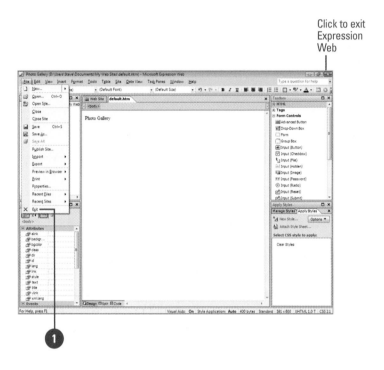

Creating a Web Site

Introduction

Before jumping in and letting your creative energy take over, it's wise to plan out what you want your Web site to accomplish. Taking the time now to plan your overall ideas and getting them down on paper will save you hours of work later on. Maybe you want to create a business site that will have a corporate style to it. Perhaps you're a hobbyist who wants to display your favorite collection. Either way, having an image and content to match your product will take some planning and research.

Microsoft Expression Web helps you create a Web site in two general ways—by a template or from scratch. A **template** opens a Web site with predefined headings, links, and placeholder text that specifies what information you should enter.

As far as content, Expression Web makes it easy to import a file, folder or an entire Web site. There is a wizard, called the Import Web Site Wizard, that can step you through the process. If you find that you need to insert a page or two into your site, you can do it through a blank page, or even using a template to add a page or two. After you finish working with a Web site, you can to save the material.

If you want to use an entire Web site or some individual Web pages in another site, you can create a Personal Web Package, which allows you to export the Web content you want from a Web site in a single file that you can import into another Web site. If you no longer need a Web site, you can delete it.

What You'll Do

Plan a Web Site

Create a Web Site Using a Template

Work with Template Content

Manage Template Content

Create a One Page Web Site

Open an Existing Web Site

Import Web Content

Add Pages to Your Web Site

Create a Personal Web Package

Save a Web Site

Rename a Web Site

Delete a Web Site

Planning a Web Site

Before you begin developing your Web site in Expression Web, there are several issues to consider and a few decisions to make. First, of course, is the question of what type of Web site you want to build. What is the focus of your design? Are you looking to create a personal site? Maybe you want to create a business or organization site.

Web Site Templates

After you've considered these questions, you need to decide whether you intend to work from a template or create your Web site from scratch. Creating a Web site one page at a time is a lot harder than using a template. Expression Web provides a variety of templates representing the most popular Web site styles. A **template** provides a complete multiple-page site with Web pages, a common look and navigation system, and placeholders for your content. After you create a site using a template, you can customize it to your specific needs by replacing the headers, textual arrangements, or graphic elements.

When you create a Web site, Expression Web creates Web page files, Cascading Style Sheets (CSS) files, script files, image files, and other folders for the purpose of organizing site files. Expression Web tracks files and folders in a Web site using hidden files known as **metadata**. The hidden files are stored in hidden folders that begin with _vti in the main Web site folder. You don't need to change anything in these folders, you just need to know why they exist if they become visible.

Types of Web Sites

When you create a Web site, you need to decide which type of site you want to create. There are three types of Web sites: Disk-based, FTP (File Transfer Protocol), and HTTP (Hyper-Text Transfer Protocol) or secure HTTP (HTTPS) with Secure Sockets Layer (SSL).

A disk-based Web site is located at a specific disk location, which can be a local hard disk or network drive, and useful for Intranets (internal Web sites) or publishing to a remote Web server later. An FTP site is typically located on a remote Web server and useful for fast file transfer and working remotely. An HTTP or HTTPS site is located on a remote Web server and useful for browsing Web pages and working remotely. If you want additional security and your Web server is configured to allow SSL visitors, you can enable SSL so credentials are encrypted.

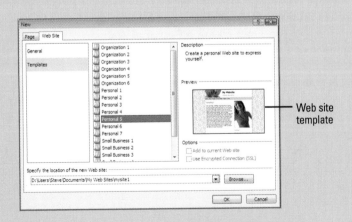

Web site template

Creating a Web Site Using a Template

Expression Web comes with templates that make it easy to create a Web site. A **template** opens a Web site with predefined headings, links, and placeholder text that specifies what information you should enter (such as your address). A Web site template includes a set of related Web pages with established links ready for you to customize the content and the necessary CSS files to create a uniform display. You can use the Web Site tab on the New dialog box to create a Web site using templates, which include One Page Web Site, Empty Web Site, and several site variations for Organization, Personal, and Small Business.

Create a Web Site Using a Template

1. Click the **New** button list arrow on the Common toolbar, and then click **Web Site**.

   The New dialog box opens, displaying the Web Site tab.

2. In the first pane, click **Templates**.

3. Click the template icon you want to use.

4. Specify the location where you want to store the Web site (click **Browse**, if necessary) and a name at the end.

   ◆ **Disk-based**. Enter a path location. For example: C:\web site\mysite

   ◆ **FTP**. Enter an ftp site address. For example: ftp://ftp.website.com/mysite

   ◆ **HTTP**. Enter an http site address. For example: http://www.website.com/mysite

5. If you specify an http site, select the **Use Encrypted Connection (SSL)** check box to create a secure site.

6. Click **OK**.

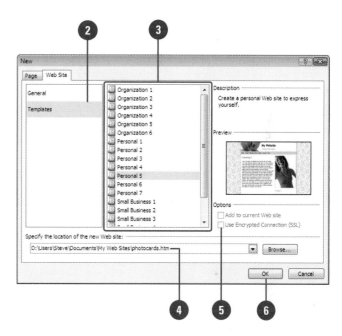

Working with Template Content

After you create a template or open an existing one, you can replace the content on any of the pages with your own material. The site's home page—the first page that appears when you type a URL—is called *default.htm*. When you open the home page, you can select elements, such as headlines, text, or images and insert new content. If an element is shared by multiple pages, such as the site's name or navigation bar, you need to open the locked content in a .dwt file (typically called *master .dwt*). When you make changes on a Web site or page, an asterisk (*) appears on the tab next to the name indicating changes have not been saved.

Open Template Pages

① Open the Web site based on a template you want to change.

② Double-click the file you want to open in the Folder List.

   ◆ **Home page**. Double-click default.htm.

   ◆ **Master page**. Double-click master.dwt.

③ Select and replace the elements you want, such as text, headings, site name, or navigation.

④ Click the **Save** button on the Common toolbar.

   TIMESAVER *To save all files at once, click the File menu, and then click Save All.*

   An alert message appears, asking if you want to save your changes.

⑤ Click **Yes**, and then click **Close** to close the status dialog box.

   Any changes made to the master appear on the home page and all other site pages.

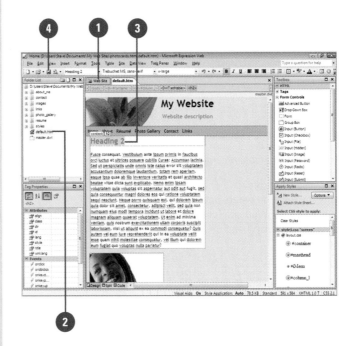

Replace Content in Template Pages

1. Open the Web page with the template content you want to replace.

2. Select the heading or paragraph text you want to change.

3. Type or paste in your own text.

4. Select an image you want to replace.

5. Click the **Insert** menu, point to **Picture**, and then click **From File**.

   The Picture dialog box opens.

6. Locate and select the picture you want to insert.

7. Click **Insert**.

   The Accessibility Properties dialog box opens.

8. Type a description.

9. Click **OK**.

   The original image is replaced by the new image. You can resize the graphic to fit where you want.

See Also

See "Resizing and Resampling Graphics" on page 128 for information on resizing graphics and using the Pictures toolbar.

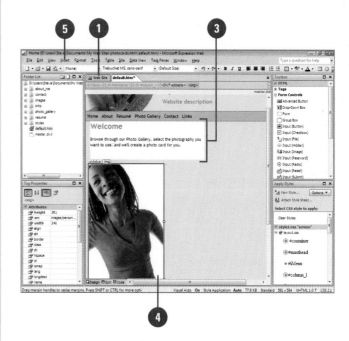

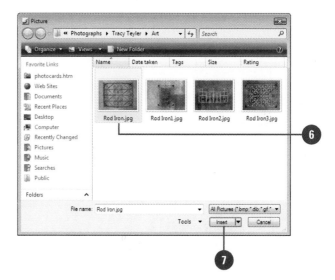

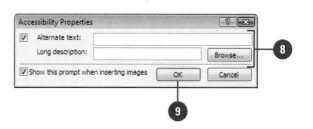

Managing Template Content

When you create a Web site from a template, you are bound to get files and folders from Expression Web you don't need. You can quickly right-click the file or folder you no longer want in the Folder List and delete it from the site. Since the template files all work together, you can copy a template file from the site and save it with a new name to create a new Web page that works with the other Web site files.

Delete a Template Page, File, or Folder

① Open the Web site based on a template you want to change.

② In the Folder List, right-click the file or folder you want to remove, and then click **Delete**.

③ Click **Yes** to confirm the deletion.

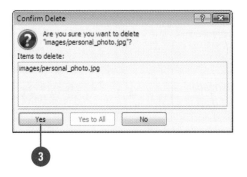

Copy a Template Page to Create a New Web Page

1. Open the Web site based on a template you want to change.

2. In the Folder List, right-click the template file you want to use as the basis for a new Web page file, and then click **New From Existing Page**.

A new untitled page appears in the Editing window with content and formats from the original template Web page.

New untitled Web page

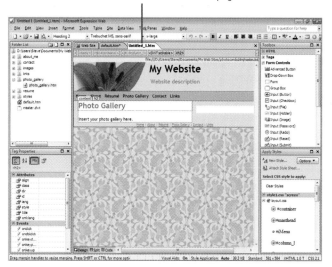

Creating a One Page Web Site

When you start Expression Web, a blank Web page opens based on a default blank template. The default blank template defines the page margins, default font, and other settings. The blank Web page doesn't become a Web site until you save it. Instead of starting Expression Web and saving the new page, you can use the New dialog box to quickly create a one page blank Web site, which you can fill in. You can then add new pages easily and link them together to create a connected Web site. If you need a blank Web site without any of the related files and folders that come along with it, you can create an empty Web site.

Create a Blank One Page Web Site

1. Click the **New** button list arrow on the Common toolbar, and then click **Web Site**.

   The New dialog box opens, displaying the Web Site tab.

2. In the first pane, click **General** if necessary.

3. Click **One Page Web Site**.

4. Specify the location where you want to store the Web site (click **Browse**, if necessary) and a name at the end.

   ◆ **Disk-based**. Enter a path location. For example: *C:\web site\mysite*

   ◆ **FTP**. Enter an ftp site address. For example: ftp://ftp.website.com/mysite

   ◆ **HTTP**. Enter an http site address. For example: *http://www.website.com/mysite*

5. If you specify an ftp or http site, select the **Use Encrypted Connection (SSL)** check box to create a secure site.

6. Click **OK**.

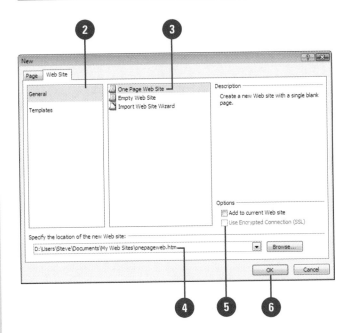

Create a Empty Web Site

1. Click the **New** button list arrow on the Common toolbar, and then click **Web Site**.

   The New dialog box opens, displaying the Web Site tab.

2. In the first pane, click **General** if necessary.

3. Click **Empty Web Site**.

4. Specify the location where you want to store the Web site (click **Browse**, if necessary) and a name at the end.

   - **Disk-based**. Enter a path location. For example: *C:\web site\mysite*

   - **FTP**. Enter an ftp site address. For example: ftp://ftp.website.com/mysite

   - **HTTP**. Enter an http site address. For example: *http://www.website.com/mysite*

5. If you specify an ftp or http site, select the **Use Encrypted Connection (SSL)** check box to create a secure site.

6. Click **OK**.

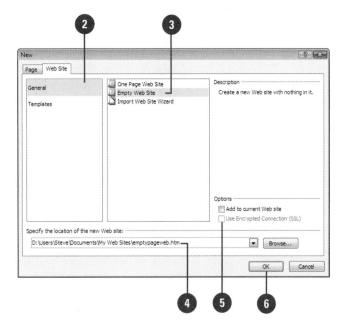

Opening an Existing Web Site

If you need to update an existing Web site, Expression Web gives you ways to open the site. You can use the Open button list arrow on the Common toolbar or the Recent Sites command on the File menu. You can open a Web site from your local hard drive, a network drive, or a Web server using a Web address, known as a **Uniform Resource Locator (URL)**. If you type a file name in the Site name box, Expression Web opens that file using the Windows file system. If you type a Web address, such as *www.mywebsite.com*, Expression Web retrieves all the files from that location just like a browser. When you open several pages at the same time, they all appear in the same window. However, if you open a new site while another site is still open, the new site opens in a new Expression Web window.

Open a Web Site from a Local Computer

1. Click the **Open** button list arrow on the Common toolbar, and then click **Open Site**.

2. Click an icon on the Navigation pane (Vista) or Places bar (XP) to open a frequently used folder.

3. Navigate to the drive and folder location where you want to open the Web site.

4. Select the Web folder with the site you want to open.

5. Click **Open**.

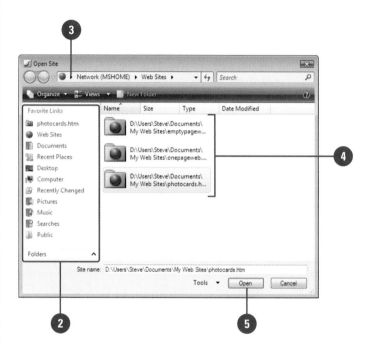

Did You Know?

You can open a recently opened Web site. If you've recently accessed a Web site, you can use the File menu to quickly open it again. Click the File menu, point to Recent Sites, and then click the site you want.

You can automatically open the last opened site. Click the Tools menu, click Applications Options, select the Open last Web site automatically when Expression Web starts check box, and then click OK.

Open a Web Site from a Web Server

1. Click the **Open** button list arrow on the Common toolbar, and then click **Open Site**.

2. Type the URL (either an http or ftp address) or select an existing shortcut to the Web site you want open.

3. Click **Open**.

4. Type the user name and password for the Web server.

5. Click **OK**.

   The Remote Web Site Editing Options dialog box opens.

6. Click the **Edit live Web site now** or **Edit local copy now, and publish changes to the server later** option.

7. Click **OK**.

   The Web site opens, displaying the site folders and files in the Folder List.

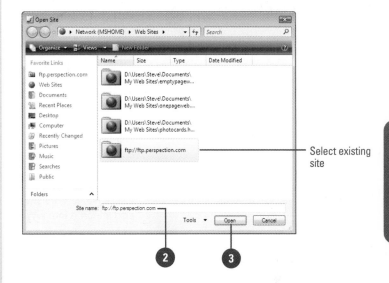

Select existing site

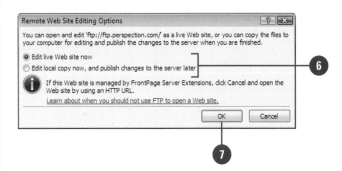

For Your Information

Internet URLs

A URL (Uniform Resource Locator) is like a postal address, each part of the address helps indicate where it's supposed to go. The entire address includes the Hypertext Transfer Protocol (HTTP), a colon, two forward slashes, and the site type (usually www for World Wide Web). This is followed by the domain address (the site's name), a period, and the domain name (refers to the type of site, such as .com for commercial). A sample URL is *http://www.quepublishing.com*.

Importing Web Content

When you're working on a Web site, you might want to import a page file (or even an entire folder) or an entire site that was created in Microsoft FrontPage or another program. Expression Web makes it easy to import a file, folder, or a Web site. When you import a Web site, Expression Web uses the Import Web Site Wizard to step you through the process. The wizards helps you transfer files using FrontPage Server Extensions, WebDAV (Distributed Authoring and Versioning), FTP (File Transfer Protocol), Windows file system, and HTTP (directly from a Web site on the Internet). When you import a site created with FrontPage, Expression Web recognizes the pages and the code (with FrontPage Server Extensions) behind it. However, you can use the code on new pages, which means you'll need to modify the pages over time to meet standard coding. If you have a Personal Web Package, which is a reusable Web site or parts of a Web site in a single file, you can also import it into a Web site.

Import Web Content from a File or Folder

1 Open the Web site in which you want to import Web content.

2 Click the **File** menu, point to **Import**, and then click **File**.

3 Click **Add File** or **Add Folder**.

4 Navigate to the location with the file, folder, or URL you want to import, and then click the file or folder.

5 Click **Open** to add it to the Import dialog box.

6 Select all the files that you want to import.

7 Click **OK**.

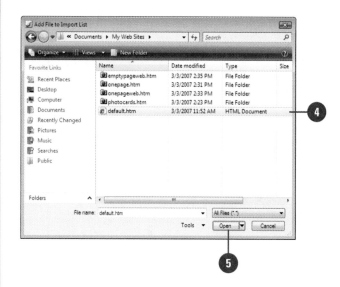

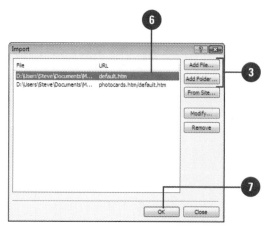

Did You Know?

You can import a Personal Web Package. Click the File menu, point to Import, click Personal Web Package, locate and select the Web Package file (.fwp), and then click Open. Expression Web creates a new folder with the same name as the imported file.

Import Web Content from a Web Site

1. Open the Web site in which you want to import Web content.

2. Click the **File** menu, point to **Import**, and then click **Import Web Site Wizard**.

   The Import Web Site Wizard dialog box opens.

3. Click the option indicating how you want to get the files.

4. Type a Web site location or click **Browse** and select one. See the example above the Web Site Location box.

5. Click **Next** to continue.

   ◆ If requested, enter a username and password, and then click **OK**.

6. If available, type the location where you want to create a local copy of the site or click **Browse** and select one.

   ◆ If a site is already open, select the **Add to current Web site** check box.

7. Click **Next**, and then specify the options you want to limit how many levels below the home page to import or limit the import to a maximize size or only HTML and image files, if available.

8. When you're done, click **Finish**.

   The wizards imports the Web files into corresponding folders in your site.

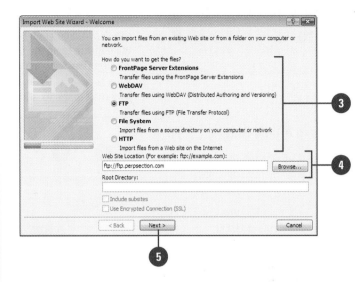

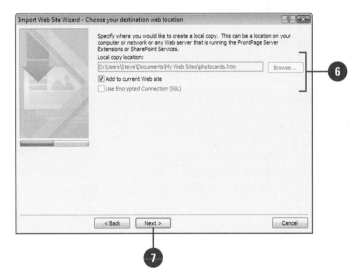

Adding Pages to Your Web Site

Whether you have a Web site created using a template, or are beginning from scratch, you will eventually need to add new pages to the site. New pages can be blank or template based, so it is also possible to integrate template pages with your own pages that you created from scratch. The New dialog box contains an extensive selection of single-page templates. After you create the new page, you need to create a hyperlink to the existing Web.

Add Pages to a Web Site

1. Click the Web Site tab for the site in which you want to add a new page.

2. If necessary, click the **View** menu, and then click **Folder List** to display the Folder List.

3. Right-click a blank area of the Folders List, point to **New**, and then click **HTML**.

   TIMESAVER *Click the New Page button on the title bar of the Folder List.*

   A new file appears in the Folder List, and is assigned a default name which is highlighted and framed in a box.

4. Type a new name (including .htm at the end) for the page, and then press Enter.

5. Drag the file name icon for the page where you want it in the Folder List.

   Expanding and contracting perforated lines appear any place where your page can be positioned.

6. When the new page is where you want it, release the mouse button to position the page.

7. Double-click the new page to open it for editing.

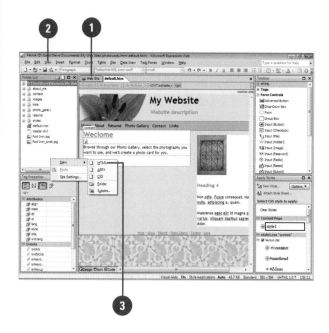

Added page open for editing

Add Pages to a Web Site Using Templates

1. Click the Web Site tab for the site in which you want to add a new page.

2. Click the **New** button list arrow on the Common toolbar, and then click **Page**.

3. Click the tab with the page template you want to use.

   ◆ **General.** Creates HTML, ASPX, PHP (**New!**), CSS, Master Page, Dynamic Web Template, JavaScript, XML, Text File, Create from Dynamic Web Template, or Create from Master Page.

   ◆ **ASP.NET.** Creates ASPX, Master Page, Web User Control, Web Configuration, Site Map, and Create from Master Page.

   ◆ **CSS Layouts.** Creates an HTML file and links it to a CSS file.

   ◆ **Style Sheets.** Initializes a cascading style sheet (CSS) file to standardize the appearance of Web pages.

   ◆ **Frames Pages.** Creates frame pages.

4. Click the template you want to use.

5. Click **OK**.

6. Click the **Save** button on the Common toolbar.

7. Navigate to the Web site folder location where you want to add pages.

8. Type a name for the page, or use the suggested name, and then click **Save**.

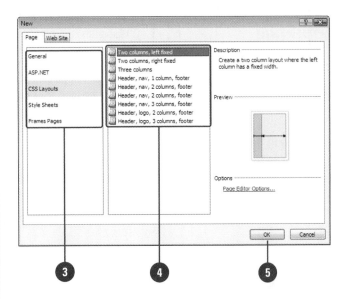

General Page Formats

Type	Description
HTML	Creates a blank standard HTML page
ASPX	Creates an ASP.NET 2.0 Web form
PHP (**New!**)	Creates a PHP (PHP Hypertext Preprocessor) file
CSS	Creates a blank CSS file
Master Page	Create an ASP.NET 2.0 master page that you can use as a template
Dynamic Web Template	Creates a Dynamic Web Template that you can attach to other pages for a consistent look
JavaScript	Creates a file for the JavaScript language
XML	Creates a blank XML file
Text File	Creates a blank text file
Create from Dynamic Web Template	Creates a Web page based on a Dynamic Web Template
Create from Master Page	Creates an ASP.NET Web form based on an ASP.NET master page

Creating a Personal Web Package

A Personal Web Package allows you to package an entire Web site or parts of a Web site in a single file that you can use (import) in another Web site. To create a Personal Web Package, you use the Personal Web Package command on the Export menu. In the Export Web Package dialog box, you select the files and folders you want to include in the Personal Web Package file (.fwp), provide property information about the files and folders, and select dependency options for use during the import process.

Create a Personal Web Package

1 Open the Web site with the files and folders you want to export into a Personal Web Package.

2 Click the **File** menu, point to **Export**, and then click **Personal Web Package**.

3 In the left pane, select the files or folders you want in the Personal Web Package.

4 Click **Properties**.

5 Enter the title, description, author, and company information you want.

6 Click **OK**.

7 To display file dependencies, click **Show Dependencies**, and then select a file in the left pane.

8 To change the dependency option, click the **Dependency Checking** list arrow, then select an option.

9 Click **OK**.

10 Navigate to the location where you want to save the Web Package.

11 Type a name for the Personal Web Package.

12 Click **Save**, and then click **OK** upon completion.

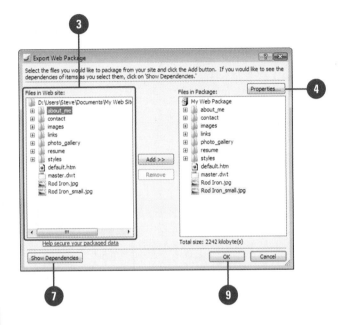

Saving a Web Site

▶

After you finish working with a Web site, you need to save the material. When you make changes on a Web site or page, an asterisk (*) appears on the tab next to the name indicating changes have not been saved. When you save a Web site, you save each Web page and any related, or embedded, files, such as graphics, included with the pages. You can use the Save All command on the File menu to quickly save all modified files. If graphics on a Web page need to be saved, the Save Embedded Files dialog box appears, asking you to select any options you want and save the files.

Save a Web Site

1. Click the **File** menu, and then click **Save All**.

2. If necessary, specify which image files you want to save with the Web page or pages, and where to save them.

   ◆ **Rename.** Rename the embedded file name.

   ◆ **Change Folder.** Change the embedded folder location.

   ◆ **Set Action.** Set option to save or not save an embedded file.

   ◆ **Picture File Type.** Change the graphic type and quality.

3. Click **OK**.

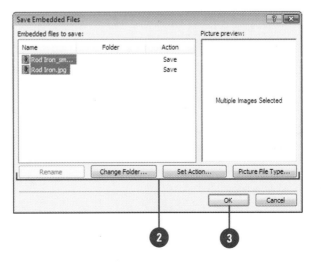

Renaming a Web Site

When you create a Web site using a template or wizard, Expression Web automatically give the site a general name (mysite1, mysite2, etc.) and saves it. You can rename the site to something more meaningful to you. You can right-click the Web site folder or use the Site Settings command on the Site menu.

Rename a Web Site

1. Click the **Site** menu, and then click **Site Settings**.

2. Click the **General** tab.

3. Type a new site name.

4. Click **OK**.

Did You Know?

You can rename the Web folder. Right-click the Web folder in Folders view or the Folder List, click Rename, type a new name, and the press Enter. You can also rename a Web folder in Windows Explorer.

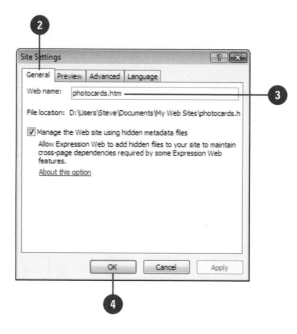

Deleting a Web Site

If you no longer want or need a Web site you can delete it. When you delete a Web site, Expression Web deletes everything it contains, including Web pages, pictures, text files, Expression Web files, and all folders. If you want to save any files in the Web site folder, you need to back them up before deleting the site.

Delete a Web Site

1 Open the Web site you want to delete.

2 If necessary, click the **View** menu, and then click **Folder List** to display the Folder List.

3 Right-click the Web site you want to remove, and then click **Delete**.

4 Click the **Delete this Web site entirely** option.

5 Click **OK**.

Did You Know?

You can delete only the hidden data for a Web site. If you want to keep Web pages and related content, such as images, for a Web site, yet remove the hidden tracking and organization files used by Expression Web, the Delete command allows you the option to do it. Right-click the Web site you want in the Folder List, click the Delete only hidden metadata files from this Web site preserving all other files and folders option, and then click OK.

Working with Web Pages

3

Introduction

Once on the Web, you can open other Web pages in the Folder List or Folders views, or you can even open up another page using the Windows menu. Microsoft Expression Web provides several ways to navigate between pages. After you open a Web page, you can use the document tabs at the top of the editing window in Design view, choose the Web page's name from the Window menu, or press Ctrl+Tab until the page you want appears in the window to navigate between pages.

One of the most user-friendly components of Expression Web is its capability to automatically convert text and images into HTML format. When you save a Web site or Web page, it is actually being saved in HTML format. After you create a Web site, you can use the Folder List view to quickly and easily manage individual Web pages.

When looking at a Web site, there are certain details that can make your Web pages a site that visitors will return to. Microsoft Expression Web helps you generate that type of site. Visitors might notice a washed out background picture called a watermark. Or maybe it's a soothing color or light sound as you pass over certain feature of the page. Having a custom feel will express to your visitors that you've spent time and looked at every detail of your site.

You can preview your Web pages in a browser, or in Design view. Because each browser can display your site differently, you will want to examine your site using several of the most popular browser formats. You can also create your own template, instead of using one of the built-in page templates that comes with Expression Web.

What You'll Do

Create an HTML Page

Open Web Pages from Within a Web

Navigate Web Pages

Display Web Pages in the HTML Format

Manage Web Pages

Set the Home Page

Change the Web Page Title

Change Web Page Properties

Insert Background Pictures and Watermarks

Change Background Colors

Add Background Sound

Set Page Size

Preview and Print Web Pages

Export Web Content

Create a Page Template

Use a Dynamic Page Template

Create a Master and Content Page

Save a Web Page with Different Formats

Animate Page Transitions

Creating an HTML Page

An HTML page is a common Web page. HTML is a coding language that describes the elements on a Web page and instructs a Web browser how to display it. As you add elements to an HTML page in Design view, Expression Web creates the HTML code behind it. If you are familiar with the HTML language, you can use the Code view to make code changes. Split view allows you to display Design and Code view at the same time, which makes it a beneficial learning tool. When you add an element in Design view, you can view the related code in Code view. You can use the New submenu on the File menu or the New button on the Common toolbar to create a new HTML page. With the Page Editor Options dialog box, you can set the default type for new documents and the default file extension—either .html or .htm—for new HTML documents (**New!**).

Create an HTML Page Quickly

① Click the Web Site tab for the site in which you want a new page.

② Use any of the following methods:

◆ Click the **File** menu, point to **New**, and then click **HTML**.

◆ Click the **New** button list arrow on the Common toolbar, and then click **HTML**.

◆ Click the **New** button on the Common toolbar (applies when HTML is set as the default document type).

TIMESAVER *Press Ctrl+N to create a new HTML page.*

An untitled Web page appears without the use of New dialog box.

③ Click the **Save** button on the Common toolbar, type a name for the page, and then click **Save**.

New HTML page

Create an HTML Page

1. Click the Web Site tab for the site in which you want a new page.

2. Click the **New** button list arrow on the Common toolbar, and then click **Page**.

3. In the left pane, click **General**.

4. Click **HTML**.

5. Click **OK**.

   An untitled Web page appears.

6. Click the **Save** button on the Common toolbar, type a name for the page, and then click **Save**.

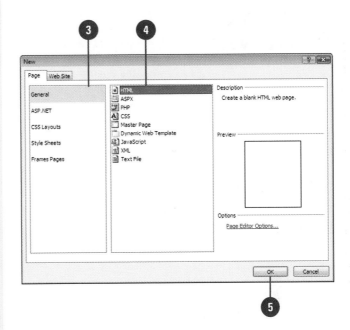

Set the Default Document Type

1. Click the **Tools** menu, and then click **Page Editor Options**.

2. Click the **Authoring** tab.

3. Click the **Default Document** list arrow, and then select the document type you want.

4. Click the **.html** or **.htm** option for the default HTML file extension (**New!**).

5. To add a byte order mark (BOM) to a new UTF-8 document, select the check boxes next to the extensions you want, or deselect the ones you don't want (**New!**).

6. Click **OK**.

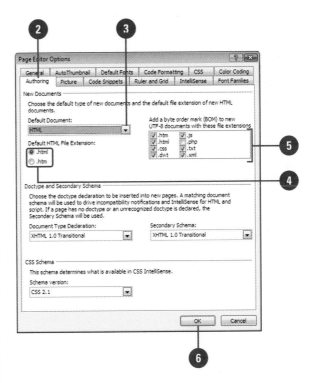

Opening Web Pages from Within a Web

Expression Web allows you to multi-task, which means you can have more than one Web page open at the same time. After you open a Web site, you can quickly open Web pages in Folders view, or from the Folder List instead of using the Open button on the Common toolbar or the Open command on the File menu. If you want to view open Web pages in a separate Expression Web window, you can display the page, and then choose Open in New Window from the Window menu. You can press Alt+Tab to switch between the separate windows. Instead of starting from scratch to create a new page, you can open a copy of an existing page with the default new Web page title of Untitled_1.htm.

Open a Web Page in Folders View

1. Open the Web site with the Web page you want to open.

2. Click the Web Site tab.

3. Click the **Folders** button.

4. Double-click the icon or file name representing the page you want to access.

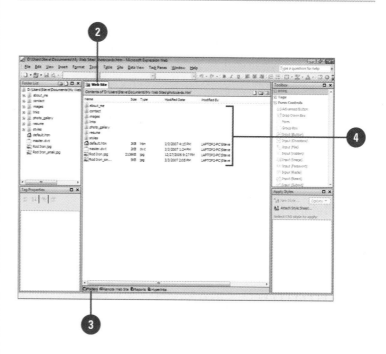
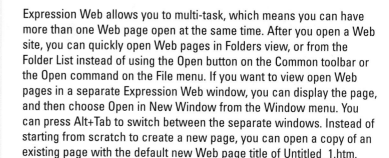

Did You Know?

You can open a linked page from Design view. Press and hold Ctrl and click a hyperlink in the page, or right-click a hyperlink in a page that's already open, and then click Follow Hyperlink.

See Also

See "Opening an Existing Web Page" on page 13 for information on opening an external Web page.

Open a Web Page Using the Folder List

1. Open the Web site with the Web page you want to open.

2. If necessary, click the **View** menu, and then click **Folder List** to display the Folder List.

3. Double-click the page you want to open.

Web page opened from Folder List

Open a Copy of a Web Page Using the Folder List

1. Open the Web site with the Web page you want to open.

2. If necessary, click the **View** menu, and then click **Folder List** to display the Folder List.

3. Right-click the page you want to copy, and then click **New From Existing Page**.

A new untitled page appears in the Editing window with content and formats from the original template Web page.

4. Click the **Save** button on the Common toolbar.

5. Navigate to the Web site folder location where you want to add pages.

6. Type a name for the page, or use the suggested name, and then click **Save**.

Navigating Web Pages

Expression Web provides several ways to navigate between pages. After you open a Web page, you can use the document tabs at the top of the Editing window, choose the Web page's name from the Window menu, or press Ctrl+Tab until the page you want appears in the window to navigate between pages.

Navigate Web Pages Using Document Tabs

① Open the Web site with the Web page you want to display, and then open the Web page.

② Click the document tab with the page you want to display.

Navigate Web Pages Using the Windows Menu

① Open the Web site with the Web page you want to display, and then open the Web page.

② Click the **Window** menu.

This displays a list of up to nine open Web pages.

③ Click the page you want to open. The Web page opens in Page view.

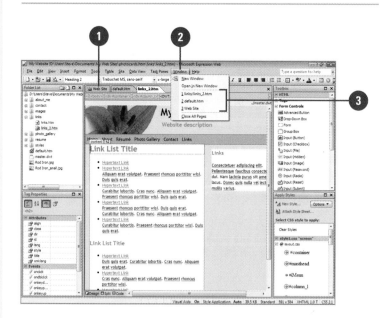

Displaying Web Pages in the HTML Format

One of the most user-friendly components of Expression Web is its capability to automatically convert text and images into HTML format. If you're familiar with HTML, you might be comfortable enough to work in this mode. HTML adds a series of format instructions to your content using tags, such as <i>, that indicate how to format the text for display on the Web. Use the Quick Tag Selector to select any tag in your Web page. Use the Quick Tag Editor to insert, wrap, and edit HTML tags. Expression Web uses colored text to distinguish between elements when working in HTML format.

Display a Web Page in HTML

1. Open the Web page you want to display in the HTML format.

2. Click the **Split** or **Code** button at the bottom of the window.

    The Web page appears in HTML coded form.

Display HTML Tags in Design View

1. Open the Web page you want to display HTML tags.

2. Click the **View** menu, and then click **Quick Tag Selector**.

    HTML tags appear in capsule-size, six-sided frames within the text.

3. To turn off HTML tags, click the **View** menu, and then click **Quick Tag Selector** again.

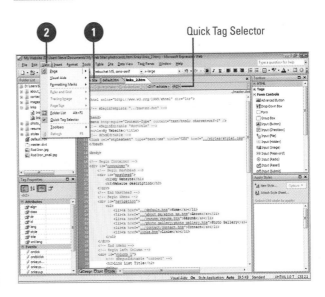

Quick Tag Selector

Managing Web Pages

After you create a Web site, you can use the Folder List to quickly and easily manage individual Web pages, files and folders. If a page name is not exactly what you want, you can quickly rename it. The page name is the file name in your folder list, such as default.htm. You can create and name a new folder and move pages to a different location. If you no longer need or want a Web page, you can remove it. You can determine whether you want the page deleted from your hard drive or just from the Web.

Rename a Web Page

1. Open the Web site with the Web page you want to rename.

2. If necessary, click the **View** menu, and then click **Folder List** to display the Folder List.

3. In the Folder List, right-click the page you want to rename, and then click **Rename**.

   TIMESAVER *Click the file name in the Folder List, click the file again to highlight it.*

4. Select the name of the Web page file, except the extension, such as *.htm*.

5. Type a new name, and then press Enter.

> **Did You Know?**
>
> **You can delete a Web page.** In the Folder List, right-click the Web page you want to delete, click Delete, and then click Yes.

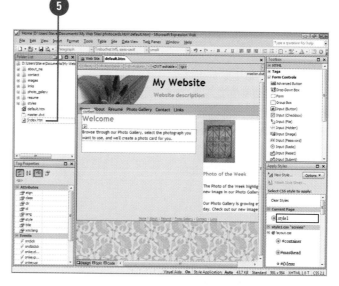

Create a New Folder

1. Open the Web site with the Web page you want to rename.

2. If necessary, click the **View** menu, and then click **Folder List** to display the Folder List.

3. Click the **New Folder** button.

4. Type a new name, and then press Enter.

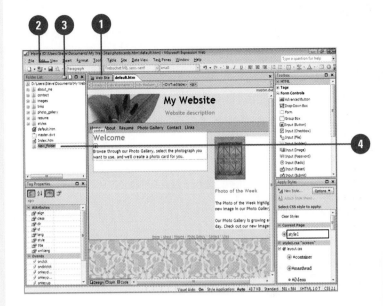

Move a Web Page

1. Open the Web site with the Web page you want to move.

2. If necessary, click the **View** menu, and then click **Folder List** to display the Folder List.

3. In the Folder List, display the page you want to use.

4. Drag the page icon to the position where you want it to occupy on your site.

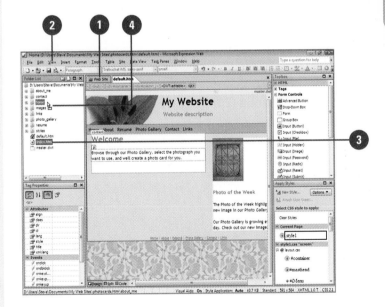

Setting the Home Page

When you create a Web site using a template, Expression Web automatically creates a home page called *default.htm*, which is the first page visitors see when they visit your site. If you already have a home page or want to create a different one, you can quickly set the one you want as the new home page using the Folder List.

Set a Web Page as the Home Page

1. Open the Web site with the Web page you want to change.

2. If necessary, click the **View** menu, and then click **Folder List** to display the Folder List.

3. In the Folder List, right-click the page you want to set as the new home page, and then click **Set as Home Page**.

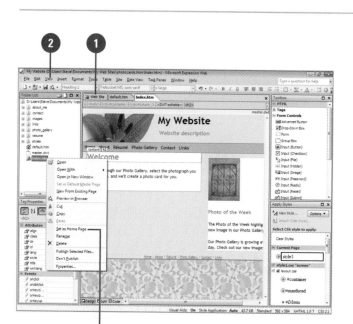

Changing the Web Page Title

A Web page title is the text that visitors see on the title bar of their Web browser when they display the Web page. Expression Web automatically sets the Web page title to the same text as the Web page file name. However, the two perform different tasks. The Web page title displays a message, while the Web pane name identifies a file. When you save a Web page, you can change the title. If you didn't change the title during the save process or you want to change it, you can use the Properties dialog box.

Change the Web Page Title

1. Open the Web site with the Web page you want to change.

2. If necessary, click the **View** menu, and then click **Folder List** to display the Folder List.

3. In the Folder List, right-click the page you want to change, and then click **Properties**.

   The Properties dialog box opens, displaying the General tab with the current title selected.

4. Type a new name for the title.

5. Click **OK**.

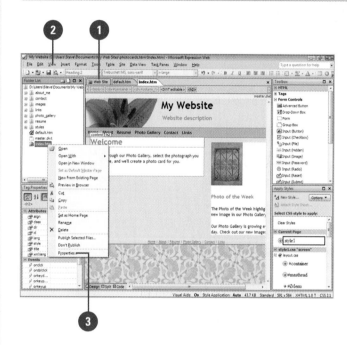

> **Did You Know?**
>
> **You can change a Web page title in the Title column.** If the Title column in the Editing window is enabled, you can select the title text, and then type a new title.

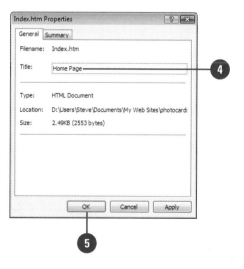

Changing Web Page Properties

Expression Web allows you to change individual Web page properties using the Page Properties dialog box. You can change the Web page title, add a page description, and specify keywords for search engines (which aren't used to much anymore; most search engines use other methods). You can also insert a background sound or image, make the background image a transparent watermark, or change the color. When you insert a background sound, it plays once when you open the Web page unless you select the Loop option. In addition, you can change the color of page text and hyperlinks. For advanced feature, you can set page margins, work with code snippets, or specify a language.

Change Web Page Properties

1. Open the Web site with the Web page you want to change, and then click the Web page tab.

2. Click the **File** menu, and then click **Properties**.

3. Click the tab you want to use, and then select the options you want:

   ◆ **General.** Use this tab to change the Web page title, add a page description, specify keywords for search engines, and insert a background sound. You can also specify a base location, which changes the root location (where your home page is typically located).

   ◆ **Formatting.** Use this tab to insert a background image, and make it a watermark (transparent). To delete a background, select the image path and delete it. You can also use this tab to change the background, text, or link colors on the current page. If you insert a background sound, you can also select the look option.

   Continue Next Page

General properties

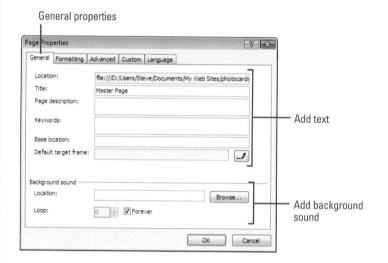

Add text

Add background sound

Formatting properties

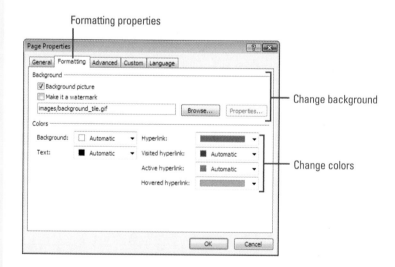

Change background

Change colors

◆ **Advanced.** Use this tab to set margins for the current page. However, it's more efficient to make margin changes using CSS.

◆ **Custom.** Use this tab to add, modify, or remove custom code snippets based on system and user variables. A code snippet is a reusable segment of code.

◆ **Language.** Use this tab to specify the page language and HTML encoding you want to use. These options make sure your Web browser and Expression Web uses the right characters set for the selected language. The default for HTML encoding is Unicode (UTF-8). You can also include a byte order mark (BOM) (**New!**).

⑤ Click **OK**.

Advanced properties

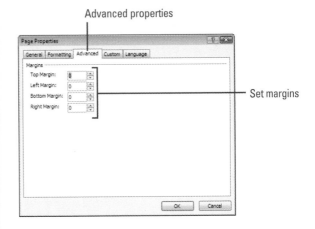

Set margins

Language properties

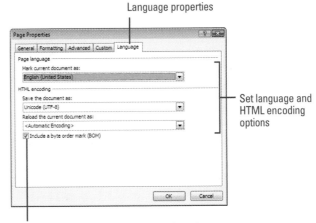

Set language and HTML encoding options

Select to include a byte order mark (BOM)

Did You Know?

What is a Unicode? A character coding standard that defines a set of letters, numbers, and symbols that represent almost all of the written languages in the world.

See Also

See "Adding and Removing Byte Order Marks" on page 366 for information on byte order marks (BOM).

Inserting Background Pictures and Watermarks

You can use a picture as the background for a page. Pictures can be taken from elsewhere on your site, a file, clip art, or the Web. You can also use a background picture in watermark form. A watermark is a background effect that displays a graphic in a light shade behind your text on your page. You can use a washed out version of your company logo, or you can add graphical text such as Under Construction. Pictures and watermarks display in the background titled across the page. Be aware that not all Web browsers support watermarks.

Insert a Background Picture

1. Open and display the Web page you want to use.

2. Right-click anywhere on the page to which you want to insert a background picture, and then click **Page Properties**.

3. Click the **Formatting** tab.

4. Select the **Background Picture** check box.

    TROUBLE? *If the option is grayed out, you need to open the master page.*

5. Click **Browse**.

6. Locate and select the picture you want to insert, and then click **Open**.

    The picture you selected now opens as a background image.

7. Click **OK**.

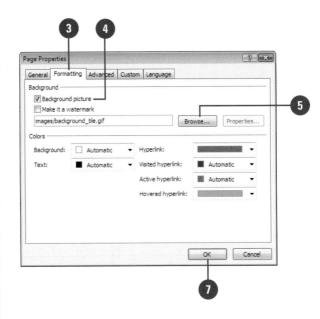

Insert a Background Picture Watermark

1. Open and display the Web page you want to use.

2. Right-click anywhere on the page to which you want to insert a background picture, and then click **Page Properties**.

3. Click the **Formatting** tab.

4. Select the **Background Picture** check box.

5. Select the **Make it a watermark** check box.

6. Click **Browse**.

7. Locate and select the picture you want to insert, and then click **Open**.

   The picture you selected now opens as a background image.

8. Click **OK**.

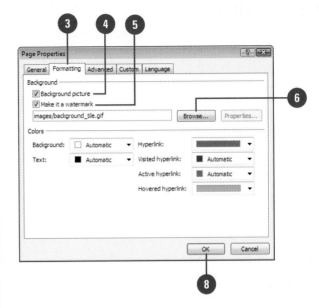

Changing Background Colors

If you'd like to add some interest to your pages, you can add background colors. When selecting background colors, some creative judgment is required. For example, if you choose a dark color for your background, make sure you use a light color for your text (the most commonly used is white) to generate the appropriate contrast required for easy reading.

Change the Background Color of a Web Page

1. Open and display the Web page you want to use.

2. Right-click the page to which you want to change a background color, and then click **Page Properties**.

3. Click the **Formatting** tab.

4. Click the **Background** list arrow.

5. Click the color you want on the color palette.

6. Click **OK**.

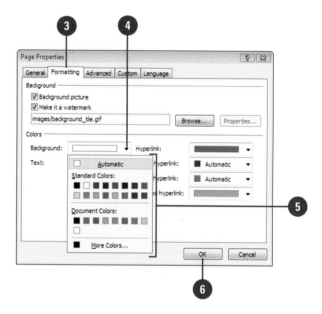

Adding Background Sound

You can introduce background sounds to accompany and enhance your Web page. There's nothing like hearing a favorite tune when you enter a site or visit a particular page. The sound can be played continuously in a loop, or you can set it for a desired number of plays. Be aware that not all browsers support background sound.

Add a Background Sound to a Web Page

1 Open and display the Web page you want to use.

2 Right-click the page to which you want to add a background sound, and then click **Page Properties**.

3 If necessary, click the **General** tab.

4 Type the sound file name or click **Browse**, locate and select the sound file you want to use, and then click **Open**.

5 To set the sound to repeat continuously, clear the **Forever** check box, and then click the number arrows in the Loop box to set the number of times you want the sound to play.

6 Click **OK**.

Whenever a visitor opens the page, they will hear the sound effect you chose.

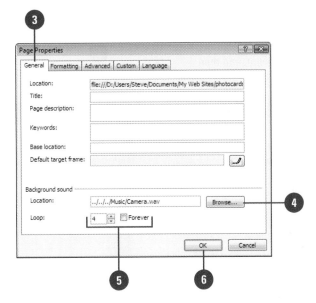

Setting Page Size

Since visitors to your Web site can use different screen resolutions or window sizes, you need to develop Web pages so a variety of users can view it without having to zoom in or scroll to much. You can use the Page Size command to simulate different page size to see how your pages look. The page sizes available using the Page Size command correspond to standard screen resolutions, which include 640 x 480, 800 x 600 and 1024 x 768 (all maximized).

Change the Page Size View

1. Click the **View** menu, and then point to **Page Size**.

2. Click the page size you want.

    TIMESAVER *Click the current page size on the status bar, and then click a new size.*

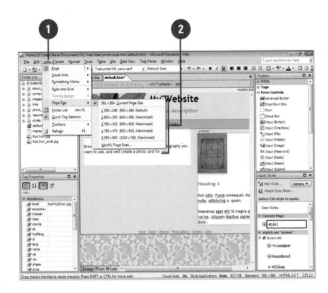

Change the Page Size

1. Click the **View** menu, point to **Page Size**, and then click **Modify Page Sizes**.

2. Perform the page size commands you want:

   ◆ **Add.** Click **Add**, enter width, height and a description, and then click **OK**.

   ◆ **Modify.** Select a page size, click **Modify**, make changes, and then click **OK**.

   ◆ **Remove.** Select a page size, and then click **Remove**.

   ◆ **Reset.** Click **Reset** to return to default page sizes.

3. Click **OK**.

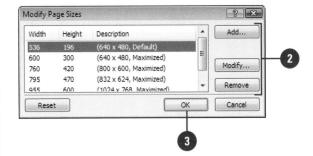

Previewing Web Pages

Because each browser can display your site differently, you will want to examine your site using several of the most popular browser formats and different sizes. When you are ready to see how your page will look to visitors, click the Preview in Browser button arrow on the Common toolbar and then select a browser and a window size. When you select a browser, the program starts and displays your Web page as you would see it on the Web. If you want to add additional browsers to the list, you can select them using the Edit Browser List dialog box. You can also simulate the page size of a browser as you work in Design view by selecting different page sizes on the Page Sizes submenu on the View menu.

Add Browsers to the Preview

1. Click the **File** menu, point to **Preview in Browser**, and then click **Edit Browser List**.

2. Click **Add**.

   The Add Browser dialog box opens.

3. Type the browser's name.

4. Click **Browse**.

5. Navigate to the location where the browser program is stored, select it, and then click **Open**.

6. Click **OK**.

7. To automatically save a Web page before previewing, select the **Automatically save page before previewing** check box.

8. To specify the window sizes you want, select the **640 x 480**, **800 x 600**, or **1024 x 768** check boxes.

9. Click **OK**.

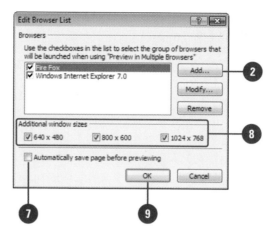

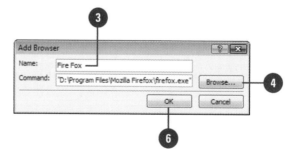

Preview a Web Page Using a Browser

① Open the Web page you want to preview.

② Click the **Preview in Browser** button arrow.

③ Click the browser with the specific size you want to use to preview your site or page.

TIMESAVER *Press F12 to preview the Web page in the most recently used browser and size.*

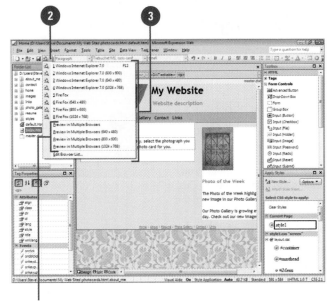

Click to preview selected page in multiple browsers

Preview in Internet Explorer

Previewing and Printing Web Pages

Printed pages are helpful when you are working in Preview view. Rather than toggling between a page in progress and a Browser Preview of that page, for example, you can print the Preview so that you have it in hard copy format. Printouts are also helpful when editing your pages. Before printing, you can preview the page to determine that there are no obvious errors.

Print Preview Web Pages

1 Open and display the Web page you want to preview.

2 Click the **File** menu, point to **Print**, and then click **Print Preview**. This opens a scaled-down image of the page you want to print and a series of buttons. The button choices are:

◆ **Print button.** Engages the printing process. The preview closes and the Print dialog box opens.

◆ **Next Page button.** Displays the next page in the sequence for multiple-page printing.

◆ **Previous Page button.** Takes you to the previous page in a sequence.

◆ **Two Page button.** Toggles between a single-page and a two-page spread in Preview mode.

◆ **Zoom In button.** Magnifies the preview image.

◆ **Zoom Out button.** Reduces the size of the characters to show more of the page preview.

◆ **Close button.** Closes the Preview mode.

3 When you're done, click the **Close** button.

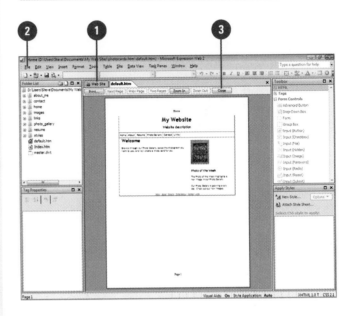

Print Web Pages

① Open and display the Web page
   you want to print.

② Click the **File** menu, point to **Print**,
   and then click **Print**.

③ Select the print options you want.

④ Click **OK**.

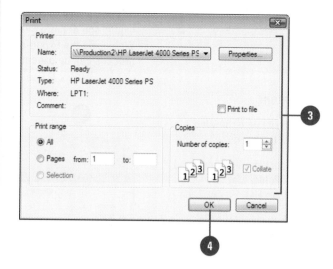

Exporting Web Content

When you export Web content, you save the information in a new format so that it can be opened in an entirely different program. You can export one or more files from Expression Web to a location outside your Web using the Export command or Copy and Paste commands. This process can be executed using the Folder List or Folders view.

Export Web Content

1. Open the Web site with the Web page you want to change.

2. If necessary, click the **View** menu, and then click **Folder List** to display the Folder List.

3. In the Folder List, select the file you want to export.

4. Click the **File** menu, point to **Export**, and then click **File**.

5. Navigate to the drive and folder location where you want to export the Web content.

6. Type a name for the page, or use the suggested name.

7. Click the **Save as type** list arrow, and then click the file type you want.

   ◆ **HTML (.htm, .html)**

   ◆ **GIF and JPEG (.gif, .jpg)**

   ◆ **Microsoft Office Files (.doc, .xls, .ppt)**

8. Click **Save**.

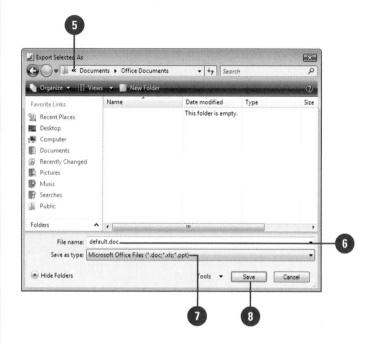

Export Web Content Using Copy and Paste

1. Select the information you want to copy.

2. Click the **Edit** menu, and then click **Copy**.

3. Display the location in which you want to move the content.

4. Click the area where you want to place the content.

5. Click the **Paste** button on the toolbar.

   The source files or folders are copied into their new location.

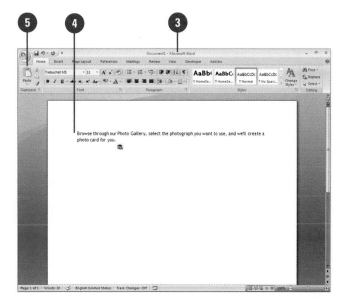

Creating a Page Template

Instead of using one of the built-in page templates that comes with Expression Web, you can create your own. There are two kinds of page templates: static and dynamic. A **static template** is a Web page you create and design, which is completely editable. After you save a static page template, you can access it in the My Templates tab of the Page Templates dialog box. A **dynamic template** is a Web page with editable areas like a static template, yet also contains non-editable areas with content that changes based on circumstances, such as actions taken by a user or the date.

Create a Static Template

1. Design and display the Web page you want to create into a static template.

2. Click the **File** menu, and then click **Save As**.

3. Type a name for the template.

4. Click the **Save as type** list arrow, and then click **Page Template**.

   The folder location changes to the Pages folder, where Expression Web stores page templates.

5. Click **Save**.

6. Type the title you want for the template.

7. Type a description for the template.

8. To save the template in the current Web site, select the **Save Template in Current Web site** check box.

9. Click **OK**.

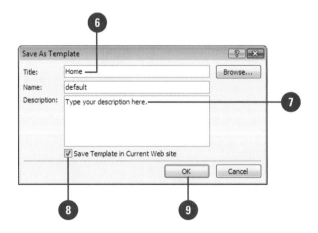

Create a Dynamic Template

1. Design and display the Web page you want to create into a dynamic template. Be sure to leave areas open to create editable regions.

2. Click the **File** menu, and then click **Save As**.

3. Type a name for the template.

4. Click the **Save as type** list arrow, and then click **Dynamic Web Template**.

   The folder location changes to the Pages folder, where Expression Web stores page templates.

5. Click **Save**.

Create Editable Regions for a Dynamic Template

1. Display the Dynamic Web Template you want to change.

2. Select the page area you want to vary from page to page.

3. Click the **Format** menu, point to **Dynamic Web Template**, and then click **Manage Editable Regions**.

4. Type a name for the area you selected.

5. Click **Add**.

6. Click **Close**.

   You can repeat Steps 2 through 6 to designate other dynamic areas.

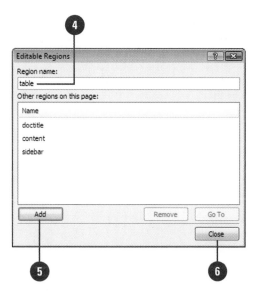

Using a Dynamic Page Template

After you create a dynamic Web template, you can apply, or attach, the template to an open Web page. When you attach a dynamic Web template to a Web page, Expression Web tries to map regions on the ordinary Web page to editable regions in the template. If you don't like the initial mapping, you can modify or skip it. After you attach a dynamic Web template to an ordinary Web page, you can modify non-editable regions in Code view, or any editor other than Design view to create updatable content.

Attach a Dynamic Web Template

1. Display the Web page in which you want to apply a dynamic page template.

2. Click the **Format** menu, point to **Dynamic Web Template**, and then click **Attach Dynamic Web Template**.

3. Locate and select the dynamic Web template you want to apply.

4. Click **Open**.

5. Select which regions in the new page will receive content/regions from the old page.

6. Click **Modify**, select a new mapping, and then click **OK**.

7. Click **OK** to attach the template.

8. Click **Close**.

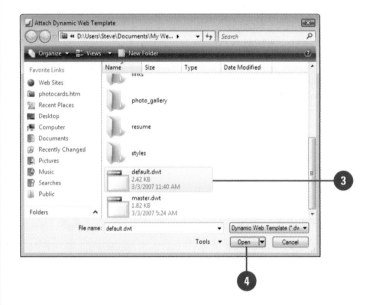

> ### Did You Know?
>
> **You can manage editable regions.**
> Click the Format menu, point to Dynamic Web Template, and then click Manage Editable Regions.

Update a Dynamic Web Template

1. Open the dynamic Web page template, and then make the changes you want to update on other pages.

2. Click the **Format** menu, and then point to **Dynamic Web Template**.

3. Click the update command you want.

   ◆ **Update Selected Page**

   ◆ **Update All Pages**

   ◆ **Update Attached Pages**

Did You Know?

You can detach a Dynamic Web Template from a Web page. Open and display the Web page with the Dynamic Web Template attached, click the Format menu, point to Dynamic Web Template, and then click Detach from Dynamic Web Template. If you want to open an attached Dynamic Web Template page, click Open Attached Dynamic Web Template on the submenu.

Creating a Master and Content Page

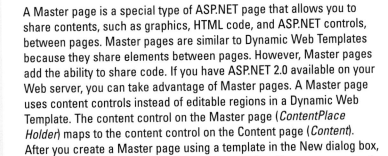

A Master page is a special type of ASP.NET page that allows you to share contents, such as graphics, HTML code, and ASP.NET controls, between pages. Master pages are similar to Dynamic Web Templates because they share elements between pages. However, Master pages add the ability to share code. If you have ASP.NET 2.0 available on your Web server, you can take advantage of Master pages. A Master page uses content controls instead of editable regions in a Dynamic Web Template. The content control on the Master page (*ContentPlace Holder*) maps to the content control on the Content page (*Content*). After you create a Master page using a template in the New dialog box, you need to save it with the .master file extension. Now, you can create a Content page and link it to a Master page.

Create a Master Web Page

1. Click the **File** menu, point to **New**, and then click **Page**.

2. In the left pane, click **General** or **ASP.NET**.

3. Click **Master Page**.

4. Click **OK**.

   An Untitled_1.master page appears in the Editing window.

5. Click the **File** menu, and then click **Save As**.

6. Type a name for the master page.

7. Click the **Save as type** list arrow, and then click **Master Page**.

8. Click **Save**.

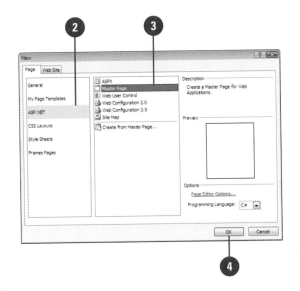

Did You Know?

You can manage content regions. Click the Format menu, point to Master Pages, and then click Manage Content Regions.

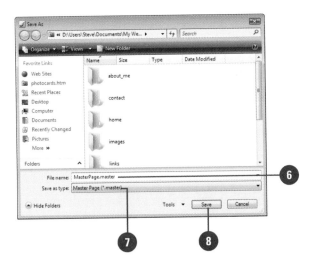

Create a Content Web Page

1. Click the **File** menu, point to **New**, and then click **Page**.

2. In the left pane, click **General** or **ASP.NET**.

3. Click **Create from Master Page**.

4. Click **OK**.

5. Click the **Specific Master Page** option.

6. Click **Browse**, locate and select the master page, and then click **Open**.

7. Click **OK**.

   An Untitled_1.aspx content page appears in the Editing window.

   The Content page pulls in the content from the Master page in the ControlPlaceHolder control.

8. Click the **File** menu, and then click **Save As**.

9. Type a name for the content page.

10. Click the **Save as type** list arrow, and then click **Web Pages**.

    This saves the content page with the .aspx extension.

11. Click **Save**.

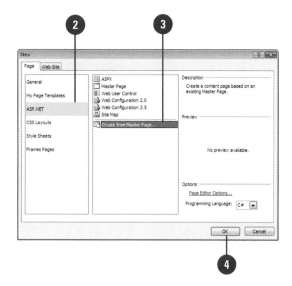

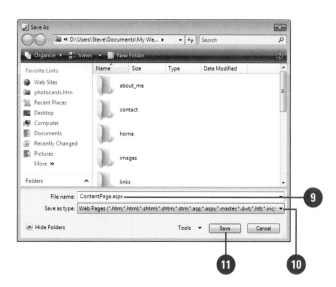

Did You Know?

You can detach a Master page. Open and display the Content page, click the Format menu, point to Master Pages, and then click Detach from Master Page. If you want to open an attached Master page, click Open Attached Master Page on the submenu.

Saving a Web Page with Different Formats

A file type specifies the file format (for example, a template) as well as the program and version in which the file was created (for example, Expression Web). You might want to change the type if you're creating a custom template or sharing files with someone who needs them for use in another program. You use the Save As dialog box to change the file type for a page. The Save as type list arrow displays a list of the available formats for the program or current selection.

Save a Web Page as a Different Type

1. Open and display the Web page you want to save in a different format.

2. Click the **File** menu, and then click **Save As**.

3. Navigate to the drive and folder location where you want to save the Web page.

4. Type a name for the page, or use the suggested name.

5. Click the **Save as type** list arrow, and then click the file type you want.

6. Click **Save**.

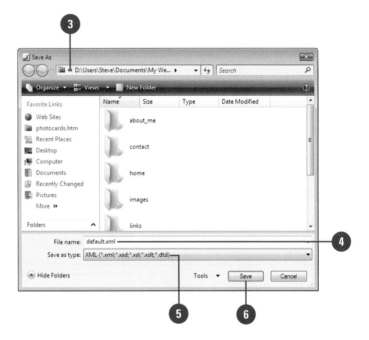

See Also

See "Expression Web Formats" on page 75 for information on selecting the right file format.

Expression Web Formats

Expression Web Save File Formats

Save As file type	Extension	Used to save
All Files	*.*	Complete Web site
Web Pages		Files in their native format; includes the formats in this list and the ones in the side bar on the previous page
HTML Files	.htm, .html	Web pages as a HTML file
Dynamic Web Template	.dwt	Web pages as a changeable Expression Web template
ASP and ASPX Files	.asp, .aspx	Web pages as a Microsoft Active Server Page
Master Page	.master	Web pages as Expression Web master page file; a special type of ASP.NET file
JScript Files	.js	Scripts as a Microsoft Scripting Language "JScript" file
VBScript Files	.vba	Scripts as a Visual Basic for Applications file
PHP Files (**New!**)	.php	Web pages as a PHP file
CSS Files	.css	Web pages as a cascading style sheet
XML	.xml, .xsd,.xsl, .xslt, .dtd	Web pages as an XML file
Text	.txt	Web pages as a text file
Page Template	.tem	Web pages as a static Expression Web template

Expression Web Open File Formats

Files of type	Extension	Used to open
All files in the above table are included in this list		*All files from the above list*
Recover Text from Any file	*.*	Text files not supported (from this list below)
WordPerfect 5.x	.doc	WordPerfect 5.0 files
WordPerfect 6.0	.wpd, .doc	WordPerfect 6.0 files
Word 2007 Document	.docx	Word 2007 documents
Word 2007 Macro-Enabled Document	.docx	Word 2007 documents that contains Visual Basic for Applications (VBA) code
Word 97 - 2003 Document	.doc	Word 97 to Word 2003 documents
Works 6.0 - 9.0	.wps	Works 6.0-9.0 files

Animating Page Transitions

You can use animation in your Web site to provide interest and call attention to important information. When you move from one Web page to another, you can display a transition effect between the two pages. You can select a transition effect, and then specify when the page transition occurs, and how long it lasts. The only disadvantage of page transitions is that the browser must wait for the entire Web page to load before it can apply the transition effect. Be aware that animated page transitions are not supported by all browsers.

Apply a Page Transition

① Open and display the Web page you want to use.

② Click the **Format** menu, and then click **Page Transition**.

③ Click the **Event** list arrow, and then click an event type: **Page Enter**, **Page Exit**, **Site Enter**, or **Site Exit**.

④ Click the transition effect you want.

⑤ Set the duration (in seconds) of the transition effect.

⑥ Click **OK**.

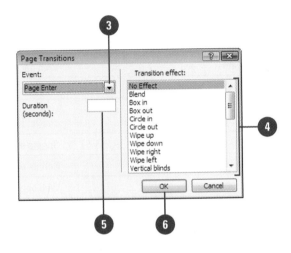

Working with Web Page Text

Introduction

As you build your Web pages, you'll find that entering, selecting, correcting, moving, and copying will become commonplace. You can use all of the text functions as you do in any other Microsoft program. With Microsoft Expression Web, you can use all the common moving, deleting, and copying functions that you have already grown accustom to. You can also find and replace and format text just as you would in Word or Excel.

When entering text, you might find it necessary to add a bulleted or numbered list. You can also create sublists and collapsible lists to use on your pages. Choosing the alignment of your text, your line spacing, and paragraph indents all work the same way as other Microsoft programs.

A style is a collection of formatting settings saved with a Web site or template that you can apply to text, graphics, and tables at any time. Expression Web comes with a standard set of styles you can apply to text. If you modify a style, you make the change once, but all text tagged with that style changes to reflect the new format. In Chapter 12, you'll learn how to create a Cascading Style Sheet (CSS), which is style information that can be referenced by individual or multiple Web pages.

Of course, while working with all of this text, using Expression Web's spell checker is a must. You can spell check, add familiar or custom words to your dictionary, check for common grammatical errors, or use the Thesaurus to enhance your Web pages. International Microsoft Expression Web users can change the language that appears on their screens by changing the default language settings.

What You'll Do

Enter and Select Text in a Web Page

Edit Text and Make Corrections

Insert a Line or Paragraph Break

Move and Copy Text

Set Text Indention and Spacing

Set Text Alignment

Insert Symbols and Horizontal Lines

Create Bulleted and Numbered Lists

Create Sublists

Apply Styles

Find and Replace Text

Format Text and Add Text Effects

Access More Colors

Find and Replace Text, Code, or HTML Tags

Check Spelling and Use Custom Dictionaries

Find the Right Words

Change Default Text

Create and Change Font Families

Insert Text from a File

Entering Text in a Web Page

There are two methods of entering text on a Web page: as part of a template or from scratch. When starting out, we strongly recommend that you work from a template. If you are working with templates, you can begin by editing the boilerplate text that opens as part of the template.

Select the template text that you wish to replace and begin typing. The boilerplate text disappears and your text begins flowing into that section of the template. Be sure to constrain your text to the original area provided in the template and, if necessary, edit what you wish to say to make the copy fit within the allotted space.

The other way to enter text is on a blank page. Create a new Web page, and then start typing. When you enter text, Expression Web automatically places text inside a **container** as an HTML tag. An HTML **tag** is code inserted in a document that specifies how the document, or a portion of the document, should be formatted. HTML defines the structure and layout of a Web document by using a variety of tags and attributes. The opening tag (<p>) marks the start of the paragraph code and a closing tag (</p>) marks the end of the paragraph, denoted by the forward slash (/). When you select a container, the tag type appears as a tab identifying the container.

Template heading text

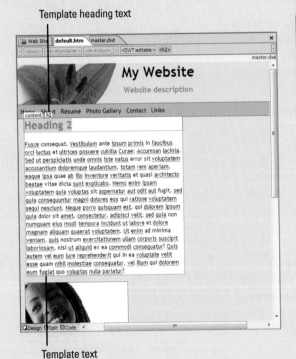

Template text

Common Tags

Symbol	Defines
<html>	Start of the HTML document
<head>	The document heading
<body>	The body of the document
<title>	The document title
<div>	A section in a document
<span>	A section in a document
<h1>	Text heading
<p>	A paragraph
<style>	Format of text
<img>	An image placeholder
<a>	A hyperlink
<iframe>	An inline frame
<!-- comment -->	A comment

Selecting Text in a Web Page

The first step in working with text is to highlight, or select, the text you want. Once you've selected it, you can format, replace, delete, copy, and move (cut) words, sentences, and paragraphs within one Web page or between Web pages. When you finish with or decide not to use a selection, you can click anywhere in the page to deselect the text.

Select Text

1. Position the pointer in the word, paragraph, line, or part of the page you want to select.

2. Choose the method that accomplishes the task you want to complete in the easiest way.

   Refer to the table for methods to select text.

See Also

See "Working with Template Content" on page 26 for information on working with content from a template.

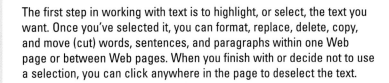

Selecting Text	
To Select	**Do This**
A single word	Double-click the word.
A single paragraph	Triple-click a word within the paragraph.
A single line	Click in the left margin next to the line.
Any part of a page	Click at the beginning of the text you want to highlight, and then drag to the end of the section you want to highlight.
A large selection	Click at the beginning of the text you want to highlight, and then press and hold Shift while you click at the end of the text that you want to highlight.

Editing Text

You can edit text in Expression Web several ways. First, you can select the text you want to edit, and then type text to replace it or press the Delete key to remove it. Another way to edit text is to place the insertion point in the text, and then type to insert text or press the Backspace or Delete keys to remove it. The Backspace key deletes text to the left, while the Delete key deletes text to the right.

Select and Edit Text

1. Select the text you want to edit.

2. Perform one of the following editing commands:

   ◆ To replace text, type your text.

   ◆ To delete text, press the Backspace key or the Delete key.

Insert and Edit Text

1. Click in the page to place the insertion point where you want to make the change.

   ◆ To insert text, type your text.

   ◆ To delete text, press the Backspace key or the Delete key.

   TIMESAVER *Press Ctrl+ Backspace or Ctrl+Delete to delete one word at a time left or right.*

Making Corrections

Everyone makes mistakes and changes their mind at some point, especially when creating or revising a document. With Expression Web, you can instantly correct typing errors by pressing a key. You can also reverse more complicated actions, such as typing an entire word, formatting a paragraph, or creating a chart. With the Undo button, if you change your mind, you can just as easily click the Redo button to restore the action you reversed.

Undo or Redo an Action

◆ Click the **Undo** button to reverse your most recent action, such as typing a word, formatting a paragraph, or creating a chart.

   TIMESAVER *Press Ctrl+Z to undo.*

◆ Click the **Redo** button to restore the last action you reversed.

   TIMESAVER *Press Ctrl+Y to redo your undo.*

◆ Click the **Undo** button list arrow, and then select the consecutive actions you want to reverse.

◆ Click the **Redo** button list arrow, and then select the consecutive actions you want to restore.

Undo button ———— Undo button list arrow

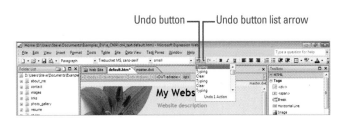

Redo button ———— Redo button list arrow

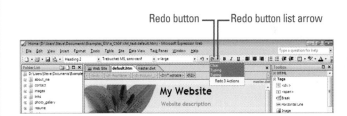

Inserting a Line or Paragraph Break

As you enter or modify text on a Web page, the text automatically wraps within a container to create a paragraph. If you want to create a paragraph, all you need to do is press Enter, which inserts a paragraph break. When you insert a paragraph break, Expression Web automatically creates a new paragraph container, which is denoted with a tab labeled with a p. If you want to insert a line, yet still remain in the same paragraph, you can insert a line break. Sometimes it's hard to see the difference between a paragraph or line break, so Expression Web provides the option to show or hide formatting marks. In addition to showing or hiding line breaks and paragraph marks, you can also show or hide spaces, comments, script blocks, container position, aligned elements, and other code-related elements.

Show or Hide Line and Paragraph Marks

◆ **Show or Hide All Formatting Marks.** Click the **View** menu, point to **Formatting Marks**, and then click **Show**.

  ◆ You can also click the **Show Formatting Marks** button on the Standard toolbar.

  TIMESAVER *Click Ctrl+Alt+/ to show or hide all formatting marks.*

◆ **Show or Hide Line Breaks.** Click the **View** menu, point to **Formatting Marks**, and then click **Line Breaks**.

  ◆ You can also click the **Show Formatting Marks** button arrow on the Standard toolbar.

◆ **Show or Hide Paragraph Marks.** Click the **View** menu, point to **Formatting Marks**, and then click **Paragraph Marks**.

  ◆ You can also click the **Show Formatting Marks** button arrow on the Standard toolbar.

Click to show or hide formatting marks

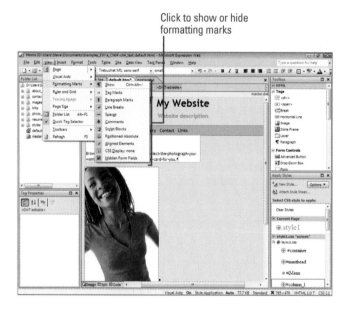

Insert a Line Break

◆ Click where you want the text to break, and then press Shift+Enter.

◆ Click where you want the text to break, click the **Insert** menu, point to **HTML**, click **Break**, click the break option you want, and then click **OK**.

◆ Click where you want the text to break, click the plus sign (+) next to Tags in the Toolbox task pane, and then double-click the **Break** icon.

Line Break

Double-click to insert a line break

Insert a Paragraph Break

◆ Click where you want a new paragraph, and then press Enter.

◆ Click where you want the text to break, click the **Insert** menu, point to **HTML**, and then click **Paragraph**.

◆ Click where you want the text to break, click the plus sign (+) next to Tags in the Toolbox task pane, and then double-click the **Paragraph** icon.

New paragraph

Double-click to insert a new paragraph

Moving and Copying Text

Text can be moved and copied in Expression Web just like in other word processing software. You can move or copy text within a Web page, between Web pages, or to another program. When you cut (for a move) or copy text or graphics, Expression Web places it on the Clipboard. To complete the copy or move, you paste the data stored on the Clipboard in another location. You can use the commonly used **Paste** command or the **Paste Text** command, which provides options to control line breaks and white space. When you paste an item with the Paste command, the Paste Options button appears allowing you to keep or remove formatting or keep HTML or Text only. When you use the Paste Text command, the Paste Text dialog opens allowing you to select the option you want. To copy or move text or graphics without using the Clipboard, you can use a technique called **drag-and-drop**. Drag-and-drop makes it easy to copy or move text or graphics short distances on your Web page.

Move or Copy Text Using Drag-and-Drop

1. Select the text you want to move or copy.

2. To move the text from its current location, drag the selection to the new location, and then release the mouse button.

3. To copy the text to a new location, hold down Ctrl and drag the selection to the new location, and then release the mouse button.

> ### Did You Know?
>
> **You can copy and paste between documents.** You can cut or copy text between pages and even between Expression Web and other Microsoft programs. Switch between programs on the system taskbar at the bottom of the screen.

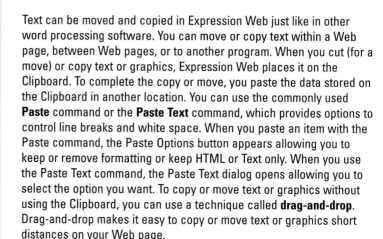

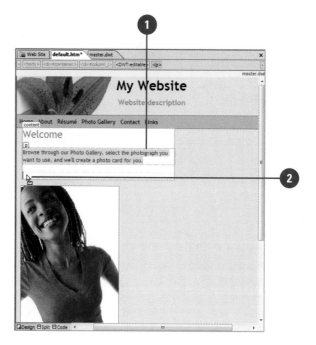

Move or Copy Text

1. Select the text you want to move or copy.

2. To move the text from its current location, click the **Edit** menu, and then click **Cut**. The text is removed from its current location and placed on the Clipboard.

3. To copy the text to a new location, click the **Edit** menu, and then click **Copy**. A copy of the text is placed on the Clipboard.

4. Click to position the insertion point where you want to place the cut or copied text.

   TIMESAVER *The Copy, Cut, and Paste buttons are available on the Standard toolbar.*

5. Click the **Edit** menu, and then click one of the following:

   ◆ **Paste**. Pastes the text and retains the source formatting.

   ◆ **Paste Text**. Select a paste option in the Paste Text dialog box, and then click **OK**.

   The text is copied from the Clipboard to the new location, but also remains on the Clipboard for future placements.

6. If necessary, click the **Paste Options** button, and then click an option to adjust the pasted item.

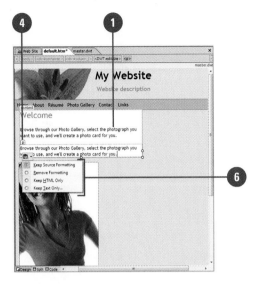

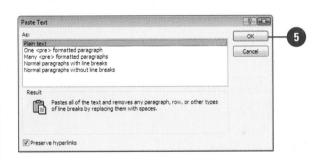

Did You Know?

You can turn on or off paste options. Click the Tools menu, click Page Editor Options, click the General tab, select or clear the Show Paste Options buttons check box, and then click OK.

Paste Text Options

Select	To Do This
Plain text	Insert plain text with spaces replacing any line breaks in pasted text
One <pre> formatted paragraph	Use <pre> (preformatted) tag to maintain all line breaks of pasted text
Many <pre> formatted paragraph	Use <pre> tag to maintain all line and paragraph breaks of pasted text
Normal paragraphs with line breaks	Convert any lines breaks to (line break) tag and any paragraph breaks to <p> tag
Normal paragraphs without line breaks	Pastes text without line breaks

Setting Text Indention and Spacing

Indenting paragraph text allows you to shift text to make it stand out. You can indent text to create an outline or indent the first line of a paragraph. You can use the Increase Indent Position and Decrease Indent Position buttons on the Formatting toolbar to quickly change text position or use the Paragraph dialog box to set more precise positioning. Line spacing is another way to vary the look of a Web page. The lines in a Web page are single-spaced by default, but you can easily change line spacing to double or 1.5 lines to allow extra space between every line. Sometimes, you'll want to add space above and below certain paragraphs, such as for headlines or indented quotations to help set off the text.

Change Paragraph Indention

1. Open and display the Web page you want to use.

2. Select the paragraph you want to change.

3. Click an indent button on the Formatting toolbar to apply the attribute that you want the selected text.

   ◆ **Increase Indent Position button.** Increase the indent position to the right.

   TIMESAVER *Press Tab to increase the indent position.*

   ◆ **Decrease Indent Position button.** Decrease the indent position to the left.

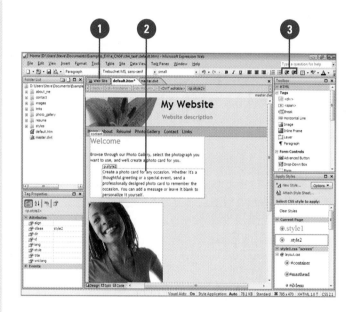

Did You Know?

You can change character spacing.
Select the text you want to change, click the Format menu, click Font, click the Character Spacing tab, click the Spacing list arrow, click Normal, Expanded, or Condensed, click the Position list arrow, click a vertical position option, and then click OK.

Change Paragraph Indents

1. Open and display the Web page you want to use.

2. Select the paragraph you want to change.

3. Click the **Format** menu, and then click **Paragraph**.

4. Type the space you want indented on the left side of the selected paragraph (in points).

5. Type the space you want indented on the right side of the selected paragraph (in points).

6. Type the space you want indented before the first line of the selected paragraph (in points).

7. Click **OK**.

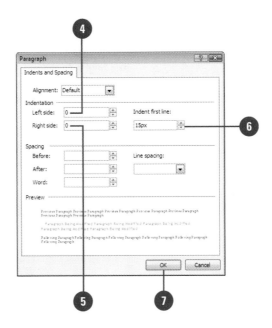

Change Line Spacing

1. Open and display the Web page you want to use.

2. Select the paragraph you want to change.

3. Click the **Format** menu, and then click **Paragraph**.

4. Click the **Line Spacing** list arrow, and then click the spacing you want.

5. Type the space you want to add before (above) each selected paragraph (in points).

6. Type the space you want to add after (below) each selected paragraph (in points).

7. Click **OK**.

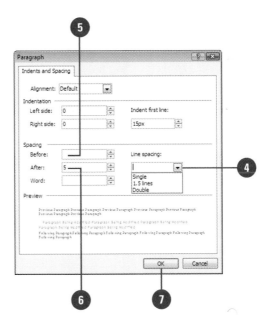

Setting Text Alignment

Text alignments vary the look of a Web page and help lead the user through the text. You can align text along the left or right margin, in the center, or equally across the page. Left-aligned text works well for body paragraphs in most cases, but other alignments vary the look of a page and help lead the reader through the text. **Right-aligned text**, which is even along the right margin and ragged at the left margin, is good for adding a date to a letter. **Justified text** spreads text evenly between the margins, creating a clean, professional look, often used in articles. **Centered text** is best for titles and headings. You can quickly change text alignment using alignment buttons on the Formatting toolbar.

Change Text Alignment

1. Open and display the Web page you want to use.

2. Select the text you want to align.

3. Click an alignment button on the Formatting toolbar to apply the attribute that you want the selected text.

   ◆ **Align Left button.** Aligns text along the left margin. The text is uneven along the right margin.

   ◆ **Center button.** Aligns text in the middle of the page.

   ◆ **Align Right button.** Aligns text along the right margin. The text is uneven along the left margin.

   ◆ **Justify button.** Aligns text evenly between the two margins.

See Also

See "Setting Text Indention and spacing" on page 86 for information on changing text indention and spacing.

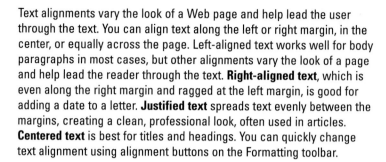
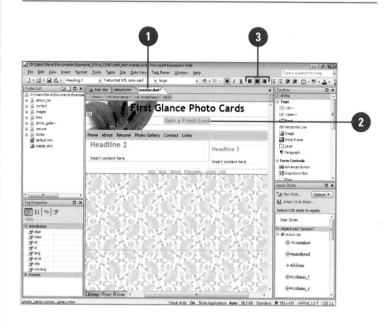

Inserting Symbols

Expression Web comes with a host of symbols and special characters for every need. Insert just the right one to keep from compromising a Web page's professional appearance with a hand-drawn arrow («) or missing mathematical symbol (å). Before you insert a symbol, be aware that not all browsers support all symbols. Be sure to test your pages on several browsers.

Insert Symbols and Special Characters

1. Open and display the Web page you want to use.

2. Click where you want to insert a symbol or character.

3. Click the **Insert** menu, and then click **Symbol**.

   TIMESAVER *Recently used symbols appear at the bottom of the dialog box.*

4. To see other symbols, click the **Font** list arrow, and then click a new font.

5. To select a subset, click the **Subset** list arrow, and then select the subset you want.

   ◆ Some common subsets include Currency symbols, Arrows, and General Punctuation.

6. Click a symbol or character.

7. Click **Insert**.

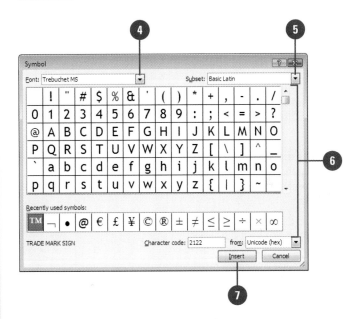

See Also

See Chapter 5, "Working with Web Page Graphics" on page 117 for information on inserting graphics.

Inserting Horizontal Lines

Horizontal lines have a variety of uses in the construction of a Web page. Whether they're used to separate sections of a page or to underline an important piece of text, you have several decisions to make. Lines have a variety of properties that you can modify, including width, height, alignment, and color.

Insert a Horizontal Line

1. Open and display the Web page you want to use.

2. Click where you want to insert a horizontal line.

3. Click the **Insert** menu, point to **HTML**, and then click **Horizontal Line**.

   ◆ You can also click the plus sign (+) next to Tags, and then double-click the **Horizontal Line** icon.

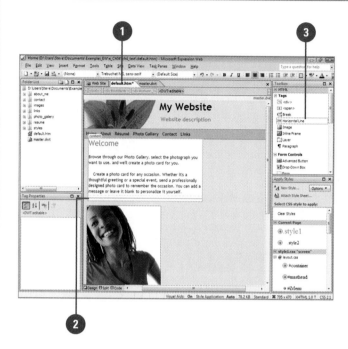

Modify a Horizontal Line

1. Open and display the Web page with the horizontal line you want to change.

2. Double-click the horizontal line you want to modify.

3. Select the formatting options you want.

   ◆ **Width.** Width of the line. Specified in pixels or as a percentage of the window width.

   ◆ **Height.** Height of the line in pixels.

   ◆ **Alignment.** Alignment of the line on the page.

   ◆ **Color.** Color of the line, unless you want it shaded. If you select a color, shading is no longer an option.

   ◆ **Solid Line.** Select the check box to create a solid line. Clear it to create a shaded line.

4. Click **OK**.

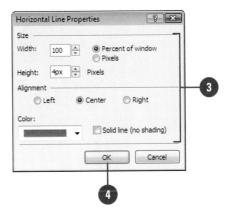

Creating Bulleted and Numbered Lists

The best way to draw attention to a list is to format the items with bullets or numbers. For different emphasis, you can change any bullet or number style to one of the predefined formats. You can also customize the list style or insert a picture as a bullet. If you move, insert, or delete items in a numbered list, Expression Web sequentially renumbers the list for you. Every time you press Enter, a new bullet will appear. To end a list, press Enter twice.

Create Bulleted and Numbered Lists from Scratch

1. Open and display the Web page you want to use.

2. Select the text you want to change into a bulleted or numbered list, or click where you want to start a list.

3. Click the **Bullets** or **Numbering** button on the Common toolbar.

4. If you're starting a list, type the first entry, and then press Enter.

5. Type the next entry, and then press Enter.

6. To end the list, press Enter twice.

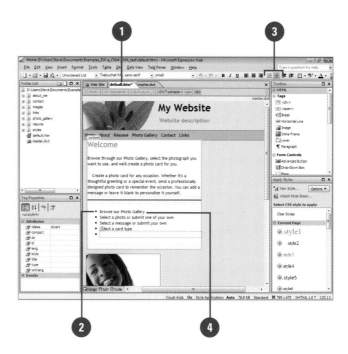

Did You Know?

You can remove bullets or numbering from a list. Select the list with the bullets or numbering, and then click the Bullets or Numbering button on the Common toolbar.

You can add more items to a list. Click at the end of the line above where you want to add an item to the list, and then press Enter. To create a sublist, press Tab.

Change the Format of a Bulleted or Numbered Lists

1. Open and display the Web page you want to use.

2. Select the list you want to format.

3. Click the **Format** menu, and then click **Bullets and Numbering.**

4. Click the tab (**Picture Bullets, Plain Bullets, Numbers,** or **Other**) for the type of change you want to make.

5. Click the style change you want.

6. Click **OK.**

Did You Know?

You can insert a custom bullet. Produce a custom bullet, and then save it, preferably in either GIF (.gif) or JPEG (.jpg) format. In Expression Web, place the insertion point at the place where you want to start the list. Click the Format menu, click Bullets and Numbering, click the Picture Bullets tab, click the Specify picture option button, click Browse to locate your creation, double-click a picture, and then click OK. You can proceed as you would with any other bullet style.

You can use the Style list arrow to format a bullets or numbered list. Click the Style list arrow on the Common toolbar, and then click Unordered List <ul> or Ordered List <ol>. An unordered list is a bulleted list, while an ordered list is a numbered list.

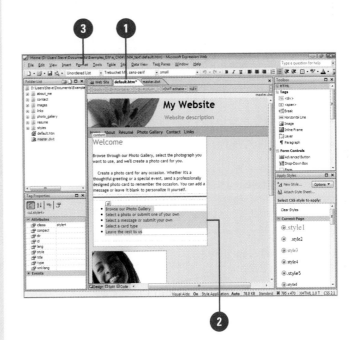

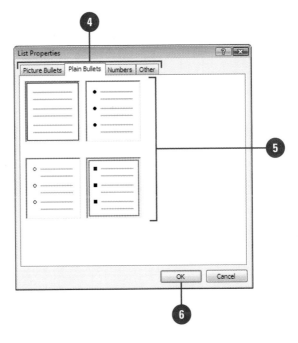

Creating Sublists

In addition to the standard bulleted and numbered lists, you can also create indented lists, or sublists. A sublist creates multilevels in a list. You can create a sublist with a bulleted or numbered list. You use the Increase Indent button on the Formatting toolbar to create the multi-levels. If you want to insert a line to create a sublist, you can press Tab or use the Increase Indent button.

Create a Sublist List

1. Open and display the Web page you want to use.

2. Select the text you want to change into a sublist, or click where you want to start the sublist (press Enter to create a new line).

3. Click the **Increase Indent** button on the Formatting toolbar.

    ◆ If you create a new line, you can press Tab to create a sublist.

    Expression Web creates a sublist bullet.

4. If you're starting a sublist, type the first entry, and then press Enter.

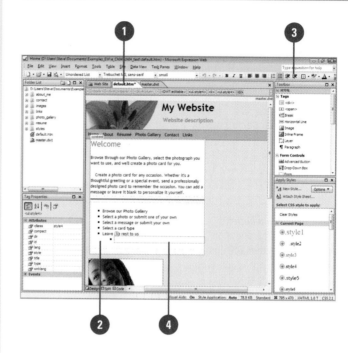

Applying Styles

A **style** is a collection of formatting settings saved with a Web site or template that you can apply to text, graphics, and tables at any time. If you modify a style, you make the change once, but all text tagged with that style changes to reflect the new format. Expression Web provides you with **Built-In Styles**, or you can create your own **User-Defined Styles**. Both built-in and user-defined styles are available from the same style list while you edit a page. When you create a user-defined style, you can also create an embedded Cascading Style Sheet (CSS), which is style information that is applied to the open Web page.

Apply a Style to Text

① Open and display the Web page you want to use.

② Select the text you want to apply a style.

③ Click the **Style** list arrow on the Common toolbar.

④ Click a style from the drop-down list. The default styles include:

- ◆ (None)
- ◆ Paragraph <p>
- ◆ Heading1 <h1> through Heading 6 <h6>
- ◆ Unordered List <ul>
- ◆ Ordered List <ol>
- ◆ Defined Term <dt>
- ◆ Definition <dd>
- ◆ Address <address>
- ◆ Preformatted <pre>
- ◆ Block Quote <blockquote>

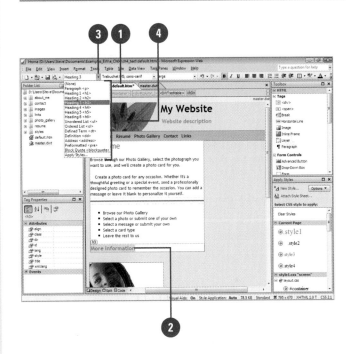

Did You Know?

You can remove a style. Select the text, click the Style list arrow on the Common toolbar, and then click (None).

Creating Heading and Definitions

You can use the Styles list arrow on the Common toolbar to quickly format text as a heading or definition list. A heading provides structure for a Web page by providing visual indicator of what is important. The default styles include six different headings, labeled Heading1 <h1> through Heading6 <h6>. Heading1 is the largest size and Heading6 is the smallest size. If you have a list of definitions you want to include in a Web page, you can use the Define Term <dt> and Definition <dd> styles to format the information you want to provide.

Create a Heading

1. Open and display the Web page you want to use.

2. Select the text you want to change into a heading or subheading.

3. Click the **Style** list arrow on the Common toolbar.

4. Click a style (such as Heading 1, Heading 2, etc.) from the drop-down list.

   The text is defined with the heading tag associated with it (<h1> to <h6>).

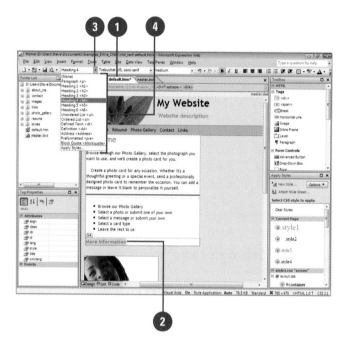

Create a Definition List

1. Open and display the Web page you want to use.

2. Click to place the insertion point where you want to place a definition.

3. Click the **Style** list arrow on the Common toolbar, and then click **Defined Term**.

4. Type the term name, and then press Enter.

   The term is defined with the <dt> tag and the definition is indented.

5. Type the definition for the term name, and then press Enter.

   The definition is defined with the <dd> tag.

6. Type the next term name, press Enter, type the definition, and then press Enter.

7. To end the definition list, press Enter twice.

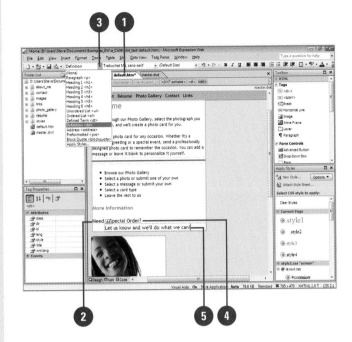

Formatting Text

You'll often want to format, or change the style of text to add emphasis to part of a Web page. **Boldface**, *italics*, <u>underlines</u>, and other text effects are toggle switches, which means you simply click to turn them on and off. For special emphasis, you can apply multiple formats, such as bold and italics. You can also change the font typeface and size. Using one font typeface for headings and another for main text adds a professional look to your Web page.

Format Text Quickly

1. Open and display the Web page you want to use.

2. Select the text you want to format.

3. Click a formatting button on the Common toolbar to apply the attribute you want.

   ◆ **Bold** button.

   ◆ **Italic** button.

   ◆ **Underline** button.

   ◆ **Font Color** button list arrow, and then select a color.

   ◆ **Highlight** button list arrow, and then select a color.

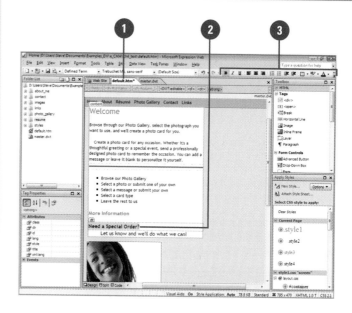

Change the Font Quickly

1. Open and display the Web page you want to use.

2. Select the text you want to format.

3. Click the **Font** list arrow, and then click a font typeface.

See Also

See Chapter 12, "Creating Styles and Layouts with CSS" on page 285 for information on formatting text using cascading style sheets, which provides consistent formatting for Web pages.

Change the Font Size of Text Quickly

1. Open and display the Web page you want to use.

2. Select the text you want to format.

3. Select the font sizing option you want.

   ◆ Click the **Font Size** list arrow on the Common toolbar, and then click a font typeface.

   ◆ Click the **Increase Font Size** or **Decrease Font Size** button on the Formatting toolbar.

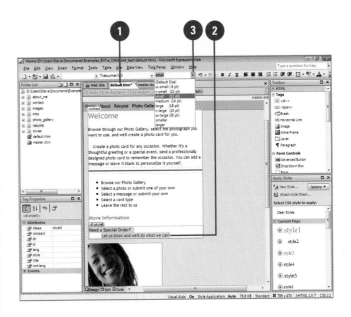

Format Text Using the Font Dialog Box

1. Open and display the Web page you want to use.

2. Select the text you want to format.

3. Click the **Format** menu, and then click **Font**.

4. Select the formatting options you want.

   ◆ Select a font.

   ◆ Select a font style.

   ◆ Select a font size.

   ◆ Select a font color on the Color list.

   ◆ Under Effects, select the effect of your choice, if any.

5. Click **OK**.

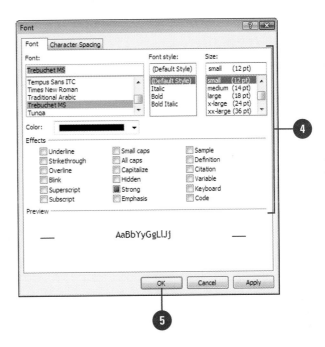

Adding Text Effects

Expression Web comes with simple special effects you can quickly add to text on your Web pages. Some of the effects add style to your text, such as Blink or Overline, while others define the type of text, such as Definition or Citation, on your Web pages.

Add Font Effects to Text

1. Open and display the Web page you want to use.

2. Select the text you want to format.

3. Click the **Format** menu, and then click **Font**.

4. Select or clear the font special effects check boxes. The unique effects to Expression Web include:

    ◆ **Overline.** Draws a line above the text.

    ◆ **Blink.** Applies blinking animation to the text.

    ◆ **Capitalize.** Capitalizes the first letter in each word.

    ◆ **Strong.** Applies a stronger emphasis to the text.

    ◆ **Emphasis.** Applies a subtle emphasis to the text.

    ◆ **Sample.** Applies a fixed width font to the text.

    ◆ **Definition.** Specifies the text as a definition.

    ◆ **Citation.** Specifies the text as a reference to other sources.

    ◆ **Variable.** Specifies the text as a variable or program argument.

    ◆ **Keyboard.** Specifies the text that is entered by a user.

    ◆ **Code.** Specifies the text as a programming code.

5. Click **OK**.

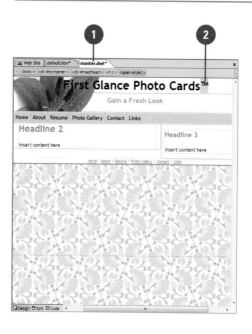

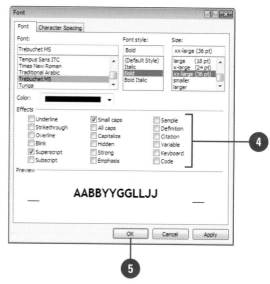

Accessing More Colors

Expression Web comes with a standard set of 16 colors. In addition to the standard colors, Expression Web allows you to add more colors to the set for use on your Web pages. More Colors are additional colors that you can add to each color menus—the Font Color button menu, for example. More Colors are useful when you want an object or picture to always have the same color. They are also useful when you want to change the color of an object to a specific color, but the standard colors don't not have that color. Colors that you add to a specific color menu appear in all color menus and remain in the menu even if the color scheme changes.

Add a Color to the Menus

1. Open and display the Web page you want to use.

2. Click any color list arrow (such as **Font Color** button list arrow) to open a color palette.

3. Click **More Colors** on the color palette.

4. Do one of the following:

   ◆ Click a color from the expanded palette. Every time you click a color, its corresponding hexadecimal value appears in the Value box.

   ◆ Enter a hexadecimal value in the Value box. An example of such a value would be HEX={99,FF,CC}.

   ◆ To select a color from anywhere on the screen, click **Select**, and then click any color on the screen.

   ◆ To select a color that represents the color average of an area of the palette, click **Select**, and then drag the eye dropper cursor to create a box encompassing the colors you want to average.

5. Click **OK**, and then click **OK** again.

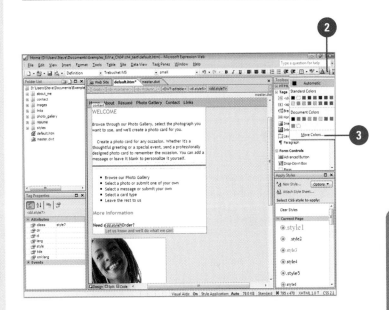

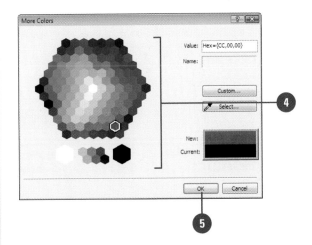

Finding and Replacing Text or Code

Suppose that you discover you have misspelled or want to change a word throughout an entire Web page. You do not need to read through the document to find every instance of the word and manually change it. The Find and Replace commands can do that for you. Expression Web can find every instance for you, and walk you through the Web site from page to page until all the corrections have been made. In addition to text, you can also find and replace code. You can search one or more Web page or an entire Web site. When you search multiple pages, the results appear in a Find task pane.

Find and Replace Text or Code on a Web Page

1. In the Folder List, open or select the one or more pages you want to search.

   ◆ To select multiple pages, use Ctrl+click.

2. Click the **Edit** menu, and then click **Find**.

3. Enter the text for which you are searching, or click the **Regular expression** list arrow, and then select a special character or option.

4. If you want to replace the text or code found, click the **Replace** tab, and then enter the replacement text.

5. Click the **Current page** option.

6. Select the search parameters you want (Match case, Find whole word only, etc.).

7. Select one of the following buttons:

   ◆ **Find All** or **Find Next button.** Locates all instances or the next instance of the text.

   ◆ **Replace All** or **Replace button.** Replaces all instances or the selected instance of the text.

8. When you're done, click **Close** in the dialog box and task pane.

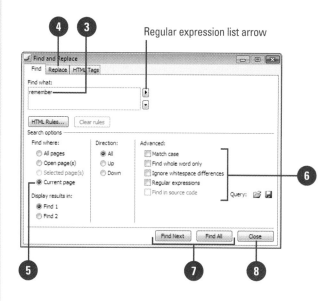

Regular expression list arrow

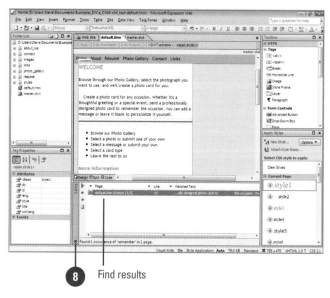

Find results

Find and Replace Text or Code on a Web Site

1. In the Folder List, open or select the Web site you want to search.

2. Click the **Edit** menu, and then click **Find**.

3. Enter the text for which you are searching.

4. If you want to replace the text or code found, click the **Replace** tab, and then enter the replacement text.

5. Click the **Selected Pages** option or the **All Pages** option.

6. Click **Find All**.

   The list of pages containing the selected word(s) opens in the Find pane at the bottom of the Editing window.

7. When Expression Web lists the pages in which the text you're seeking was found (step four), you can open any of these pages by double-clicking the page from the list. The first instance of the text you're looking for is highlighted. This text can be replaced via the Replace command.

8. To continue searching the page, click the blue **Next** or **Back** arrows in the Find pane.

9. When you're done, click **Close** in the dialog box and task pane.

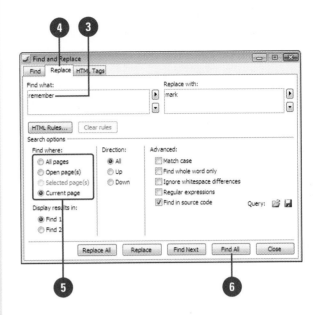

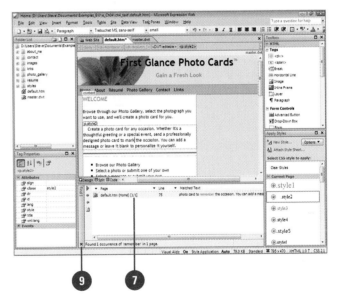

Did You Know?

You can perform a search on part of a Web page. Perform an initial find with the criteria you want. Click the Edit menu, click Incremental Search, and then click the text you want to search.

Finding and Replacing HTML Tags

In addition to finding and replacing text and code, you can also find and replace HTML tags. The Find and Replace dialog box includes an HTML Tags tab, which you can use to search for and replace HTML tags. You can search one or more Web page or an entire Web site. When you search multiple pages, the results appear in a Find task pane, which makes it easy to view and work with the results in different page view. The Split view allows you to search for tags without having to change your view.

Find and Replace HTML Tags

1. In the Folder List, open or select the one or more pages you want to search.

   ◆ To select multiple pages, use Ctrl+click.

2. Click the **Edit** menu, and then click **Find**.

3. Click the **HTML Tags** tab.

4. Click the **Find tag** list arrow, and then select the tag you want to find.

5. If you want to replace the tag, click the **Replace action** list arrow, select an action, and then specify what you want to replace it with.

6. Click the find where and direction options you want.

7. Select the search parameters you want (Match case, Find whole word only, etc.).

Continue Next Page

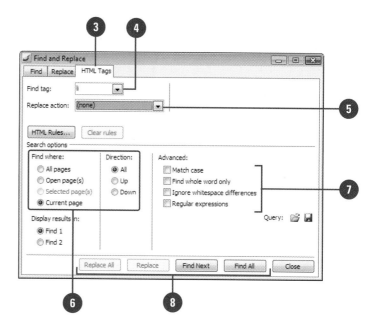

Did You Know?

You can open the Find and Replace dialog box from the Find pane. Click the green arrow at the top of the Find pane to open the Find and Replace dialog box.

8. Select one of the following buttons:

   ◆ **Find All** or **Find Next button.**
   Locates all instances or the next instance of the text.

   ◆ **Replace All** or **Replace button.**
   Replaces all instances or the selected instance of the text.

   The list of pages containing the selected tags opens in the Find pane at the bottom of the Editing window.

9. When Expression Web lists the pages in which the text you're seeking was found (step four), you can open any of these pages by double-clicking the page from the list. The first instance of the text you're looking for is highlighted. This text can be replaced via the Replace command.

10. To continue searching the page, click the blue **Next** or **Back** arrows in the Find pane.

11. When you're done, click the **Close** button in the Find pane.

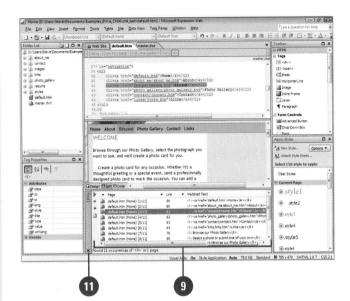

Did You Know?

You can display two different find results. Expression Web provides two Find panes. In the Find and Replace dialog box, you can select the one you want to use. This means you can work with two different find results at the same time.

You can save searches as a query. Perform a search using the Find and Replace dialog box, and then click the Save Query button. To open a previously save query, click the Open Query button.

Checking Spelling

Using Expression Web, you can correct spelling errors on a Web site immediately, or create a task for each page with an error and correct them later. Begin by opening the page whose spelling you want to examine. If you commonly use words unique to a hobby or profession that would not appear in a normal dictionary, or are unlikely to be part of the common vernacular, consider adding them to your dictionary so that they will not repeatedly be called into question during spell checks.

Check Spelling in a Web Page

1. Open and display the Web page you want to check, and then click where you want to start checking.

2. Click the **Tools** menu, point to **Spelling**, and then click **Spelling**.

    The program begins scanning the pages for words that aren't in its dictionary.

3. Click the suggested word or type the correct word, and then click **Change**. Click **Change All** to correct all instances of the word.

4. If the unrecognized word is correctly spelled but the program doesn't know it (as with a name, for example), click **Ignore** to ignore this instance of the word, or click **Ignore All** to ignore all instances of this word.

5. Click **Add** to add this word to your custom dictionary.

6. When the spell checker reaches the end of the document, if it hasn't searched the beginning, a prompt will ask if you want it to resume the search at the start of the document.

7. When you're done, click **OK**.

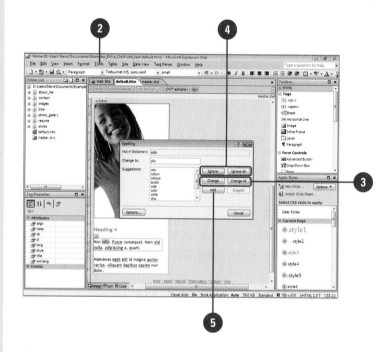

Spell Checking in a Web Site

1. If necessary, click the **View** menu, and then click **Folder List** to display the Folder List.

2. Select the Web site or the pages you want to check. To select multiple pages, click the first page, and then press and hold down Ctrl while clicking the other pages.

3. Click the **Tools** menu, point to **Spelling**, and then click **Spelling**.

4. Click the **Entire Web Site** option or the **Selected Page(s)** option.

5. Click **Start**.

6. Double-click the first misspelled word in the list. If a misspelled word needs to be corrected, the Spelling dialog box opens. Otherwise, the Continue With The Next Page? dialog box opens.

7. To correct a misspelled word, use the buttons in the Spelling dialog box to change or ignore the misspelled word. To continue spell checking the next page, click **Next Page**.

8. If you want to stop the spell check or it is done checking all the pages, click **Back To List**.

9. Click **Cancel** to close the Spelling dialog box.

Did You Know?

You can add a task for misspelled words. By assigning spelling corrections to Tasks, you can come back and correct them at your convenience. Click the Add a Task for Each Page With Misspellings check box to select it in the Spelling dialog box.

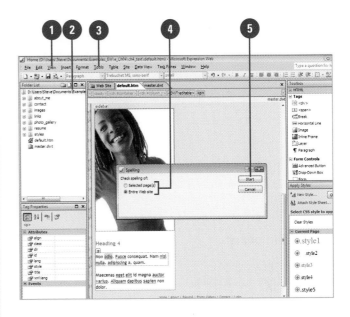

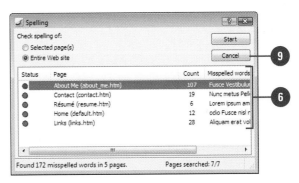

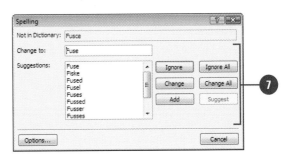

Using Custom Dictionaries

Before you can use a custom dictionary, you need to enable it first. You can enable and manage custom dictionaries by using the Custom Dictionaries dialog box. In the dialog box, you can change the language associated with a custom dictionary, create a new custom dictionary, or add or remove an existing custom dictionary. If you need to manage dictionary content, you can also change the default custom dictionary to which the spelling checker adds words, as well as add, delete, or edit words. If you mistakenly type an obscene or embarrassing word, such as *ass* instead of *ask*, the spelling checker will not catch it because both words are spelled correctly. You can avoid this problem by using an exclusion dictionary. When you use a language for the first time, Expression Web automatically creates an exclusion dictionary. This dictionary forces the spelling checker to flag words you don't want to use.

Use a Custom Dictionary

1 Click the **Tools** menu, point to **Spelling**, and then click **Spelling Options**.

2 Click **Custom Dictionaries**.

3 Select the check box next to **CUSTOM.DIC (Default)**.

4 Click the **Dictionary language** list arrow, and then select a language for a dictionary.

5 Click the options you want:

   ◆ Click **Edit Word List** to add, delete, or edit words.

   ◆ Click **Change Default** to select a new default dictionary.

   ◆ Click **New** to create a new dictionary.

   ◆ Click **Add** to insert an existing dictionary.

   ◆ Click **Remove** to delete a dictionary.

6 Click **OK** to close the Custom Dictionaries dialog box.

7 Click **OK**.

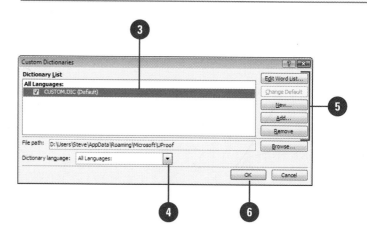

Find and Modify the Exclusion Dictionary

1. In Windows Explorer, go to the folder location where the custom dictionaries are stored.

   - **Windows Vista.** C:\Users*user name*\AppData\Roaming\Microsoft\UProof

   - **Windows XP.** C:\Documents and Settings*user name*\Application Data\Microsoft\UProof

   TROUBLE? *If you can't find the folder, change folder settings to show hidden files and folders.*

2. Locate the exclusion dictionary for the language you want to change.

   - The file name you want is ExcludeDictionary *Language Code Language LCID*.lex.

     For example, ExcludeDictionary EN0409.lex, where EN is for English.

     Check Word Help for an updated list of LCID (Local Identification Number) number for each language.

3. Open the file using Microsoft Notepad or WordPad.

4. Add each word you want the spelling check to flag as misspelled. Type the words in all lowercase and then press Enter after each word.

5. Save and close the file.

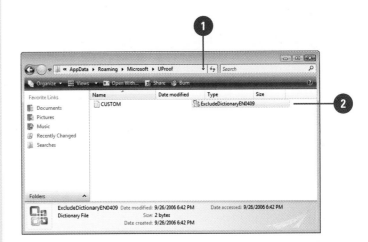

Checking Spelling for Languages

International Expression Web users can change the language that appears on their screens by changing the default language settings. Before you can use a different language, you need to install the Microsoft Expression Web Language Pack for the languages you want to use in a Web site. After you install a language, you can set the default language for a Web page, Web site, and a custom dictionary. If the text in your Web page is written in more than one language, you can designate the language of selected text so the spelling checker uses the right dictionary. However, the keyboard you use to enter text determines the language used by the spelling checker.

Mark Text as a Language

1. Open and display the Web page you want to use.

2. Select the text you want to mark.

3. Click the **Tools** menu, and then click **Set Language**.

4. Click the language you want to assign to the selected text.

5. Click **OK**.

Did You Know?

You can specify your keyboard layout. After you enable editing for another language, such as Hebrew, Cyrillic, or Greek, you might need to install the correct keyboard layout so you can enter characters for that language. The keyboard you use to enter text determines the language used by the spelling checker. In the Control Panel (Classic view), double-click the Regional and Language Options icon, click the Language (XP) or Keyboards and Languages (Vista) tab, and then click Details (XP) or Change Keyboards (Vista) to check your keyboard.

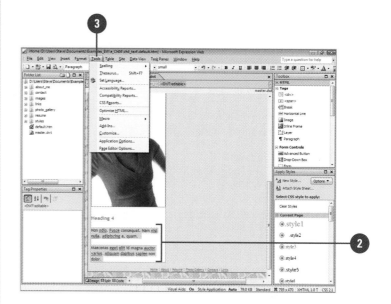

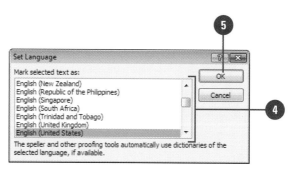

Set Default Spelling Language for a Web Site

1️⃣ Open and display the Web site you want to use.

2️⃣ Click the **Tools** menu, and then click **Page Editor Options**.

3️⃣ Click the **General** tab.

4️⃣ Click the **Default Page Language** list arrow, and then select a language.

5️⃣ Click **OK**.

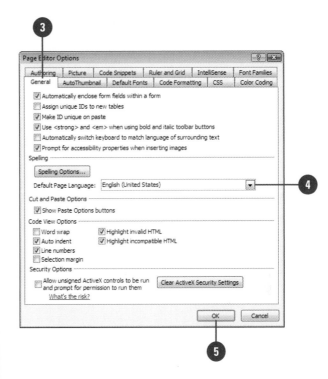

See Also

See "Changing Web Page Properties" on page 54 for information on setting the language used for spell checking on a Web page.

See "Using Custom Dictionaries" on page 108 for information on setting the language used for a custom dictionary.

Checking Spelling as You Type

As you type, a red wavy line appears under words not listed in Expression Web's dictionary (such as misspellings or names) or duplicated words (such as the the). You can correct these errors as they arise. When Expression Web learns the spellings of words you use regularly, it even automatically corrects some errors as you type. If the unrecognized work is correct, you can add it to the dictionary.

Enable Check Spelling and Grammar Options

1. Click the **Tools** menu, point to **Spelling**, and then click **Spelling Options**.

2. Select the **Check spelling as you type** check box.

3. Click **OK**.

Correct Spelling and Grammar as You Type

1. In a Web page, right-click a word with a red wavy underline.

2. Click a substitution, or click **Ignore All** to skip any other instances of the word.

Did You Know?

You can remove the red wavy line. Click the Tools menu, point to Spelling, click Spelling Options, select the Hide spelling errors check box, and then click OK.

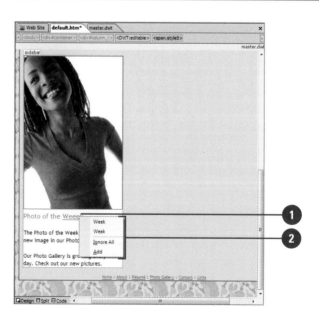

Finding the Right Words

Repeating the same word in a Web page can reduce a message's effectiveness. Instead, replace some words with synonyms, words with similar meanings, or find antonyms, words with opposite meanings. If you need help finding exactly the right word, you can use the Thesaurus.

Use the Thesaurus

1. Open and display the Web page you want to use.

2. Select the word you want to look up.

3. Click the **Tools** menu, and then click **Thesaurus**.

4. Click a word to display its synonyms and antonyms.

5. Click the word you want to use or type one you want.

6. Click **Replace**.

7. Click **Cancel**.

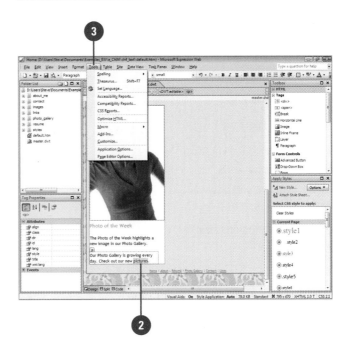

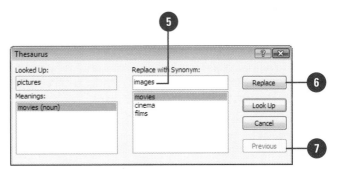

Changing Default Text

When you type text in a page, Expression Web applies a set of default text attributes. You can change the default text for Design and Code views. In Design view, you can change the default proportional and fixed-width fonts. A proportional font has variable spacing between letters, while a fixed-width font has the same spacing between letters. Proportional fonts are typically used for Web page text, while fixed-width fonts are typically used for working with code. When you are working with large amounts of text, a fixed-width font is easier to read.

Change Default Text

① Click the **Tools** menu, and then click **Page Editor Options**.

② Click the **Default Fonts** tab.

③ Click the language you want as the default.

④ Select the defaults fonts you want for Design view.

⑤ Select the default font and size you want for Code view.

⑥ Click **OK**.

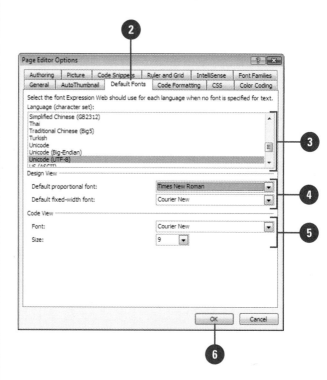

Creating and Changing Font Families

Instead of applying one font to text in a Web page, you can apply a set of fonts, known as a font family, in order to increase the likelihood that the visitor's computer system will have one of the fonts you specify. Expression Web comes with a few font families when you install the program, such as Arial, Helvetica, sans-serif. You can modify an existing font family or create your own. When you create your own, use fonts that are the same relative size, so using any of the fonts in the font family looks the same on any computer.

Create and Change Font Families

1. Click the **Tools** menu, and then click **Page Editor Options**.

2. Click the **Font Families** tab.

3. Click **(New Font Family)** to create a new one or click an existing one to change it.

4. To add a font to a family, select a font, and then click **Add**.

5. To remove a font families, select the font family, and then click **Remove**.

6. To change the priority order, select a font family, and then click **Move Up** or **Move Down**.

7. Click **OK**.

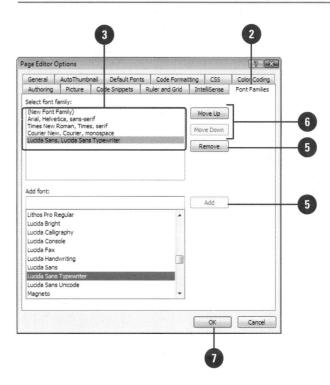

Inserting Text from a File

If you have a word processing document that you want to use as a Web page, you can insert the entire file. You use the File command on the Insert menu to select the file and insert the contents. The Select File dialog box works just like the Open dialog box. Expression Web allows you to insert files in several formats, including Rich Text Format (.rtf), Text Files (.txt), Word 2007 (docx), Word 97-2003 (.doc), and HTML (.htm, .html).

Insert a File

1. Open and display the Web page you want to use.

2. Click where you want to insert the content of the file.

3. Click the **Insert** menu, and then click **File**.

   ◆ If the File command is not available, see "Customizing the Menu bar" on page 368 to add it to the Insert menu.

   The Select File dialog box opens.

4. Click the **Files of type** list arrow, and then select the type of file you want to insert.

5. Locate and select the file.

6. Click **Open**.

7. If necessary, select an option, and then click **OK**.

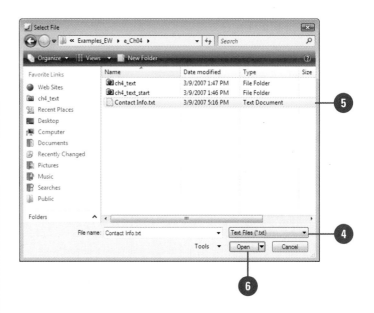

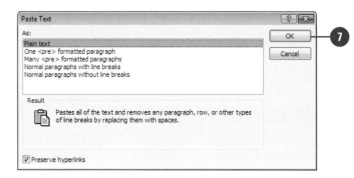

Working with Web Page Graphics

5

Introduction

As you begin to include graphics into your Web pages, it's important to understand all the different types of graphics and how they can be used in Microsoft Expression Web. There are company logos for business sites, banner graphics, special bullets, link bars with navigation buttons, and so forth. The most common formats for graphics are GIF and JPEG. You can insert pictures from files, digital cameras, or scanned images.

Once you get the graphic into your Web page, you can move it to the location you want. You might need to manipulate the graphic by rotating or flipping it for the perfect fit and angle. Most likely, you'll also need to crop or resize the graphic to be the size you need. You can position graphics and text elements on the page in different ways. Use absolute positioning to place an element at an exact location on the page, or relative positioning to place an element inline with text, where it can move depending on the changes you make the page. Instead of waiting for a large picture to download, you can use a small preview picture, known as a thumbnail, which downloads much faster. It's common practice to display a small preview picture and give the visitor the choice of whether to view the larger version. Other graphical features include adding page transitions to your Web site for a custom feel.

Other graphic elements such as working with layers, wrapping text, changing a graphic's contrast and brightness, changing colors, and other graphical formatting can be done in Expression Web. More technical elements such as changing a graphic's format, changing the way a graphic is displayed, and creating a low resolution graphic can also be done. If there have been too many changes to a graphic, Expression Web let's you start over by restoring the graphic and its original properties.

What You'll Do

Understand Graphics

Change Graphic Defaults

Insert Graphics

Copy and Paste Graphics from the Web

Select and Move Graphics

Resize and Resample Graphics

Create Thumbnails

Crop, Rotate, and Flip Graphics

Change Graphic Positioning

Change Graphic Stacking Order

Work with Layers

Wrap Text and Align Graphics

Adjust Graphic Contrast and Brightness

Convert Graphic Color

Add a Bevel to a Graphic

Add Margins and Padding to Graphics

Apply Borders and Shading

Change Graphic Formats

Change the Way Graphics are Displayed

Restore a Graphic

Understanding Graphics

Graphics can be used to provide visual interest, supplemental information, or even to support a theme. Whether it's the company logo on a business site or a special photo on your personal site, graphics brighten up a Web. Graphics can be used in a variety of ways in Expression Web. For example, you can use a graphic element as a background. There are company logos for business sites, banner graphics, special bullets, link bars with navigation buttons, and so forth. The most common formats for graphics are **GIF** (CompuServe's Graphics Interchange, which uses up to 256 colors) and **JPEG** (Joint Photographic Experts Group, which uses more than 256 colors). Both formats have

specific strengths and weaknesses. GIFs work best for buttons, solid blocks of color and illustrations, while JPEGs work best for photographs. With GIF format graphics, for example, you can designate one of your 256 or fewer colors as transparent, while JPEG is better suited to pictures containing thousands, or even millions of colors.

You can also determine the level of file compression by resetting the graphic quality. The lower you set the quality, the higher the file compression and the smaller the file size.

There are several other graphic formats, including:

♦ **PNG** (Portable Network Graphics, a GIF alternative that supports transparency for multiple colors)

♦ **BMP** (Bitmap Format, the native Microsoft Windows format supports graphics up to 24-bits)

♦ **WMF** (Microsoft Windows Metafile, which supports bitmapped vector and EPS data; for example, clip art from the Microsoft Clip Organizer is WMF).

When you save a graphic in a file format other than GIF or JPEG, Expression Web converts the file to GIF format if it has 256 colors or less, or to JPEG if it has more than 256 colors. You can change the default file type settings and the default file type conversion and paste setting by using the Pictures tab in the Page Editor Options dialog box.

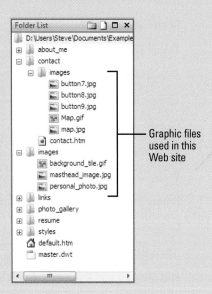

Graphic files used in this Web site

Changing Graphic Defaults

When you insert a graphic in a file format other than GIF or JPEG, such as Microsoft Office clip art in the WMF file format, Expression Web converts the file to GIF format if it has 256 colors or less, or to JPEG if it has more than 256 colors. When you save the Web page, Expression Web prompts you to save the graphics using the Save Embedded Files dialog box. The graphic file formats are set to program defaults, which you can change by using the Picture tab in the Page Editor Options dialog box. You can change the default file type settings and the default file type conversion and paste setting.

Change Graphic Defaults

1. Click the **Tools** menu, and then click **Page Editor Options**.

2. Click the **Picture** tab.

3. Click **File Types Settings**.

4. For GIF images, select or deselect the following check boxes:

   ◆ **Interlaced.** Select to paint the picture in bands rather than from top to bottom.

   ◆ **Transparent.** Select to use one color in the image as transparent; turn off and use the Set Transparent Color button on the Picture toolbar to set the color.

5. For JPEG images, specify quality and progressive settings:

   ◆ **Quality.** Specify the quality you want; higher the quality, the larger the file size.

   ◆ **Progressive Passes.** Specify the number of passes to display a low-quality version of the picture and then gradually increase the quality to set value.

6. Click **OK**.

7. Select the formats you want for the Default File Type Conversion and Paste Settings: **256 or Fewer Colors** and **More than 256 Colors**.

8. Click **OK**.

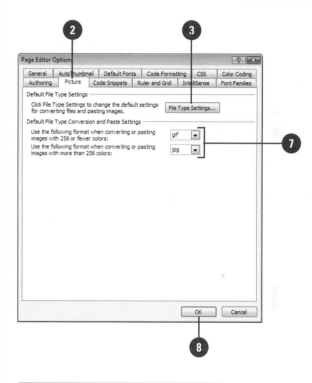

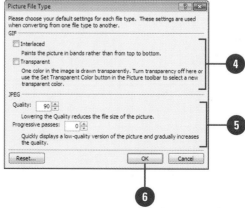

Inserting Graphics

Expression Web makes it possible for you to insert graphics, pictures, scanned or digital photographs, or artwork you scanned or created in a drawing program. You can use the Insert menu to insert files or you can drag and drop files from the Folder List. When you open your Web site, the files and folders in the Web site folder appear in the Folder List. You can use Windows Explorer to copy or move files into the Web site folder and then drag files onto your Web pages from the Folder List.

Insert Graphics from a File

1. Open and display the Web page you want to use.

2. Position the insertion point where you want to insert a graphic.

3. Click the **Insert** menu, point to **Picture**, and then click **From File**.

   TIMESAVER *Click the Insert Picture from File button on the Pictures toolbar.*

4. Navigate to the drive and folder location of the file you want to insert.

5. Click the file(s) you want to insert.

6. Click **Insert**.

7. For accessibility purposes, type a brief description of the graphic in the Alternate text box or a more detailed using a file (such as a .htm) in the Long description box.

8. Click **OK**.

9. Click the **Save** button on the Common toolbar.

   If the graphics are not already included in the Web site folder, the Save Embedded Files dialog box opens.

10. If you want to change folder location, click **Change Folder**, navigate to the Web site folder, and then click **OK**.

11. Click **OK**.

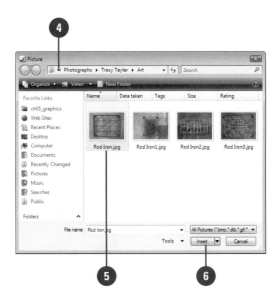

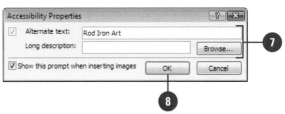

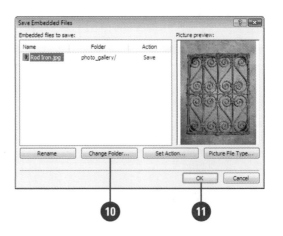

Insert Graphics from the Folder List

1. Use Windows Explorer to copy or move the graphic files you want to use into the Web site folder.

2. Open and display the Web site in which you want to insert graphics.

3. If necessary, click the **View** menu, and then click **Folder List** to display the Folder List.

4. If necessary, double-click the folder with the graphics you want to use.

5. Drag a graphic file to a location on the Web page.

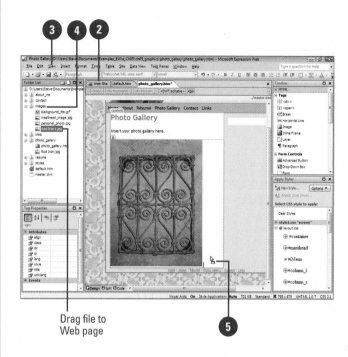

Drag file to
Web page

See Also

See "Resizing and Resampling Graphics" on page 128 for information on resizing a graphic.

Did You Know?

You can display thumbnail images in the Picture dialog box. In the Picture dialog box, click the View button list arrow, and then click Thumbnails (XP) or one of the Icon views (Vista).

You can have the alternate text read aloud. Some programs for the visually impaired read aloud the text in the Alternate text box.

For Your Information

Tracing Graphics

If you have a scanned image of a Web page layout or an existing document that you want to use on a Web page, you can use Trace Image to make it easier for you to re-create. Trace Image sets a copy of the image as a background picture in Design view. Open the Web page in which you want to trace an image, click the View menu, point to Trace Image, click Configure, click Browse and locate the image you want to use, set the x and y (distance from the left (x) and top (y) edge of Design view to the left and top edge of the tracing image), set the Opacity, and then click OK. After you specify a tracing image, you can use Show Image on the Trace Image submenu to display and hide the image.

Inserting Photoshop Graphics

Expression Web makes it possible for you to insert graphics and layers from an Adobe Photoshop PSD file (**New!**). Adobe Photoshop is a graphics design and image enhancement program developed by Adobe System Incorporated. In Photoshop, you can manipulate an image thousands of ways, everything from color correction, reducing dust and scratches in an old image, to removing a tree, or adding a missing friend. You can generate a PNG, GIF, or JPEG file from a Photoshop PSD file and select which layers to include and which to exclude from the graphic image. After you insert a PSD file, you can edit the original file in Photoshop and then update it later into your Web page.

Insert Photoshop Graphics and Layers from a PSD File

1. Open the Web site and display the Web page you want to use.

2. Position the insertion point where you want to insert a graphic.

3. Click the **Insert** menu, point to **Picture**, and then click **From Adobe Photoshop (.psd)**.

4. Navigate to the drive and folder location of the file you want to insert.

5. Click the file(s) you want to insert.

6. Click **Open**.

7. Click the **All Layers Image** option or click the **Selected Layers** option, and then select the check boxes with the layers you want to import.

8. Click the **Encoding** list arrow, select the file format you want, and then specify a quality setting if you select the JPEG format.

9. Click the **Optimized** tab to view the modified image, or click the **Original** tab to view the original file.

10. Click **Import**.

11. Type alternative text and a brief description for accessibility purposes, and then click **OK**.

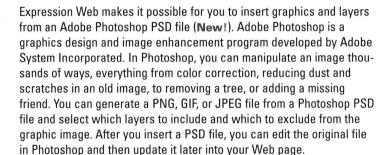

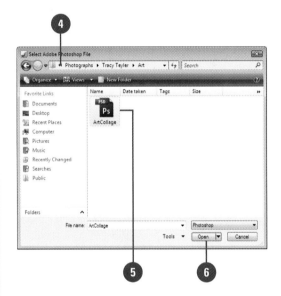

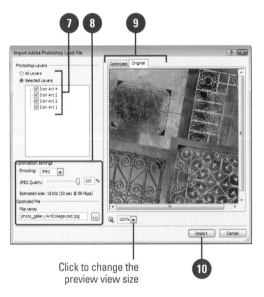

Click to change the preview view size

Edit a Graphic in Photoshop and Update the Web Page

1. Open and display the Web page that contains the graphic imported from Adobe Photoshop.

2. In Design view, right-click the graphic, point to **Adobe Photoshop PSD**, and then click **Edit Source (... file name)**.

   The default application, such as Adobe Photoshop or Adobe Photoshop Elements, for editing PSD files launches and opens the PSD file from your Web page.

3. Make and save the changes you want to the PSD file, and then exit Photoshop.

   The Photoshop graphic is updated back in Expression Web.

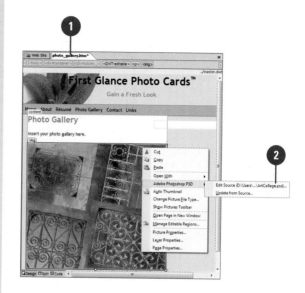

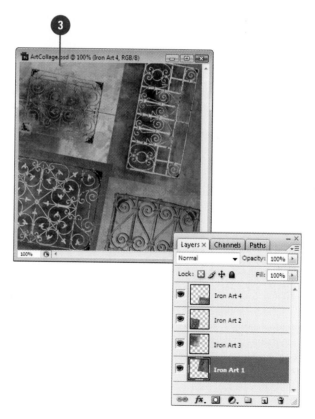

Did You Know?

You can edit and update the graphic independently. Instead of accessing Photoshop from Expression Web, you can open, edit, and save the graphic separately in Photoshop, and then update the graphic later in your Web page. To update the graphic in your Web page, right-click the graphic, point to Adobe Photoshop PSD in Design view, click Update from Source, set the options you want, and then click Import.

You can also import Adobe Photoshop files. Click the File menu, point to Import, click Adobe Photoshop (.psd), select the PSD file, click Open, specify the import options you want (see previous page for details), and then click Import.

Inserting a Graphic from a Scanner or Camera

If you have a scanner or digital camera connected to your computer, you can scan or download a picture into a Web page. You can use a digital still or video camera, or a live Web camera. For a video or Web camera, you can capture an image and use it in a Web page. When you scan an image, you can use default or custom settings to scan and insert the image. Check the instructions that come with your digital camera or scanner to make sure it is set up correctly and is compatible with Expression Web. Images from a scanner or digital camera are typically large, so if you have a lot of images you may be better off scanning or moving the image file to your hard disk and resizing them in a graphics program and then insert them into Expression Web. However, you can also resize and resample images in Expression Web too.

Insert a Graphic from a Scanner or Camera

1 Open and display the Web page you want to use.

2 Click to place the insertion point where you want to insert the graphic.

3 Click the **Insert** menu, point to **Picture**, and then click **From Scanner or Camera**.

> **IMPORTANT** *Your steps may vary depending on your scanner and operating system.*

4 Click the **Device** list arrow, and then select the device connected to your computer.

5 Select the resolution (the visual quality of the image) you want.

6 To use default settings, click **Insert**.

7 To specify your own settings to scan a picture or capture and select a camera image, click **Custom Insert**, and then follow the device instructions.

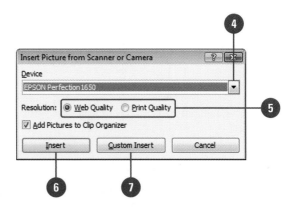

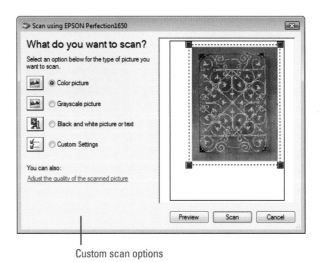

Custom scan options

Copying and Pasting Graphics from the Web

Copying and pasting objects is another integral part of Web design. In a Web page, you can copy and paste graphics in the same way in which you copy and paste text. When you want to copy a graphic from the Web, the process is slightly different in a Web browser; you use the right-click method. When you copy material from the Web, you need to get permission from the owner to use it. In many cases, the Web site provides conditions of use.

Copy and Paste Graphics from the Web

1. Open your Web browser, and then search the Web for a graphic as you normally would using your browser.

2. Right-click the graphic, and then click **Copy**. Depending on your browser, you command might differ.

3. Close your browser and switch back to Expression Web.

4. Open and display the Web page you want to use.

5. Click where you want to insert the graphic.

6. Click the **Edit** menu, and then click **Paste**.

    This inserts a reference on your page to the graphic on the Web site.

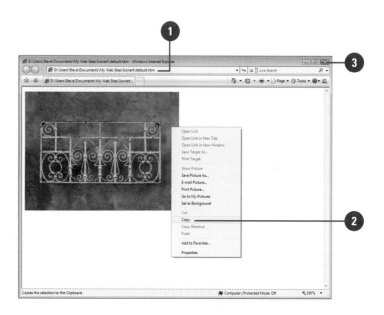

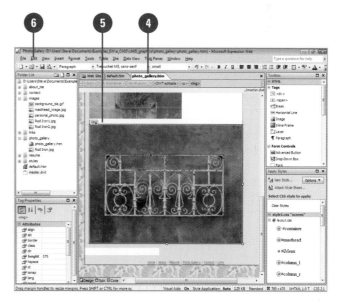

Selecting and Moving Graphics

As you learn more about and use Expression Web, you'll want to enhance your Web pages with more than just text. To do so, you can insert an object. An **object** is a picture or graphic image you create with a drawing program or insert from an existing file of another program. For example, you can insert a company logo that you have drawn yourself, or you can insert clip art. To work with an object, you need to select it first. Then you can resize or move it with its selection handles, the little circles that appear on the edges of the selected object.

Select and Deselect an Object

◆ In Page view, click an object to display its handles.

To select more than one object at a time, hold down Shift as you click each object.

◆ In Page view, click elsewhere within the document window to deselect a selected object.

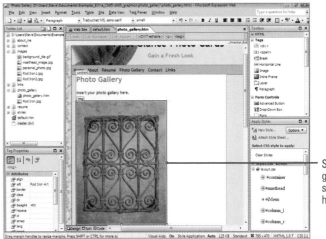

Selected graphic; sizing handles

Move an Object

1 Open and display the Web page you want to use.

2 Click an object to select it.

3 Drag the object to a new location.

4 Release the mouse button to drop the object in the new location.

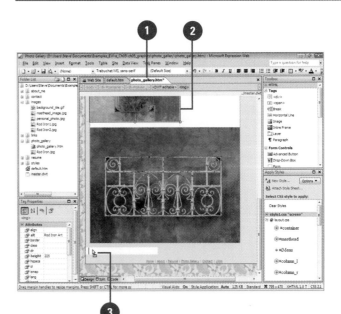

Working with Graphics

When you select a graphic, the Pictures toolbar appears by default unless you close it. The Pictures toolbar provides buttons to perform simple editing tasks, such as cropping, flipping, rotating, and adjusting brightness and contrast. If you need to perform major editing, it's best to use a graphics program designed to do the job. After you edit a graphic and save the changes, you have the option to save the graphics as a new file or replace the original using the Save Embedded Files dialog box.

Modify Graphics Using the Pictures Toolbar

1. Open and display the Web page you want to use.

2. In the Design or Split view, click the picture you want to select it.

   The Pictures toolbar displays when you select a picture.

3. If the Pictures toolbar doesn't open, click the **Edit** menu, point to **Toolbars**, and then click **Pictures**.

4. Click the buttons you want on the Pictures toolbar to make changes to the graphic.

5. Click the **Save** button on the Common toolbar.

   If the graphics are not already included in the Web site folder, the Save Embedded Files dialog box opens.

6. Click **Change Folder**, navigate to the Web site folder, and then click **OK**.

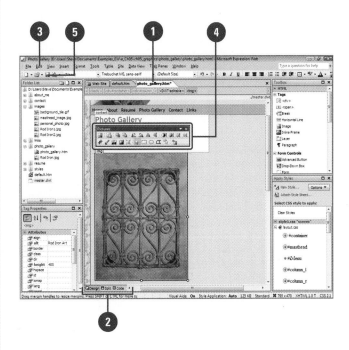

See Also

See "Restoring a Graphic" on page 152 for information on restoring a graphic back to its original state.

Resizing and Resampling Graphics

When you insert a graphic from a scanner or digital camera, the graphic typically comes in large, so you'll need to resize it. You can resize graphics, using both numerical and graphic-direct techniques. However, if you enlarge a graphic too much, you lose image details. After you resize a graphic, the Picture Actions button appears, where you have the option to retain the picture file's original size, but tell the browser to use the new size, or to change the picture's physical size to the new size, known as **resampling**. The next time you save the page, Expression Web prompts you to save the picture at the new size.

Resize Graphics Directly

1. Open and display the Web page you want to use.

2. Select the graphic you want to resize. Resize handles appear on the graphic.

3. Drag a resize handle (small squares) to the size you want. To resize a graphic while preserving its proportions (that is, its aspect ratio), hold down the Shift key while you drag a handle located in the graphic's corners diagonally.

4. Click the **Picture Actions** button, and then click an option to resample or not.

   ◆ **Only Modify Size Attributes.** Modifies the picture size attributes in the HTML code yet retains the original picture size.

   ◆ **Resample Picture To Match Size.** Changes the physical picture size on the page and in the file.

> **Did You Know?**
>
> *You can use the Resample button later.* If you want to resample a picture later, select the picture, and then click the Resample button on the Pictures toolbar.

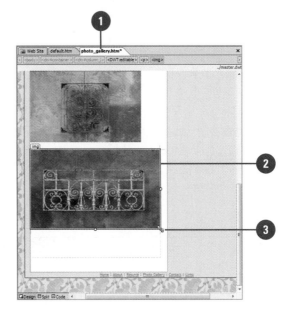

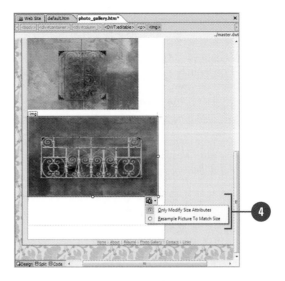

Resize Graphics Numerically

1. Open and display the Web page you want to use.

2. Right-click the graphic, and then click **Picture Properties**.

3. Click the **Appearance** tab.

4. Select the **Specify size** check box.

5. If you want to preserve the height-to-width proportions of the picture, select the **Keep aspect ratio** check box. The aspect ratio refers to the proportions of a graphic. If you select this option, you only need to change the width or height, not both.

6. Decide whether you want to change the size in pixels or in percentage, and then enter values in the Width and Height boxes.

7. Click **OK**.

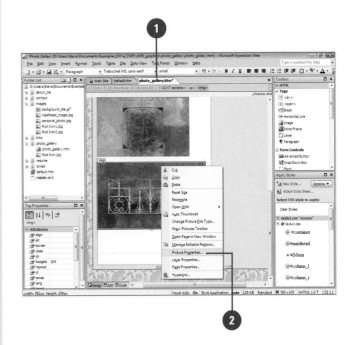

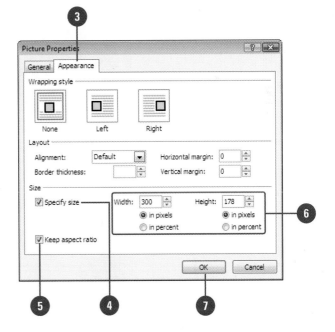

Creating Thumbnails

Instead of waiting for a large picture to download, you can use a small preview picture, known as a thumbnail, which downloads much faster. It's common practice to display a small preview picture and give the visitor the choice of whether to view the larger version. Expression Web makes it easy to create a thumbnail using the Auto Thumbnail feature. The command removes the large graphic, creates the thumbnail in its place, and then sets up a hyperlink from the thumbnail to the large graphic. Expression Web creates a thumbnail based on the default setting in the Page Editor Options dialog box. You can change the default graphic size in pixels and add a border or bevel edge.

Create a Thumbnail

1. Open and display the Web page you want to use.

2. Select the graphic you want to use to create a thumbnail.

3. Click the **Auto Thumbnail** button on the Pictures toolbar.

   TIMESAVER *Press Ctrl+T to use Auto Thumbnail.*

   ◆ You can also right-click the graphic, and then click Auto Thumbnail.

   The original graphic is replaced by a thumbnail image.

4. To view the thumbnail and larger image, press F12 to start your Web browser, and then click a thumbnail.

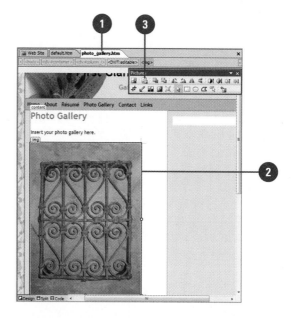

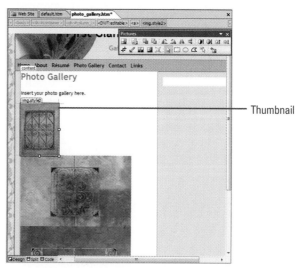

Thumbnail

Set AutoThumbnail Properties

1. Click the **Tools** menu, and then click **Page Editor Options**.

2. Click the **AutoThumbnail** tab.

3. Select the general and usage options you want. Some of the common options include:

   ◆ **Set.** Controls the size of the thumbnail picture. You can choose to make all the thumbnail pictures the same width, height, shortest side, or longest side.

   ◆ **Pixels.** Specifies the fixed size applied to the edge.

   ◆ **Border Thickness.** Create borders around each thumbnail picture.

   ◆ **Beveled Edge.** Creates beveled edges for each thumbnail picture.

4. Click **OK**.

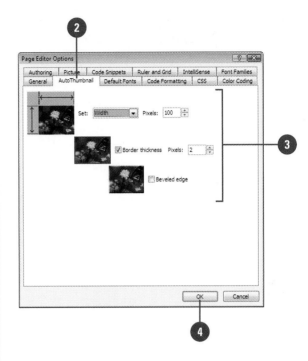

Cropping Graphics

Cropping is the process of framing a portion of a photo and eliminating any unnecessary visual elements. If, for example, you have a photo that is not centered properly, you can crop out the side to center it. You can use the Crop button on the Pictures toolbar to drag a resize handle on a graphic to crop out part of the image. The graph remains unchanged and you can uncrop it at any time.

Crop a Graphic

1 Open and display the Web page you want to use.

2 Select the graphic you want to crop.

Resize handles appear on the graphic and the Pictures toolbar opens.

3 Click the **Crop** button on the Pictures toolbar.

A cropping box appears inside the graphic.

4 Drag a resize handle on the cropping box to include the part of the graphic that you want to keep.

5 Click the **Crop** button on the Pictures toolbar again to eliminate the area outside of the cropping box.

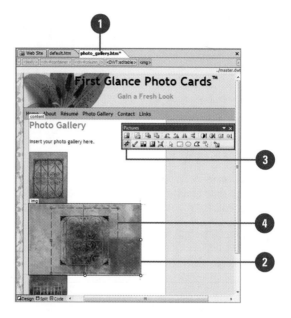

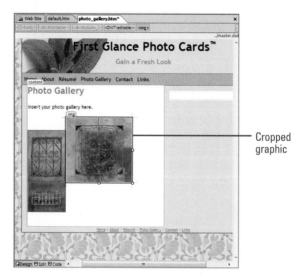

Cropped graphic

Rotating and Flipping Graphics

After you insert a graphic or create an object, you can change its orientation on the page by rotating or flipping it. Rotating a graphic keeps the original front to back positioning and rotates the graphic clockwise or counter-clockwise to achieve the desired affect, while flipping a graphic creates a mirror graphic of a graphic, oriented either horizontally or vertically. Rotating turns an object 90 degrees to the right or left; flipping turns an object 180 degrees horizontally or vertically.

Rotate and Flip Graphics

① Open and display the Web page you want to use.

② Select the graphic you want to flip or rotate.

③ To rotate the graphic, click either the **Rotate Right 90** button or the **Rotate Left 90** button on the Pictures toolbar.

④ To flip the graphic, click either the **Flip Horizontal** button or the **Flip Vertical** button on the Pictures toolbar.

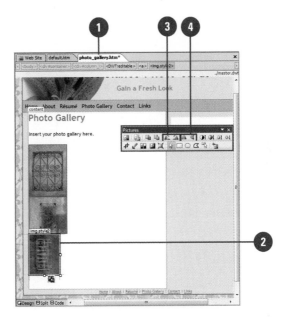

Changing Graphic Positioning

Expression Web gives you the control you need to place graphics and text on the page in exactly the place where you want them. You can position graphics and text elements on the page in different ways. You can use absolute positioning to place an element at an exact location on the page, or relative positioning to place an element inline with text, where it can move depending on the changes you make on the page. When you change positioning, Expression Web creates a separate layer (identified by a blue border and a name tag in the upper-left corner) for the element, which you can resize, move, and name. An element placed using absolute positioning appears in a fixed location relative to the top-left corner of the page.

Change Graphic Positioning

1 Open and display the Web page you want to use.

2 Select the graphic you want to change positioning.

3 Click the **Format** menu, and then click **Position**.

4 Click the **Absolute** or **Relative** box.

5 Click **OK**.

A blue layer appears with the graphic.

6 To move or resize the positioning layer, click the edge of the layer (if necessary), and then drag the edge or a handle.

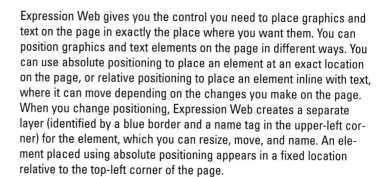
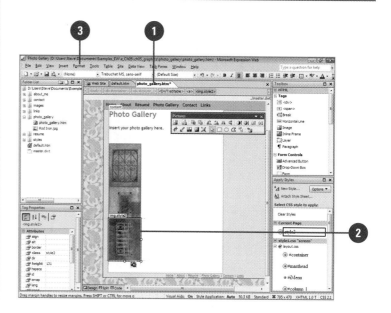

> ### Did You Know?
>
> **You can use the Positioning or Pictures toolbar to set absolute positioning options.** Right-click any toolbar, and then click Positioning or Pictures. Select the Web page elements you want, click the Position Absolutely button, and then drag the handles to resize the positioning layer.

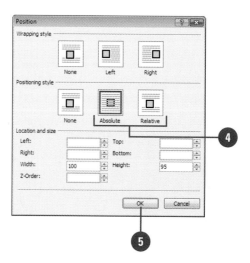

Changing Graphic Stacking Order

Absolute positioning allows you to position graphics in a stacking order relative to each other. Stacking is the placement of objects one on top of another to overlay each other. You can create overlapping graphics by applying absolute positioning to each graphic you want to arrange, selecting individual graphics, and using the Bring Forward and Send Backward buttons on the Pictures toolbar. The stacking position is indicated by the z-value in the Position dialog box or the Layers task pane, where you can change it. A higher z-value appears on top. You can set positioned graphics in front of or behind both regular page content and each other. However, at different solutions, absolute elements might not appear exactly where you intended. Be sure to test the page.

Change Graphic Stacking Order

1. Open and display the Web page you want to use.

2. Select the object or objects you want to arrange.

   ◆ If necessary, click the **Format** menu, click **Position**, click **Absolute**, and then click **OK** for each graphic, so you can arrange them.

3. Click the **Bring Forward** or **Send Backward** button on the Pictures toolbar.

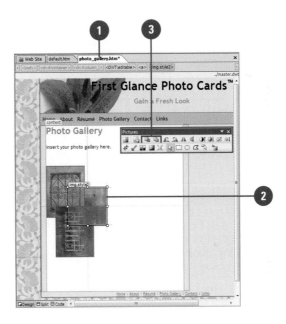

Did You Know?

You can move or resize the positioning layer. Click the edge of the layer (if necessary) to select it, and then drag the layer edge to move it or a handle to resize it.

See Also

See "Setting Position Properties" on page 305 for more information on position properties and setting them using CSS.

Working with Layers

Expression Web provides the Layers task pane to make it easy to work with layers. You can use the Layers task pane to create, name, and control the display of layered elements. In addition to creating a layer when you apply positioning, you can also insert or draw empty layers and then insert graphics and text. In the task pane, you can click the Eye icon to toggle between visible (eye open), hidden (eye closed), and inherit (no icon). The inherit state takes its visibility from the positioned element. The z-value in the task pane identifies the overlap (where the higher z-value appears on top). The ID value is the layer name referred to by scripts and style sheets.

Create and Name a Layer

1. Open and display the Web page you want to use.

2. Click the **Format** menu, and then click **Layers** to display the Layers task pane.

3. Click the **New Layer** button on the Layers task pane.

4. Double-click the layer name you want to change.

5. Type a new name (no spaces), and then press Enter.

6. To insert a graphic or text, click in the layer, and then use the **Insert Picture** button on the Pictures toolbar or type text.

7. When you're done, click the **Close** button on the task pane.

Did You Know?

You can delete a layer quickly. Click the layer edge or ID value, and then press Delete.

See Also

See "Setting Position Properties" on page 305 for information on setting position properties for layers.

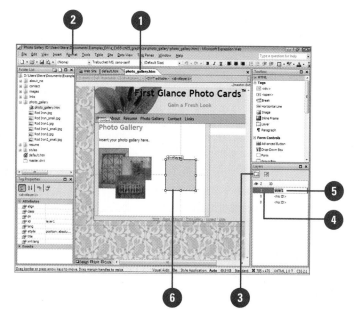

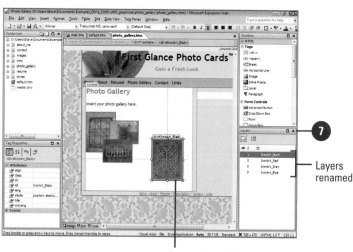

Layers renamed

Inserted graphic

Create an Attached Layer

1. Open and display the Web page you want to use.

2. Click the **Format** menu, and then click **Layers** to display the Layers task pane.

3. Click the layer to which you want to attach another one.

4. Click the **New Layer** button on the Layers task pane.

5. Drag to position the new layer where you want it relative to the other layer.

    When you move the initial layer, the attached layer moves too.

6. To collapse the attached layer, click the plus sign (+).

7. When you're done, click the **Close** button on the task pane.

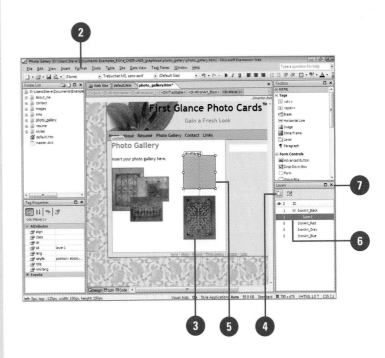

Change the Layer Display

1. Open and display the Web page you want to use.

2. Click the **Format** menu, and then click **Layers** to display the Layers task pane.

3. Click the **Eye** icon to toggle between visible (eye open), hidden (eye closed), and inherit (no icon).

4. Click another layer on the task pane to apply the change.

5. When you're done, click the **Close** button on the task pane.

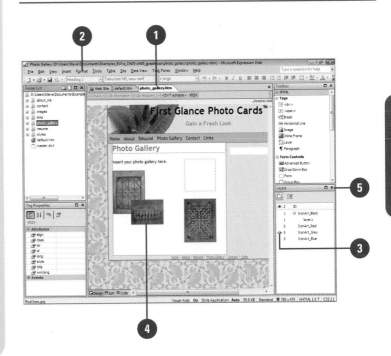

Wrapping Text and Aligning Graphics

You can wrap text around a graphic to attractively integrate text and graphics in a Web page. You can use the Wrapping Style options (also known as horizontal alignment) in the Pictures Properties dialog box to have text flow around the right or left side of a graphic. You can also set the vertical alignment in the Pictures Properties dialog box. The vertical alignment controls where the graphics aligns above or below the elements on either side of it. The effect of your vertical alignment depends on the selected Wrapping style.

Wrap Text Around a Graphic

1 Open and display the Web page you want to use.

2 Right-click the graphic you want to wrap around text, and then click **Picture Properties**.

The default is set to None, which removes any text wrapping.

3 Click the **Appearance** tab.

4 Click the **Left** or **Right** box.

5 Click **OK**.

See Also

See "Setting Position Properties" on page 305 for more information on position properties and setting them using CSS.

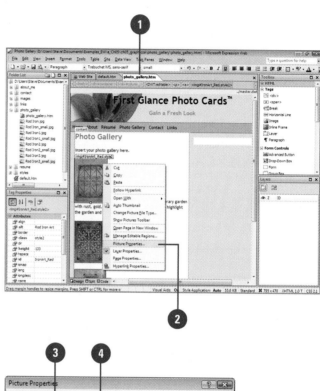

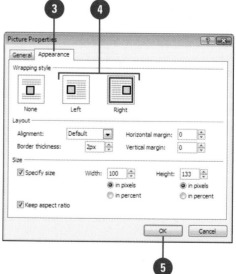

Set Vertical Alignment

1. Open and display the Web page you want to use.

2. Right-click the graphic you want to align, and then click **Picture Properties**.

3. Click the **Appearance** tab.

4. To set the vertical alignment, click the **Alignment** list arrow, and then select an option. The Default, Top, Middle, or Bottom option is recommended.

5. Click **OK**.

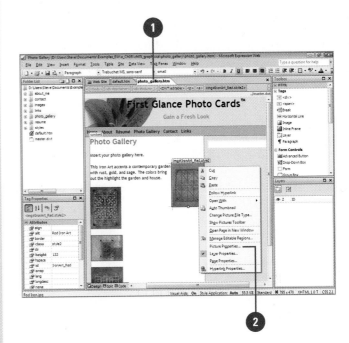

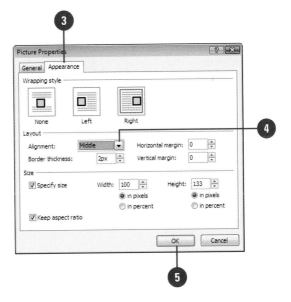

Adjusting Graphic Contrast and Brightness

Once you have inserted clip art and other objects into a Web page, you can adapt them to meet your needs. Perhaps the clip is too small to be effective, or you don't quite like the colors it uses. You can increase or decrease the brightness of a graphic, as well as the color contrast using the Pictures toolbar. In addition, you can introduce a wash, a gray art effect that increases the brightness but dims the contrast and serves as an excellent background.

Adjust Graphic Contrast and Brightness

1. Open and display the Web page you want to use.

2. Select the graphic you want to adjust.

   Resize handles appear on the graphic and the Pictures toolbar opens.

3. To alter the color contrast, click the **More Contrast** button or the **Less Contrast** button on the Pictures toolbar.

4. To change the brightness, click the **More Brightness** button or the **Less Brightness** button on the Pictures toolbar.

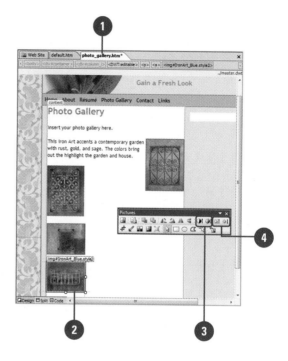

Wash Out the Color in a Graphic

① Open and display the Web page you want to use.

② Select the graphic you want to change. Resize handles appear on the graphic and the Pictures toolbar opens.

③ Click the **Color** button on the Pictures toolbar.

A list menu opens.

④ Click **Wash Out**.

The picture has now been faded, or washed out.

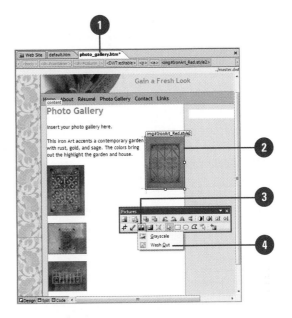

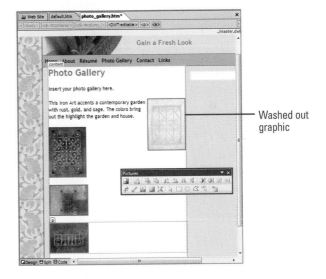

Washed out graphic

Converting Graphic Color

You can also convert color graphic to grayscale. Grayscale applies black and white shading values to color graphics, using a variety of gray tones in place of the different colors. When a color is designated as transparent, whenever that color appears in the graphic, the background is visible through it. Graphics can have only one transparent color, and if you select a transparent color for a graphic that already has a transparent color selected, the original transparent color will revert to its original form. When you close the page, Expression Web prompts you to save the page in GIF format.

Convert a Graphic to Grayscale

1 Open and display the Web page you want to use.

2 Select the graphic you want to convert to grayscale.

Resize handles appear on the graphic and the Pictures toolbar opens.

3 Click the **Color** button on the Pictures toolbar.

A list menu opens.

4 Click **Grayscale**.

The picture is now in black and white.

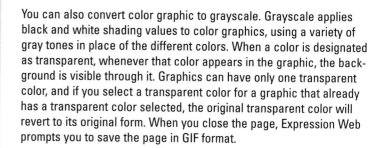

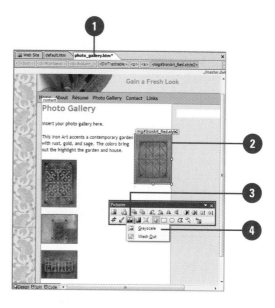

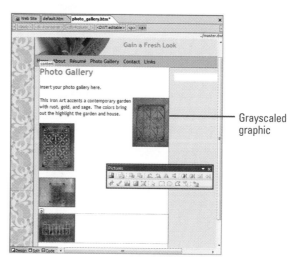

Grayscaled graphic

Make Colors in a Graphic Transparent

① Open and display the Web page you want to use.

② Select the graphic you want to change.

Resize handles appear on the graphic and the Pictures toolbar opens.

③ Click the **Set Transparent Color** button on the Pictures toolbar.

When you move your cursor onto the graphic, it becomes an eye dropper.

④ Click the color within the graphic that you want to make transparent.

Every pixel of that color is now rendered transparent, creating a speckling effect.

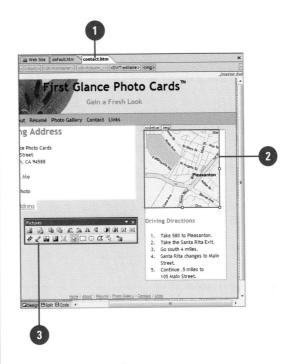

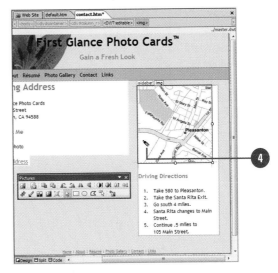

Adding a Bevel to a Graphic

Special effects can be used to bevel the border or create the illusion of dimensionality. In addition to adding a border to a graphic, you can also add a bevel-style frame. When you click the Bevel button on the Pictures toolbar, Expression Web transforms the edge of your graphic into a bevel-style frame. You can continue to click the Bevel button until you are satisfied with the degree of the bevel.

Add a Beveled Edge Around a Graphic

1. Open and display the Web page you want to use.

2. Select the graphic in which you want to add a beveled edge.

3. Click the **Bevel** button on the Pictures toolbar.

4. Continue to click the **Bevel** button until you achieve the look you want.

> ### Did You Know?
>
> ***You can undo bevel changes.*** If you don't like a bevel change, you can click the Undo button on the Standard toolbar to reverse the last change or several changes.

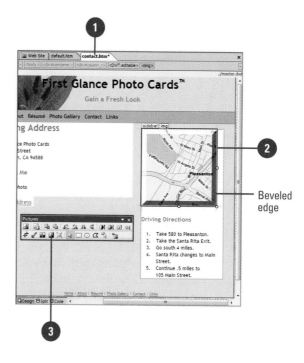

Beveled edge

Adding Margins and Padding to Graphics

Graphic margins are the space outside of the border and graphic padding is the space inside of the border. If you want to change the margins or padding for a specific graphic, you can quickly click and drag the margin or padding line. When you select a graphic, a set of beige lines that cross at the corners appear outside the graphic border. To change the graphic margins, drag the beige lines to the location you want. When press the Shift key with a selected graphic, a set of blue lines that cross at the corners appear inside the graphic border. To change the graphic padding, press and hold Shift and drag the blue lines to the location you want.

Add Margins and Padding to Graphics

1. Open and display the Web page you want to use.

2. Select the graphic you want to adjust.

3. To change graphic margins, drag the beige lines around the graphic.

   As you drag, a ScreenTip appears indicating the margin size in pixels.

4. To change graphic padding, hold down Shift, and then drag the blue lines around the graphic.

   As you drag, a ScreenTip appears indicating the padding size in pixels.

> ### Did You Know?
>
> **You can set exact graphic padding in the Borders and Shading dialog box.** Select the graphic, click the Format menu, click Borders and Shading, click the Borders tab, specify the padding you want, and then click OK.

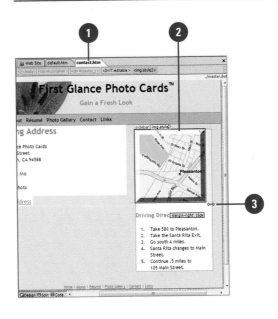

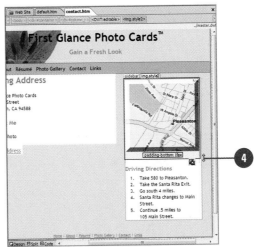

Applying Borders and Shading

To enhance the appearance of a graphic on a Web page, you can quickly add a border using the Borders button on the Common toolbar. When you add a border, you can specify what sides you want to include or exclude. For example, you can add a border on just the top and the bottom and leave the sides open. Shading colors the background behind the selected graphic. If you want to customize borders and add shading by changing line style, color, and width preferences, you can make changes in the Borders and Shading dialog box.

Apply a Border

1. Open and display the Web page you want to use.

2. Select the graphic you want to add borders and shading.

3. Click the **Borders** button arrow on the Common toolbar, and then click to select the border commands to add or remove a border.

Did You Know?

You can also specify border width and height in pixels. Right-click the graphic you want to change, click Picture Properties, click the Appearance tab, enter a value for the width and height of the border in pixels, and then click OK. To remove the border, type 0 (zero).

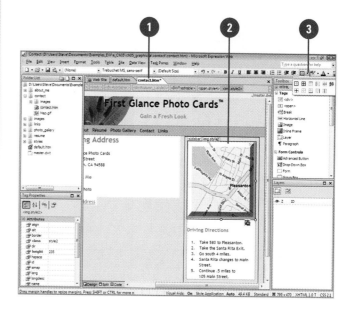

Add Borders and Shading to Graphics

1. Open and display the Web page you want to use.

2. Select the graphic you want to add borders and shading.

3. Click the **Format** menu, and then click **Borders and Shading**.

4. Click the **Borders** tab.

5. Click to select the type of Setting you want for your border.

6. Click to select the type of Style.

7. Apply any other options you want.

8. Look in the preview box to see the new border; you can also click the buttons to show or hide individual sides of a graphic.

9. Click the **Shading** tab.

10. Click to select the shading background and foreground fill color you want to apply to your graphic.

11. Look in the preview box to see the new shading color.

12. Click **OK**.

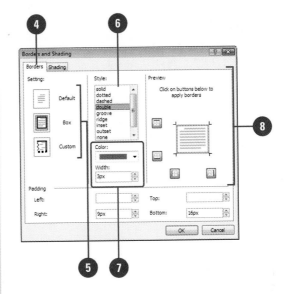

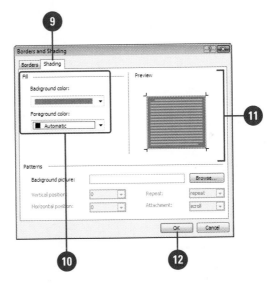

Changing Graphic Formats

Expression Web allows you to insert graphics with the WMF (Windows Metafile) format, such as clip art. However, the file format is not optimal for use on Web pages. When you save a Web page with WMF files or any other non Web graphic, Expression Web prompts you to save the graphics on that page, and set the file format to JPEG, GIF, or PNG through the Save Embedded Files dialog box. This dialog box automatically opens any time you attempt to save a page containing a graphic element. If you want more control over the formats and settings, you can convert individual graphics yourself to one of four Web friendly formats: GIF, JPEG, PNG-8, and PNG-24. If you change the graphic format to GIF or JPEG, you can set additional options.

Change a Graphic File Format

1. Open and display the Web page you want to use.

2. Right-click the graphic you want to change, and then click **Change Picture File Type**.

3. Click the file type option you want.

4. Click **OK**.

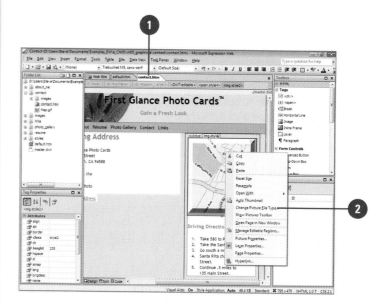

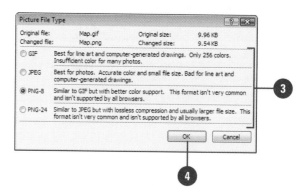

Change Graphic Format During a Web Page Save

1. Open and display the Web page with the graphics you want to change.

2. Click the **Save** button on the Common toolbar to save the page with the graphic on which you want to change the properties.

3. Click the name of the graphic whose properties you want to reset.

4. Click **Picture File Type**.

5. For GIF or JPEG, select the applicable additional settings.

   ◆ **Interlaced.** Displays a coarse version of a picture until the full version is downloaded.

   ◆ **Transparent.** Displays one color (typically the background) of the picture as transparent.

   ◆ **Quality.** Specifies a degree of compression. Typical values are 70 through 90.

   ◆ **Progressive Passes.** Specifies the number of coarse versions of a picture before the full version appears. Specify 0 to display the picture at full resolution as it arrives.

6. Click **OK**.

7. Click **OK**.

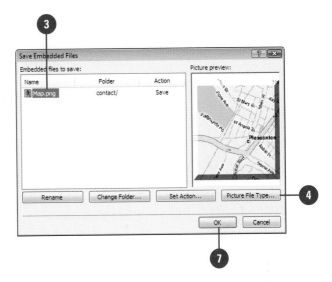

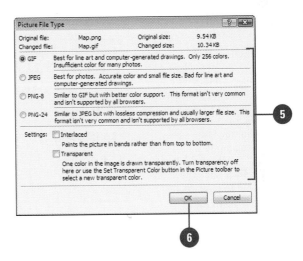

Changing the Way Graphics are Displayed

For a variety of reasons, the quality of the graphics you display on your Web site or page will have a major impact on the experience visitors have on your Web site. High quality graphics, for example, take much longer to load than lower resolution graphics, so you will lose some visitors before they even finish loading. Concurrently, very low quality graphics give a less than professional appearance to your Web site. Good designs strive for balance between these two considerations. For that reason, you will sometimes want to change the way graphics are displayed. To create a low resolution version of a graphic by editing it in a third party graphics editor program, you must first configure the editor that you want to use in conjunction with graphic files. You only need to perform this operation once. After you configure your graphic's editor program, you are ready to create a low resolution version of the graphic. Be aware that some Web browsers do not support low resolution graphics.

Configure a Graphics Editor Program

1. Click the **Tools** menu, and then click **Application Options**.

2. Click the **Configure Editors** tab.

3. Add a new extension or change an existing one.

   ◆ **Add an extension.** Click the **New Extension** button, and then type an extension.

   ◆ **Change an extension.** Click the extension you want to change, and then click the **New Editor** button.

4. Click a program from the list to associate with GIF or click **Browse for more** to locate the one you want.

5. Click **OK**.

   The file association is added to the list.

6. Click **OK**.

New Extension button ② New Editor button

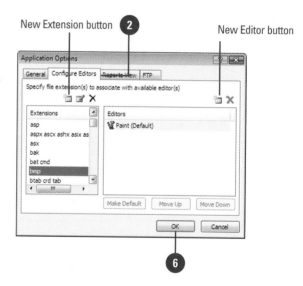

⑥

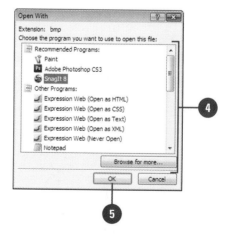

⑤

Create Low Resolution Graphics

1. Open and display the Web page you want to use.

2. Right-click the graphic you want to change, point to **Open With**, and then click the program you want to use.

   The graphic editor program opens.

3. Create a low resolution version of the graphic you want to use by following the instructions that are specific to the graphic editor program that you are using.

4. Returning to Expression Web, right-click the graphic to open the shortcut menu, and then click **Picture Properties**.

5. Click the **General** tab.

6. Enter the file name for the alternate low-resolution graphic you created, or click **Browse** to locate it.

7. Double-click the graphic to associate it.

8. Click **OK**.

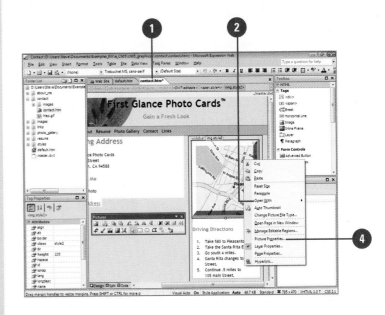

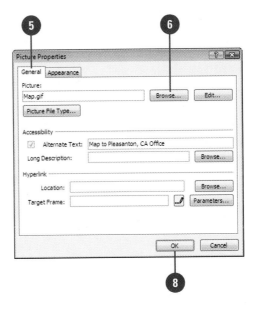

Restoring a Graphic

If you make several changes to a graphic that you don't want to keep, you can click the Restore button on the Pictures toolbar to return the graphic back to its original state since it was last saved. This gives you the ability to try different or interesting effects with a graphic without having to worry about keeping the changes if you don't like the result.

Restore Graphic Changes

① Open and display the Web page you want to use.

② Click the graphic in which you want to restore.

③ Click the **Restore** button on the Pictures toolbar to undo the most recent change made to a graphic.

IMPORTANT *The Restore button only works if you have not saved your changes.*

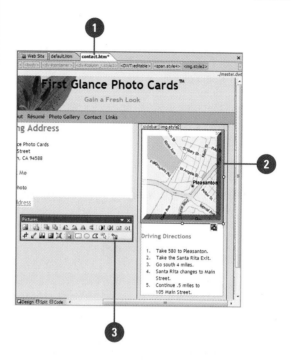

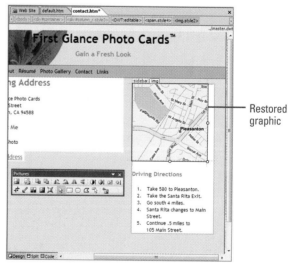

Restored graphic

Working with Web Page Media

Introduction

As you begin to include media into your Web pages, it's important to understand the different types of media you can use in Microsoft Expression Web. Expression Web 2 supports Adobe Flash SWF movie files, Microsoft Windows Media files, and Microsoft Silverlight application and related XAML (eXtensible Application Markup Language) files.

Adobe Flash SWF movies are vector-based animations and media that you can scale, rotate, and modify without losing any degree of sharpness or quality. Windows Media files —WMV (Windows Media Video) and WMA (Windows Media Audio)—are standard video and audio formats that you can create using Windows Movie Maker and other programs, and play using Windows Media Player. Microsoft Silverlight is an exciting new technology that helps you design, develop, and deliver media-enabled experiences and rich interactive applications on the Web using your browser with the Silverlight plug-in. When you create a Silverlight application, an authoring program, such as Microsoft Expression Blend 2, also creates an XAML file.

You can use the Media submenu on the Insert menu or the Media control in the Toolbox in Expression Web to quickly add these media types directly to your Web pages. After you insert a media type into a Web page, you can set properties and preview it.

If you want to run other media, such as Apple QuickTime (MOV), Adobe Reader (PDF), RealVideo (RAM), or Motion Picture Experts Group (MPEG), you can do it by enabling Expression Web to run unknown or unsigned ActiveX controls and opening the Web page with the media in Expression Web. You cannot insert these media types directly into a Web page in Expression Web. However, if the media is already on a Web page, you can open it in Expression Web, set ActiveX properties, and preview the media.

What You'll Do

Insert Flash Movies

Set Flash Movie Properties

Insert Windows Media

Set Windows Media Properties

Work with Silverlight

Insert Silverlight Media

Set Security for ActiveX Controls

Run ActiveX Controls

Preview and Play Media

Preview Silverlight Media

Inserting Flash Movies

Expression Web includes the ability to import Flash movies in the SWF format created in Adobe Flash from the Insert menu or the Toolbox (**New!**). Adobe Flash movies are vector-based animations and media that you can scale, rotate, and modify without losing any degree of sharpness or quality. Flash movies are especially suited for playback over the Web because they have a small file size, which loads and plays quickly.

Insert Flash Movies

1. Open and display the Web page you want to use.

2. Position the insertion point where you want to insert a Flash movie.

3. Click the **Insert** menu, point to **Media** and then click **Flash Movie**.

4. Navigate to the drive and folder location of the file you want to insert.

5. Click the file(s) you want to insert.

6. Click **Insert**.

   A Flash object placeholder appears, displaying a lightening bold icon and the name of the Flash movie file name.

7. Click the **Save** button on the Common toolbar.

   If the movie isn't already included in the Web site folder, the Save Embedded Files dialog box opens.

8. If you want to change folder location, click **Change Folder**, navigate to the Web site folder, and then click **OK**.

9. Click **OK**.

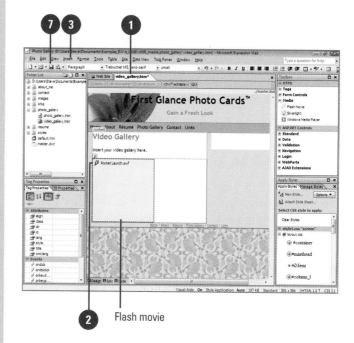

Flash movie

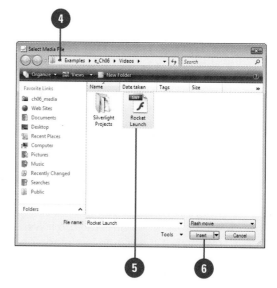

Insert a Flash Movie from the Toolbox Task Pane

1. Open and display the Web page you want to use.

2. Expand the **HTML** and **Media** categories in the Toolbox task pane.

3. Position the insertion point where you want to insert a Flash movie.

4. Double-click the media in the Toolbox.

   TIMESAVER *Drag media icon to your Web page in Design or Code view.*

5. Navigate to the drive and folder location of the file you want to insert.

6. Click the file(s) you want to insert.

7. Click **Insert**.

   A Flash object placeholder appears, displaying a lightening bold icon and the name of the Flash movie file name.

8. Click the **Save** button on the Common toolbar.

   If the movie isn't already included in the Web site folder, the Save Embedded Files dialog box opens.

9. If you want to change folder location, click **Change Folder**, navigate to the Web site folder, and then click **OK**.

10. Click **OK**.

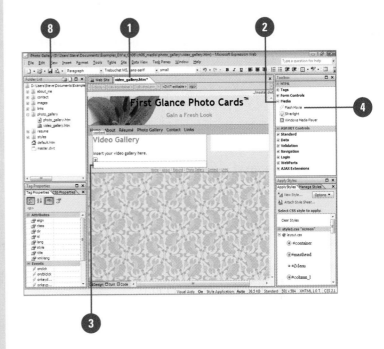

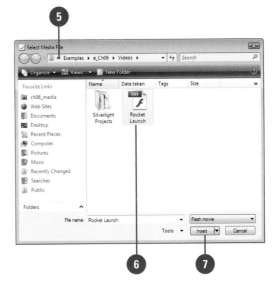

Setting Flash Movie Properties ▶

After you insert a Flash movie, a Flash object placeholder appears, displaying a lightening bold icon and the name of the Flash movie file name. Now, you can set general and appearance properties for Flash Movies (**New!**). Since Flash movies are vector-based animations and media, you can scale, rotate, and modify them without losing any degree of sharpness or quality and their small file size makes them load and play quickly. Before you can play Flash movies or edit movie properties, you need to have Adobe Flash Player installed on your computer, which you can download for free at *www.adobe.com*.

Set Flash Movie General Properties

1. Open and display the Web page with the Flash movie you want to change.

2. Right-click the Flash movie object, and then click **Flash SWF Properties**, or double-click it.

3. Click the **General** tab.

4. Type a name or ID for the Flash movie object.

5. Specify the Source (or root) URL and Base URL (optional) for the flash movie; click **Browse** to select a location. The Source URL is relative to the Base URL when you set both.

6. Specify the following options under Playback settings:

   ◆ **Auto Play.** Select to automatically play when the browser loads the page.

   ◆ **Loop.** Select to automatically play the movie again when it ends.

   ◆ **Show Menu.** Select to show all available playback controls or clear to show only About and Settings options.

   ◆ **SWLiveConnect.** Specify the Java file to start when loading the Flash player.

7. Click **OK**.

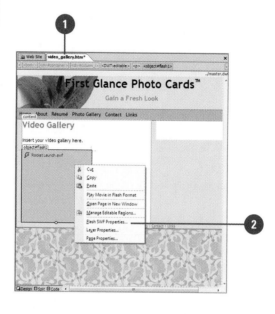

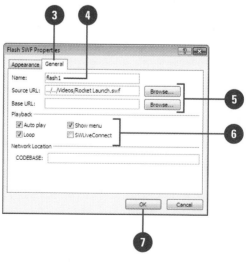

Change Flash Movie Appearance Properties

1. Open and display the Web page with the Flash movie you want to change.

2. Right-click the Flash movie object, and then click **Flash SWF Properties**.

3. Click the **Appearance** tab.

4. Specify the following options:

   ◆ **Quality.** Sets the anti-aliasing level in the movie. A higher setting means a higher quality and slower download. **Auto Low** gives priority to playback over quality, while **Auto High** gives equal priority to both.

   ◆ **Scale.** Sets movie dimensions; **Default** displays the entire movie; **No Border** resizes the movie to the specified size, yet maintains proportions; and **Exact Fit** resizes the movie to the specified size.

   ◆ **Background Color.** Sets the color in the movie background.

   ◆ **Transparent.** Select to make the background transparent.

   ◆ **Alignment.** Sets movie alignment within the movie object.

5. Specify the following options:

   ◆ **Specify Size.** Select to set CSS width and height.

   ◆ **Keep Aspect Ratio.** Select to maintain movie proportions.

6. Click **OK**.

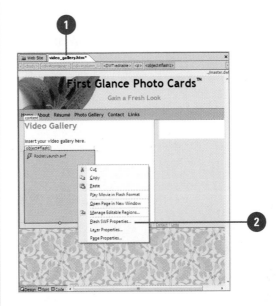

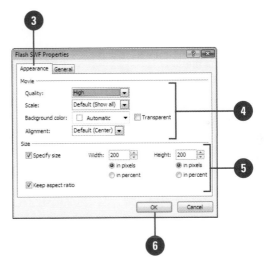

Inserting Windows Media

Expression Web includes the ability to import a variety of Windows Media formats—including multimedia (ASF), video (WMV), audio (WMA), playlist, MIDI, and picture—from the Insert menu or the Toolbox (**New!**). WMV (Windows Media Video) and WMA (Windows Media Audio) are standard video and audio formats that you can create using Windows Movie Maker and play using Windows Media Player. ASF (Advanced System Format) is the preferred Windows Media format, which compressed WMV or WMA content. After you insert a Windows media file, a media object placeholder appears, displaying a miniature Windows Media Player.

Insert Windows Media

① Open and display the Web page you want to use.

② Position the insertion point where you want to insert the Windows media.

③ Click the **Insert** menu, point to **Media** and then click **Windows Media Player**.

④ Click the **Format** list arrow, and then select **Windows Media file** or a Windows media format.

⑤ Navigate to the drive and folder location of the file you want to insert.

⑥ Click the file(s) you want to insert.

⑦ Click **Insert**.

A media object placeholder appears, displaying a miniature Windows Media Player.

⑧ Click the **Save** button on the Common toolbar.

If the movie isn't already included in the Web site folder, the Save Embedded Files dialog box opens.

⑨ If you want to change folder location, click **Change Folder**, navigate to the Web site folder, and then click **OK**.

⑩ Click **OK**.

Windows media

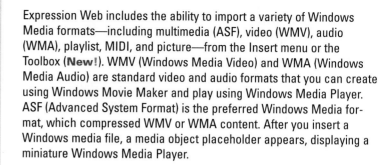

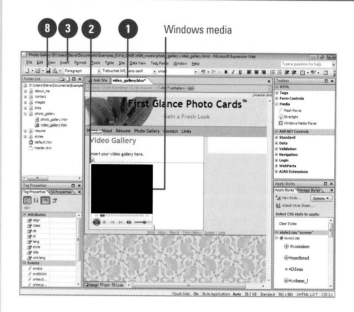

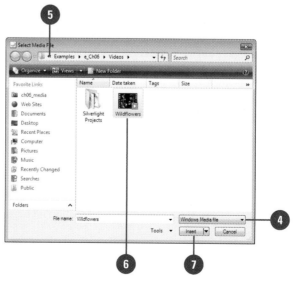

Insert Windows Media from the Toolbox Task Pane

1 Open and display the Web page you want to use.

2 Expand the **HTML** and **Media** categories in the Toolbox task pane.

3 Position the insertion point where you want to insert a movie.

4 Double-click the media in the Toolbox.

> **TIMESAVER** *Drag media icon to your Web page in Design or Code view.*

5 Click the **Format** list arrow, and then select **Windows Media file** or a Windows media format.

6 Navigate to the drive and folder location of the file you want to insert.

7 Click the file(s) you want to insert.

8 Click **Insert**.

A media object placeholder appears, displaying a miniature Windows Media Player.

9 Click the **Save** button on the Common toolbar.

If the movie isn't already included in the Web site folder, the Save Embedded Files dialog box opens.

10 If you want to change folder location, click **Change Folder**, navigate to the Web site folder, and then click **OK**.

11 Click **OK**.

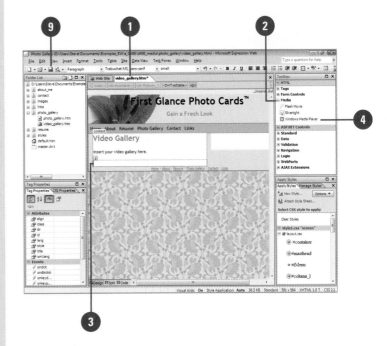

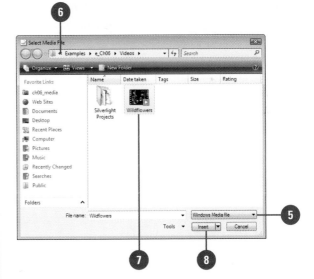

Setting Windows Media Properties

After you insert a Windows media file, a media object placeholder appears, displaying a miniature Windows Media Player. Now, you can set properties for Windows Media files (**New!**) and some common HTML options. You can set general options for layout controls, playback, and volume. If you have experience with Windows Media, you can set Advanced and Parameter properties. If you want to set HTML options for object tags and CSS, you can set Object Tag properties. Before you can play Windows media or edit media properties, you need to have the latest Windows Media Player installed on your computer, which you can download for free at *www.microsoft.com*.

Set Windows Media Properties

① Open and display the Web page with the Windows media you want to change.

② Right-click the Windows media object, and then click **ActiveX Control Properties**, or double-click it.

③ Click the **General** tab.

④ Specify any of the following options:

◆ **File Name or URL.** Specify a file name or the URL address.

◆ **Controls Layout.** Select a mode: None, Mini, Full (default), or Invisible.

◆ **Auto Start.** Select to automatically start playing the media.

◆ **Stretch To Fit.** Select to resize media object to fit object area.

◆ **Play Full Screen.** Select to play in full screen; deselect to play in a separate window.

◆ **Play Count.** Specify the number of times to play.

◆ **Mute.** Select to turn off sound.

◆ **Volume.** Drag to specify a volume level; select 0 for no volume.

◆ **Balance.** Drag to specify audio for left and right channels.

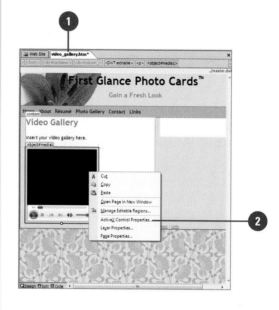

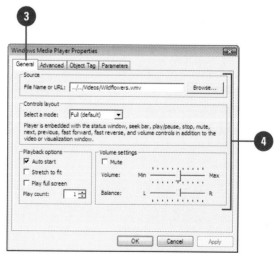

5 Click the **Advanced** tab.

6 Specify options in any of the following areas:

   ◆ **Control Settings.** Select to enable the controls and specify play rates and other options if you have specific requirements.

   ◆ **Script Command Settings.** Select to use scripts at a specific URL.

   ◆ **Closed Caption Settings.** Specify a closed caption file, language, style, and ID.

7 Click the **Object Tag** tab.

8 Specify any of the following options:

   ◆ **Name.** Sets the ID of the media.

   ◆ **Alignment.** Sets the CSS float property to align movie object.

   ◆ **Border Thickness.** Sets the CSS border-width property.

   ◆ **Horizontal and Vertical Spacing.** Sets the CSS margin property.

   ◆ **Height and Width.** Sets media object dimensions.

   ◆ **HTML.** Provides an alternative if the browser cannot play the media file; you can enter text and HTML code.

   ◆ **Source Code.** Sets the URL to automatically install the correct version of the player if it is not installed.

9 Click the **Parameters** tab.

10 Use the **Add**, **Remove**, and **Modify** buttons to edit PARAM elements.

The Player uses PARAM elements to define specific startup conditions for the control.

11 Click **OK**.

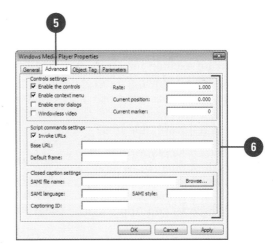

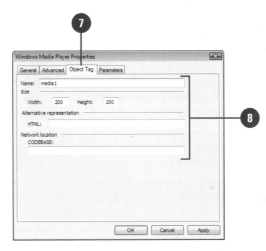

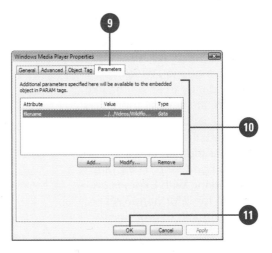

Working with Silverlight

Microsoft Silverlight is an exciting new technology that helps you design, develop, and deliver media-enabled experiences and rich interactive applications on the Web. Silverlight provides the following features:

- ◆ A cross-browser, cross-platform plug-in that runs in all popular browsers, including Microsoft Internet Explorer, Mozilla Firefox, and Apple Safari, and on Microsoft Windows and Apple Mac OS X.

- ◆ A consistent experience no matter where it runs.

- ◆ A small download that installs in seconds.

- ◆ Streaming video and audio that scales video quality to everything from mobile devices to desktop browsers to 720p HDTV video modes.

- ◆ Compelling graphics that users can manipulate—drag, turn, zoom—directly in the browser.

- ◆ Reads data and updates the display without refreshing the whole page.

You can create a Silverlight media application using authoring programs, such as Microsoft Expression Blend, Microsoft Expression Encoder, or Microsoft Visual Studio. A Silverlight authoring program creates a media application in XAML (eXtensible Application Markup Language), which you can also edit independently in an editor, like HTML. However, there are several more files that make up the application, including a silverlight.js file, an HTML file that references the Silverlight browser plug-in, and a JavaScript file that supports the HTML file. See Chapter 16, "Working with Expression Studio" on page 385 for information on using Expression Blend and Expression Encoder.

Silverlight integrates multimedia, graphics, animations, and interactivity into a single runtime. Silverlight supports playback of WMV, WMA, and MP3 media across all supported browsers without requiring Windows Media Player, the Windows Media Player ActiveX control or Windows Media browser plug-ins. In addition, text in a Silverlight application is searchable and indexable, so it's easy for visitors to find.

After you create a Silverlight media application, you can insert into Web pages with Expression Web (**New!**) and display it in a Web browser with the Microsoft Silverlight cross-browser, cross-platform plug-in, which is available free for download at *www.microsoft.com/silverlight*.

There are currently two versions of Silverlight, Silverlight 1.0 and Silverlight 1.1 Alpha (still in development at the first printing of this book). Silverlight 1.0 uses XAML markup language and JavaScript to create applications, while version 1.1 uses XAML and .NET Framework.

Inserting Silverlight Media

After you create a Silverlight 1.0 media application using a Silverlight authoring program, such as Microsoft Expression Blend or Microsoft Expression Encoder, you can insert it into a Web page with Expression Web (**New!**). A Silverlight authoring program creates a media application in XAML (eXtensible Application Markup Language). A typical Silverlight application consists of several files, which includes an XAML file, a silverlight.js file, an HTML file that references the Silverlight browser plug-in, and a JavaScript file that supports the HTML file. After you insert a Silverlight application into a Web page, you can display it in a Web browser with the Microsoft Silverlight cross-browser, cross-platform plug-in.

Insert Silverlight Media

1. Open and display the Web page you want to use. Make sure the Web page is saved to a Web site.

2. Position the insertion point where you want to insert the media.

3. Click the **Insert** menu, point to **Media** and then click **Silverlight**.

4. Click **Select Folder**.

5. Navigate to and select the drive and folder that contains the Web page, XAML files, and JavaScript files created by your Silverlight authoring program.

6. Click **Open**.

7. If the folder contains more than one Web page, select the homepage of your Silverlight media, and then click **Select**.

The folder is added to the Folders list and it contains the imported assets for your Silverlight media. The Silverlight media appears blank in an iframe object. *See "Previewing Silverlight Media" on page 168 to see the results.*

IMPORTANT *Do not move or rename the imported files and folders in Expression Web. Otherwise, your Silverlight media application will not work.*

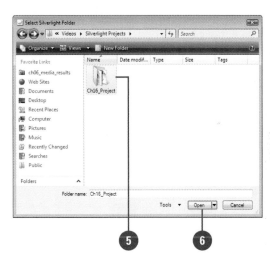

Setting Security for ActiveX Controls

Expression Web supports ActiveX controls—add-ins, plug-ins, and extensions—to run Silverlight applications, XAML, Windows Media, and Flash SWF files. If you open a Web page with other ActiveX controls, you need to give Expression Web permission to run the control on your computer (**New!**). For example, you can open a Web page that supports other media, such as Apple QuickTime (MOV), Adobe Reader (PDF), RealVideo (RAM), or Motion Picture Experts Group (MPEG). Before you grant permission for an ActiveX control to run on your computer, you need to set security options and make sure it's authentic from a trusted publisher and has a valid digital signature, which helps verify the publisher's identity and determines whether its been tampered with after its been signed. An unsigned or unknown ActiveX control can cause problems on your computer, like a virus.

Set Security Options for ActiveX Controls

1. Click the **Tools** menu, and then click **Page Editor Options**.

2. Click the **General** tab.

3. Select the **Prompt for unsigned ActiveX** control check box to have Expression Web prompt you for permission to run unsigned ActiveX controls.

   If you deselect this option, unsigned ActiveX controls appear as an unavailable box in Design view. The controls won't run and you won't be prompted for permission to run them.

4. To clear the list of unknown and unsigned ActiveX controls you have given permission to run and trust, click **Clear ActiveX Security Settings**.

5. Click **OK**.

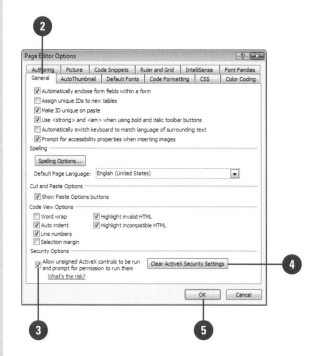

Running ActiveX Controls

When you set the security option to prompt you for permission to run an unknown or unsigned ActiveX control (**New!**), which is any ActiveX control other than Silverlight media, XAML, Windows Media and Flash SWF files, you can run it by opening the Web page with the embedded ActiveX control object and granting permission. However, if an ActiveX control isn't installed on your computer, you cannot run it and you won't be prompted for permission to run it, so make sure it's installed before you open the Web page. If you use and trust an ActiveX control on a regular basis, you can set an option when Expression Web prompts you for permission to always trust the ActiveX control and prevent prompts in the future (**New!**).

Run Unknown or Unsigned ActiveX Controls

1. Set the security option to prompt for unsigned ActiveX controls; see the previous page for specific instructions.

2. Open and display the Web page with an unknown or unsigned ActiveX control.

   An Expression Web dialog box appears, asking you for permission to run the control.

3. To prevent this dialog box from appearing in the future when you open this ActiveX control, select the **Always trust and display this ActiveX control** check box.

4. Click **Yes** to run the control or click **No** to not run the control.

   When you run a control, it appears in Design view, where you can preview it and set properties.

   ◆ To set properties, right-click the ActiveX control, click **ActiveX Control Properties**, specify the options you want, and then click **OK**.

   When you don't run a control, it appears as a grey box in Design view and only HTML properties are editable.

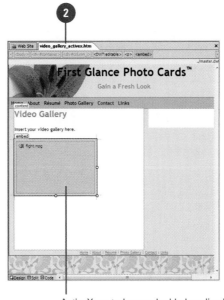

ActiveX control: an embedded media object

Previewing and Playing Media

After you insert a media object into a Web page, you can preview it in Design view (**New!**) and in your Web browser. Before you can play Flash or Windows media or edit media properties, you need to have the latest Adobe Flash Player or Windows Media Player installed on your computer, which you can download for free at *www.adobe.com* or *www.microsoft.com*. If you open a Web page with an unsigned or unknown media-related ActiveX control, such as Apple QuickTime (MOV), Motion Picture Experts Group (MPEG), or RealVideo (RAM), and grant permission to run it, you can preview and play the media objects.

Preview and Play a Flash Movie in Design View

1. Open and display the Web page with the media you want to preview.

2. In Design view, select the media you want to preview.

   If the Flash movie appears as a placeholder with a lightening bold icon and the name of the Flash movie file name, you can play the Flash movie in Design view.

3. Right-click the media object, and then click **Play Movie in Flash Format**.

   The Flash movie plays in Design view. The movie continues to play until you deselect the Play Movie in Flash Format command.

4. To stop the movie, right-click the media object, and then click **Play Movie in Flash Format** with the check mark to deselect it.

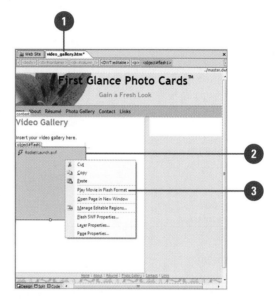

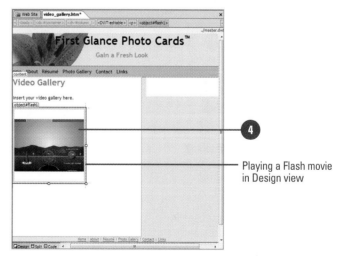

Playing a Flash movie in Design view

Preview and Play Media in a Web Browser

1. Open and display the Web page with the media you want to preview.

    ◆ **Flash movies.** Files with the SWF extension.

    ◆ **Windows media.** Files with the WMV or WMA extensions.

    ◆ **ActiveX controls.** Files related to an ActiveX control, which can include the following extensions: MOV, MPEG, or RAM.

2. Click the **File** menu, point to **Preview in Browser**, and then select a browser command.

3. If prompted, click **OK** to save your changes before previewing your page in a Web browser.

    The media appears on your Web page in your Web browser.

4. For Windows media, use the controls provided by Windows Media Player to playback the media.

Did You Know?

You can change ActiveX properties for a media object. In Design view, right-click the ActiveX media object, click ActiveX Control Properties, specify the options you want, and then click OK.

See Also

See "Setting Security for ActiveX Controls" on page 164 for information on using ActiveX controls.

Windows Media Player

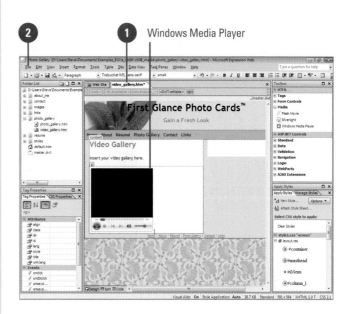

Windows media

Previewing Silverlight Media

When you insert a Silverlight media application into a Web page, Expression Web places it into an inline frame and appears with a placeholder in Design view. You can preview the Silverlight media application as you would see it on the Web by previewing the Web page in your Web browser. The Preview in Browser submenu on the File menu provides a list of available browsers and different screen sizes. You can also add more browsers to the list.

Preview Silverlight Media in a Web Browser

1. Open and display the Web page with the media you want to preview.

2. Click the **File** menu, point to **Preview in Browser**, and then select a browser command.

3. If prompted, click **OK** to save your changes before previewing your page in a Web browser.

   The Silverlight media appears on your Web page in your Web browser.

See Also

See "Changing Frame Properties" on page 248 for information on modifying the frame with Silverlight media.

See "Previewing Web Pages" on page 62 for information on previewing Web pages in a Web browser with different browsers and sizes

Silverlight media in an inline frame

Placeholder for Silverlight media in Design view

Silverlight media

Adding Hyperlinks to Web Pages

Introduction

When you are surfing the Web, a bookmark in your browser is a shortcut to a favorite Web site or page. In Expression Web, the term **bookmark** is used to denote a link that helps the reader navigate a long Web page quickly, rather than having to scroll through it. **Hyperlinks**, also known as **links**, connect you to information in other documents. Rather than duplicating the information stored in other documents, you can create hyperlinks to the relevant material. Web sites are continually changing as new content and hyperlinks provide greater functionality and ease of use for users.

Graphics, like text, can contain hyperlinks. If you set a default hyperlink for a graphic, the Web browser displays the hyperlink destination when the graphic is clicked. A **hotspot** is defined as an invisible region on a graphic or other Web area to which you have assigned a hyperlink. In Expression Web, hotspots can be shaped as rectangles, circles, or polygons. If you're having trouble viewing hotspots within a graphic, you can use the Highlight Hotspots button on the Pictures toolbar to temporarily remove the graphic so you can see the hotspots.

Expression Web provides different ways to view hyperlinks. Hyperlinks view offers a simplified presentation of the source and destination of internal and external hyperlinks that appear on a given page. Hyperlinks view displays your links, but it doesn't assure that they are correct. If a link becomes outdated or unnecessary, you can easily revise or remove it using the Hyperlinks task pane.

What You'll Do

Create Bookmarks

Create Hyperlinks Within a Web Page

Create Hyperlinks to Files and Web Pages

Create Hyperlinks to E-Mail Addresses

Create Target Hyperlinks

Edit Hyperlinks

Add Hyperlinks to Graphics

Add Graphic Hotspots

Highlight Graphic Hotspots

Modify Graphic Hotspots

Add ScreenTips to Hyperlinks

Work with Hyperlinks View

Verify Hyperlinks

Repair Broken Hyperlinks

Creating Bookmarks

When you are surfing the Web, a bookmark or favorite in your browser is a shortcut to a Web site or page, a placeholder so that you can quickly access a favorite location in cyberspace. In Expression Web, the term bookmark (as known as an **HTML anchor**) is used to denote a link that helps the reader navigate a long Web page quickly, rather than having to scroll through it. After you have placed one or more bookmarks, they are available to navigate to in the Bookmark dialog box. If you no longer need a bookmark, you can delete it. However, when you delete a bookmark, any hyperlinks that are connected to the deleted destination are not automatically adjusted and are now dead links that you need to locate and repair.

Create a Bookmark

① Open the Web page you want to change in Design view.

② Select the text or graphic element within the page that you want to bookmark. If you have broken the page into sections, section headers make excellent bookmarks.

③ Click the **Insert** menu, and then click **Bookmark**.

④ Type a bookmark name.

⑤ Click **OK**.

In Design view, the bookmark appears with a perforated underline.

Did You Know?

You can rename a bookmark. Right-click the bookmark, click Bookmark Properties, type the new name, and then click OK. Expression Web does the rest, reconfiguring any relevant hyperlinks.

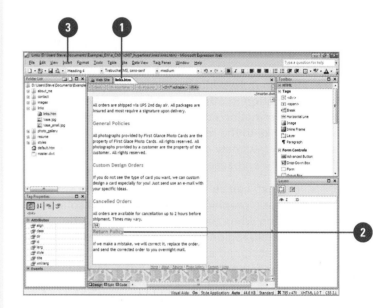

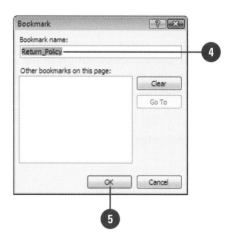

Navigate to Bookmarks

1. Click the **Edit** menu, and then click **Go To Bookmark**.

2. Click the bookmark in which you want to navigate.

3. Click **Go To**.

4. Click **OK**.

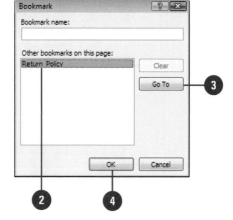

Delete Bookmarks

1. Click the **Edit** menu, and then click **Go To Bookmark**.

2. Click the bookmark you want to remove.

3. Click **Clear**.

4. Click **OK**.

See Also

See "Verifying Hyperlinks" on page 187 for information on verifying hyperlinks after you delete a bookmark.

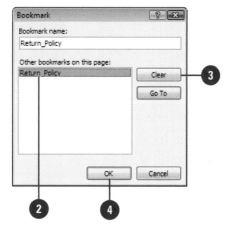

Creating Hyperlinks Within a Web Page

After you create bookmarks in a Web page, you can create hyperlinks to them. This is useful when you want to create an easy way for users to jump to different points within a Web page. Sometimes during the development process, you want to create a hyperlink, but the Web page file that doesn't exist yet. You can create a hyperlink now and then create the Web page file later.

Create a Hyperlink to a Bookmark Within a Web Page

① Open the Web page you want to change in Design view.

② Select the word or words you want to link from.

③ Click the **Insert Hyperlink** button on the Common toolbar.

④ Click the **Place in This Document** button on the Link to bar.

The words you entered as the link on your Web page appear in the Text to display box.

⑤ Select the bookmark within the Web page you want to link.

⑥ Click **OK**.

The selected text appears as a hyperlink.

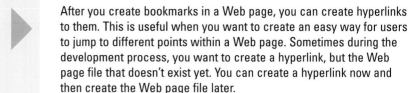

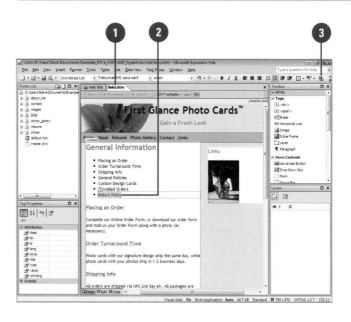

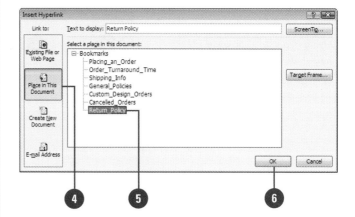

Create a Hyperlink to a Web Page Not Available

1. Open the Web page you want to change in Design view.

2. Select the word or words you want to link from.

3. Click the **Insert Hyperlink** button on the Common toolbar.

4. Click the **Create New Document** button on the Link to bar.

   The words you entered as the link on your Web page appear in the Text to display box.

5. Enter a name for the new document.

6. Click the **Edit the new document later** option.

7. Click **OK** to complete the link.

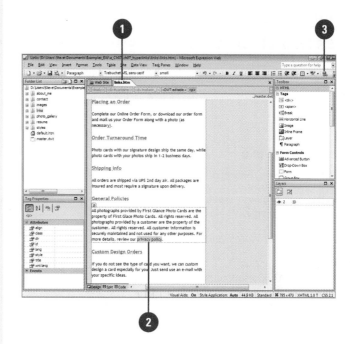

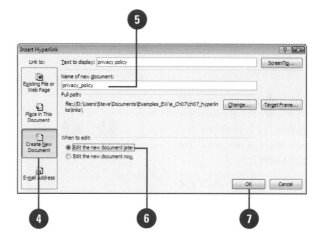

Creating Hyperlinks to Files and Web Pages

Hyperlinks connect you to information in other documents. Rather than duplicating the important information stored in other documents, you can create hyperlinks to the relevant material. You can create hyperlinks to pages in your Web site or to external files and pages from a local or Internet location. The Insert Hyperlink dialog box makes it easy to create hyperlinks to files and Web pages by keeping track and displaying the current folder (typically the Web site folder), and recently used files and browsed Web pages.

Create a Hyperlink to a Web Page

1. Open the Web page you want to change in Design view.

2. Select the word or words you want to link from.

3. Click the **Insert Hyperlink** button on the Common toolbar.

4. Click the **Existing File or Web Page** button on the Link to bar.

    The words you entered as the link on your Web page appear in the Text to display box.

5. Click **Current Folder** or **Browsed Pages** to locate a Web page.

    ◆ If the Web page is not available in the list, click the **Browse the Web** button, go to the Web page you want to use, and then click the **Close** button.

6. Select the Web page to which you want to link, or type a URL to access an Internet location in the Address box.

7. Click **OK**.

    The selected text appears as a hyperlink.

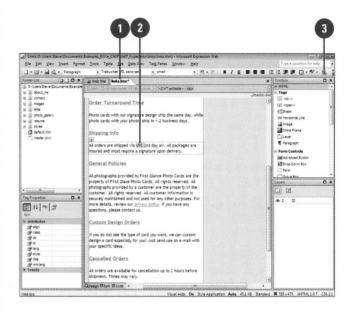

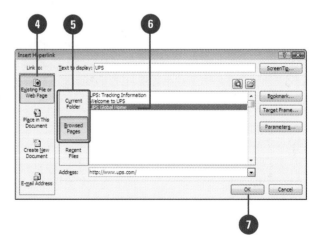

Create a Hyperlink to a File

1. Open the Web page you want to change in Design view.

2. Select the word or words you want to link from.

3. Click the **Insert Hyperlink** button on the Common toolbar.

4. Click the **Existing File or Web Page** button on the Link to bar.

   The words you entered as the link on your Web page appear in the Text to display box.

5. Click **Recent Files** to locate a file.

   ◆ If the file is not available in the list, click the **Browse for File** button, locate and select the file you want to use, and then click **Open**.

6. Select the file to which you want to link, or type the location to the file in the Address box.

7. Click **OK**.

   The selected text appears as a hyperlink.

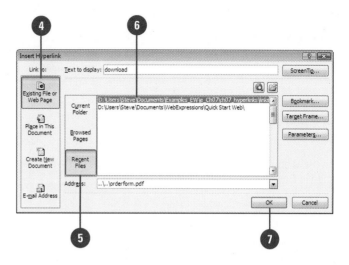

For Your Information

Hyperlinking to Adobe Acrobat and Other Files

In addition to Web pages, you can create hyperlinks to Adobe Acrobat (PDF) files, Microsoft Office documents, and ZIP files to name a few. When a user clicks a hyperlink to a file, the related program starts and opens the file directly from the Web page. If the user's computer doesn't have the program, the file doesn't open. To avoid this problem, you need to inform users what software they need to view the file. In many cases, you can provide a link to obtain the software.

Creating Hyperlinks to E-mail Addresses

Creating a hyperlink to an e-mail address allows users of your Web page to contact you, or any other e-mail recipient that you specify. When a user on one of your Web pages selects a hyperlink to an e-mail address, their default e-mail program opens with a new message already filled in. The new message includes the specified e-mail address and subject you specified in the Insert Hyperlink dialog box.

Create a Hyperlink to an E-mail Address

① Open the Web page you want to change in Design view.

② Select the word or words you want to link from.

③ Click the **Insert Hyperlink** button on the Common toolbar.

④ Click the **E-mail Address** button on the Link to bar.

The words you entered as the link on your Web page appear in the Text to display box.

⑤ Enter the e-mail address you want to use or select one from the recently used list.

⑥ Enter a subject for the e-mail message.

⑦ Click **OK**.

The selected text appears as a hyperlink.

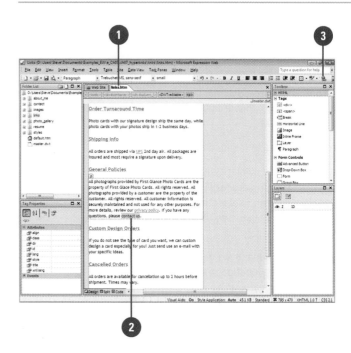

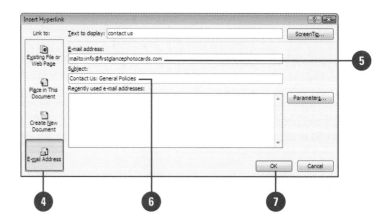

Creating Target Hyperlinks

When you create a hyperlink, a Web browser normally replaces the current Web page with the new Web page. Instead of replacing the current Web page with the new Web page, you can keep the current page display and open the new page in a new window. This is useful for hyperlinks to external Web sites. Users stay at your site, yet they can still view another Web page. This is known as a target hyperlink. In Besides New Window, other common targets include Page Default, Same Frame, Whole Page, and Parent Frame.

Create a Hyperlink to a Target Frame

1. Open the Web page you want to change in Design view.

2. Right-click an existing hyperlink, and then click **Hyperlink Properties**.

3. Click **Target Frame**.

4. Click the target you want to use.

5. If you want all your hyperlinks to use the target frame, select the **Set as page default** check box.

6. Click **OK**.

7. If you want to change the hyperlink, select the file or Web page to which you want to link, or type a URL to access an Internet location in the Address box.

8. Click **OK**.

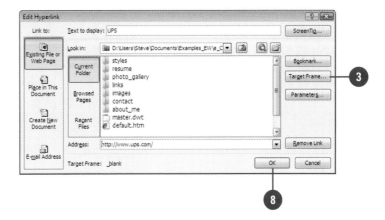

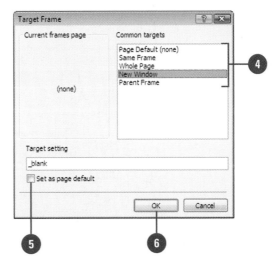

Editing Hyperlinks

Web site are continually changing as new content and hyperlinks provide greater functionality and ease of use for users. If a link becomes outdated or unnecessary, you can easily revise or remove it. When you click a hyperlink for the first time (during a session), the color of the hyperlink changes, indicating that you have accessed the hyperlink. If you prefer a different color, you can change the color of the hyperlink in different states.

Change a Hyperlink

1 Right-click the hyperlink, and then click **Hyperlink Properties**.

2 Change the address for the link (use the **Browse the Web** or **Browse for File** buttons if necessary).

3 Click **OK**.

Browse for file or Web buttons

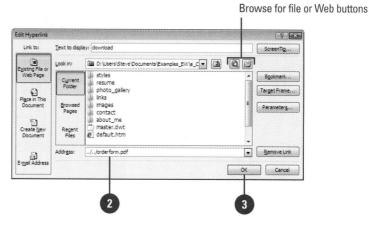

Remove a Hyperlink

1 Right-click the hyperlink, and then click **Hyperlink Properties**.

2 Click **Remove Link**.

Change Hyperlink Colors

1. Right-click a blank area in a Web page, and then click **Page Properties**.

2. Click the **Formatting** tab.

3. Click the list arrow next to the corresponding hyperlink option, and then click a color.

   ◆ **Hyperlink.** The color used for a hyperlink that hasn't been used yet.

   ◆ **Visited Hyperlink.** The color used after a hyperlink has been used.

   ◆ **Active Hyperlink.** The color used while the user is actually clicking the hyperlink.

   ◆ **Hovered Hyperlink.** The color used while the user points to the hyperlink.

4. Click **OK**.

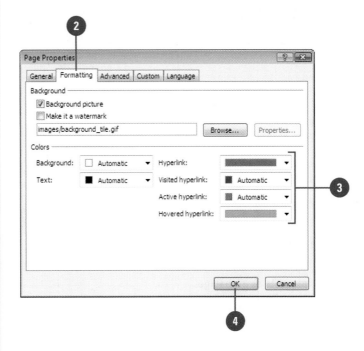

Adding Hyperlinks to Graphics

Graphics, like text, can contain hyperlinks. If you set a default hyperlink for a graphic, the Web browser displays the hyperlink destination when the graphic is clicked. When creating a button that is linked to your home page, for example, you can define a default hyperlink that leads to a specific destination, instead of drawing a hotspot around the entire button.

Create a Hyperlink to an Existing Internal Web Page

① Open the Web page you want to change in Design view.

② Select the graphic you want to use.

③ Click the **Insert Hyperlink** button on the Common toolbar.

④ Click **Existing File or Web Page**.

⑤ Browse to select the target page. The URL for the designated page appears in the Address box.

⑥ Click **OK**.

> ### See Also
>
> See "Adding Graphic Hotspots" on page 182 for information on creating hyperlink regions on a graphic.

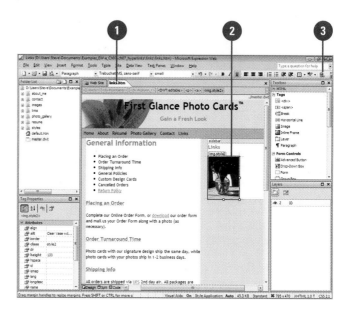

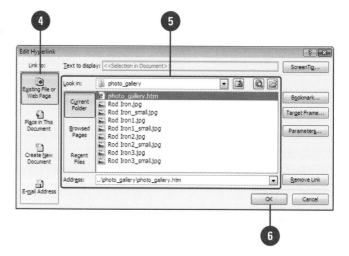

Create a Hyperlink to a New Internal Page

1. Open the Web page you want to change in Design view.

2. Select the graphic you want.

3. Click the **Insert Hyperlink** button on the Common toolbar.

4. Click **Create New Document**.

5. Enter the name of the new document.

6. Click the **Edit the new document later** option.

7. Click **OK**.

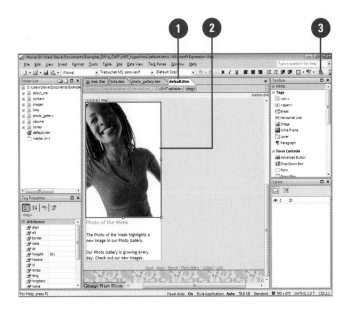

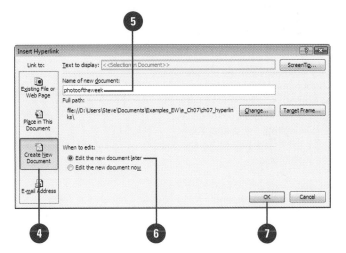

Adding Graphic Hotspots

A hotspot is defined as an invisible region on a graphic or other Web area to which you have assigned a hyperlink. When a site user clicks their cursor over that hyperlink, the link's destination is displayed in the Web browser. In Expression Web, hotspots can be shaped as rectangles, circles, or polygons. However, a hotspot cannot overlap or extend beyond the image boundaries. A graphic containing one or more hotspots is an Image map. Image maps typically provide clues so that you know where to click. The areas of the graphic that doesn't contain hotspots can be assigned a default hyperlink; when the user clicks anywhere outside a hotspot, they are directed to the destination you set as the graphic's default hyperlink.

Add a Hotspot to a Graphic

① Open the Web page you want to change in Design view.

② Select the graphic you want to add a hotspot.

③ Click a hotspot button (**Rectangular**, **Circular**, or **Polygonal**) on the Pictures toolbar that conforms to the shape you want.

④ Move the cursor over the picture until it becomes a drawing implement. Drag a hotspot to the shape you want, and then double-click to complete the shape. You can size the hotspot by dragging the sizing handles.

When you're done, the Insert Hyperlink dialog box opens.

⑤ Enter or browse for the URL in which you want to link the hotspot.

⑥ Click **OK**.

> **Did You Know?**
>
> **_You can return a hotspot to its original position._** Select the hotspot, and then press Esc.

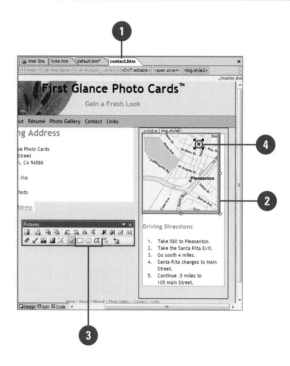

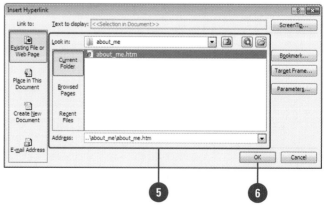

Highlighting Graphic Hotspots

If you're having trouble viewing hotspots within a graphic, you can use the Highlight Hotspots button on the Pictures toolbar to temporarily remove the graphic so you can see the hotspots. Once you have identified the location of the hotspots you want to modify, you need to click the Highlight Hotspots button again to turn it off before you can edit the hotspot.

Highlight Hotspot Hyperlinks

1. Open the Web page you want to change in Design view.

2. Select the graphics that contains the hotspot you want to modify.

3. Click the **Highlight Hotspots** button on the Pictures toolbar. The graphic disappears so you can see the hotspots.

4. Click the button again to view the graphic.

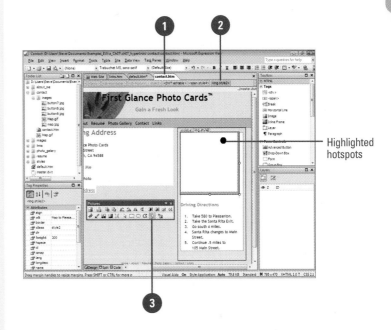

Highlighted hotspots

Modifying Graphic Hotspots

After you create a graphic hotspot using the buttons (Rectangle Hotspot, Circular Hotspot, or Polygonal Hotspot) on the Pictures toolbar, you can select, move, or resize the hotspot. You can edit the size and shape of a hotspot the same way you edit an object. To edit the URL for a hotspot, you need to double-click the hotspot. If you no longer need a hotspot, you can select it and press Delete.

Edit Hotspot Hyperlinks

1. Open the Web page you want to change in Design view.

2. Select the graphics that contains the hotspot you want to modify.

3. Perform one or more of the following:

   ◆ **Edit the URL for a hotspot.** Double-click the hotspot, and then alter the destination in the Address box.

   ◆ **Resize the hotspot.** Drag the selection handles.

   ◆ **Delete a hotspot.** Press the Delete key on the keyboard.

   ◆ **Move the hotspot.** Drag it to a new position, or press the arrow keys to move the hotspot in small increments.

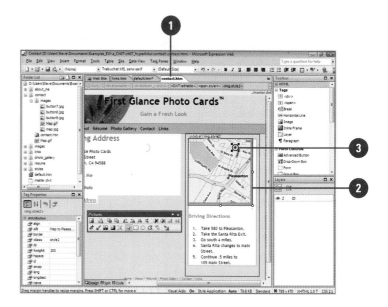

Adding ScreenTips to Hyperlinks

A ScreenTip (also known as tooltips) provides helpful information to users when they point to a hyperlink. When a user points to a hyperlink in a Web browser, a small tag appears displaying information you provide about the hyperlink. ScreenTips are not required, but they are useful for users.

Add a ScreenTip to a Hyperlink

① Open the Web page you want to change in Design view.

② Right-click an existing hyperlink, and then click **Hyperlink Properties**.

③ Click **ScreenTip**.

④ Type the ScreenTip text you want users to see.

⑤ Click **OK**.

⑥ Click **OK**.

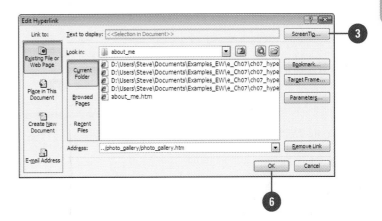

Working with Hyperlinks View

Hyperlinks view offers a simplified presentation of the source and destination of internal and external hyperlinks that appear on a given page. These links are displayed in a flowchart fashion. Clicking the plus sign (+) box for any page displays that page's links. This provides a quick, easy method to expand or shrink the link view to display the entire link structure of the pages, or only those that link directly to the home page. Double-clicking a page automatically displays that page and moves it to the center of the hyperlink display when you revert to Hyperlinks view.

Display Hyperlinks View

1. Open the Web site in which you want to display hyperlinks.

2. Click the **Web Site** tab.

3. Click the **Hyperlinks** button at the bottom of the window.

4. Click a plus sign (+) to display the entire link structure of a page.

Did You Know?

Hyperlinks are displayed using a variety of buttons. In Hyperlinks view, a page containing a globe button represents the presence of a link to the Web. A page featuring a picture button signifies a link to a visual element, and an envelope button indicates the hyperlink leads to a piece of e-mail.

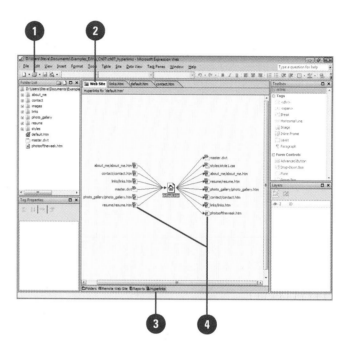

Verifying Hyperlinks

When you have a layout of your hyperlinks, you'll want to confirm that they're accurately linked. Because sites are purchased, re-started, and even shut down on a regular basis, URLs to external links can change. Hyperlinks view displays your links, but it doesn't assure that they are correct. To verify links, use the Verify Hyperlinks button in the Hyperlinks task pane. If Expression Web discovers a problem with a link, you can open and fix it from the Hyperlinks task pane.

Verify Hyperlinks in Reports View

1. Click the **Task Panes** menu, and then click **Hyperlinks**.

2. Click the **Verify Hyperlinks** button.

3. Click the **Verify all hyperlinks** option.

4. Click **Start**.

5. If prompted to connect to the Web, click **Yes**.

    Expression Web automatically checks any links that haven't been confirmed as correct and generates a report. Scan the Status column and make sure you don't have any broken links. If there are none, the process is over.

Did You Know?

You can check a single hyperlink. In Hyperlinks view, right-click then hyperlink you want to check, and click Verify Hyperlink. If the hyperlink is broken, the arrow connecting the file displays a break.

You can recalculate hyperlinks to correct property data associated with a Web page. The Recalculate Hyperlinks commands updates property data, known as metadata, to correct any data problems. Click the Site menu, click Recalculate Hyperlinks, and then click Yes.

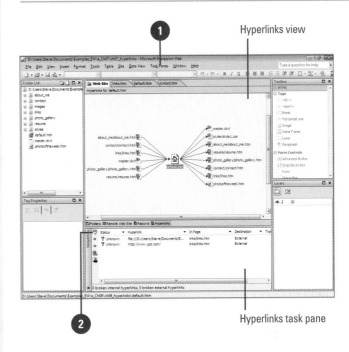

Hyperlinks view

Hyperlinks task pane

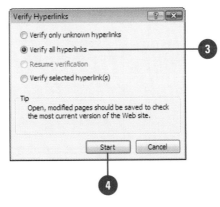

Repairing Broken Hyperlinks

If a hyperlink is broken, the arrow connecting the file displays a break in Hyperlink view, while a broken chain icon displays a break in the Hyperlinks task pane. If an external hyperlink is unverified, a question mark appears next to it in the Hyperlinks task pane. To repair a broken hyperlink, you can use the Edit Hyperlink dialog box to select the correct hyperlink. If you're repairing an external hyperlink, you also need to verify the hyperlink to change its status from Unknown to OK.

Repair Broken Hyperlinks

① Click the **Task Panes** menu, and then click **Hyperlinks**.

② Select a broken hyperlink in the Hyperlinks task pane.

③ Click the **Edit Hyperlink** button.

The Edit Hyperlink dialog box opens with the link of the page in question, and a blank space for you to enter the correct address.

④ Click **Browse**, and then locate and select the correct Web page.

⑤ Click the **Change in all pages** or **Change in selected pages** option.

⑥ Click **Replace**.

The hyperlink is repaired. If a question mark appears next to a hyperlink, you need to verify the hyperlink.

⑦ Click the **Verify Hyperlinks** button.

The Verify Hyperlink dialog box opens with the Verify only unknown hyperlinks option selected by default.

⑧ Click **Start**, and then click **Yes** if prompted to connect to the Web.

Expression Web automatically checks any links that haven't been confirmed as correct and generates a report.

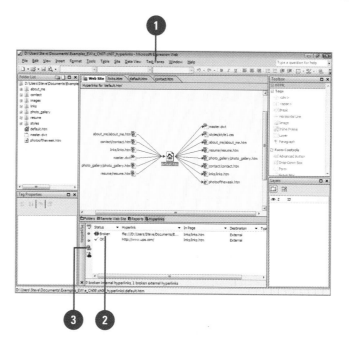

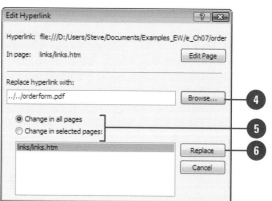

Adding Interactive Behaviors

Introduction

Implementing the use of interactive buttons makes moving around a site an easy experience for a visitor. You can customize these buttons, and define hyperlinks for them. These animation effects are triggered by an event, such as clicking on a link.

Behaviors are timesavers because they give you sections of code for common tasks. In addition, behaviors are a great way to introduce yourself to the wonderful world of scripting without having to write all the code. For example, if you want to add a play script to a button, you can do it using the Insert button in the Behaviors task pane, or you can write out the code on your own. Using Behaviors, as opposed to writing the code by hand, is not better, they're simply faster. The more time you save doing common scripting tasks using Behaviors, the more time you will have for the creative process.

You use the Behaviors task pane to apply the behavior to a triggering object, such as a button. You specify the event that triggers the behavior, such as releasing the mouse, select a target object, such as a graphic, and then select settings for behavior parameters, such as a URL address or element property.

Inserting Interactive Buttons

An interactive button gives you the ability to link one page to another page in the current Web site, a Web site, or an e-mail address. You don't have to know HTML code to create, modify, and link an interactive button. You can select a button style from a pre-defined list and then add button text, select button and background colors, and specify the font style, size, and color for all states of the button including the original, hover, and pressed states. After you create the button, you can define a hyperlink for a button.

Create an Interactive Button

1. Open and display the Web page you want to use.

2. Position the insertion point where you want to insert an interactive button.

3. Click the **Insert** menu, and then click **Interactive Button**.

4. Click the button type you want.

5. Type the button title.

6. Type a hyperlink location or use **Browse** to locate and select it.

7. Click the **Font** tab.

8. Select the font options you want.

   ◆ **Font, Font Style, and Size.** Specifies the button text font type, style, and size.

   ◆ **Font Color.** Specifies the text font color for the original, hovered, and pressed button.

   ◆ **Alignment.** Specifies the horizontal and vertical alignment of the text.

Continue Next Page

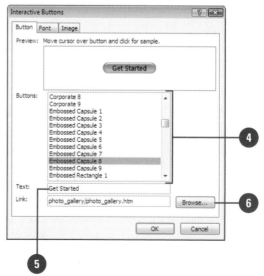

9 Click the **Image** tab.

10 Specify the image options you want.

- ◆ **Width and Height.** Controls the width and height of the button.

- ◆ **Create Hover Image.** Select to change the button when the mouse pointer passes over it.

- ◆ **Create Pressed Image.** Select to change the button when a visitor clicks it.

- ◆ **Preload Button Images.** Select to load all the button pictures in memory.

11 Click the **JPEG image** option to choose a solid background color, or choose the **GIF image** option to set a transparent background.

12 Click **OK**.

13 Click the **Save** button on the Common toolbar, and then click **OK** (if necessary) to save any embedded and related files.

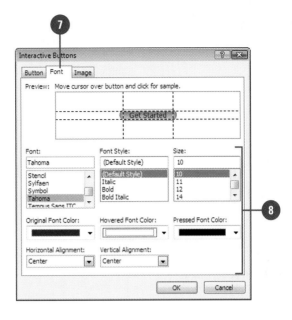

> ### See Also
>
> See "Adding Hyperlinks to Graphics" on page 180 for information on creating a hyperlink to a button graphic.

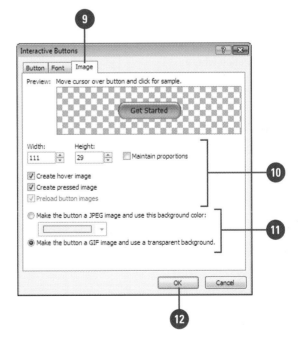

Working with Interactive Buttons

If you want to create a navigation bar with buttons with the same style and height, it's faster and easier to make a copy of an existing interactive button and edit the button label and link location than to create new ones from scratch. When you create a copy of an interactive button and change the text label, the text may get cut off. To maintain the button height and change the width, use the Image tab in the Interactive Buttons dialog box to turn off the Maintain proportions option and change the Width of the button to make the text fit the way you want.

Copy an Interactive Button

1. Open and display the Web page you want to use with the interactive buttons.

2. Right-click the button you want to duplicate, and then click **Copy**.

3. Position the insertion point where you want to place a copy of the button.

4. Click the **Edit** menu, and then click **Paste**.

   The interactive button is pasted into the specified location where you can edit it.

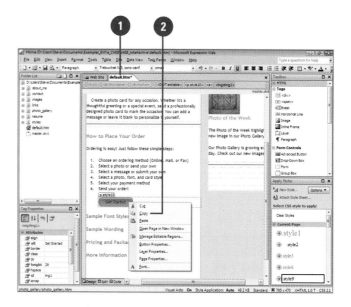

Edit an Interactive Button

1. Open and display the Web page you want to use with the interactive buttons.

2. Double-click the interactive button or right-click the button, and then click **Button Properties**.

3. Change the button title.

4. Change the hyperlink location or use **Browse** to locate and select it.

5. If you want to change the font, click the **Font** tab, and then make the changes you want.

6. Click the **Image** tab.

7. Clear the **Maintain proportions** check box, and then change the Width and Height to the size you want for the button.

8. Click **OK**.

9. Click the **Save** button on the Common toolbar, and then click **OK** (if necessary) to save any embedded and related files.

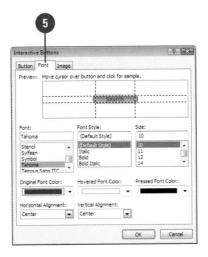

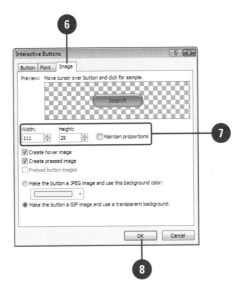

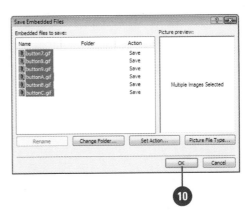

Adding Behaviors to Elements

Behaviors are timesavers because they give you sections of code for common tasks. A behavior consists of an **action** triggered by a specific **event**. For example, an interactive button executes the Swap Images behavior action when a user points to the button event. You use the Behaviors panel to apply the behavior to a triggering object, such as a button. You specify the event that triggers the behavior, such as hovering the mouse, select a target object, such as a swap an image, and then select any related action property settings for the behavior, such as a preload images. Action property settings vary depending on the action. You can add more than one behavior to an element; the Behavior task pane lists the behaviors in the order in which they occur. When you add a behavior to an element, it doesn't alter the element or show any visual indicator that a behavior is applied.

View a Behavior to an Element

1. Click the **Task Panes** or **Format** menu, and then click **Behaviors**.

   The Behaviors task pane appears as a tab in the lower right-corner of the screen.

2. Select the element with a behavior. For example, an interactive button.

   The Behaviors task pane displays the behaviors associated with the element.

Did You Know?

You can change available behaviors on the Insert button. The behaviors available on the Insert button are based on a CSS schema. To change the CSS schema, click the Tools menu, click Page Editor Options, click the Authoring tab, click the Schema version list arrow, and then select a schema version.

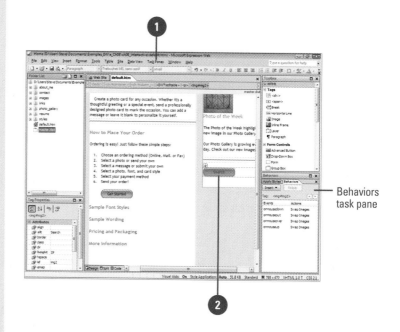

Behaviors task pane

Add a Behavior to an Element

1. Open and display the Web page you want to use.

2. If necessary, click the **Task Panes** or **Format** menu, and then click **Behaviors** to display the Behaviors task pane.

3. Click the element you want to add a behavior.

4. In the Behaviors task pane, click **Insert**, and then select an action from the list.

   A dialog box appears, allowing you to set the details of the action.

5. Specify the action details and set the options you want.

6. Click **OK**.

   The Behaviors task pane displays the event and action linked to the selected element.

7. To change the trigger, point to the event, click the list arrow, and then select the event you want.

8. Click the **Save** button on the Common toolbar, and then click **OK** (if necessary) to save any embedded and related files.

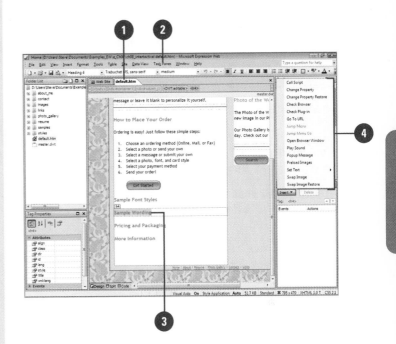

Did You Know?

You can change the order of behaviors associated with an element. Open the Behaviors task pane, select the element with the behaviors, select the action-event you want to change, and then click the Up or Down buttons in the task pane. If the buttons are grayed out, the action-event cannot be reorder.

For Your Information

Adding Behaviors to Text Within a Paragraph

If you want to add a behavior to text within a paragraph, you need to add some HTML code to isolate the text you want to use. Otherwise the behavior is added to the entire paragraph. In Split or Code view, you need to enclose the words in a span tag, including a unique ID.

For example, change the paragraph from <p>Click here for help.</p> to <p><span id="helplink">Click here</span> for help.</p>

Now, select the text "Click here" and add the behavior as shown on this page.

Modifying Behaviors

After you apply a behavior to an element, you can use the Behaviors task pane to change any of the actions or events. You can change action property settings or change the event associated with an action. Action property settings vary depending on the action. If you no longer want to use an action-event, you can delete it from the element.

Change a Behavior to an Element

① Click the **Task Panes** or **Format** menu, and then click **Behaviors**.

The Behaviors task pane appears as a tab in the lower right-corner of the screen.

② Select the element with the behavior you want to change.

The Behaviors task pane displays the behaviors associated with the element.

③ Perform the changes you want.

◆ **Action.** Double-click the action in the Behaviors task pane to open its dialog box, change action properties, and then click **OK**.

◆ **Event.** Point to the event in the Behaviors task pane, click the list arrow, and then select a new event.

◆ **Delete.** In the Behaviors task pane, click the action you want to remove, and then click **Delete**.

④ Click the **Save** button on the Common toolbar, and then click **OK** (if necessary) to save any embedded and related files.

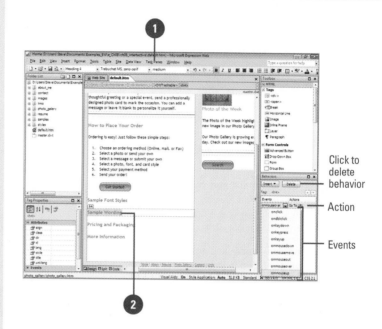

Click to delete behavior

Action

Events

Going to Another Web Page

The Go To URL behavior gives you the ability to link an element on a Web page to a URL address. For example, you can create a Web page, and then use the Go To URL behavior to direct visitors to other sites and pages, or you could create a set of interactive buttons for use on a standard HTML driven Web site. Whichever option you choose, the ability to direct a visitor to other Web sites is essential to creating Internet-oriented documents.

Use the Go To URL Behavior

① Open and display the Web page you want to use.

② If necessary, click the **Task Panes** or **Format** menu, and then click **Behaviors** to display the Behaviors task pane.

③ Click the element you want to add the Go To URL behavior.

④ In the Behaviors task pane, click **Insert**, and then click **Go To URL**.

A dialog box appears, allowing you to set the details of the action.

⑤ Type the URL or click **Browse**, select the URL from the Edit Hyperlink dialog box, and then click **OK**.

⑥ Click **OK**.

The action appears, using the *onmouseover* event as the default.

⑦ To change the trigger, point to the event, click the list arrow, and then select the event you want.

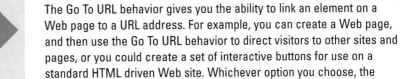

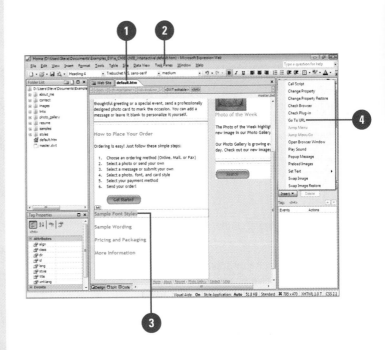

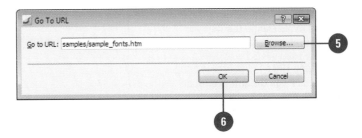

Creating a Jump Menu

The Jump Menu behavior allows you to add a drop-down menu to a Web page. When you use the Jump Menu behavior, you can specify the text for each item on the drop-down menu and where to link each one. After you insert a Jump Menu, you can create a new style in the Manage Style task pane using the element ID in the Selector box. Along with the Jump Menu behavior, you can also use the Jump Menu Go behavior, which allows you to not jump as soon you select an item in the drop-down menu.

Create a Jump Menu

1. Open and display the Web page you want to use.

2. If necessary, click the **Task Panes** or **Format** menu, and then click **Behaviors** to display the Behaviors task pane.

3. In the Behaviors task pane, click **Insert**, and then click **Jump Menu**.

4. Click **Add**.

5. Type a name for the first item in the menu.

6. Enter the URL or use the **Browse** button to select a Web page.

7. Click **OK**.

8. Repeat steps 4 through 7 to add more items to the menu.

9. Use the **Move Up** and **Move Down** buttons to rearrange the items in the menu.

10. Click **Open URLs in** list arrow, and then click **Page Default (None)** or **New Window**.

11. Click **OK**.

12. To modify the Jump Menu, double-click the Jump Menu, make any changes, and then click **OK**.

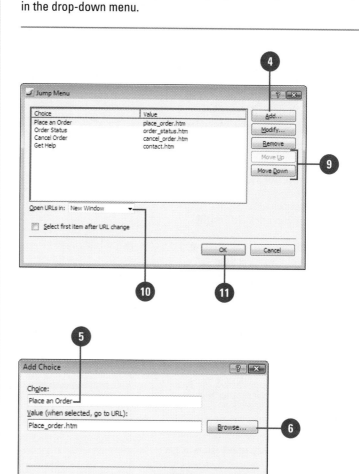

Format the Jump Menu Using a Style

1. Open and display the Web page you want to use.

2. If necessary, click the **Task Panes** menu, and then click **Manage Styles** to display the Manage Styles task pane.

3. In the Manage Styles task pane, click **New Style**.

4. Type the ID name for the Jump Menu in the Selector text box. For example, type **#id1**.

5. In the left pane, click **Font**, **Block**, and **Position** to change the Jump Menu font size, menu width, and other formatting you want.

6. Click **OK**.

See Also

See "Working with Styles" on page 301 for information on formatting an element using a style.

Did You Know?

You can use the Jump Menu Go behavior. To use the Jump Menu Go behavior, insert a Jump Menu behavior and then insert or select an element to use for the trigger. In the Behaviors task pane, click Insert, click Jump Menu Go, and then select the jump menu from the list.

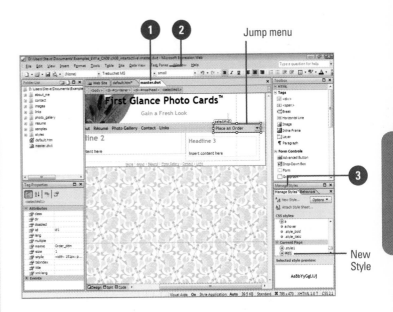

Jump menu

New Style

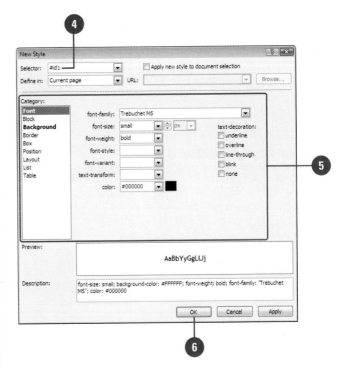

Displaying Text Messages

Expression Web provides several behaviors to display user text messages, including Popup Message and Set Text. The Set Text behavior consists of four individual behaviors: Set Text of Frame, Set Text of Layer, Set Text of Status Bar, and Set Text of Text Field. These behaviors allow you to display text in an alert dialog box, a specific frame, layer, text field, or the status bar.

Create a Popup Message Window

1. Open and display the Web page you want to use.

2. If necessary, click the **Task Panes** or **Format** menu, and then click **Behaviors** to display the Behaviors task pane.

3. Click the element you want to add a behavior.

4. In the Behaviors task pane, click **Insert**, and then click **Popup Message**.

5. Type the message you want.

6. Click **OK**.

   The action appears, using the *onclick* event as the default.

7. To change the trigger, point to the event, click the list arrow, and then select the event you want.

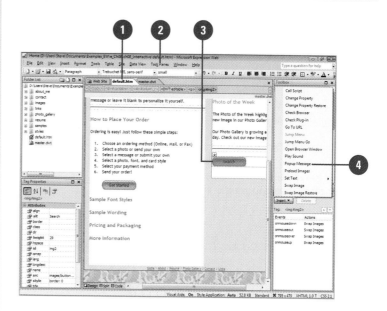

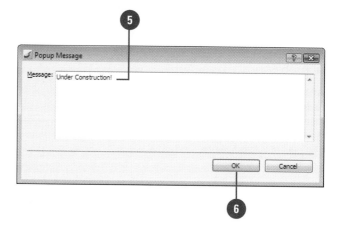

Create a Status Bar Message

1. Open and display the Web page you want to use.

2. If necessary, click the **Task Panes** or **Format** menu, and then click **Behaviors** to display the Behaviors task pane.

3. Click the element you want to add a behavior.

4. In the Behaviors task pane, click **Insert**, point to **Set Text**, and then click **Set Text of Status Bar**.

5. Type the message you want.

6. Click **OK**.

   The action appears, using the *onmouseover* event as the default.

7. To change the trigger, point to the event, click the list arrow, and then select the event you want.

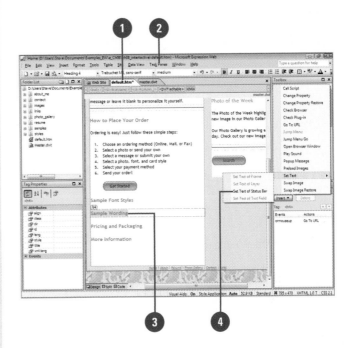

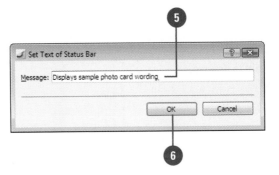

Preloading and Swapping Images

The Preload Images behavior allows you to preload images when a Web page initially loads. This is useful when you want to swap images on mouse rollover buttons. The Preload Images behavior loads the rollover image when the page initially loads, so visitors will not experience a delay while the image loads the first time a visitor points to the button. The Swap Images behavior allows you to swap one image for another when an event occurs. The most common use of this behavior is to create rollover buttons. When you insert an Interactive Button, Expression Web uses the Swap Images behavior. Along with the Swap Image behavior, you can also use the Swap Image Restore behavior, which restores the images that were swapped by the Swap Image behavior.

Preload Images

① Open and display the Web page you want to use.

② If necessary, click the **Task Panes** or **Format** menu, and then click **Behaviors** to display the Behaviors task pane.

③ In the Behaviors task pane, click **Insert**, and then click **Preload Images**.

④ Click **Browse**, locate and select the image you want to preload, and then click **OK**.

⑤ Click **Add**.

⑥ To add more images, repeat steps 4 and 5.

⑦ Click **OK**.

The action appears, using the *onchange* event as the default.

⑧ To change the trigger, point to the event, click the list arrow, and then select the event you want.

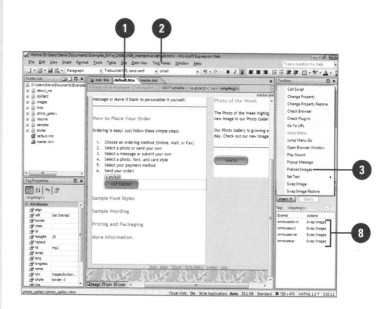

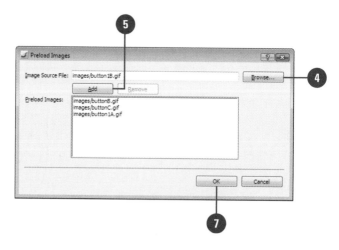

Swap Images

1. Open and display the Web page you want to use.

2. If necessary, click the **Task Panes** or **Format** menu, and then click **Behaviors** to display the Behaviors task pane.

3. Click the image you want to swap.

4. In the Behaviors task pane, click **Insert**, and then click **Swap Image**.

   The selected image appears highlighted in the Swap Images dialog box.

5. Click **Browse**, locate and select the image you want to swap it with, and then click **Open**.

6. To insert a Preload Images behavior, select the **Preload Images** check box.

7. To insert a Swap Image Restore behavior, select the **Restore on mouseout event** check box.

8. To remove a swap, select an image in the list, and then delete the file and path in the Swap Image URL box.

9. Click **OK**.

   The action appears, using the *onclick* event as the default.

10. To change the trigger, point to the event, click the list arrow, and then select the event you want.

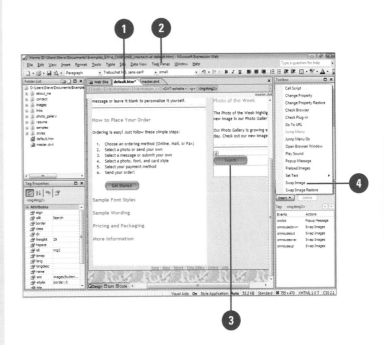

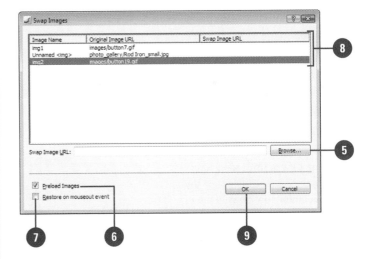

Checking for Browsers and Plug-ins

Web browser functionally vary depending on your version and don't always display information and execute HTML code in the same way, so you may want to check a visitor's browser before displaying a Web page. The Check Browser behavior allows you to detect a user's Web browser and version and then redirect the visitor to another page. You can check for versions of Internet Explorer, Netscape Navigator, Opera, AOL, WebTV, AOL TV, and HotJava. If you want to check for FireFox (Mozilla 5.0), use Netscape Navigator for the browser type and a version later than 5. In addition to checking browsers, you can also check for plug-ins. The Check Plug-in behavior allows you to check for the existence of Adobe Flash, Apple QuickTime, RealNetworks RealPlayer, Adobe Shockwave, and Microsoft Windows Media Player, and then redirect a visitor.

Check the Browser Version

1. Open and display the Web page you want to use.

2. If necessary, click the **Task Panes** or **Format** menu, and then click **Behaviors** to display the Behaviors task pane.

3. Click the element you want to add a behavior.

4. In the Behaviors task pane, click **Insert**, and then click **Check Browser**.

5. Use the list arrows to select the browser type and version you want.

6. Select the **Go to URL** check box, and then enter the URL or use the **Browse** button for use with the specified browser.

7. Select the **Go to URL** check box, and then enter the URL or use the **Browse** button for use with all other browsers.

8. Click **OK**.

   The action appears, using the *onclick* event as the default.

9. To change the trigger, point to the event, click the list arrow, and then select the event you want.

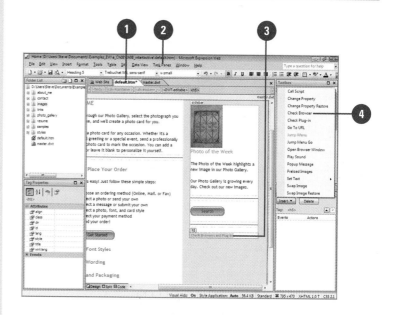

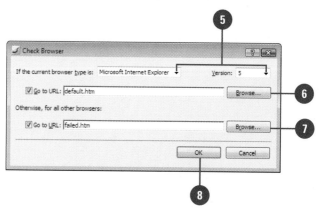

Check for Plug-ins

1. Open and display the Web page you want to use.

2. If necessary, click the **Task Panes** or **Format** menu, and then click **Behaviors** to display the Behaviors task pane.

3. Click the element you want to add a behavior.

4. In the Behaviors task pane, click **Insert**, and then click **Check Plug-in**.

5. Use the list arrow to select the plug-in type you want.

6. Select the **Go to URL** check box, and then enter the URL or use the **Browse** button for use with the specified plug-in.

7. Select the **Go to URL** check box, and then enter the URL or use the **Browse** button for use with all other plug-ins.

8. Click **OK**.

   The action appears, using the *onmouseover* event as the default.

9. To change the trigger, point to the event, click the list arrow, and then select the event you want.

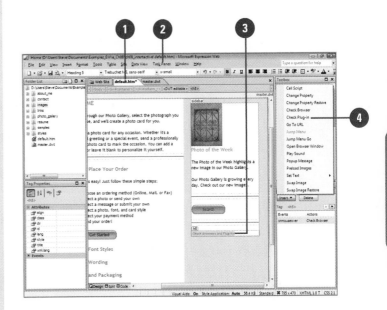

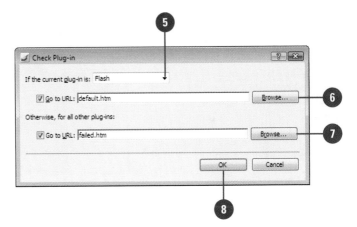

Changing Element Properties

The Change Property behavior allows you to change properties, such a font styles, borders or visibility, for an element on a Web page. The Change Property behavior is useful for adding interactivity to a Web page. For example, you can have the Change Property behavior display a text description or link address when a user points to a picture on a page. Along with the Change Property behavior, you can also use the Change Property Restore behavior, which restores the most recent property changes made by the Change Property behavior. When you use the Change Property Restore behavior, Expression Web displays a message dialog box acknowledging the use of the behavior. You can double-click the behavior to display a list of properties being restored.

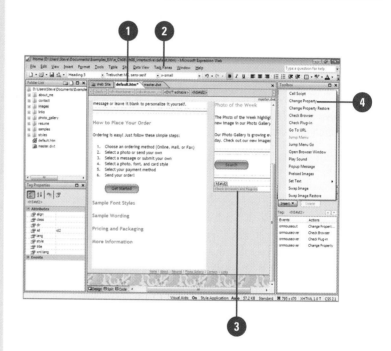

Use the Change Property Behavior

1. Open and display the Web page you want to use.

2. If necessary, click the **Task Panes** or **Format** menu, and then click **Behaviors** to display the Behaviors task pane.

3. Click the element you want to add a behavior.

4. In the Behaviors task pane, click **Insert**, and then click **Change Property**.

   A dialog box appears, allowing you to set the details of the action.

5. Click the **Current Element** or **Select Element** option.

6. If you selected the Select Element option, click the **Element Type** list arrow, select a type, click the **Element ID** list arrow, and then select an ID.

7. Use the following property buttons to change the property you want.

   ◆ **Font.** Click **Font**, use the Font and Character Spacing tabs to select the font, font size, font style you want, and then click **OK**.

Continue Next Page

- ◆ **Position.** Click **Position**, select the wrapping and positioning options you want, and then click **OK**.

- ◆ **Border and Shading.** Click **Borders**, use the Borders and Shading tabs to select the options you want, and then click **OK**.

- ◆ **Visibility.** Click **Visibility**, click the **Inherit**, **Visible**, or **Hidden** option, and then click **OK**.

8 To not insert a Change Property Restore behavior, clear the **Restore on mouseout event** check box.

9 Click **OK**.

10 To change the trigger, point to the event, click the list arrow, and then select the event you want.

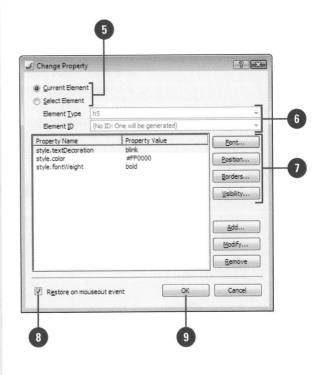

Add, Modify, or Remove Properties

1 Open and display the Web page with the behaviors.

2 In the Behaviors task pane, double-click the change property behavior you want to edit.

3 Perform any of the following options.

- ◆ **Add.** Click **Add**, type a property name and value, and then click **OK**.

- ◆ **Modify.** Select the property, click **Modify**, change the property name and value, and then click **OK**.

- ◆ **Remove.** Select the property, and then click **Remove**.

4 Click **OK**.

Opening Another Browser Window

The Open Browser behavior allows you to set a hyperlink to open in a new browser window. When you use the Open Browser behavior, you need to specify the URL you want to open in the new browser window and any window attributes, such as width, height, navigation and location toolbar, status bar, menu bar, scrollbar as needed and resize handles. If you want to use this behavior with text, you can also use the Change Property and Change Property Restore behaviors to change the pointer to a hand when visitors hover over you text link.

Open Another Browser Window

1 Open and display the Web page you want to use.

2 If necessary, click the **Task Panes** or **Format** menu, and then click **Behaviors** to display the Behaviors task pane.

3 Click the element you want to add a behavior; typically link text or graphic.

4 In the Behaviors task pane, click **Insert**, and then click **Open Browser Window**.

5 Type the URL or click **Browse**, select the URL from the Edit Hyperlink dialog box, and then click **OK**.

6 Enter a window name and size (width and height in pixels). The window name is used in the behavior script, so it cannot have any spaces.

7 Select the check boxes with the window attributes you want to use; it's recommended to keep the defaults: Status bar, Scrollbars as needed, and Resize handles.

8 Click **OK**.

The action appears, using the *onclick* event as the default.

9 To change the trigger, point to the event, click the list arrow, and then select the event you want.

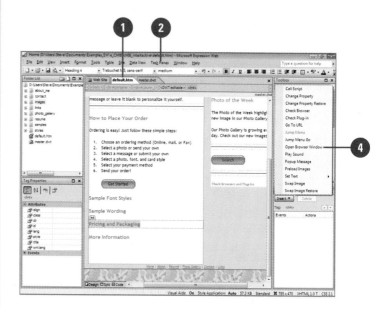

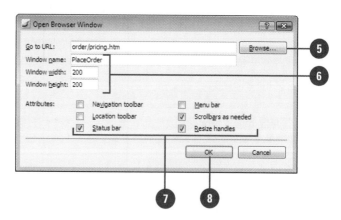

Executing a Script

Use the Call Script Behavior

1. Open and display the Web page you want to use.

2. If necessary, click the **Task Panes** or **Format** menu, and then click **Behaviors** to display the Behaviors task pane.

3. Click the element you want to add a behavior.

4. In the Behaviors task pane, click **Insert**, and then click **Call Script**.

5. Type the line of script you want to run.

6. Click **OK**.

7. To change the trigger, point to the event, click the list arrow, and then select the event you want.

The Call Script behavior runs a line of script when an event occurs. The behavior only runs one line of script, which means you can execute a single line of code or a procedure that calls a section of code. To use the Call Script behavior, you need JavaScript experience and coding knowledge, which is outside the scope of this book.

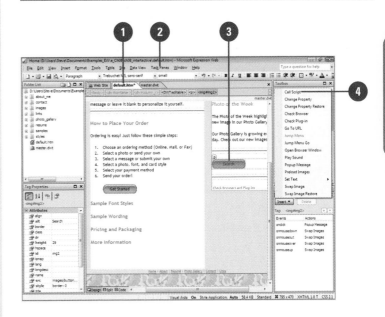

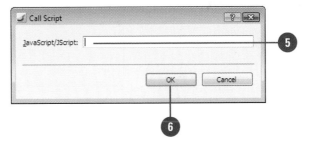

Playing a Sound

The Play Sound behavior allows you to play a sound when an event occurs. With the Play Sound behavior, you can play a variety of sounds including WAV (.wav), MIDI (.mid), RealAudio (.ram or .ra), AIFF sound (.aif, .aifc, or .aiff), and AU sound (.au or .snd).

Use the Sound Behavior

1. Open and display the Web page you want to use.

2. If necessary, click the **Task Panes** or **Format** menu, and then click **Behaviors** to display the Behaviors task pane.

3. Click the element you want to add a behavior.

4. In the Behaviors task pane, click **Insert**, and then click **Play Sound**.

5. Click **Browse**, locate and select the sound file, and then click **Open**.

6. Click **OK**.

   The action appears, using the *onchange* event as the default.

7. To change the trigger, point to the event, click the list arrow, and then select the event you want.

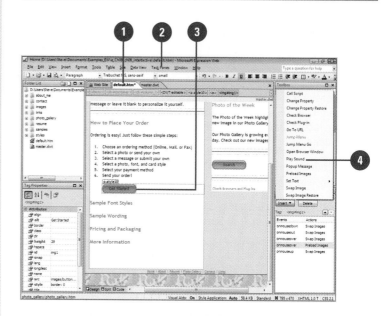

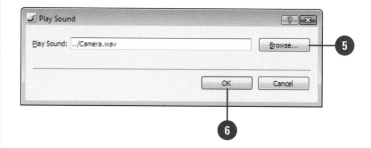

Adding Tables and Layout Tables

Introduction

Tables are a useful tool for laying out and formatting Web pages in Microsoft Expression Web. Tables consists of horizontal rows and vertical columns. The intersection of a row and column is called a cell, which contains the information you want to present. A table in Expression Web has two main uses: page layout and data formatting.

A layout table creates a grid on your page, which you can use to position various elements—text and graphics—on the page to create an overall look. Due to limitations in HTML for arranging information, page layout is one of the most important aspects of using a table in Expression Web.

In addition to page layout, tables also make it easy to manage and present your data. These conventional tables that format your data in a tabular way, are like the ones you might create in some of the other Office programs, such as Microsoft Excel, PowerPoint or Word.

The main difference between layout tables and conventional tables is the additional page layout options to arrange and modify cell properties. If you create one type of table, yet determine later you need the other, you can switch between the two types.

Once you have your table designed, you can modify it by changing the cell formatting, and the way cells are viewed on your page. You can also add, modify and delete various cells, rows, and columns in your table. Adding a rounded corner or a shadow effect to your cells could provide that extra touch. You might even have a table where you need to split a cell into two cells, or merge other cells into one cell.

Some of the final touches such as formatting your overall table, adding color, and including some graphical images to the table can really make your data stand out.

What You'll Do

Create a Layout Table

Draw a Layout Table and Cells

Modify a Layout Table

Create a Table Using Microsoft Excel Data

Create a Conventional Table

Enter Text in a Table

Convert Text to a Table

Fill a Table with Information

Create Table Captions

Add Cells, Rows, or Columns to Tables

Resize Rows and Columns

Split and Merge Cells

Delete Table Elements

Align Cell Contents

Change Table and Cell Properties

Format a Table

Add Color to a Table

Add Images to Tables

Creating a Layout Table

A layout table helps you organize data and design the overall look of a Web page. A layout table creates a grid on the page, which you can use to map out the location for each element you want to display on the page. You can create your own layout table grid or use one of the table layout templates that comes with Expression Web. The templates provides a quick and easy way to create a table grid. Once you create a layout table, you can create additional cells and insert your content.

Create a Layout Table

1. Open and display a blank Web page.

2. Click the **Task Panes** menu, and then click **Layout Tables** to display the Layout Tables task pane.

    ◆ If you want to display more information, click the **Maximize** button in the Layout Tables task pane.

3. Use one of the following methods to create a layout table.

    ◆ Click the **Insert Layout Table** link to create a one cell layout table.

    ◆ Click the **Draw Layout Table** button, and then drag to create a table.

    ◆ Click any of the templates in the Choose Layout area.

4. Click in a cell, and then add content.

Did You Know?

You can switch between table types quickly. Click the Show Layout Tool button on the Layout Tables task pane.

You can remove a table layout from a page. Click the No Layout on the Layout Tables task pane.

Draw Layout Table button

Insert Layout Table link

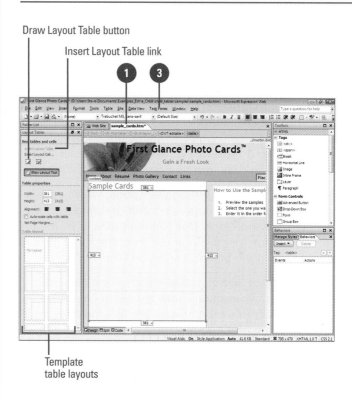

Template table layouts

Change Layout Table Properties

1. Open and display the Web page with the layout table you want to change.

2. Click the **Task Panes** menu, and then click **Layout Tables** to display the Layout Tables task pane.

3. Use the Table properties area to change the layout table.

   - ◆ **Width.** Changes table width.

   - ◆ **Height.** Changes table height.

   - ◆ **Alignment buttons.** Changes table alignment on the page to the left, center, or right.

   - ◆ **Auto-Scale Cells With Table.** Select to keep the width of the table equal to the sum of its cell width.

4. To set page margins, click **Set Page Margins** on the task pane, enter the margins you want, and then click **OK**.

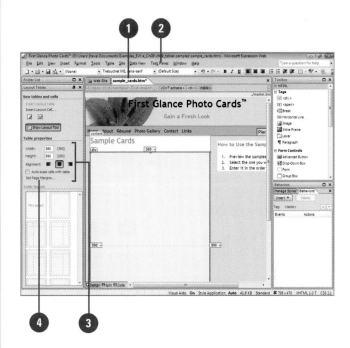

Did You Know?

You can also use the size label in the table layout to resize a cell. Click the size label on the top or at the side, and then select the option you want on the menu. To enter an exact row height or column width, click Change Row Height or Change Column Width. To have the cell shrink or grow at content changes, click Make Row Autostretch or Make Column Autostretch.

Drawing a Layout Table and Cells

Expression Web makes a distinction between conventional cells and layout cells. Conventional cells contain no special properties, while layout cells do. These special properties, for example, allow you to have individual borders, rounded corners, shadows, and resize or reposition layout cells without affecting other layout cells. When you add a layout cell in a layout table, Expression Web adds and sizes rows and columns to create the cell in the location where you want it. The rows and columns serve only to position the cell. When you add more layout cells, the rows and columns change. After you create a layout cell, you can move and resize it to create the layout you want. Before you can move or resize a layout cell, you need to first select it (point to the edge, and then click the blue edge).

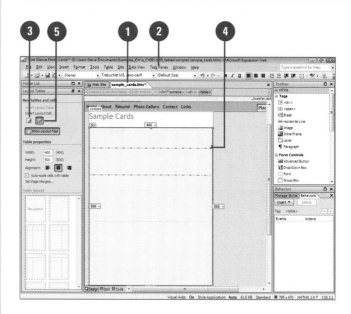

Draw a Layout Table and Cell

1 Open and display the Web page with the layout table you want to use.

2 Click the **Task Panes** menu, and then click **Layout Tables** to display the Layout Tables task pane.

3 Click the **Draw Layout Table** button on the task pane.

4 Drag a layout table on the page.

5 Click the **Draw Layout Cell** button on the task pane.

6 Drag a layout cell in the layout table.

- ◆ To draw multiple cells, press and hold Ctrl while you drag each cell.

Resize a Layout Table

1. Open and display the Web page with the layout cells you want to change.

2. Point to the edge of the layout table to display a green edge.

3. Click the green edge to select the layout table.

4. To resize the layout table, drag a handle to the desired size.

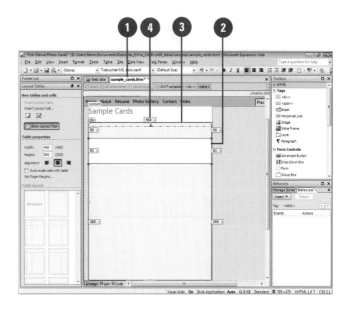

Move or Resize a Layout Cell

1. Open and display the Web page with the layout cells you want to change.

2. Point to the edge of the layout cell to display a blue edge.

3. Click the blue edge to select the layout cell.

4. To move the layout cell, drag the tab at the top of the cell with the cell size or the blue edge.

5. To resize the layout cell, drag a handle to the desired size.

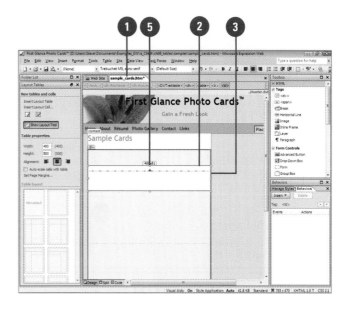

Modifying a Layout Table

Before you can modify a layout table, you need to first select it and you must not be in drawing mode. You can click the Draw Layout Cell button to change modes. To select a layout table, point to the table edge, and then click the green edge. When you select a layout table, list arrows appear at the edges, indicating the size of the row or column. You can click the list arrows to change row and column properties.

Modify a Layout Table

1. Open and display the Web page with the layout table you want to use.

2. Point to the edge of the layout table to display a green edge.

3. Click the green edge to select the layout table.

4. Click the list arrow for the row or column you want to modify, and then click **Change Column Height** or **Change Width Height** to open a dialog box. You can select some options directly from the submenu without opening the dialog box (if so, skip Steps 5 and 6).

5. Select the row or columns options you want. The column options include:

   ◆ **Column Width.** The column width.

   ◆ **Clear Contradicting Width.** Select to correct two or more cells in the same column with different heights.

   ◆ **Make Column Autostretch.** Select to let the browser determine the width of the column.

   ◆ **Use Column Spacer Image.** Select to control the width of the column by adding a transparent picture to the last row.

6. Click **OK**.

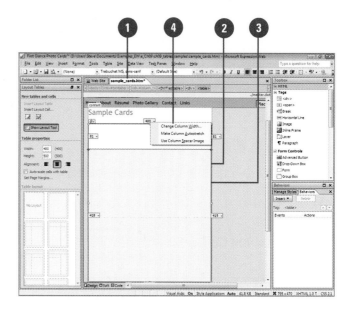

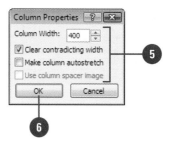

Creating a Table Using Microsoft Excel Data

You can create a table based on Microsoft Excel data by importing the information as static data or using Active Server Pages (ASP) and Microsoft's Internet Information Services (IIS) to provide live data. This task focuses on importing Excel data into a table. During the import process Expression Web translated the file data to HTML. Depending on the file, the headers and column labels and table may be large, which you can change using the font commands on the Common toolbar and the Table Properties dialog box.

Create a Table Using Excel Data

1. Open and display a blank Web page to insert the data.

2. Click the **Insert Table** button on the Standard toolbar, and then click the first cell to create a single-cell table.

3. Click in the single-cell table.

4. Click the **Insert** menu, and then click **File**.

   ◆ If the File command is not available, see "Customizing the Menu bar" on page 368 to add it to the Insert menu.

   The Select File dialog box opens.

5. Click the **Files as type** list arrow, and then click **All Files**.

6. Locate and select the Microsoft Excel file you want to insert, and then click **Open**.

   A status dialog box appears as the file is converted to HTML. The data is inserted as a borderless table indicated by the dashed outline.

7. To change the table size, right-click the table, click **Table Properties**, change the table size and any other options you want, and then click **OK**.

8. To change the font type and font size, use the list arrows on the Common toolbar.

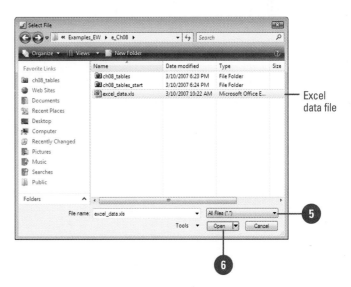

Excel data file

Creating a Conventional Table

Though you might want to reference and analyze information, the best way to initially display large amounts of data is through the use of tables. Tables are defined by their various components; the cell, the row, and the column. The number of rows determines the height of the table, and the number of columns the width. The combination of the two determines the total number of cells that can hold information. You can quickly create a table by using the Insert button on the Standard toolbar and choosing how many rows and columns you want, or by using the Insert Table command and selecting the options you want in the Insert Table dialog box.

Create a Conventional Table

1. Open and display the Web page you want to use.

2. Click where you want to create a table.

3. Click the **Insert Table** button on the Standard toolbar.

4. Drag to choose how many rows and columns you want.

Did You Know?

You can resize a row or column quickly. Position the pointer (which changes to the double-headed arrow) on the row or column border you want to resize, and then drag the border to the size you want.

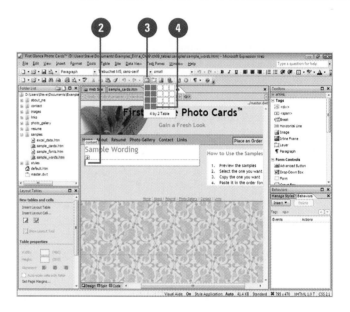

Table

Create a Conventional Table by Setting Properties

1 Open and display the Web page you want to use.

2 Click where you want to create a table.

3 Click the **Table** menu, point to **Insert**, and then click **Table**.

4 Define the attributes of the table, some options include:

- ◆ **Rows.** The number of rows you want in your table.

- ◆ **Columns.** The number of columns you want in your table.

- ◆ **Alignment.** The position you want to assign the table text.

- ◆ **Specify Width.** The width of the table in pixels or percentages.

- ◆ **Cell Padding.** The space, in pixels, between the data and the inside of the table cell.

- ◆ **Cell Spacing.** The space (in pixels) between the cells.

- ◆ **Border Size.** The thickness level (in pixels) you want to assign to the table's border box.

- ◆ **Background color or picture.** The color or picture you want in the background of the table.

- ◆ **Set as Default.** Select to set current options as the default for all new tables.

5 Click **OK**.

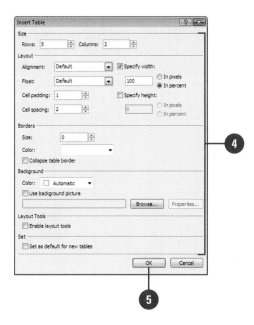

Entering Text in a Table

Once you create your table, you enter text into cells just as you would in a paragraph, except pressing the Tab key moves you from cell to cell. The first row in the table is good for column headings, whereas the left-most column is good for row labels. To enter text in cells, you need to know how to move around the table and select the rows and columns.

Enter Text and Move Around a Table

① Open and display the Web page you want to use.

② Position the insertion point in the table where you want to enter text.

The insertion point shows where text you type will appear in a table.

③ Type your text, and then perform one of the following:

◆ Press Enter to start a new paragraph within that cell.

◆ Press Tab to move the insertion point to the next cell to the right (or to the first cell in the next row).

◆ Press the arrow keys or click in a cell to move the insertion point to a new location.

Type and format text just as you would in a paragraph.

Press Tab to move to the first cell in the next row.

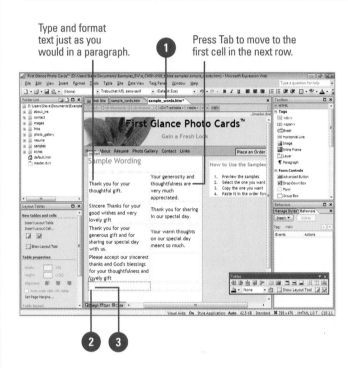

Select Table Elements

Refer to this table for methods of selecting table elements, including:

- ◆ The entire table
- ◆ One or more rows and columns
- ◆ One or more cells

Did You Know?

You can see the selection difference between layout and conventional tables. When you select a conventional table in Design view, it appears with a solid black background. When you select a layout table, it appears with a green border.

Selecting Table Elements

To Select	Do This
The entire table	Click in a cell, click the Table menu, point to Select, and then click Table.
One or more rows	Position the pointer along the left edge of the row you want to select (a black arrow appears), and then drag to select the rows you want, or click the Table menu, point to Select, and then click Row.
One or more columns	Position the pointer along the top edge of the column you want to select (a black arrow appears), and then drag to select the columns you want, or click the Table menu, point to Select, and then click Column.
A single cell	Drag a cell or click the cell with the black arrow, or click the Table menu, point to Select, and then click Cell.
More than one cell	Drag with the black arrow to select a group of cells.

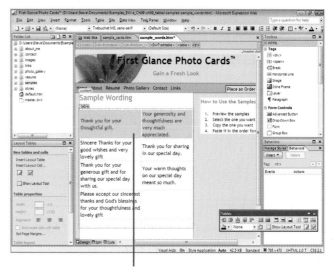

Selected row

Converting Text to a Table

If you have existing text separated by paragraphs, tabs, or commas, you can convert the text to a table. When text is separated by paragraphs, tabs, or commas, it's known as delimited text, which is commonly used to delineate data for tables, spreadsheets, and databases. During the conversion process, you can select the character used to separate the text on your page to create a table.

Convert Delimited Text to a Table

1. Open and display the Web page you want to use.

2. Select the text you want to convert to a table.

3. Click the **Table** menu, point to **Convert**, and then click **Text to Table**.

4. Click the option to designate the character used to separate the text (commas, paragraphs, etc.).

5. Click **OK**.

Did You Know?

You can create a one-celled table. Click the None option in the Convert Text to Table dialog box.

HTML doesn't support tabs as a character separator. HTML doesn't directly support tabs as a character to separate text, so we recommend avoiding them, if possible, despite their presence on the Convert Text to Table dialog box.

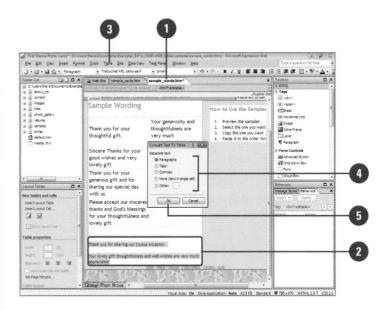

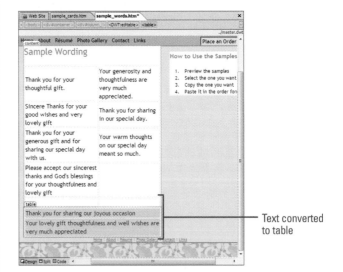

Text converted to table

Filling a Table with Information

A table needs information, and while you will normally enter most of that data manually when creating a new table, text can also be easily copied into a row or column of cells. The Fill Down and Fill Right commands allow you to propagate repeating content to table cells below or right of the currently selected cell.

Fill Cells with Information

① Open and display the Web page you want to use.

② Select the cell with the text to be copied along with the adjacent cells in a row or a column by dragging the cursor either to the right (row) or down (column).

③ Click the **Table** menu, point to **Fill**, and then click **Right** or **Down**. All selected cells, in the row, or column now contain the text from the original cell.

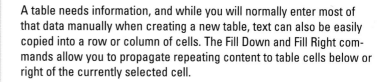

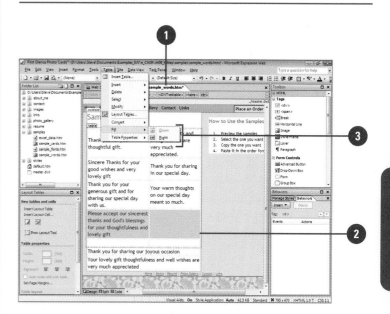

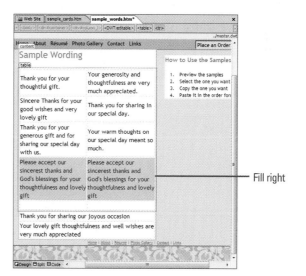

Fill right

Creating Table Captions

A caption is an important way to provide information about the data in a table. When you insert a table caption, it appears at the top of the table, but you can move it to the bottom. When you enter caption text, the rows and columns in the table grow to accommodate the cell contents.

Add a Caption to a Table

1. Open and display the Web page you want to use.

2. Position the insertion point anywhere inside the table.

3. Click the **Table** menu, point to **Insert**, and then click **Caption**.

   The text insertion point appears at the top of the table (top is the default selection).

4. Type the caption for the table at the insertion point.

Did You Know?

You can change caption alignment on the Formatting toolbar. Select the caption, and then click Align Right, Align Left, or Center on the Formatting toolbar.

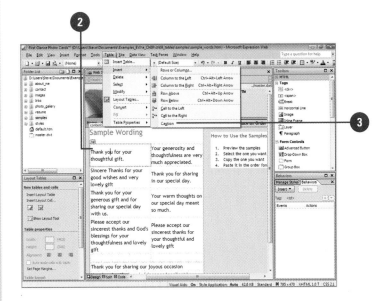

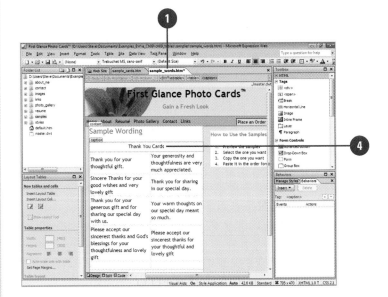

Change the Position of a Caption

① Open and display the Web page you want to use.

② Right-click the caption, and then click **Caption Properties**.

③ Click the **Top of table** option or the **Bottom of table** option.

④ Click **OK**.

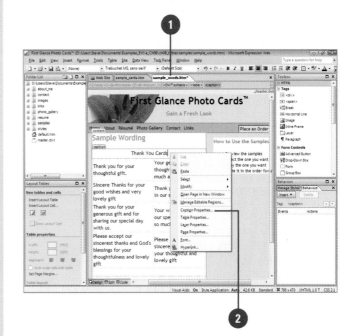

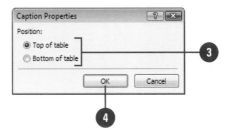

Adding Cells, Rows, or Columns to Tables

As you begin to work on a table, you might need to modify its structure by adding more rows, columns, or cells to accommodate new text, graphics, or other tables. The table realigns as needed to accommodate the new structure. When you insert rows, columns, or cells, the existing rows shift down, the existing columns shift right, and you choose what direction the existing cells shift. Similarly, when you delete unneeded rows, columns, or cells from a table, the table realigns itself.

Add a Cell, Row, or Column to a Table

1 Open and display the Web page you want to use.

2 Click to position the insertion point to the right of the cell where you want to add another cell.

3 To add a single cell, click the **Table** menu, point to **Insert**, and then click **Cell to the Left** or **Cell to the Right**.

4 To add multiple rows or columns, click the **Table** menu, point to **Insert**, and then click **Rows Or Columns**.

◆ To add a single row or column, click the **Table** menu, point to **Insert**, and then click **Columns to the Left**, **Column to the Right**, **Row Above**, or **Row Below**.

TIMESAVER *Use buttons on the Tables toolbar to perform the commands.*

5 Enter the number of columns or rows you want to add to the table, and the related options.

6 Click **OK**.

The new columns or rows are added to the table underneath or to the right of the insertion point.

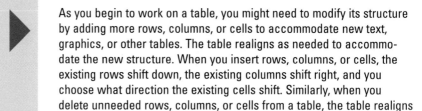

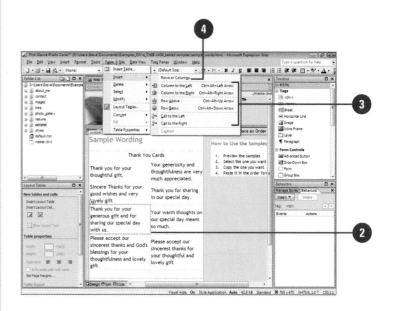

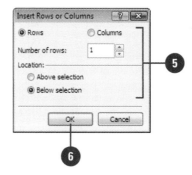

Resizing Rows and Columns

Expression Web provides three commands—Distribute Rows Evenly, Distribute Columns Evenly, and AutoFit To Contents—you can use to create evenly spaced rows and columns in a table. However, due to limitations in HTML regarding table dimensions, browsers often override table alignment settings, so its important to test pages with tables in several browsers. If you need to adjust a single row or column, you can use the mouse pointer to drag the border to a new location.

Resize Table Rows and Columns

1. Open and display the Web page you want to use.

2. Select the rows and columns you want to resize.

3. To distribute rows or columns evenly, click the **Table** menu, point to **Modify**, and then click **Distribute Rows Evenly** or **Distribute Columns Evenly**.

4. To minimize the size of rows and columns to fit the cell contents, click the **Table** menu, point to **Modify**, and then click **AutoFit To Contents**.

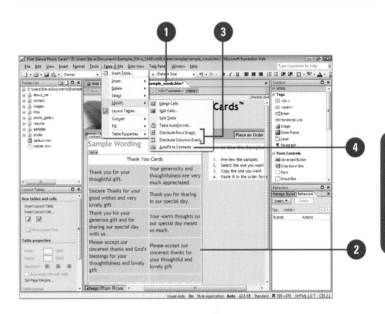

Resize Table Rows and Columns Using the Mouse

1. Open and display the Web page you want to use.

2. Position the pointer over the border between rows or columns you want to resize (cursor changes to a double-headed arrow), and then drag the border to resize it.

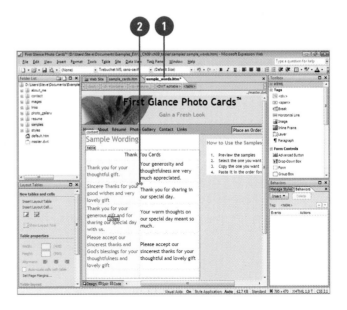

Splitting and Merging Cells

Cells can also be split or combined (also known as merged). Often there is more to modifying a table than adding or deleting rows or columns; you need to make cells just the right size to accommodate the text you are entering in the table. For example, a title in the first row of a table might be longer than the first cell in that row. To spread the title across the top of the table, you can merge (combine) the cells to form one long cell. Sometimes to indicate a division in a topic, you need to split (or divide) a cell into two.

Split a Cell into Two Cells

1. Open and display the Web page you want to use.

2. Select the cell or cells you want to split.

3. Click the **Table** menu, point to **Modify**, and then click **Split Cells**.

   TIMESAVER *Click the Split Cells button on the Tables toolbar to perform the command.*

4. Click the **Split into columns** option or the **Split into rows** option.

5. Type the number of columns or rows into which you want the cells split.

6. Click **OK**.

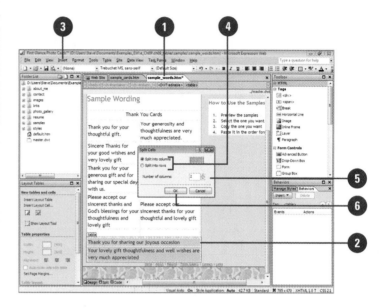

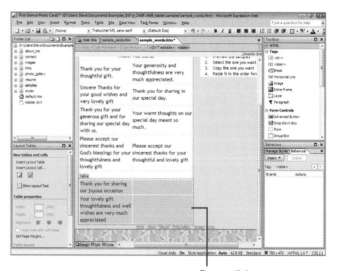

Rows split in two

Merge Cells Together

1. Open and display the Web page you want to use.

2. Click a column, row, or group of adjacent cells, and then drag to select them. You can begin with two cells or select an entire group of adjacent cells.

3. Click the **Tables** menu, and then click **Merge Cells**.

   TIMESAVER *Click the Merge Cells button on the Tables toolbar to perform the command.*

   The cells merge into a single, larger cell.

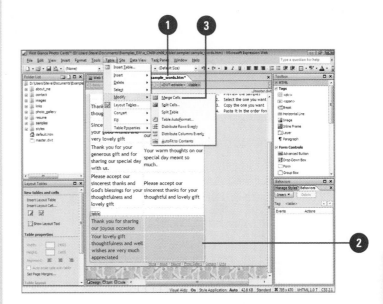

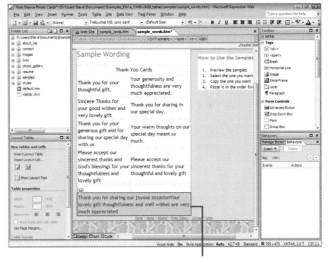

The two rows merged into one

Deleting Table Elements

If you no longer need a table element, you can remove it. Tables, cells, rows, columns, and captions can all be easily deleted in Page view. You can use the commands on the Table menu or the Backspace and Delete keys. The Backspace key deletes the selected table, cell, column, or row and its contents, while the Delete key deletes only the contents of the selected table, cell, column, or row.

Delete a Table Element

1. Open and display the Web page you want to use.

2. Select the table, cell, row, column, or caption you want to delete.

3. Click the **Table** menu, point to **Select**, and then:

   ◆ To delete a table, click **Table**.

   ◆ To delete a cell, click **Cell**.

   ◆ To delete a row, click **Row**.

   ◆ To delete a column, click **Column**.

4. Click the **Table** menu, and then click the delete command you want: **Table**, **Delete Columns**, **Delete Rows**, or **Delete Cells**.

   TIMESAVER *Click the Delete Cells button on the Tables toolbar to perform the command.*

> ### Did You Know?
>
> *You can delete a table caption.* Select the caption, and then press Delete.

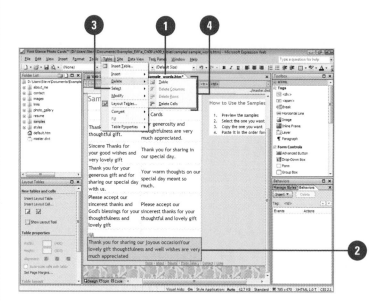

Aligning Cell Contents

You can align the cell content in a table to any border. Expression Web makes it easy with the alignment buttons on the Formatting and Tables toolbars. The Formatting toolbar contains the Align Left, Center, and Alight Right buttons and the Tables toolbar contains the Align Top, Center Vertically, and Align Bottom buttons.

Align Cell Contents

1 Open and display the Web page you want to use.

2 Select the rows or columns in which you want to align cell contents.

3 Use the alignment buttons on the Formatting or Common toolbar.

◆ **Align Left.** Aligns to the left edge of the cell.

◆ **Center.** Aligns to the horizontal center of the cell.

◆ **Align Right.** Aligns to the right edge of the cell.

4 If necessary, right-click any toolbar, and then click **Tables** to display the Tables toolbar.

5 Use the alignment buttons on the Tables toolbar.

◆ **Align Top.** Aligns to the top of the cell.

◆ **Center Vertically.** Aligns to the vertical center of the cell.

◆ **Align Bottom.** Aligns to the bottom of the cell.

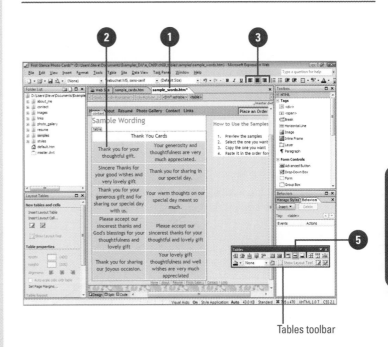

Tables toolbar

Changing Table Properties

Once you create a table and enter information, you can modify a variety of elements in the table, including alignment, cell spacing, cell padding (the space around the cell contents), height and width, border size, and color. You can change all of these properties in the Table Properties dialog box.

Change Table Properties

1. Open and display the Web page you want to use.

2. Right-click the table, and then click **Table Properties**.

3. You can set the table's layout modifying the following parameters or accepting the default settings.

   ◆ **Alignment.** Set the position for the table on the page (left, right, center).

   ◆ **Float.** Indicate whether you want text surrounding the table to flow around the left or right side of the table. If you do not want text to flow around the table at all, select Default.

   ◆ **Cell Padding.** Change the space between a cell border and its content by entering a number in the box.

   ◆ **Cell Spacing.** Change the space between the table cells by entering a number in the box.

   ◆ **Specify Width.** Set the width of the columns in pixels or percentage of the available screen space.

   ◆ **Specify Height.** Set the height of the columns in pixels or percentage of the available screen space.

Continue Next Page

④ You can set the table's borders modifying the following parameters or accepting the default settings.

◆ **Size.** Enter the width of your table border in pixels. If you don't want a border, enter 0 (zero).

◆ **Color.** Select one color for the table border from the dialog box's list color menu.

⑤ To select a color for the table background, in the Background area, click the **Color** list arrow, and then select a color from the Color palette.

⑥ Click **OK**.

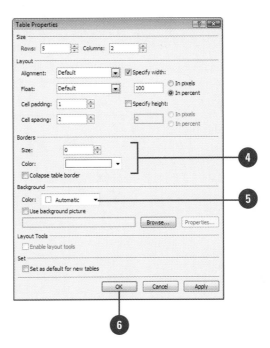

Changing Cell Properties

You can use the Cell Properties dialog box to resize rows or columns of cells and change the span between cells in a table. You can also change the cell alignment, size, and border or background color. If the text or images in a cell are larger than the set values, the table or its elements will be upsized to contain the content. The cell span feature is designed to create various widths or heights within cells on the same table.

Resize Cells, Rows, or Columns

1. Open and display the Web page you want to use.

2. Click to place the insertion point within a row or column you want to resize.

3. Click the **Table** menu, point to **Select**, and then click **Row**, **Column**, or **Cell**.

4. Right-click the selected element, and then click **Cell Properties**.

5. To set the width, click the **Specify width** check box to select it, and then enter a value in pixels or in percent.

6. To set the height, click the **Specify height** check box to select it, and then enter a value in pixels or in percent.

7. Click **OK**.

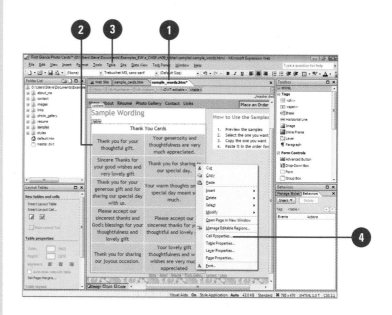

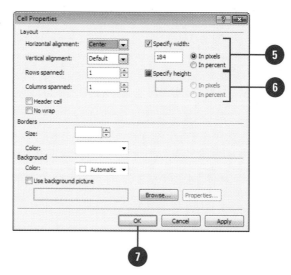

Change Cell Span

1. Open and display the Web page you want to use.

2. Right-click the selected cell, and then click **Cell Properties**.

3. Enter the number of rows and columns you want in the **Rows spanned** and **Columns spanned** boxes.

4. Click **OK**.

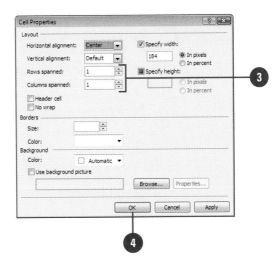

Change Cell Layout

1. Open and display the Web page you want to use.

2. Select the cell you want to change, right-click the cell, and then click **Cell Properties**.

3. Set the cell alignment options you want.

   ◆ **Horizontal Alignment.** Click the **Horizontal Alignment** list arrow, and then select an alignment.

   ◆ **Vertical Alignment.** Click the **Vertical Alignment** list arrow, and then select an alignment.

4. You can set the cell's layout using the following parameters:

   ◆ To set cells as header cells, select the **Header cell** check box.

   ◆ To wrap your text within a cell, clear the **No wrap** check box.

5. Click **OK**.

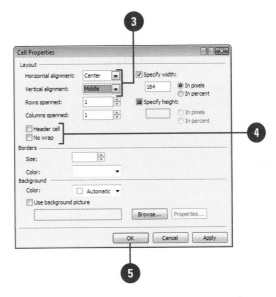

Formatting a Table

A uniform background color isn't always the best solution. For example, if you have a large table with a lot of columns, it might be easier for the reader to follow particular rows of information if your table uses alternating background colors for each row. Or perhaps you just want to have a different color in the first row or column (or both) to pull out the key terms that organize the data. Either way, you can use a color template to format your table, regardless of the number of cells it contains, or their arrangement.

Format a Table Quickly

① Open and display the Web page you want to use.

② Click the table to select it.

③ Click the **Table AutoFormat Combo** button list arrow on the Tables toolbar.

④ Click the table format style you want.

> ### Did You Know?
>
> **You can view the Tables toolbar.**
> Right-click any toolbar, and then click Tables, or click the View menu, point to Toolbar, and then click Tables.

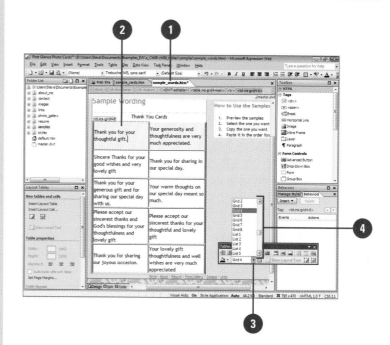

Format a Table Using AutoFormat

1. Open and display the Web page you want to use.

2. Click the table to select it.

3. Click the **Table AutoFormat** button on the Tables toolbar.

4. Click the table format you want.

5. Click the format check boxes to select or clear additional formatting options.

6. Click **OK**.

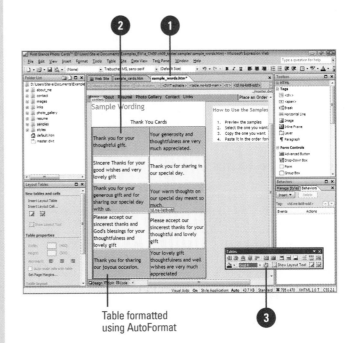

Table formatted using AutoFormat

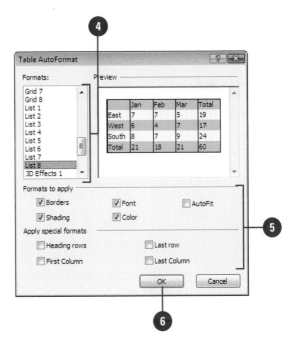

Adding Color to a Table

Tables are transparent by default, showing the background color or pattern of the Web page as the background of the table. If this is not the best design choice, consider adding a different color as the background. You can change the color table elements quickly using the Fill Color button on the Tables toolbar. If you want to change several color options at once, you can use the Table Properties dialog box. You can also add color to cells and borders. A cell border can contain one or two colors (the second color adds depth, or a 3-D type), and each individual cell within a table can have its own one or two-colored border.

Add Color to Table Elements Quickly

1. Open and display the Web page you want to use.

2. Select the table, column, row, or cell you want to add color.

3. Click the **Fill Color** button list arrow on the Tables toolbar.

4. Select a color on the menu.

Did You Know?

You can add color to a table using Table Properties. Right-click the table, click Table Properties, click the background color, select a color, and then click OK.

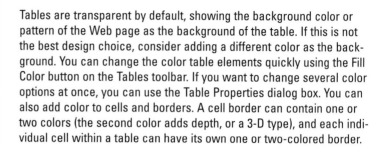
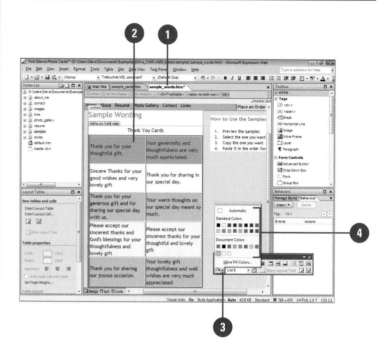

Change Cell Border or Background Color

1. Open and display the Web page you want to use.

2. Right-click the table cell, and then click **Cell Properties**.

3. Click the **Color** list arrow, and then select a color.

4. You can set the cell's background using the following parameters in the Background area:

   ◆ Click the **Color** list arrow, and then select a color.

5. Click **OK**.

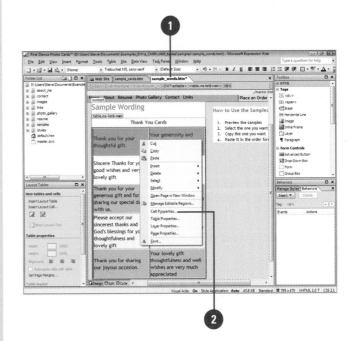

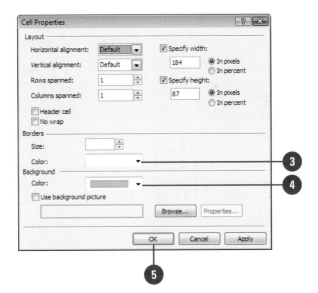

Adding Images to Tables

Because tables are supported by many browsers, they can be used to help lay out a page's text and graphics. Tables provide an ideal way to present images in a unified manner, which browsers can consistently display in the same way. You can insert pictures into a single cell or an entire table using the Cell Properties and Table Properties dialog boxes.

Add an Image to a Table or Cell

1. Open and display the Web page you want to use.

2. Right-click the table or cell, and then click **Table Properties** to add a table image or **Cell Properties** to add a cell image.

3. Select the **Use background picture** check box.

4. Click **Browse**.

5. Locate and select the picture you want to use, and then click **Open**.

6. Click **OK**.

Adding Frames and Borders

Introduction

A frames page is a type of HTML page that breaks up the browser display into different areas, known as **frames**. Each frame can display a different page. Pages are shown in frames by creating a hyperlink to the page and indicating the frame as a portion of the link. Frames are useful to Web masters because the user interface is stable and the frames contain built-in navigation. Frames pages are used for many different types of Web sites and pages, such as catalogs or sites containing a collection of articles.

Frames pages don't actually contain content; they are holders that indicate which content pages to display within the boundaries the frames page defines. It is much like a picture frame without a picture. For example, you can click a hyperlink within a frame, and have the linked page open in a different frame, called a target frame because it is the target of the link. Frames can also be split (vertically or horizontally), resized, or deleted by dragging frame borders. Frame borders can be seen or hidden by the user. You, as the Webmaster, can determine the size of the margins inside each frame, the amount of space between frames, and whether a frame can be resized within a browser or if scroll bars should be included.

If you continually use the same frame page to create Web pages for your site, you can save time by creating a template. You can modify an existing frames page template to create a customized one, or you can create one from scratch. Expression Web comes with a variety of frames page templates—Banner and Contents, Vertical Split, Header, Footer, and Footnotes—from which you can create a customized template.

Viewing a Frames Page

Frames page   Frame borders

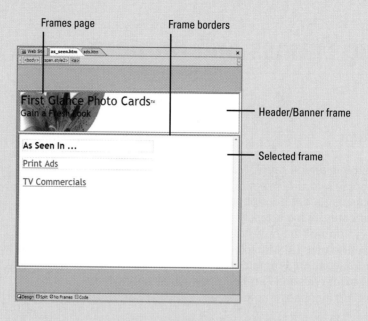

Header/Banner frame

Selected frame

Inline frame

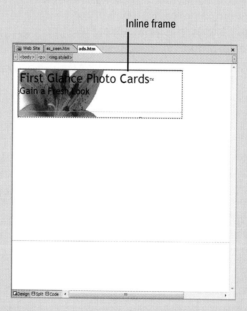

Creating a Frames Page Using a Template

When you first work with borders you should use a frames page template, because templates are pre-configured so that you can easily move between frames. The New dialog box comes with a set of built-in templates—Banner and Contents, Contents, Footer, Footnotes, Header, and Vertical Split to name a few—from which you can create a frames page. With a template, you decide what occupies the initial page (the page that is visible in each frame when you first visit a frames page), which can either be a new page or one you've previously created.

Create a Frames Page

① Click the **New** button list arrow, and then click **Page**.

② In the left pane, click **Frames Pages**.

③ Click the frames page template you want to use.

④ Click **OK**.

The page opens in template form.

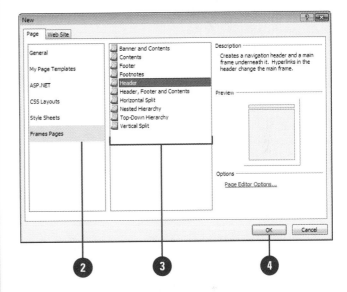

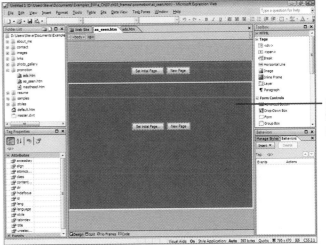

New frames page

Customizing a Frames Page Template

If you continually use the same frames page to create Web pages for your site, you can save time by creating a template. You can modify an existing frames page template to create a customized one, or you can create one from scratch. Expression Web comes with a variety of frames page templates—Banner and Contents, Vertical Split, Header, Footer, and Footnotes—from which you can create a customized template.

Customize an Existing Frames Page Template

1. Open a frames page template that you want to use as the basis for a new frames page template.

2. Right-click in any frame, and then click **Frame Properties**.

3. Make any modifications to the size of the frame, margins, name and so forth that you desire, and then click **OK**.

4. Click the **File menu**, and then click **Save As**.

5. Click the **Save as type** list arrow, and then click **Page Template**.

6. Navigate to the **frames_t** folder (which is already in the Expression Web Pages folder) to store the template along with the other frame templates.

7. Type the file name for your custom template.

8. Click **Save**.

9. Type the name you want to use as a title for the template. This is the title that will appear in the list of templates under Frames Pages in the New dialog box.

10. Type the text describing what the template does. This text is displayed in the Description area in the list of templates.

11. Click **OK**.

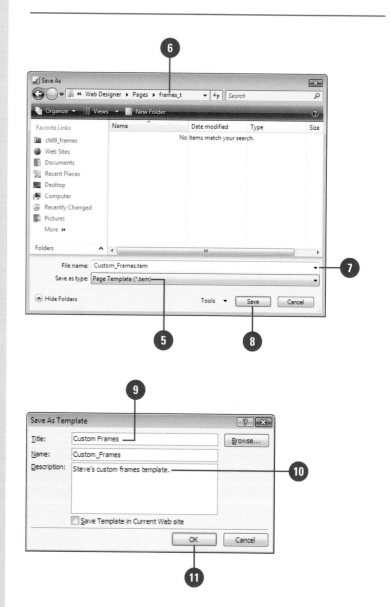

Inserting an Inline Frame

Inline frames resemble normal frames pages except an inline frame and its contents are embedded in an existing Web page. So you don't have to create a separate frames page to introduce embedded content. An **inline frame** can also create a frame within a frame. And anything you can do with a regular page can be done with an inline frame. Just as with any other frame, inline frames are customizable. Using the Inline Frame command on the Insert menu, you can add multiple inline frames to your Web page quickly.

Add an Inline Frame in a Web Page

1. Open and display the Web page you want to use.

2. Click to place the insertion point where you want to insert an inline frame.

3. In the Toolbox task pane, click the plus sign (+) to expand Tags.

4. In the Toolbox task pane, double-click **Inline Frame**.

   An inline frame appears on your page.

5. Click **Set Initial Page**.

6. Browse and locate the page you want to embed in the selected frame, and then click the page to be imported. The URL for the page appears in the Address box.

7. Click **OK**.

   The selected page is now imported into the frame.

8. Click the outside edge of the frame to select it, and then drag a resize handle to the desired size.

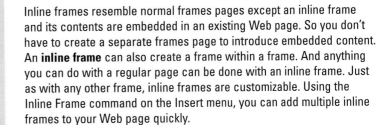

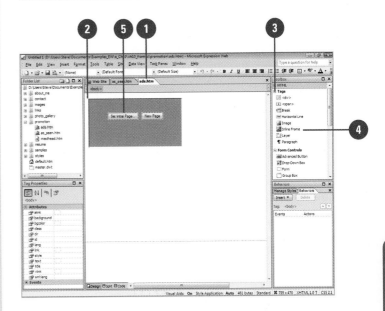

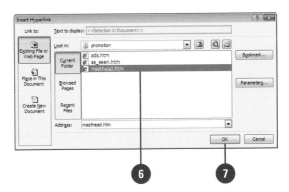

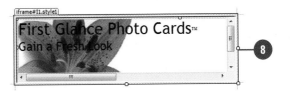

Adding Content to Frames

After you create a frames page using a template or insert an inline frame, you can add content to the frames. Each frame offers two option buttons: Set Initial Page or New Page. Using Set Initial Page, you can insert an existing page. Using New Page, you can create the contents of the frame from scratch.

Insert an Existing Page in a Frame

1. Open and display the frames page you want to add content.

2. Click **Set Initial Page**.

3. Select a file or Web page to insert in a frame.

4. Click **OK**.

   The selected page is now imported into the frame.

> ### Did You Know?
>
> **You can open a framed page in a new window.** Click in the frame, click the Format menu, point to Frames, and then click Open Page in New Window. The framed page appears in a new window all by itself.

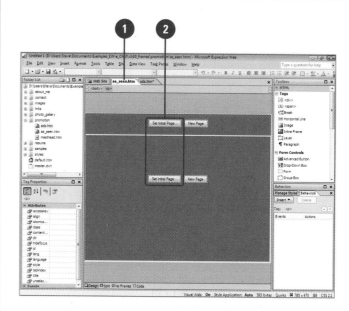

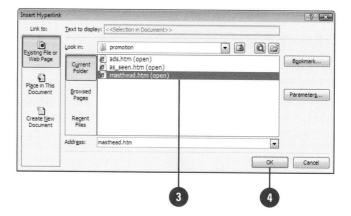

Insert a New Page in a Frame

1. Open and display the frames page you want to add content.

2. Click **New Page**.

3. Enter and format content on the page like any other Web page.

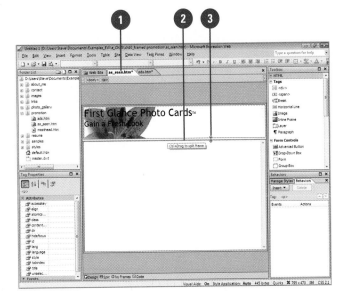

Resize a Frame

1. Open and display the frames page you want to modify.

2. Position the pointer over the frame border you want to resize.

3. Drag the frame border to a new location.

Changing Frame Properties

You can edit the properties of a normal or inline frame at any time. The Frame Properties dialog box allows you to change all aspects of working with a frame in one place. You can specify or change the frame name, the initial page, long description, title, frame size, margins, and other browser related options. These options allow you to customize the overall appearance of your frames page.

Change Frame Properties

1. Open and display the frames page you want to change.

2. Right-click the frame, and then click **Frame Properties**.

3. Change the frame properties you want.

   ◆ **Name.** The name that hyperlinks specify to load their contents in the frame.

   ◆ **Initial Page.** The page that is first displayed in a frame when a visitor browses the site.

   ◆ **Long Description.** The URL that contains more information about the current frame.

   ◆ **Title.** The description of the frame.

   ◆ **Frame Size.** The width and height of the frame in pixels, percentages, or units that create proportional spacing.

   ◆ **Margins.** The margins of the frame in pixels.

   ◆ **Resizeable In Browser.** Select to allow visitors to resize frames in a browser.

   ◆ **Show Scrollbars.** When the scrollbars appear on screen. Set to Never Appear, Always Appear, or Appear If Needed.

4. Click **OK**.

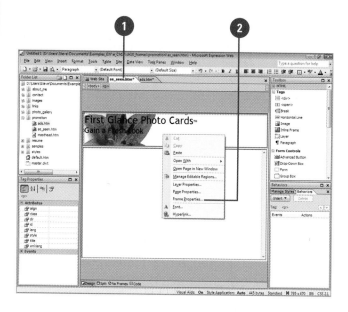

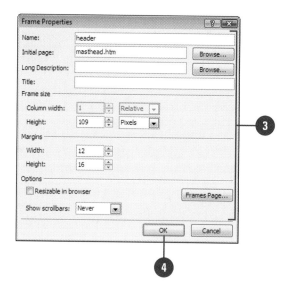

Change Inline Frame Properties

1. Open and display the frames page you want to change.

2. Right-click the frame, and then click **Inline Frame Properties**.

3. Change the inline frame properties you want.

   - **Name.** The name that hyperlinks specify to load their contents in the frame.

   - **Initial Page.** The page that is first displayed in a frame when a visitor browses the site.

   - **Title.** The description of the frame.

   - **Frame Size.** The width and height of the frame in pixels or percentages.

   - **Margins.** The margins of the frame in pixels.

   - **Alignment.** The position for the inline frame on the page (left, right, or center).

   - **Scrollbars.** When the scrollbars appear on screen. Set to Never Appear, Always Appear, or Appear If Needed.

   - **Alternate Text.** The text that you want the browser to display if the browser doesn't support frames.

4. Click **OK**.

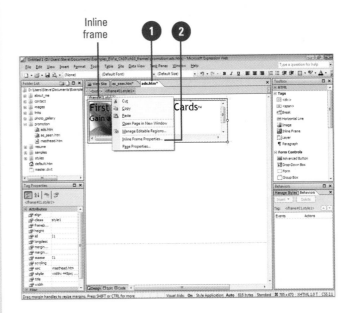

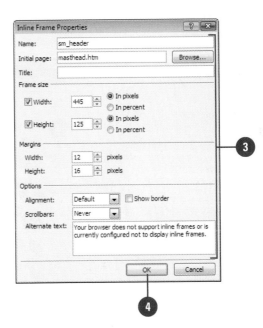

Saving Frames Pages

After you've prepared your frames page, you need to save it. Saving pages in a frames page involves a few more steps than simply a normal Web page. You need to save each page in a frame as well as the entire frames page itself. When you save a frames page, or the **frameset**, you're also saving instructions for the placement and sizing of individual frames on the page.

Save a Page in a Frame

1 Open and display the frames page you want to save.

2 Click the frame displaying the page you want to save.

3 Click the **Format** menu, point to **Frames,** and then click **Save Page As**.

4 Enter (or click) the file name for the page displayed in the thumbnail's selected frame.

5 To edit the page title, click **Change title**, type a title for the page, and then click **OK**.

6 Select the type of Web page you want saved.

7 Specify a location where you want the page saved.

8 Click **Save**.

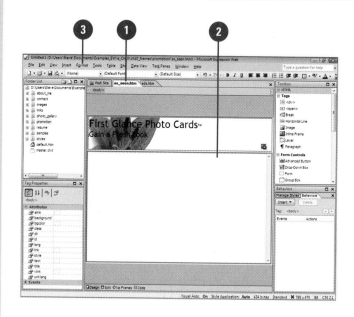

Did You Know?

The title is different from the file name. The title you see in the browser's title bar is the title of the frames page, not the title of the page displayed in that frame.

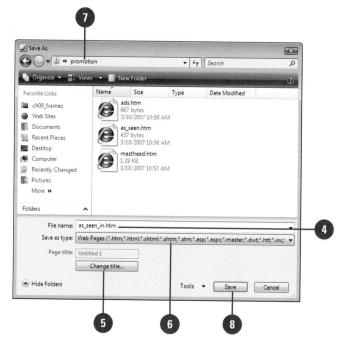

Save a Frameset

1. Open and display the frames page you want to save.

2. Click the **File** menu, and then click **Save As**.

   The Save As dialog box opens, complete with a thumbnail showing the layout of the page with the affected elements highlighted with a dark blue box.

3. Type a file name for the highlighted frames page.

4. To edit the page title, click **Change title**, type a title for the page, and then click **OK**.

5. Specify a location where you want to save the frameset.

6. Click **Save**.

   If any pages in a frame have not been saved, the Save As dialog box opens, asking you to save the page.

7. If necessary, click **Save** for each additional page in a frame.

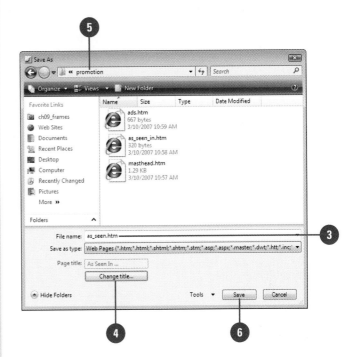

Did You Know?

You can reselect the frames page.
Press and hold Shift while you click any frame border.

Targeting a Frame

Sometimes you want a link in one frame to display content in another frame. This type of link is called a target frame. When you link a target page to a frame, you need to know the name of the frame you want to target, and the name of the Web page file you want to link to the frame.

Create or Edit the Target Frame

1 Open and display the frames page you want to use.

2 Select the normal (create) or hyperlinked (edit) text or graphic.

3 Click the **Insert Hyperlink** button on the Common toolbar.

4 Enter or verify the file name for the targeted frame.

5 Click the **Target Frame** button.

6 Select the option you want.

◆ In the Current frames page area (a map of your frames page), click the frame you want to designate as the target frame.

◆ In the Common targets box, click the target frame you want to designate as the target.

7 Click **OK**.

8 Click **OK**.

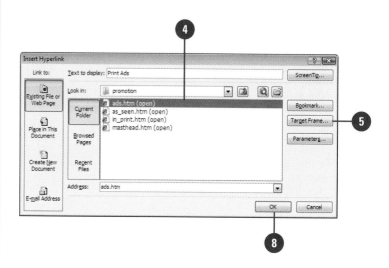

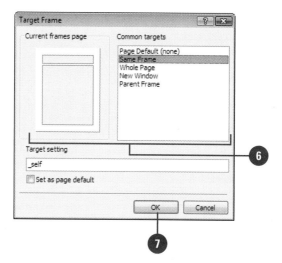

Editing Frames Pages

Editing the content of a frame is another key in developing a solid site. When working in Page view, select the frame you want to edit by clicking it. The frame might be too small for you to work in easily. If this is the case, you'll want to open it in a larger window. Frame margins set the distance between the frame content and the border.

Open a Frame in a Window for Editing

1 Open and display the frames page you want to change.

2 Right-click anywhere in the frame. A dark blue border appears around the frame you're editing and a shortcut menu opens.

3 Click **Open Page in New Window**.

The frame is now large enough to work in easily.

4 Click the **File** menu, and then click **Close** to return the page to its original size.

Did You Know?

You can show or hide scrollbars. Right-click in the frame, click Frame Properties, click the Show Scrollbars list arrow, click If Needed, Never, or Always, and then click OK.

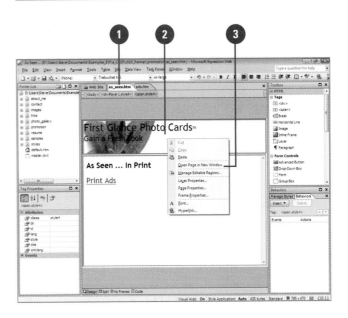

Splitting Frames

There are two ways to split a frame: by dragging its border, or by using the Split Frame command on the Frames menu. When you split a frame, Expression Web creates a new frame and the content in the original frame remains intact.

Split a Frame Quickly

1. Open and display the frames page you want to change.

2. Click the frame you want to split to select it.

3. Hold down Ctrl while you drag the frame border.

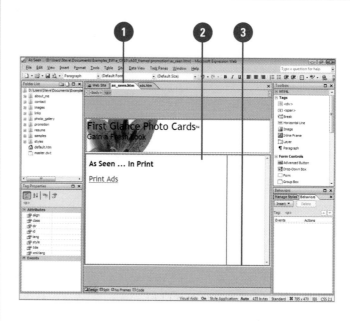

Split Frames in Columns or Rows

1. Open and display the frames page you want to change.

2. Click the frame you want to split to select it.

3. Click the **Format** menu, point to **Frames**, and then click **Split Frame**.

4. Click the **Split into columns** option to split the frame vertically, or click the **Split into rows** option to divide the frame horizontally.

5. Click **OK**.

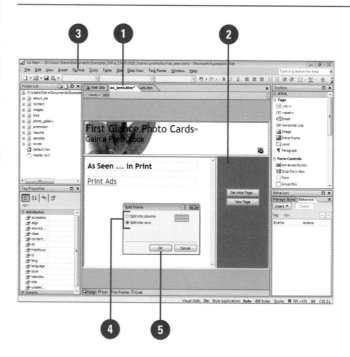

Deleting a Frame

When you no longer need a frame, you can delete it from a frames page. When the frame is deleted, the Web page in the frame is deleted, but the page is still available in your Web site folders. After you delete a frame, the remaining frames on the Web page expand to fill the space left by the frame you deleted. If the frames page contains only one frame, you cannot delete that frame.

Delete a Frame

1 Open and display the frames page you want to change.

2 Click the frame you want to remove.

3 Click the **Format** menu, point to **Frames**, and then click **Delete Frame**.

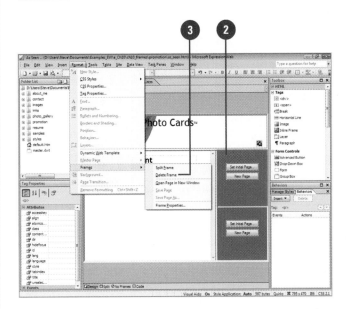

Show or Hide Border Frames

You can display or hide borders around frames. When you display a border, you can also set the spacing between borders to achieve the look you want. If you hide borders, you can still see them when you work on the page in Design view. The hidden frame borders appear as a thin gray line.

Display or Hide Borders Around Frames

1. Open and display the frames page you want to change.

2. Right-click anywhere on the frames page, and then click **Frame Properties**.

3. Click **Frames Page**.

4. If necessary, click the **Frames** tab.

5. Select or clear the **Show Borders** check box to display or hide border frames.

6. If you select the **Show Borders** check box, enter the amount of space, in pixels, you want between borders.

7. Click **OK**.

8. Click **OK**.

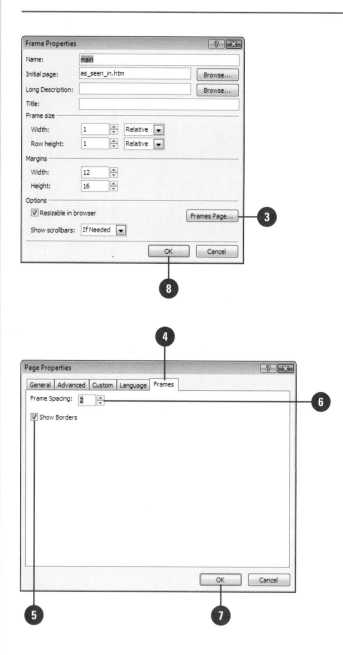

Gathering User Input Using Forms

Introduction

In this chapter, you're going to create Web page forms using Microsoft Expression Web. Forms that appear on Web pages are similar to paper forms. Web page forms share the same purpose (gathering information about your users) and use many of the same devices (check boxes, information fields, etc.) as paper forms. The most popular types of forms include:

- ◆ Request
- ◆ Registration
- ◆ Feedback
- ◆ Contact information
- ◆ Survey
- ◆ Guest book
- ◆ Order (shipping and billing information)
- ◆ Log On (prompts users to enter name and password)
- ◆ Search (enables users to search your site)

After some initial design and thought for your form page, you can get started by adding it to your Web site, and then you can design and display all the various information that you want to gather using text boxes, check boxes, option buttons, labels, list menus, and push buttons. You can also further customize your form by adding pictures, and setting certain rules for entering the data in certain fields.

Creating Forms

Expression Web offers numerous types of forms so that you can collect information from users to your site. You can start from scratch and create the form by adding information fields to a blank form, or you can use one of the wizard templates. When you first create a form, Expression Web inserts a rectangular box with a perforated line-dash perimeter. Inside this box, you can add everything from check boxes and text fields to list boxes and submit buttons. To help with the layout of the form, you can insert a table. If you no longer need a form or form field, you can select and then delete it.

Create a Form

1. Open and display the Web page you want to use.

2. Click to place the insertion point where you want to insert a form.

3. In the Toolbox task pane, click the plus sign (+) to expand Form Controls.

4. In the Toolbox task pane, double-click the **Form** button.

   A form appears on the page with a dashed outline around the border.

5. Insert a table or press Enter to add space between form elements, and then type any text you want.

6. To resize the form, click the edge of the form to select it, and then drag a resize handle to the desired size.

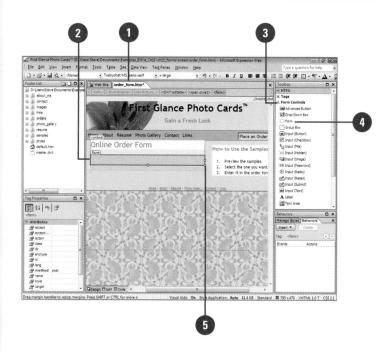

Did You Know?

Expression Web helps you out. When inserting a form field before you've created the form, Expression Web automatically creates a form area and places it within the form. While editing the page, the form border appears as a perforated line.

Insert a Table in a Form

1. Open and display the Web page with the form you want to insert.

2. Click in the form where you want to create a table.

3. Click the **Insert Table** button on the Standard toolbar.

4. Drag to choose how many rows and columns you want.

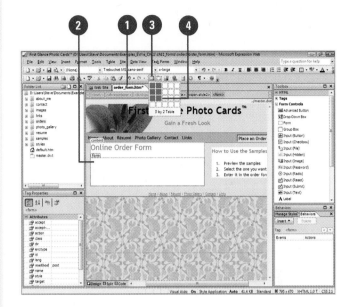

Delete a Form or Form Field

1. Open and display the Web page with the form you want to delete.

2. Click the form or the field you want to delete to select it.

3. Press Delete.

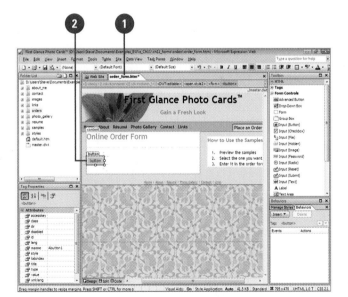

Setting Form Properties

After you create a form, you can set form properties to name the form, specify a target frame and save the form results to a file or database, or send the form results in an e-mail message. When a site visitor fills out a form and submits it, Expression Web enters the data directly into a database or file, or sends an e-mail message. The form name you specify identifies the form in scripts. If you are using frames, you can specify a target frame.

Set Form Properties

1. Open and display the Web page with the form you want to set properties.

2. Right-click the form, and then click **Form Properties**.

3. Type a name to identify the form.

4. If you are using frames, type the target frame, or click the **Browse** button, select a target, and then click **OK**.

5. Click **OK**.

See Also

See "Saving Form Results to a File" on page 274, "Sending Form Results as E-mail" on page 276, "Saving Form Results to a Database" on page 280, or "Saving Form Results to a Custom Form Handler" on page 278 for information on saving form results to different locations.

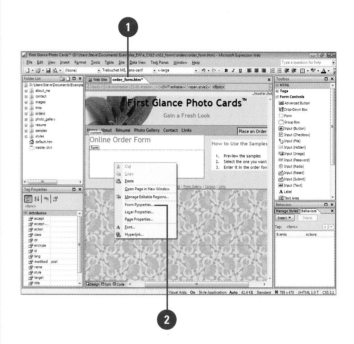

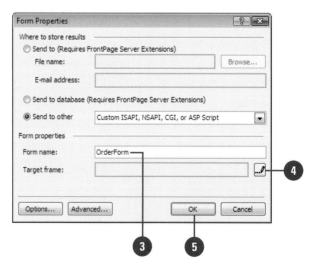

Understanding Form Fields

One of the keys to creating a form is the creation of fields. There are many different types of fields, including text boxes, text areas, option buttons, list menus, and push buttons. In addition to these fields, there are also Advanced Buttons, which you can customize through font and color selection, and Group Boxes, which you can use to segregate clusters of related controls into one group. Password fields are basically one-line text boxes used to add passwords to your site so that you can restrict access (to charge for membership, for example). When a site user enters their password, it appears on screen as a collection of dots or asterisks to secure confidentiality.

After you've decided what types of fields to add to the form, you can define what you want them to do and how you want them to look. You can even set properties for each field, such as the length of a text field, or the available options on a list menu. You can insert form fields using the Form submenu on the Insert menu. If an item on the Form submenu is grayed out, the command is not available. You need a Web server equipped with FrontPage Server Extensions to activate the commands. After you create a form, you have to determine how to collect and display the user data.

Form Field Element Types

Field Element Type	Description
Advanced Button	A button that executes an action, yet also embeds HTML content
Drop-Down Box	Select an item from a list of several choices
Form	Create a form to place form field elements
Group Box	A titled border that surrounds a group of related elements
Input (Button)	A button that executes an action using JavaScript
Input (Check Box)	Select between two values, such as yes/no or true/false
Input (File)	Browse and upload a file provided by the user
Input (Hidden)	A text box that is invisible to users, yet available for data or execute an action
Input (Image)	A picture as a button
Input (Password)	A text field that inputs a password with dots instead of characters
Input (Radio)	Select one value from a list of values
Input (Reset)	A button that clears form fields
Input (Submit)	A button that submits form field data
Input (Text)	Enter short, one line text, such as a name
Label	A text label that associates with a form control
Text Area	Enter multiple line text, such as a comment

Setting Form Tab Order

When you fill out a form, many times it is easier for users to move from field to field using the Tab key instead of clicking the mouse each time. Many form elements have a Tab Order field. Tab order determines which fields in a form receive the focus (active where you can enter data) when the user presses the Tab key. A form field with lower tab values receives the focus before any fields with higher values.

Set Tab Order

1. Open and display the Web page you want to use.

2. Double-click the form field in which you want to change the tab order field value.

3. Type the tab order value you want (lower numbers appear before higher numbers).

4. Click **OK**.

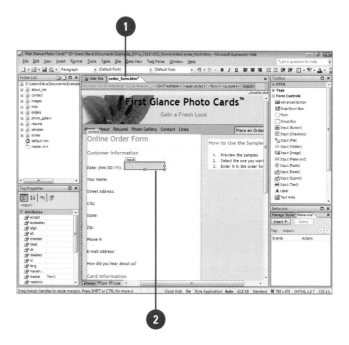

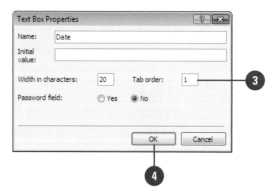

Inserting Labels

After you type a label next to a check box or option button, you can specify whether Web site users select the check box or option button by clicking the box or button, or its label. If you want your users to click the label, you need to active the label.

Insert a Label

1. Open and display the Web page you want to use.

2. Click in the form where you want to place the label.

3. In the Toolbox task pane, click the plus sign (+) to expand Form Controls.

4. In the Toolbox task pane, double-click the **Label** button.

   The text label appears surrounded by a perforated border, which indicates the label is active.

5. Type the text you want in the label.

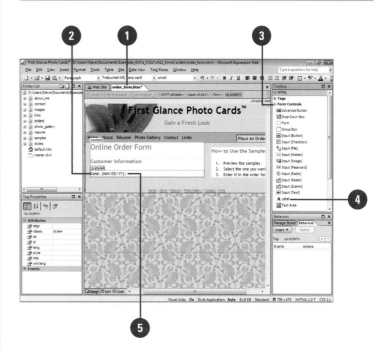

Inserting Text Boxes

You can insert two types of text boxes in a form, Text Box and Text Area. Text boxes ask for information and provide a field where a user can type an answer. Text boxes are used for collecting relatively small quantities of information, such as the user's online name. Text areas are small text windows best suited for brief text entries. This window scrolls vertically and horizontally to maximize its available space. They are ideal for use as guest books.

Insert a Text Box or Text Area

① Open and display the Web page you want to use.

② Click in the form where you want to place the text box or text area.

③ In the Toolbox task pane, click the plus sign (+) to expand Form Controls.

④ In the Toolbox task pane, double-click the **Input (Text)** button, **Input (Password)** button, or **Input (Text Area)** button.

◆ The Input (Text) and Input (Password) buttons both create a text box. The only difference is an option in the Text Properties dialog box.

A text box or text area appears in the form with an insertion point next to it. You can click to place the insertion point before or after the text box.

⑤ To resize a form field, click to select it, and then drag the sizing handles to the desired size.

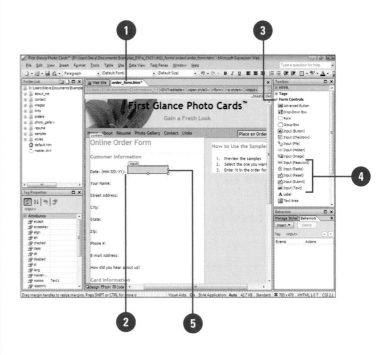

Change Text Properties

① Open and display the Web page you want to use.

② Double-click the text box or text area.

◆ You can also right-click the text box or text area, and then click **Form Field Properties**.

The Text Box or Text Area Properties dialog box opens.

③ Enter a name that will identify the text box.

④ Enter the text to be displayed in the text box when a site user first opens the form. As you type, the characters will be counted in the Width in characters box.

⑤ Specify the field specific options for text boxes or text areas.

◆ For text boxes, click the **Yes** option to create a password to your Web site so that you can restrict access. When a Web site user enters their password, it appears as asterisks for confidentiality.

◆ For text areas, type the number of lines in which you want the area.

⑥ Click **OK**.

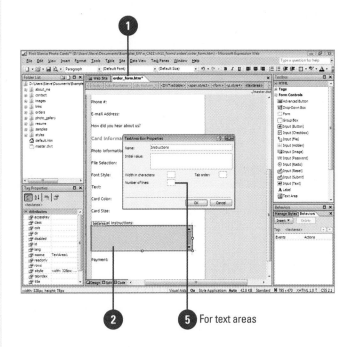

⑤ For text areas

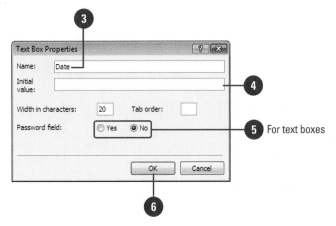

⑤ For text boxes

Inserting Drop-Down Boxes

The drop-down box allows users to choose one option from a scrollable list of choices. For example, you can create a list of all 50 states from which the user can choose one. The advantage of using a drop-down box is that the users are forced to select an option from the list, which prevents data input errors.

Insert a Drop-Down Box

1. Open and display the Web page you want to use.

2. Click in the form where you want to place the drop-down box.

3. In the Toolbox task pane, click the plus sign (+) to expand Form Controls.

4. In the Toolbox task pane, double-click the **Input (Drop-Down Box)** button.

5. Double-click the drop-down box.

6. Type a name for the drop-down box.

7. Click **Add**.

8. Type the name of the list item you want to list.

9. To have the item selected initially, click the **Selected** option.

10. Click **OK**.

11. Perform Steps 7 through 10 for each item you want to include in the list.

12. Enter a height for the drop-down box.

13. Click the **Yes** or **No** option to allow multiple selections.

14. Click **OK**.

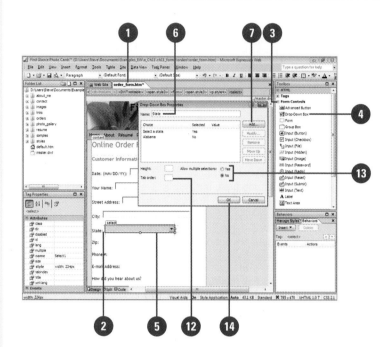

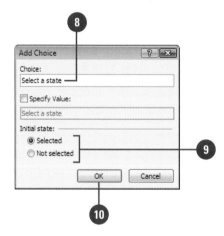

Inserting Group Boxes

A Group box allows you to group related form elements into a separate area on the form, which provides some organization for the form elements and avoids confusion for the user. The Group box is useful for check boxes and option buttons. A Group box is a separate container on the form, so you can easily move it along with its contents.

Insert a Group Box

1. Open and display the Web page you want to use.

2. Click in the form where you want to place the Group box.

3. In the Toolbox task pane, click the plus sign (+) to expand Form Controls.

4. In the Toolbox task pane, double-click the **Group Box** button.

5. To resize the Group box field, click the edge of the field to select it, and then drag a resize handle to the desired size.

6. Right-click the Group box field, and then click **Group Box Properties**.

7. Type the label you want to appear at the top of the Group box.

8. Click the **Align** list arrow, and then select an alignment option.

9. Click **OK**.

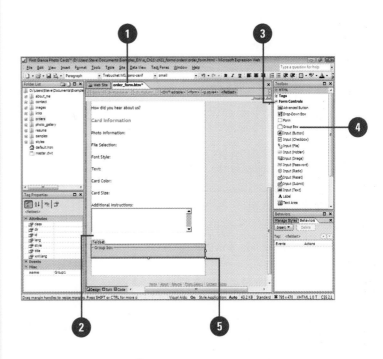

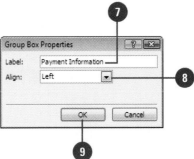

Insert Radio Buttons

Radio buttons (also known as Option buttons) are used when asking a user a question with more than one possible answer. Only one option button in a group can be selected at a time. Expression Web groups option buttons within a form with the same name. Typically assigning the same name to fields creates errors, but not with the option button. You need to assign option buttons in the same group with the same name to function properly.

Insert a Radio Button

1. Open and display the Web page you want to use.

2. Click in the form where you want to place the option button.

3. In the Toolbox task pane, click the plus sign (+) to expand Form Controls.

4. In the Toolbox task pane, double-click the **Input (Radio)** button.

5. Click next to the option, and then type a label.

6. Double-click an option button within the group.

7. Type a group name (the same one for each option button in the group).

8. Enter a value to associate with the option.

    This value is returned with the form results and is displayed on the default confirmation page.

9. Click the **Selected** option or the **Not selected** option to set up the default state when a user opens the form.

10. Click **OK**.

11. Repeat steps 6 through 10 for each option button in the group.

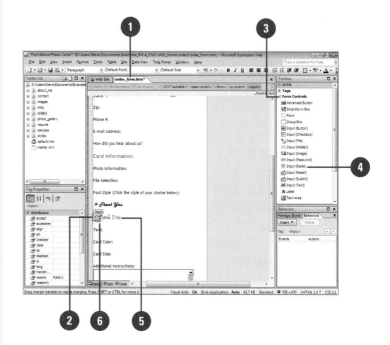

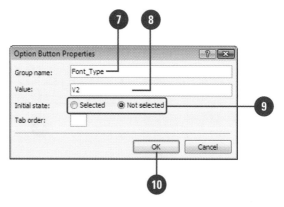

Inserting Check Boxes

Check boxes are provided to allow users multiple choices from a list or series of options. Check boxes are just what they sound like—a statement which you can either confirm, by checking the box, or decline by leaving the box blank.

Insert a Check Box

1. Open and display the Web page you want to use.

2. Click in the form where you want to place the check box.

3. In the Toolbox task pane, click the plus sign (+) to expand Form Controls.

4. In the Toolbox task pane, double-click the **Input (Checkbox)** button.

5. Click next to the check box, and then type a label.

6. Double-click the check box you want to change.

7. Enter a name that identifies the check box in the form results.

   The name is not displayed on the form.

8. Enter a value to associate with the check box.

   This value is returned with the form results and is displayed on the default confirmation page.

9. Click the **Checked** option or the **Not checked** option to set up the default state when a user opens the form.

10. Click **OK**.

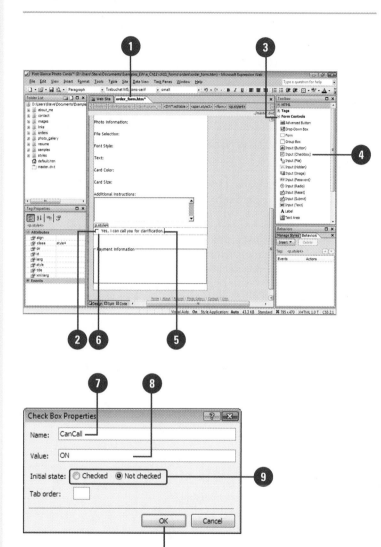

Inserting Buttons

Push buttons are functional components that are used when the user needs to do something. When you insert a form field, two buttons appear, Submit and Reset. The Submit button is a command that a user has to click to submit the form when completed, while the Reset button is a command that a user has to click to reset the form and start over. You can create a push button to perform an action.

Insert a Push Button

1. Open and display the Web page you want to use.

2. Position the insertion point in the form where you want to place the push button.

3. In the Toolbox task pane, click the plus sign (+) to expand Form Controls.

4. In the Toolbox task pane, double-click the **Input (Button)**, **Input (Submit)**, or **Input (Reset)** button.

   A push button appears in the form.

5. Double-click the button.

6. Enter a name that identifies the push button in the form results.

   The name is not displayed on the form.

7. Type the label that appears on the button.

8. Click the button type you want (**Normal** is the standard button, **Submit** is a button that submits the completed form, or **Reset** is a button that clears the form so the user can start over).

9. Click **OK**.

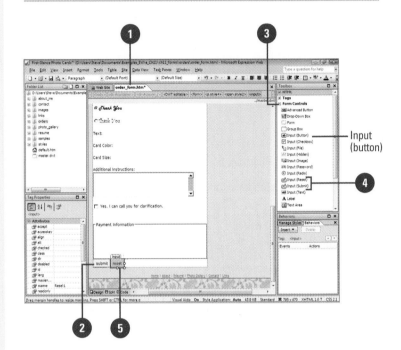

Input (button)

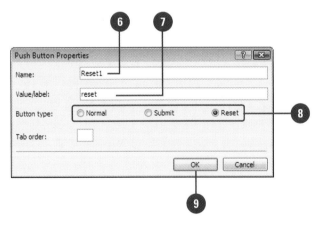

Insert an Advanced Button

1. Open and display the Web page you want to use.

2. Position the insertion point in the form where you want to place the advanced button.

3. In the Toolbox task pane, click the plus sign (+) to expand Form Controls.

4. In the Toolbox task pane, double-click the **Advanced Button** button.

   An Advanced button appears in the form with selected default button text.

5. Select the button text, and then type a name for the button.

6. Right-click the advanced button, and then click **Advanced Button Properties**.

7. Click the **Button Type** list arrow, and then select a button type.

8. Type a name to identify the button.

9. Click **OK**.

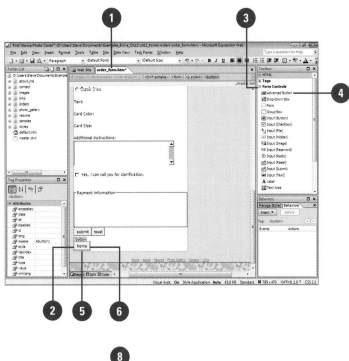

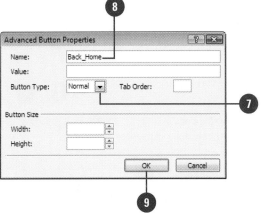

Creating Picture Buttons

You can insert a picture in a form, which you can use as a button. If you want, you can use a picture button, like a push button, to perform an operation. You can insert a picture in a form in a similar way you insert a picture in a Web page.

Insert a Picture Button

① Open and display the Web page you want to use.

② Position the insertion point in the form where you want to place the picture.

③ In the Toolbox task pane, click the plus sign (+) to expand Form Controls.

④ In the Toolbox task pane, double-click the **Input (Image)** button.

⑤ Resize the pictures field, and then double-click the picture field you want to insert a picture.

The Picture Properties dialog box opens, displaying the Form Field tab.

⑥ Type a name to identify the picture.

⑦ Click the **General** tab.

⑧ Click **Browse**, locate and select the picture you want to use, and then click **Open**.

⑨ Select the **Alternate Text** check box, and then enter descriptive text to display accessibility information.

⑩ Click the **Appearance** tab.

⑪ Select the wrapping style, layout, and size options you want.

⑫ Click **OK**.

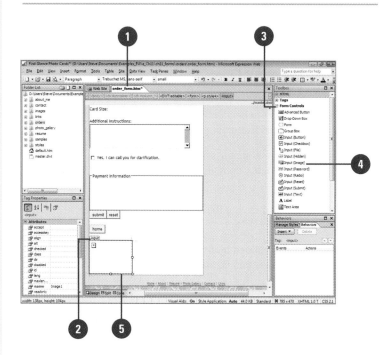

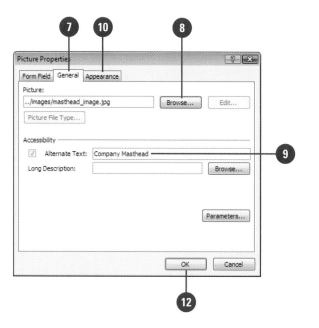

Inserting File Uploads

If you need to receive files from co-workers or users to your Web site, you can add a File Upload field to your form. When you add the File Upload field to a form, a text box and push button entitled Browse appear on the page. Users can use the text box to enter a path and file name or the Browse button to select a file to upload to your Web site. The file is transferred when you submit the form. If there is a problem, users can reset the form, and then try again.

Insert a File Upload Field

1. Open and display the Web page you want to use.

2. Click in the form where you want to place the file upload field.

3. In the Toolbox task pane, click the plus sign (+) to expand Form Controls.

4. In the Toolbox task pane, double-click the **Input (File)** button.

5. Double-click the file upload field.

6. Type an internal name for the field.

7. Specify the width of the field.

8. Click **OK**.

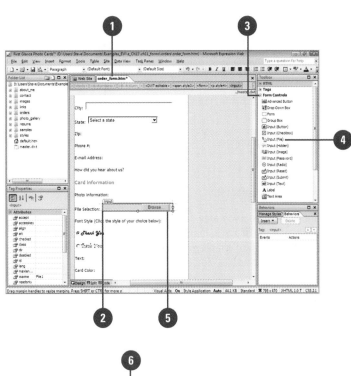

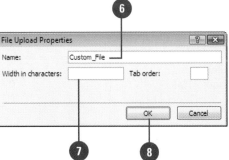

Saving Form Results to a File

Once you create a form and collect information from users on the Web, you can save the form results to a text or HTML file. When a site user fills out a form and submits it, Expression Web enters the data directly into a file. The File Results tab provides options for saving results to a file. If you want to save results to two different file formats, you have the option of selecting a second file. By default, form results are saved to a text file. In order to save results to a file Expression Web requires FrontPage Server Extensions (FPSE), both on the Web server you use to develop the site and the one users use.

Save Form Results to a File

1. Open and display the Web page you want to use.

2. Right-click the form, and then click **Form Properties**.

3. Click the **Send to** option.

4. Click **Options**.

5. Click the **File Results** tab.

6. Enter the location and name of a new file, or click **Browse**, locate and select the file to which you want to save the results, and then click **Open**.

7. Click the **File format** list arrow, and then select a file format.

   - **XML**. Select to export as XML data.

   - **HTML**. Select to create a definition list or bulleted list.

   - **Formatted Text**. Select to create with or without HTML.

   - **Text database**. Select a separator type, which you can import into a database.

8. To pair the values of each form field with it's name, select the **Include field names** check box.

9. Click **OK**.

10. Click **OK**.

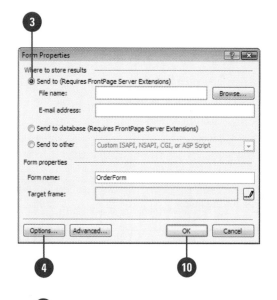

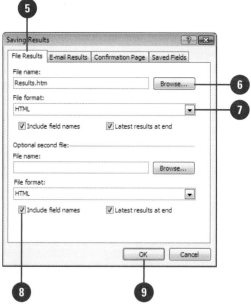

Using a Custom Confirmation Page

A confirmation page provides information to your users submit a form. When a user submits data in a form, Expression Web displays a default confirmation page. If you prefer to use a confirmation page of your own (which needs to be a static page), you can specify one on the Confirmation tab in the Options dialog box for some form handlers. You can specify two different confirmation pages: one for when a user successfully submits a form and another for when a user's input fails a validation script. Confirmation pages are optional. However, they provide good feedback for users and provide a way to thank them for submitting information.

Use a Custom Confirmation Page

① Open and display the Web page you want to use.

② Right-click the form, and then click **Form Properties**.

③ Click the **Send to** option.

④ Click **Options**.

⑤ Click the **Confirmation Page** tab.

⑥ Enter the URL of the confirmation page, or click **Browse**, locate and select the page, and then click **Open**.

⑦ Enter the URL of the validation failure page, or click **Browse**, locate and select the page, and then click **Open**.

⑧ Click **OK**.

⑨ Click **OK**.

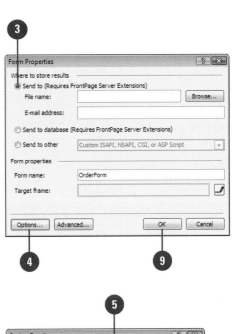

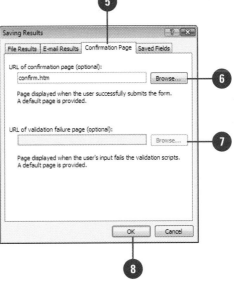

Sending Form Results as E-Mail

Once you create a form and collect information from users on the Web, you can send the form results in an e-mail message. As you send the results in an e-mail, you can also save the results to a file at the same time, so you have two records of the form results. To help automate part of the process, you can set e-mail settings and insert form field information in the e-mail message. In order to send results in an e-mail message Expression Web requires FrontPage Server Extensions (FPSE), both on the Web server you use to develop the site and the one users use.

Send Form Results as E-Mail

① Open and display the Web page you want to use.

② Right-click the form, and then click **Form Properties**.

③ Click the **Send to** option.

④ Type the e-mail address to which you are sending the form results.

⑤ If you want, specify a file to save the results in a file as well as being sent via e-mail.

⑥ Click **Options**.

The Saving Results dialog box opens, displaying the File Results tab.

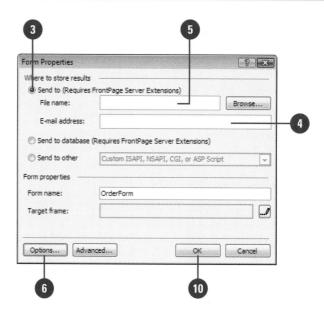

7 Click the **E-Mail Results** tab.

8 Perform one or more of the following steps:

◆ In the E-Mail format box, select the text format you want from the list menu.

◆ In the Subject line box, type the text that you want in the subject line of the e-mail (the default subject line in the e-mail is Form Results).

◆ If you want the subject line of the e-mail to contain the results of one field from the form, select the **Form Field Name** check box, and then type the name of the field in the Subject line box.

◆ In the Reply-to line box, a specific e-mail address can appear as the sender of the e-mail (the From or Reply To line in the e-mail). Enter the address.

◆ If the form contains a field that collects the site user's e-mail address, that address can be used as the sender's address. Select the **Form Field Name** check box, and then type the name of the form field in the Reply-to line box.

9 Click **OK**.

10 Click **OK** to close the Form Properties dialog box.

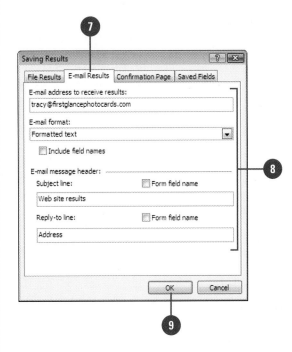

Saving Form Results to a Custom Form Handler

You can also set up a form to save results using a custom form handler. A form handler is a program on a server that is executed when a site user submits a form. You can use your custom script (ISAPI, NSAPI, CGI, or ASP Script) as a form handler. These custom scripts require scripting knowledge, which is beyond the scope of this book. In addition to the custom scripts, Expression Web also provides custom form handlers to work with a registration or discussion page. These form handlers require FrontPage Server Extensions (FPSE), both on the Web server you use to develop the site and the one users use.

Create a Custom Form Handler

1. Open and display the Web page you want to use.

2. Right-click the form, and then click **Form Properties**.

3. Click the **Send to other** option, click the list arrow, and then click **Custom ISAPI, NSAPI, CGI, or ASP Script**.

4. Click **Options**.

5. Type the URL where you stored your script.

6. Click the **Method** list arrow, and then select one of the following formats for submitting data to the form handler:

   ◆ **Post.** Passes the name-value pair to the form handler as input.

   ◆ **Get.** Encodes the form's name-value pair and assigns the data to a server variable named Query_String.

   ◆ **Default.** Leaves the Encoding type text box empty.

7. Click **OK**.

8. Click **OK**.

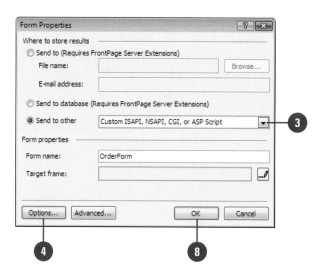

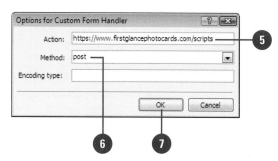

Create a Discussion Form Handler

1. Open and display the Web page you want to use.

2. Right-click the form, and then click **Form Properties**.

3. Click the **Send to other** option, click the list arrow, and then click **Discussion Form Handler**.

4. Click **Options**.

5. Fill in the information you want in the Discussion, Article, and Confirmation Page tabs.

6. Click **OK**.

7. Click **OK**.

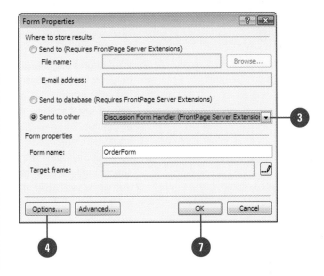

Create a Registration Form Handler

1. Open and display the Web page you want to use.

2. Right-click the form, and then click **Form Properties**.

3. Click the **Send to other** option, click the list arrow, and then click **Registration Form Handler**.

4. Click **Options**.

5. Fill in the information you want in the Registration, File Results, Confirmation Page, and Saved Results tabs.

6. Click **OK**.

7. Click **OK**.

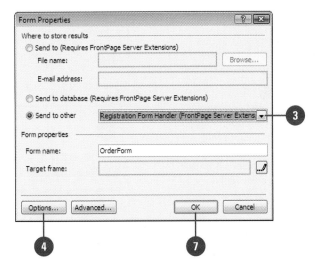

Saving Form Results to a Database

Once you create a form and collect information from users on the Web, you can also save the form results to a database. You can save the results to an ODBC-compliant database, which includes Microsoft Access. When a site user fills out a form and submits it, Expression Web enters the data directly into a database. You can save the information in a form to a database by using a database connection. A database connection is a connection that specifies the name, location, and type of database you want to access. You can create a new database or connect to an existing one. The Web site enables you to view, update, delete, or add records. To view the data once you set up the connection, your Web site must be hosted or published on a Web server configured with FrontPage Server Extensions (FPSE) and Active Server Pages (ASP), if necessary. For example, a confirmation page must be an ASP page, other page types will not work with databases.

Save Form Results to a Database

1. Open and display the Web page you want to use.

2. Right-click the form you want to save the results from, and then click **Form Properties**.

3. Click the **Send to database** option.

4. Click **Options**.

5. Click the **Database Connection to Use** list arrow, and then select an existing database connection.

   ◆ If you don't have a connection, click **Add Connection** to create a new one, or click **Create Database** to have the FrontPage Extensions create a Microsoft Access 2002 database along with a connection for you.

   IMPORTANT *If you convert the Access 2002 database to an Access 2007 database, it will not work with your forms.*

6. Click the **Table to hold form results** list arrow, and then select the table where you want to place the form results data from.

   Continue Next Page

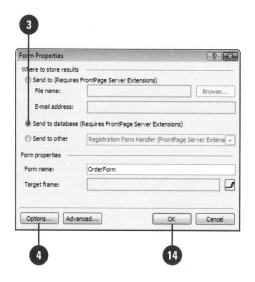

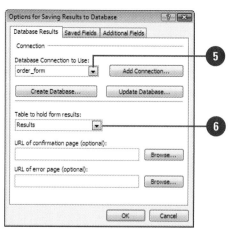

⑦ Click the **Saved Fields** tab.

The fields in the form are listed. For each field, you must specify the database column in which you want to save the data.

◆ If FrontPage Extension created the database, the form fields are mapped to the appropriate fields in the database.

⑧ Click the form field you want to modify.

⑨ Click **Modify**.

⑩ Click the **Save To Database Column** list arrow, select the column where you want to save the form field data, and then click **OK**.

⑪ Repeat steps 8 through 10 for each form field, and then click **OK**.

⑫ To view and modify additional fields provided by Expression Web, click the **Additional Fields** tab, and then change the fields you want.

⑬ Click **OK**.

⑭ Click **OK**.

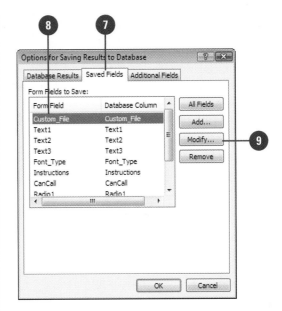

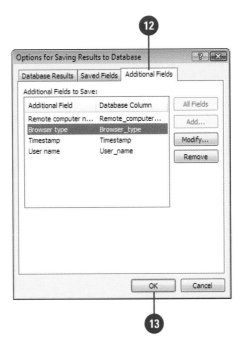

Did You Know?

You can update a database with new fields. If you add new fields to a form after you created the database, you need to update the database with the new fields. Add the new fields to the form, right-click the form, click Form Properties, click Options, and then click Update Database.

Using Other Form Handlers

If you design a great looking form and then upload it to your Web server, you'll find that when you fill out the form and click the submit button...nothing at all happens!

In order to get a form working, it is not enough to just design the form itself in HTML. You also have to create a form handler. A **form handler** is a program that runs on the Web server. The form handler takes the information entered in the HTML form by the user and does something with it. For example, you can use form handlers to send information as an e-mail or to a database. If you have FrontPage Server Extensions (FPSE) installed on your Web server, you can take advantage of Expression Web's built-in form handlers. See pages 274-281 for topics related to form handlers using FPSE. If you don't have FPSE or want to use them, you can find a form handlers on the Web.

When you add a form to a Web page, Expression Web inserts <form> tags. The <form> tag tells the browser where the form starts and ends. You can add all kinds of HTML tags between the <form> and </form> tags. When you submit a form, you need a program that can receive the information and do something with it. When you add a form to a Web page, Expression Web also adds the following properties to the <form> tag:

- **action**=address

- **method**=post or method=get

The address is the URL of a form handler, such as a CGI (Common Gateway Interface) script, where the form content is sent and processed. POST and GET are two different methods for submitting data to the script. If you use the GET method, the input values are passed as part of the URL. If you use the

Form tags in Code view   Form in Design view

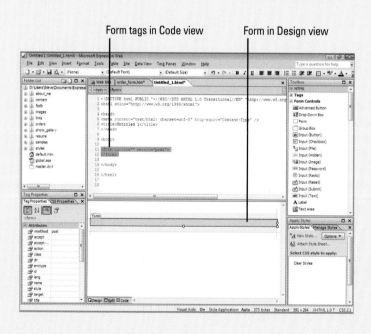

POST method, the information is sent to the server as part of the data body and will not be visible in the URL box in the user's browser. Expression Web uses POST as the default method. Here's an example of <form> tags in an HTML page:

```
<html>
  <body>
  <form action="http://www.mydomain.com/
  myformhandler.cgi"
  method="post"
  name="myform">
  <!-- Here goes form fields and HTML -->
  </form>
  </body>
</html>
```

Expression Web doesn't include a form handler. The action property is left blank. However, there are many form handlers available for free or a small fee on the Web. Simply perform a Web search for "form handlers" or "CGI scripts" to find the form handler you need for the task you want to get accomplished.

As you add form fields—such as a text box, check box, radio button, drop-down menu or submit and reset buttons—to a form, Expression Web adds the HTML code between the <form> tags.

Form tags: action and method   Selected form field tag

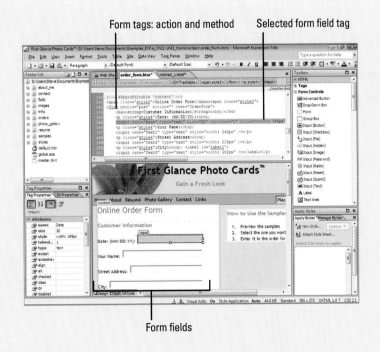

Form fields

Creating Styles and Layouts with CSS

Introduction

Cascading Style Sheets are becoming the predominant method of formatting a Web site. A Cascading Style Sheet (CSS) is style information that can be referenced by individual or multiple Web pages. The cascading part of cascading style sheets indicates different style levels and the control each one has over the other. CSS let you separate the content of a Web page from its layout and design. A CSS Web page is an HTML file with links to a CSS file. You can create the two files separately, or you can use CSS Layouts in Expression Web to create and link them.

Expression Web provides several task panes and toolbars to help you create and manage CSS. The CSS tools include four tasks panes: Manage Styles, Apply Styles, CSS Properties, and Tag Properties, and two toolbars: Style Application and Style. Expression Web also provides two different Quick Tag tools for working with tags: Quick Tag Selector and Quick Tag Editor. The Quick Tag Selector makes it easy to identify and select page elements, including CSS classes and IDs. The Quick Tag Editor allows you to modify an HTML tag using color coding and IntelliSense support. IntelliSense displays a context-sensitive dropdown list of code choices you can quickly select and insert in Code or Split view.

If you're having CSS problems, you can use CSS Reports to help identify them. CSS Reports helps you check individual pages or an entire Web site for errors relating to unused styles, undefined classes, mismatched case.

Working with HTML Code

HTML Code

Code view and Split view (upper pane) allow you to view and edit the HTML (HyperText Markup Language) code generated by Expression Web or write your own. The code in these views is indented and color-coded to make it easier to read and follow.

Write Valid Code

When you make code changes, Expression Web checks the code to make sure it's valid. If the code is invalid, Expression Web adds a wavy red underline to it. If your code has structure problems, Expression Web highlights the code in yellow. To help you enter valid code, Expression Web uses **IntelliSense**, which provides a pop-up menu with commands. As you type code, IntelliSense recognizes what you're doing and provides a pop-up menu with valid commands. You can select the command and press Enter or double-click it to insert it.

Use Code Snippets

Instead of retyping the same code on multiple pages, you can reuse a code segment, known as a **code snippet**. To insert a code snippet in Code or Split view, click to place the insertion point, press Ctrl+Enter, and then select the code snippet you want from the pop-up menu. You can add, delete, or modify code snippets as well as change code formatting and color coding in the Page Editor Options dialog box. To open the dialog box, click the Tools menu, and then click Page Editor Options.

In addition to these tools, you can also right-click a HTML tag to access many helpful tools and commands, including Find Matching Tab, Select Block (of code), and Find Matching Brace.

HTML Tags

An HTML tag is code inserted in a document that specifies how the document, or a portion of the document, should be formatted. HTML defines the structure and layout of a Web document by using a variety of tags and attributes.

Tag Properties

The Tag Properties task pane allows you to examine the attributes related to HTML tags. When you select an HTML element in Design or Code view, the properties associated with the selected tag appear in the Tag Properties task pane. The Tag Properties task pane shows you properties grouped into three categories: attributes, events, and misc (short for miscellaneous).

An **attribute** defines the behavior of a tag. You can have more than one attribute for a tag. In the following example, the hyperlink is defined using the <a> tag and the attribute dis defined using the href:

<a href="http//www.perspection.com">Perspection Web Site</a>

An **event** is an attribute that is triggered by an event and **misc** is any non standards-compliant attribute.

Quick Tag Tools

Expression Web provides two different Quick Tag tools: Quick Tag Selector and Quick Tag Editor. The Quick Tag Selector makes it easy to identify and select page elements, including CSS classes and IDs. The Quick Tag Editor allows you to modify an HTML tag using color coding and IntelliSense support.

Understanding CSS Styles and Layouts

Cascading Style Sheets

Cascading Style Sheets (CSS) are becoming the predominant method of formatting a Web site. CSS let you separate the content of a Web page from its layout and design. The separation allows you to display Web content on individual or multiple Web pages with different size computer monitors and other devices, such as PDAs and cell phones.

A CSS contains style definitions, called **Selectors**, which are the HTML components linked to a specialized list of style properties and values. A selector is followed by those properties and values. For example, h1 {font-size: x-large; color: green}, h2 {font-size: large; color: blue). h1 and h2 are selectors that modify the formatting properties of standard HTML tags.

There are three types of Cascading Style Sheets in Expression Web: **external** (for multiple pages in the same file), **internal** or **embedded** (for individual Web pages), and **inline** (for individual elements), which you create when you apply a style directly to an item using the Apply Styles task pane. An external CSS file uses a .css file extension. The cascading part of cascading style sheets indicates different style levels and the control each one has over the other. The cascading control starts at the lowest level and works its way up: inline, internal, and external. If an inline style is applied to an element, it takes control. If no inline style is applied, then an internal style sheet takes control. If no inline or internal style is applied, then an external style sheet takes control. An inline style is applied to individual elements using tags, such as <p> and </p>. An internal style sheet is applied to an entire page. The coding appears at the top of the page between <head> and </head>. An external sheet links to a file where all the code styles are located. Since the styles are external, you can apply them to multiple files.

CSS allows you to create three different styles: tag-based, class-based, and ID-based. **Tag-based** styles apply to a specific HTML element, such as paragraph <p> or any of the headings <h1> through <h6>. **Class-based** styles are not associated with an HTML element, which means you can apply them multiple times to the same page. **ID-based** styles are similar to Class-based styles, except they are only to be applied once per Web page.

CSS Layouts

CSS Layouts depend on two things working together: div tags (short for page divisions) and ID-based styles. ID-based styles, unlike the element- or class-based styles, can only be used once per Web page, which makes them good for styling navigation bars, banners, layout columns, and footers.

CSS Tools

Expression Web provides several task panes and toolbars to help you create and manage CSS. The CSS tools include four tasks panes: Manage Styles, Apply Styles, CSS Properties, and Tag Properties, and two toolbars: Style Application and Style. The Manage Styles task pane allows you to create and organize styles, while the Apply Styles task pane makes it easy to preview and apply styles. The CSS Properties task pane provides several ways to sort through your CSS properties, which includes CSS tags, cascading styles, and CSS rules. The Tag Properties task pane displays HTML tag properties for a selected HTML element in Design or Code view and allows you set individual tag attributes. If you prefer using toolbars, you can use the Style Application toolbar to build your CSS manually, or the Style toolbar to apply classes and IDs.

Inserting Common HTML Tags

You can insert commonly used HTML tags into a page by using the HTML submenu on the Insert menu or dragging a control from the Toolbox. The common HTML tags include <div>, <span>, Break, Horizontal Line, Image, Inline Frame, Layer, and Paragraph. When you insert the Break tag from the Toolbox, a single break line is inserted into the page. However, when you insert the Break tag from the Insert menu, the Break dialog box appears, asking you to select an option to insert a normal line or clear the left, right, or both margins.

Insert Common HTML Tags from the Toolbox Task Pane

1. Open and display the Web page you want to use.

2. Expand the **Tags** category in the Toolbox task pane.

3. Click to place the cursor in Design view where you want to place the HTML tag.

4. Drag the HTML tag to your Web page in Code or Design view where you want to insert it.

   - **<div>.** Defines a section of a page. Tag: <div>

   - **<span>.** Defines a portion of a page. Tag: <span>

   - **Break.** Inserts a line break to create white space. Tag:

   - **Horizontal Line.** Inserts a horizontal line. Tag: <hr>

   - **Image.** Inserts an image placeholder. Tag: <img scr= "" />

   - **Inline Frame.** Inserts an inline frame. Tag: <iframe id="I1" name="I1">

   - **Layer.** Inserts a placeholder object that is absolutely positioned. Tag: <div id="layer" style="position: absolute">

   - **Paragraph.** Inserts a paragraph on a page. Tag: <p>

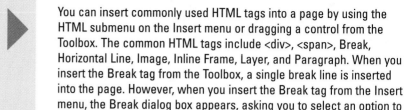

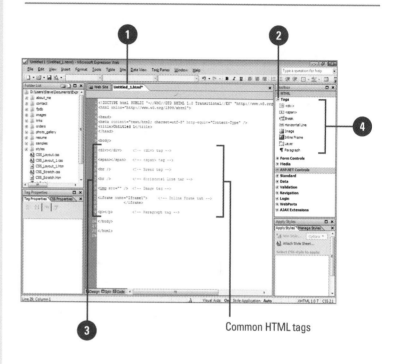

Common HTML tags

Insert Common HTML Tags from the Insert Menu

1. Open and display the Web page you want to use in Design view.

2. Click to place the cursor in Code or Design view where you want to place the HTML tag.

3. Click the **Insert** menu, and then point to **HTML**.

4. Select the tag you want on the HTML submenu.

5. If you selected the Break command, specify the options you want, and then click **OK**.

   ◆ **Normal line break.** Inserts a default line break.

   ◆ **Clear left margin.** Begins the next line at the nearest line below any items in the left margin.

   ◆ **Clear right margin.** Begins the next line at the nearest line below any items in the right margin.

   ◆ **Clear both margins.** Begins the next line at the nearest line below any items in both margins.

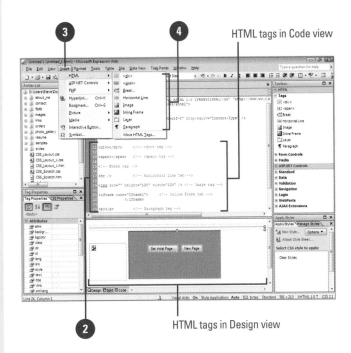

HTML tags in Code view

HTML tags in Design view

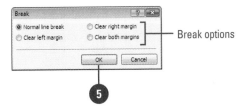

Break options

Did You Know?

You can format a horizontal line. In Design view, select the line, click the Format menu, click Properties, specify width and height, alignment, and color, and then click OK.

Using Tag Tools

The Tag Properties task pane displays HTML tag properties for a selected HTML element in Design or Code view. To display the tag properties, you select the element in Design view or click in the HTML tag in Code view. Each property in the task pane displays an icon in the left column that indicates the property type. A finger pointing to a page indicates an attribute and a lighting bolt indicates an event. If a property name appears in bolded blue text, the property is set.

Insert Tags and Comments

1. Open and display the Web page you want to use.

2. Click the **Code** or **Split** button, and then click to place the insertion point where you want.

3. To insert tag brackets or comments, click the **Edit** menu, point to **Code View**, and then click **Insert Start Tag**, **Insert End Tag**, or **Insert Comment**.

4. To insert common HTML tags, click the plus sign (+) next to Tags in the Toolbox, and then drag or double-click the tag you want.

Split view

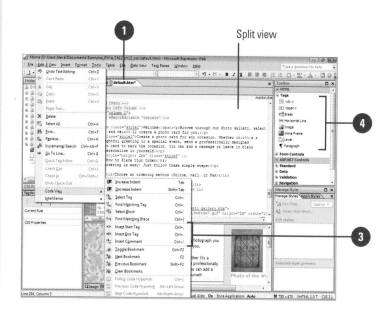

Show Tag Properties

1. Open and display the Web page you want to use.

2. Click the **Task Panes** menu, and then click **Tag Properties** to display the task pane.

3. Select the element in Design view or click in the HTML tag in Code view that you want to view tag properties.

4. Click the plus sign (+) next to the category to want to view: Attributes, Events, or Misc.

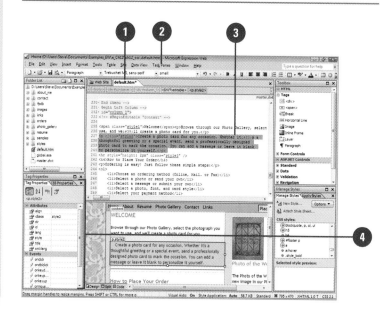

Change the Tag Properties Task Pane Display

1. Open and display the Web page you want to use.

2. Click the **Task Panes** menu, and then click **Tag Properties** to display the task pane.

3. Select the element in Design view or click in the HTML tag in Code view that you want to view tag properties.

4. Click any of the following buttons at the top of the task pane.

    ◆ **Show Categories List button.** Click to display by category as attributes, events, and misc.

    ◆ **Show Alphabetized List button.** Click to display alphabetically.

    ◆ **Show Set Properties on Top button.** Click to display specified properties at the top of the list.

    TIMESAVER *Click the Show Alphabetized List and Show Set Properties on Top buttons to display all set properties at the top.*

Show Categories List button

Show Alphabetical List button

Show Set Properties on Top button

Setting Tag Attributes

You set tag attributes in the Tag Properties task pane. The tag properties that appear in the Tag Properties task pane differ depending on the selected element. To set a tag property, select the element in Design view or the tag in Code view you want to change, click the attribute you want in the Tag Properties task pane you want to change, and then enter, select, or edit the value box next to it. Some attributes provide a drop-down menu to select a value, while others require certain value types. For other attributes, you can add any text you want, such as the alt attribute for an <img> tag, which provides text for pictures, so the visually impaired can read the text in a ScreenTip. If you are more comfortable using dialog boxes, you can click the Show Tag Properties button at the top of the task pane to display a dialog box with the attributes.

Set Tag Attributes

1. Open and display the Web page you want to use.

2. Click the **Task Panes** menu, and then click **Tag Properties** to display the task pane.

3. Select the element in Design view or click in the HTML tag in Code view that you want to view tag properties.

4. Click the plus sign (+) next to the category to want to view: Attributes, Events, or Misc.

5. To change attributes in the task pane, click the value box to the right of the attribute, and then change the value.

6. Click the **Show Tag Properties** button at the top of the task pane.

7. View the properties, and then make any changes you want.

8. Click **OK**.

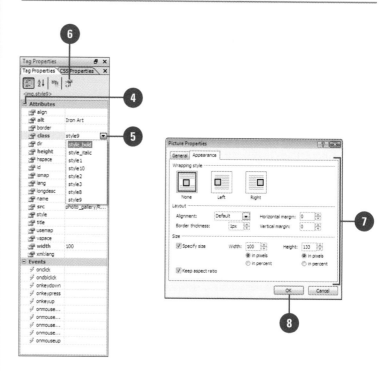

For Your Information

Managing CSS Overflow

If the content is too large to fit in the containing element, you can use the CSS Overflow property (**New!**). You can several option with the CSS Overflow property: hidden, auto, scroll, and visible. For example, #div1 {overflow: PROPERTY; width AMOUNT; height: AMOUNT; border: SIZE TYPE COLOR}

Using the Quick Tag Selector

Expression Web provides two different Quick Tag tools: Quick Tag Selector and Quick Tag Editor. The Quick Tag Selector makes it easy to identify and select page elements, including CSS classes and IDs. The Quick Tag Selector appears under the tabs in the Editing window. You can use Quick Tag Selector in any view. However, Split view allows you to quickly view and select page elements (Design view) and code elements (Code view) without having to switch.

Use the Quick Tag Selector

1 Open and display the Web page you want to use.

2 Click the **View** menu, and then click **Quick Tag Selector** to display it under the tabs in the Editing window.

3 Do any of the following:

◆ **Point to a tag selector.** Highlights the element with a border. Also, displays the tag selector arrow.

◆ **Click a tag selector.** Selects the element or code.

◆ **Click a tag selector arrow.** Point to a tag selector to display the arrow. Displays a menu where you can perform actions on the selected tag. Click **Select Tag** to select the element or code, or click **Select Tag Contents** to select only the contents of the tag, not the tag itself.

Quick Tag Selector

Tag selector arrow

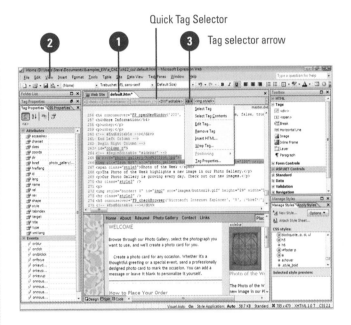

Using the Quick Tag Editor

The Quick Tag Editor allows you to modify an HTML tag using color coding and IntelliSense support. In Code view, you see all the HTML code for a given page or element. Sometimes it's hard to figure out exactly what you want to change. The Quick Tag Editor allows you to easily isolate a specific tag, where you can make changes. You can access the Quick Tag Editor by clicking a tag selector arrow or right-clicking a tag selector, and then selecting one of the following commands on the shortcut menu: Edit Tag, Insert HTML, or Wrap Tag. Other commands on the shortcut menu allow you to remove tags, change CSS positioning, and modify tag properties.

Use the Quick Tag Editor

1 Open and display the Web page you want to use.

2 Click the **View** menu, and then click **Quick Tag Selector** to display it under the tabs in the Editing window.

3 Right-click the tag selector or click the tag selector arrow you want to modify.

◆ You can also click the **Edit** menu, and then point to **Code View**.

4 Click the command on the shortcut menu you want. Each one displays the Quick Tag Editor dialog box.

◆ **Edit Tag.** Edit the HTML for the selected tag.

◆ **Insert HTML.** Enter HTML code, which is inserted on the page. The HTML code appears at the insert point or before a selected element.

◆ **Wrap Tag.** Enter HTML code, which wraps the selected tag.

5 Make the changes you want in the edit box.

6 Click the green checkmark button or press Enter to accept your changes, or click the red X to cancel your changes.

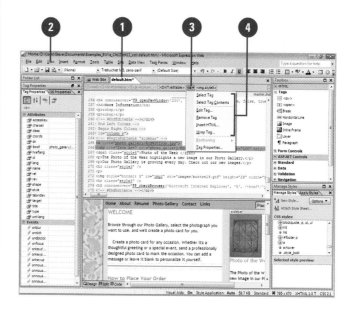

Click to switch between Insert HTML or Wrap Tag

Using CSS Tools

Expression Web provides several task panes and toolbars to help you create and manage CSS. The CSS tools include four task panes: Manage Styles, Apply Styles, CSS Properties, and Tag Properties, and two toolbars: Style Application and Style. The Manage Styles task pane allows you to create and organize styles, while the Apply Styles task pane makes it easy to preview and apply styles. The CSS Properties task pane provides several ways to sort through your CSS properties, which includes CSS tags, cascading styles, and CSS rules. If you prefer using toolbars, you can use the Style Application toolbar to build your CSS manually, or the Style toolbar to apply classes and IDs.

Use CSS Tools

1. Open and display the Web page you want to use.

2. Click the **Task Panes** menu, and then select the following task panes: **Manage Styles**, **Apply Styles**, **CSS Properties**, and **Tag Properties**.

   The Manage and Apply Styles task panes appear on separate tabs in the lower right task pane group. The CSS and Tag Properties task panes appear on separate tabs in the lower left task pane group.

3. Click the **View** menu, point to **Toolbars**, and then click **Style Application** and **Styles** to display them.

Tag Properties tab

CSS Properties tab

Apply Styles tab

Manage Styles tab

Using IntelliSense

In Code view, IntelliSense displays a context-sensitive dropdown list of choices as you enter code. From the dropdown list, you can quickly select the code item you want to use. You can customize the way IntelliSense works by using the IntelliSense tab in the Page Editor Options dialog box. You can set options to disable shortcut menus and inserting tags, quotes, and braces, and to disable code hyperlinks. By default, all check boxes are selected.

Use IntelliSense

1. Open and display the Web page you want to use.

2. Click the **Code** or **Split** button, and then click to place the insertion point where you want to edit the code.

3. Click the **Edit** menu, point to **IntelliSense**.

4. Click the command on the submenu you want:

   ◆ **List Members.** Displays a shortcut menu of valid tag properties.

   ◆ **Parameter Info.** Displays a ScreenTip that lists valid script parameters.

   ◆ **Complete Word.** Use to complete the insertion of a selected item.

   ◆ **List Code Snippets.** Displays the list of code snippets in a dropdown list; you can also press Ctrl+Enter.

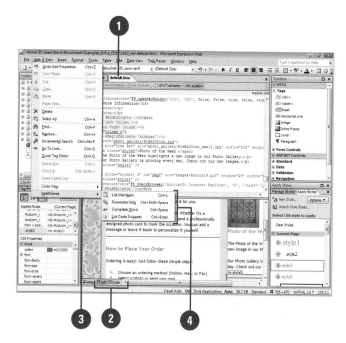

Set IntelliSense Options

1. Click the **Tools** menu, and then click **Page Editor Options**.

2. Click the **IntelliSense** tab.

3. Select the IntelliSense options for CSS that you want in the following categories:

    ◆ **Auto Popup.** Displays a shortcut menus for statement completion and display ScreenTips. Now includes PHP options (**New!**).

    ◆ **Auto Insert.** Automatically inserts the right curly brace ({}) that ends a style declaration.

    ◆ **Code Hyperlinks.** Enables the ability to go to the class-based styles by Ctrl+clicking.

4. Click the **Authoring** tab.

5. To set the CSS schema version for IntelliSense, click the **Schema version** list arrow, and then select the schema version you want.

6. Click **OK**.

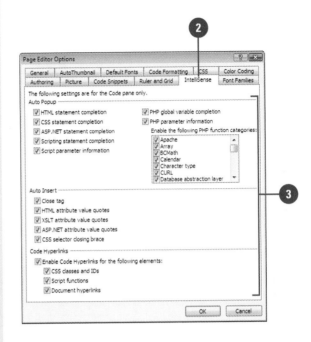

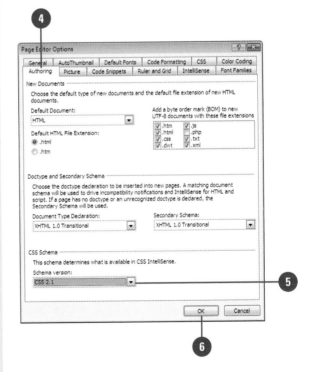

Creating Tag-based Styles

A tag-based (also known as element-based) style applies the defined style to every instance of a selected HTML element. When you create a style for a defined tag element (known as a Selector), such as a header <h1> through <h6>, paragraph <p>, or hyperlink <a:link>, it's applied to every instance of the defined tag on the page (internal) or site (external). After you define the styles you want, the style appears in the Manage Styles tab under the elements category.

Create a Tag-based Style

1. Open and display the Web page you want to use.

2. Click the **New Style** button in the Manage Styles or Apply Styles tab.

3. Click the **Selector** list arrow, and then select the type of style you want.

    The Define in box displays Current page by default.

4. Select the Categories and make changes to set the appearance of the style you want.

5. Select or clear the **Apply new style to document selection** check box.

6. Click **OK**.

    The Manage Styles tab adds the style to the elements category.

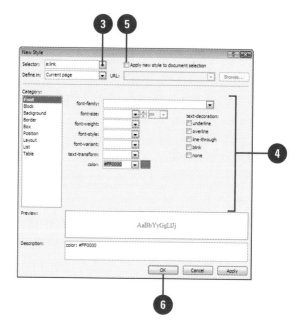

Did You Know?

You can covert a class-based style to an tag-based style. Right-click the class-based style, click Modify Style, click the Selector list arrow, select the element you want to style, and then click OK.

Creating Class-based Styles

Instead of applying a style to a specific element, such as a header, paragraph, or hyperlink, a class-based style can be applied to anything you want to define. This flexibility allows you to create custom styles for your specific purposes. For example, you can create a style called .companyname, which formats the company name with our custom look. You get to decide on the name of the style; it's best to name styles based on their function, so you can easily identify them in the Styles list. Avoid using numbers at the beginning of a style name. Class-based styles start with a dot (.) to preserve class-based syntax.

Create a Class-based Style

1. Open and display the Web page you want to use.

2. Click the **New Style** button in the Manage Styles or Apply Styles tab.

   A default name, .newStyle1, appears selected (without the period at the beginning) in the Selector box.

3. Type the name you want for the class-based style.

4. Select the Categories and make changes to set the appearance of the style you want.

5. Select or clear the **Apply new style to document selection** check box.

6. Click **OK**.

   The Manage Styles tab adds the style to the elements category.

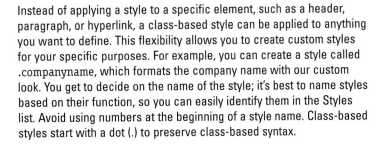

Did You Know?

You can rename a class-based style. In the Apply Styles or Manage Styles task pane, right-click the class-based style you want to rename, click Rename class "name," type a new name, and then click OK.

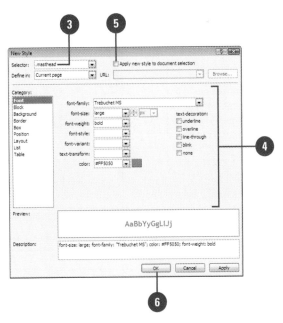

Creating Inline Styles

An inline style allows you to apply formatting directly to an element. An inline style is like an exception to the rule. It's alright to do every so often. However, it's not a good practice. It can cause formatting problems when you apply an internal or external style sheet. An inline style doesn't appear in the Manage Styles tab like the tag- and class-based styles. In the CSS Properties task pane, the style is identified by type, inline.

Create an Inline Style

1. Open and display the Web page you want to use.

2. Click in the paragraph or block you want to style.

3. Click the **New Style** button in the Manage Styles or Apply Styles tab.

4. Click the **Selector** list arrow, and then click **(inline style)**.

5. Select the Categories and make changes to set the appearance of the style you want.

6. Click **OK**.

   The CSS Properties task pane displays <inline style> as the applied rule.

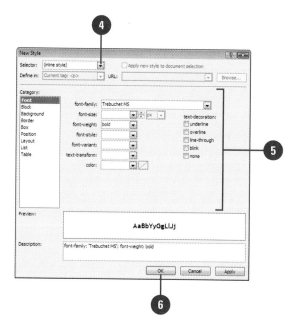

> ### Did You Know?
>
> **An inline style is different than an inline element.** An inline element, such as <em> emphasized </em>, is applied only to a few characters in a paragraph.

Working with Styles

Instead of creating a new style every time you need one, you can also copy an existing one that is close to the style you want, and then modify it to become the one you want. If you mistakenly apply a style to an element and decided you don't like it, you can remove the style from the element without deleting the style itself. However, if you want to permanently delete a style, you can certainly do it.

Work with Styles

1. Open and display the Web page you want to use.

2. Click in the paragraph or block you want to style.

- **Copy and Change a Style.** Right-click the style you want to copy in the Manage Styles tab, click **New Style Copy**, enter a new name in the Selector box, make any changes you want, and then click **OK**.

- **Modify a Style.** Right-click the style you want to modify in the Manage Styles tab, click **Modify Style**, make any changes you want, and then click **OK**.

- **Remove a Style.** Select the element with the style, and then click the **Clear Style** button in the Apply Styles tab.

- **Delete a Style.** Right-click the style you want to delete, click **Delete**, and then click **Yes** to confirm.

- **Sort and Filter Styles.** Click the Options button, and then click one of the sorting or filtering commands, such as Categorize By Order, or Show Styles Used In Current Page.

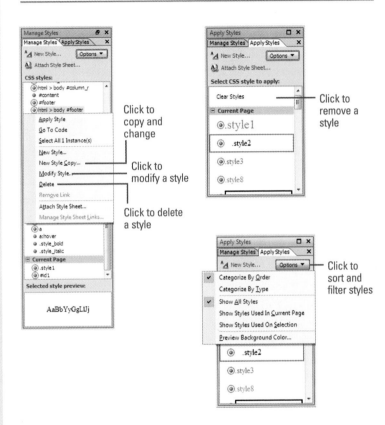

Click to copy and change

Click to modify a style

Click to delete a style

Click to remove a style

Click to sort and filter styles

Creating and Attaching Style Sheets

Cascading Style Sheets are becoming the predominant method of formatting a Web site. A Cascading Style Sheet (CSS) is style information that can be referenced by individual or multiple Web pages. A CSS contains style definitions, called Selectors, which are the HTML components linked to a specialized list of style properties and values. A selector is followed by those properties and values. There are three types of Cascading Style Sheets: external (for multiple pages in the same file), internal or embedded (for individual Web pages), and the rarely-used inline (for individual items). An external CSS file uses a .css file extension. After you create a style sheet, you can attach it to Web pages. If you no longer need a style sheet attached to a Web page, you can detach it.

Create an External Cascading Style Sheet

1. Click the **Web Site** tab for the site in which you want a new page.

2. Click the **New** button list arrow on the Common toolbar, and then click **Page**.

3. In the left pane, click **General**.

4. Click **CSS**.

5. Click **OK**.

   A blank, untitled CSS file opens in the Editing window.

6. Click the **Save** button on the Common toolbar.

7. Type a descriptive name for the CSS file.

8. Click the **Save as type** list arrow, and then click **CSS Files**.

9. Click **Save**.

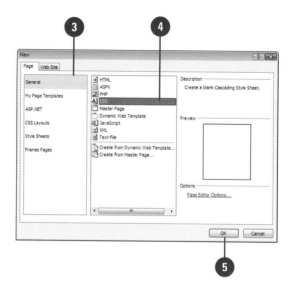

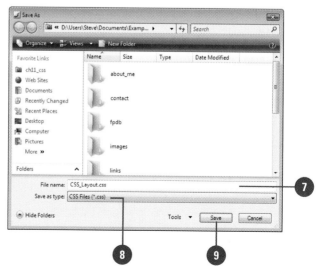

Attach a Cascading Style Sheet to a Web Page

1 Open and display the Web page(s) to which you want to attach an existing external style sheet.

> **TIMESAVER** *If the style sheet is located in the same Web site, drag it from the Folder List onto the Web page.*

2 Click the **Attach Style Sheet** button in the Apply Styles or Manage Styles task pane.

3 Type the location and CSS file name, or click **Browse** to locate and select the CSS file.

4 Click the **All HTML pages** or **Current page** option.

5 Click the **Link** or **Import** option.

6 Click **OK**.

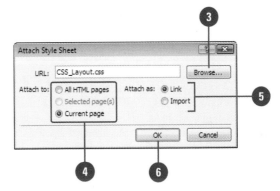

Did You Know?

You can move internal styles to an external style sheet. Attach the external style sheet to the current page, open the Manage Styles tab, select the internal styles you want to move, and then drag them onto the external style sheet's name. The styles are moved to the external style sheet and are no longer in the internal style sheet.

You can detach an external style sheet from a page. Open the page from which you want to detach an external style sheet, right-click the external style sheet in the Manage Styles tab, and then click Remove Link.

Using Rulers and Grid

You can use rulers and a visible layout grid in Design view. Turning on the visible grid makes it easier to create, modify, and align elements of all types. Within the Page Editor Options dialog box, you can select from a variety of options, such as ruler and grid measurement units and the display grid spacing and line color. To align several elements to a grid, you first turn Snap to Grid on. Then you can drag the elements to align them to the grid.

Show or Hide Rulers and Grid

1. Click the **View** menu, and then point to **Ruler and Grid**.

2. Click **Show Ruler** or **Show Grid**.

3. To have objects snap to grid, click the **View** menu, point to **Ruler and Grid**, and then click **Snap to Grid**.

4. To hide or turn the options off, choose the commands again.

Set Rulers and Grid Options

1. Click the **View** menu, point to **Ruler and Grid**, and then click **Configure**.

2. Click the **Ruler and Grid Units** list arrow, and then select a measurement.

3. Select the spacing, line style, and line color for the display grid.

4. Specify the spacing you want for the snapping grid.

5. Click **OK**.

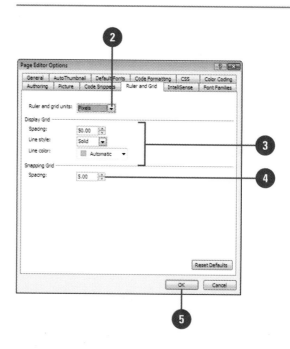

Setting Position Properties

Positioning Properties

When you're working with CSS, you can display elements on a page from top-to-bottom using five positioning properties: absolute, fixed, relative, static, and inherit.

Absolute

An absolute positioned element is placed in relation to the page's left, top corner. You can position the element anywhere on a page; it's not confined to a specific place.

Fixed

A fixed positioned element is placed in relation to the browsers window rather than the page or other elements. If you scroll the browser window, the element stays in the same place.

Relative

A relatively positioned element remains part of the placement on the page in relation to the page's code. When you move a relatively positioned element, its position changes relative to its normal spot in the code.

Static

A static positioned element stays inline (top, bottom) with other elements.

Inherit

An element inherits the positioning of the enclosing parent element.

Floating Properties

Floating properties work similarly to the wrapping styles that control how text flows around images. You can select four floating positions: Left, None, Right, and Inherit. **Left** allows other elements to flow down its right side.

None causes no wrap. The element stays in place and no other elements wrap around it. **Right** allows other elements to flow down its left side. **Inherit** uses the float settings of its enclosed parent element.

Clearing Properties

Clearing properties work in relation to Floating properties. You can select five floating positions: Both, Left, None, Right, and Inherit. **Both** blocks floats on both sides. **Left** blocks other elements from floating to its left. **None** causes no floating. The element stays in place and no other elements wrap around it. **Right** block other elements from floating to its right. **Inherit** uses the clear setting of its enclosed parent element.

Setting Position Properties

The easiest way to set positioning properties for selected elements is to use the Positioning toolbar, which provides all the positioning options in one place. To display the Positioning toolbar, click the View menu, point to Toolbars, and then click Positioning. Another way to set position properties is to use the CSS Properties tab. Click the Task Panes menu, and then click CSS Properties to display it. In the properties list, click the box to the right of the properties position, float, and clear to select the option you want. If you want to change positioning properties for a style, right-click the style in the Manage Styles tab, click Modify Styles, click the Position category, make the changes you want, and then click OK.

Positioning toolbar

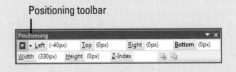

Creating a CSS Layout

Cascading Style Sheets (CSS) provide a formatting template for Web page elements. Instead of formatting individual elements, which can be time consuming, you can change and apply a CSS to make the changes you want for the entire Web site. CSS allows you to separate your content from your formatting. Using CSS also simplifies and reduces the HTML code, which speeds up download times. A CSS page is an HTML file with links to a CSS file. You can create the two files separately, or you can use CSS Layouts in Expression Web to create and link them.

Create a CSS Layout Page

1. Click the Web Site tab for the site in which you want a new page.

2. Click the **New** button list arrow on the Common toolbar, and then click **Page**.

3. In the left pane, click **CSS Layouts**.

4. Click the type of CSS layout you want.

5. Click **OK**.

   A blank, untitled HTML Web page appears along with a related untitled CSS-based page.

6. Click the **File** menu, and then click **Save All**.

7. In the Save As dialog box, name and save the HTML page and its related external CSS file.

8. Add content to the different layout sections.

9. To change a layout, right-click the style you want to modify in the Manage Styles tab, click **Modify Style**, make the changes you want to the Box, Position, and Layout, and then click **OK**.

   In the Modify Styles dialog box, boldface categories have property values already set.

10. Click the **File** menu, and then click **Save All**.

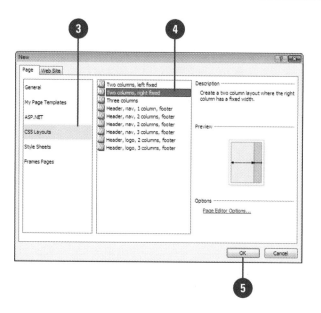

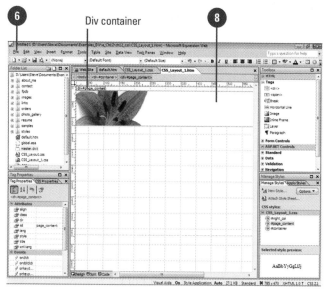

Div container

Creating Contextual Selectors

A contextual selector allows you to create styles for different situations. If you want to create a special paragraph style for a main header, you can create a contextual selector to perform the task. With contextual selectors, you can create contextual ID-based styles that only appear when particular tags are used in specific divisions. If you want to use the contextual selector on multiple pages, you can move the contextual selector style to an external style sheet.

Create Contextual Selector

1. Open and display the Web page to which you want to create a contextual selector style.

2. Click the **New Style** button in the Manage Styles tab.

3. Select the provided selector name including the period, and then type a contextual selector name using the following format:

   #div_name(space)class_name. For example, #page_content p, where p is the paragraph style.

4. Select the Categories and make changes to set the appearance of the style you want.

5. Click **Apply** to view the changes, make any adjustments, and then click **OK**.

   The new contextual style is applied in the appropriate situations and the contextual ID-based style is listed in the Manage Styles tab.

6. Click the **File** menu, and then click **Save All**.

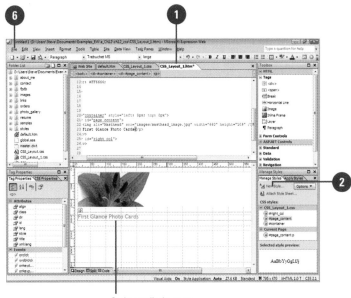

Style applied to text

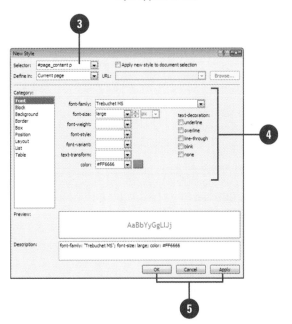

Creating a CSS Layout from Scratch

If the CSS pre-built layouts don't provide exactly what you need, you may want to create a CSS layout from scratch. It's a two step process: (1) create ID-based styles for each division, (2) insert the divisions, or divs (<div>), and then pairs them with the ID-based styles. You can insert the divs in any order. However, placing them in top to bottom order as they appear on the page helps display the page better on non-CSS browsers. After you insert the divs, you can pair them with ID styles using the Tag Properties task pane.

Create ID Styles for a CSS Layout

1. Click the Web Site tab for the site in which you want a new page.

2. Click the **New** button list arrow on the Common toolbar, and then click **HTML**.

3. Click the **New** button list arrow on the Common toolbar, and then click **CSS**.

4. Use the **Save** button on the Common toolbar to name and save the HTML page and its related external CSS file.

5. Display the HTML file.

6. Click the **Attach Style Sheet** button in the Manage Styles tab.

7. Specify the CSS file and options you want, and then click **OK**.

8. Click **New Style** in the Manage Styles tab.

9. Delete the Selector, and then type the division name. For example, #container.

10. Click the **Define in** list arrow, click **Existing style sheet**, and then click **Browse** to select the CSS file. For example, CSS_Scratch.css.

11. Set the position category to specify a position property, and then click **OK**.

12. Click the **File** menu, and then click **Save All**.

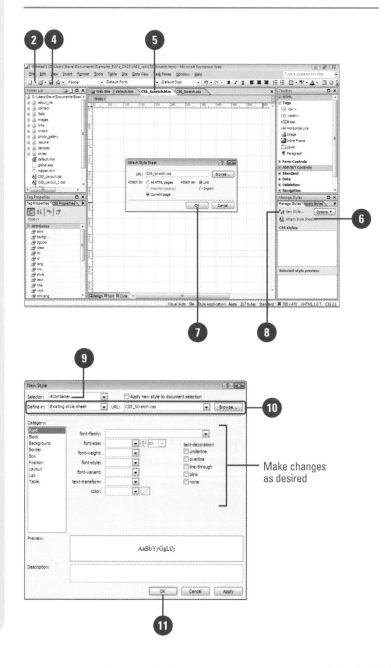

Make changes as desired

Insert div Tags and Pair with ID Styles

① Open and display the HTML page with the ID styles for a CSS layout.

② Click in the HTML page where you want to insert a div tag.

③ Click the **Insert** menu, point to **HTML**, and then click **<div>**.

◆ You can also double-click <div> in the Toolbox task pane.

An empty division, marked by a dotted border appears across the top of the page.

④ Click the box for the <div> in Design view or click in the <div> tag in Code view to select it.

◆ Changes in Code view don't appear in Design view until you press F5 to refresh the screen.

⑤ Click the **Tag Properties** tab in the task pane.

⑥ Click the blank column to the right of ID, click **container** from the list, and then press Enter.

A list of the previously created IDs appears in the list. The container ID is applied to the div tag. This connects the CSS and HTML together.

⑦ Click in the container div and repeat steps 3 through 6 to insert and ID the next division for your page.

⑧ Click the **File** menu, and then click **Save All**.

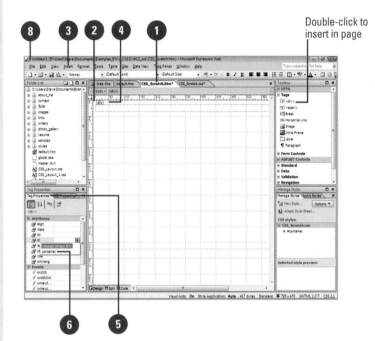

Double-click to insert in page

Checking for CSS Problems

Expression Web can help to identify CSS problems using CSS Reports. CSS Reports allows you to check individual pages or an entire Web site for errors relating to unused styles, undefined classes, mismatched case. In addition, CSS Reports also show how CSS is used in a page; it checks the usage of class selectors, ID selectors, and element selectors. After you check for CSS problems, the results appear in the CSS Reports task pane, where you can review styles and fix any problems.

Check for CSS Errors

1. Click the **Tools** menu, and then click **CSS Reports**.

2. Click the **Errors** tab.

3. Click the option to specify which pages you want to search.

4. Select or clear the Check for check boxes you want to include or exclude.

   ◆ **Unused Styles**. Shows styles not used in the style sheet.

   ◆ **Undefined Classes**. Shows styles not defined, yet still used.

   ◆ **Mismatched Case**. Shows mismatches in case between a CSS class or ID in a page and the case used in a style sheet.

5. Click **Check**.

   The Accessibility task pane opens.

6. To correct a problem, double-click the entry to open the page, where you can correct the highlighted code.

7. To sort or filter information in the task pane, click a column header, or click the column list arrow, and then click a filter or **Custom** to use AutoFilter.

8. To generate an HTML report, click the **Generate HTML Report** button in the task pane.

9. When you're done, click the **Close** button in the task pane.

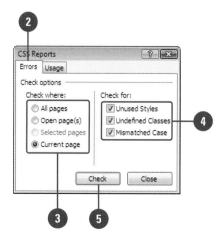

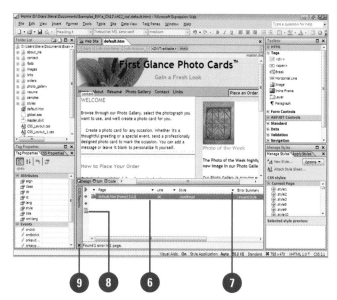

Check for CSS Usage Problems

1. Click the **Tools** menu, and then click **Accessibility Reports**.

2. Click the **Usage** tab.

3. Click the option to specify which pages you want to search.

4. Select or clear the Check for check boxes you want to include or exclude.

- ◆ **Class Selectors**. Shows the CSS classes in use.

- ◆ **ID Selectors**. Shows the CSS ID selectors in use.

- ◆ **Element Selectors**. Shows all HTML element selectors. This option generates a lot of output; use only if necessary.

5. Click **Check**.

6. To view report information, double-click the entry, and then view the highlighted code.

7. To sort or filter information in the task pane, click a column header, or click the column list arrow, and then click a filter or **Custom** to use AutoFilter.

8. To view a list of style sheet links, click the **Style Sheet Links** button in the task pane.

9. When you're done, click the **Close** button in the task pane.

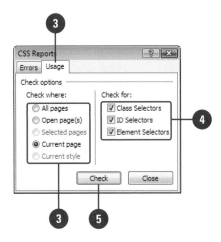

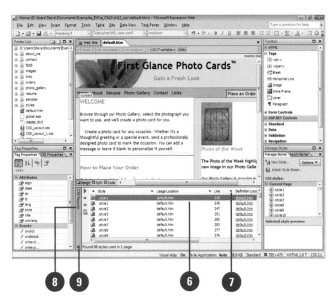

Setting CSS Options

The CSS tab in the Page Editor Options dialog box allows you to control how Expression Web uses CSS styles in your Web pages. You can use the CSS tab to override default CSS behavior in Expression Web. By default, Expression Web automatically adds CSS code to your Web pages when you apply formatting based on the options set in the CSS tab. You can set different CSS properties for different page elements, such as font and text, borders, background, sizing, positing, and floating.

Set CSS Options

1. Click the **Tools** menu, and then click **Page Editor Options**.

2. Click the **CSS** tab.

3. Select the CSS options you want. Some of the common options include:

   ◆ **Auto Style Application.** This option automatically applies CSS styles to formatting text based on the selected CSS technology properties.

   ◆ **Manual Style Application.** This option displays the Style Application toolbar so you can apply styles manually.

   ◆ **Only reuse classes with the prefix "style."** Select to change automatically added CSS classes to start with the prefix "style," which prevents Expression Web from modifying them.

   ◆ **Use width and height attributes for images instead of CSS.** Select to override CSS width and height settings.

4. Click **OK**.

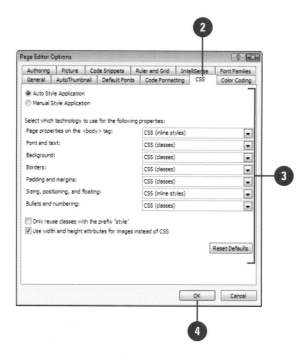

Working with Advanced Pages

Introduction

In addition to typical HTML pages, you can also create other pages—including ASP.NET, PHP, and XML—where you can take advantage of other features and technologies that HTML page don't provide.

Expression Web supports ASP.NET 2.0 and provides controls you can use directly from the Toolbox. The Toolbox in Expression Web provides seven categories of ASP.NET controls: Standard, Data, Validation, Navigation, Login, WebParts, and AJAX Extensions (**New!**). You can insert ASP.NET controls into an ASP.NET page and configure them in the same way you insert form controls. To use ASP.NET controls, you need to install ASP.NET 2.0 on your Web server and .NET Framework 2.0, 3.0, or 3.5 on your computer, which you can download from *www.microsoft.com*.

PHP is a server-side scripting language and interpreter used to create dynamic Web pages. A PHP script is embedded in an HTML Web page, and interpreted on the server before being sent to the user who requested the page. The user receives the interpreted PHP code as pure HTML code. PHP runs reliably on almost any platform currently available, including Windows, Linux and Mac servers and clients; it can perform a variety of tasks using module controls, but its strength lies in its compatibility with many types of databases, including MySQL and other SQL or ODBC databases.

XML (eXtensible Markup Language) is designed specifically for Web pages. XML is a complementary format to HTML, which is ideal for producing extensive, highly-structured data from an application in a consistent manner. XML describes the content of a Web page, while HTML tags describe how the page looks. HTML tags assign certain characteristics to the text they surround.

What You'll Do

Create an ASP.NET Page

Use ASP.NET Controls

Insert ASP.NET Controls

Insert ASP.NET AJAX Controls

Use Custom ASP.NET Controls

Get Started with PHP

Create a PHP Page

Work with PHP Code

Insert a PHP Script

Create an XML Page

Create a Data View

Work with Data in Data View

Format a Data View

Check XML Pages

Add RSS Feeds

Creating an ASP.NET Page

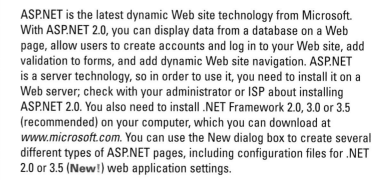

ASP.NET is the latest dynamic Web site technology from Microsoft. With ASP.NET 2.0, you can display data from a database on a Web page, allow users to create accounts and log in to your Web site, add validation to forms, and add dynamic Web site navigation. ASP.NET is a server technology, so in order to use it, you need to install it on a Web server; check with your administrator or ISP about installing ASP.NET 2.0. You also need to install .NET Framework 2.0, 3.0 or 3.5 (recommended) on your computer, which you can download at *www.microsoft.com*. You can use the New dialog box to create several different types of ASP.NET pages, including configuration files for .NET 2.0 or 3.5 (**New!**) web application settings.

Create an ASP.NET Page

1. Click the Web Site tab for the site in which you want a new page.

2. Click the **New** button list arrow on the Common toolbar, and then click **Page**.

3. In the left pane, click **ASP.NET**.

4. Click the type of ASP.NET page you want.

5. Click **OK**.

   An untitled Web page appears.

6. Click the **Save** button on the Common toolbar, type a name for the page, and then click **Save**.

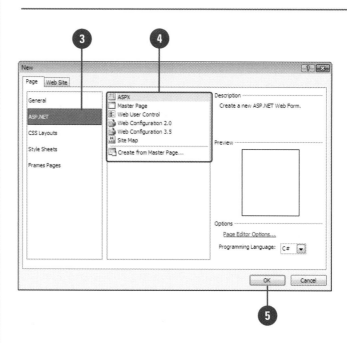

Did You Know?

You can test your ASP.NET pages without a Web server. If you don't have access to a Web server during development, Expression Web provides a MS Expression Development Server so you can test your ASP.NET pages.

See Also

See "Changing Web Site Settings" on page 352 for information on using the MS Expression Development Server.

Using ASP.NET Controls

ASP.NET Controls

Expression Web supports ASP.NET 2.0 and provides controls you can use directly from the Toolbox. You can insert ASP.NET controls into an ASP.NET page and configure them in the same way you insert form controls. To use ASP.NET controls, you need to install ASP.NET 2.0 on your Web server and .NET Framework 2.0, 3.0, or 3.5 on your computer, which you can download from *www.microsoft.com*. The Toolbox in Expression Web provides seven categories of ASP.NET controls: Standard, Data, Validation, Navigation, Login, WebParts, and AJAX Extensions (**New!**).

- ◆ **Standard.** This category provides common controls—Button, CheckBox, DropDownList, and ListBox—as well as uncommon ones—Calendar, AdRotator, and Wizard (to collect data).

- ◆ **Data.** This category provides controls to create a data-driven Web site for retrieving and displaying data. You can create data connections using the Data Source Library task pane. You can connect to data in a database, an XML file, or even a sitemap file.

- ◆ **Validation.** This category provides controls for configuring form field data validation on an ASP.NET Web form.

- ◆ **Navigation.** This category provides controls—Menu, SiteMapPath, and TreeView—for navigating in a Web site.

- ◆ **Login.** This category provides controls for creating a membership login with username and password for an ASP.NET Web site.

- ◆ **WebParts.** This category provides controls that allow users of the site to customize the appearance and layout of pages. After you insert the Web-PartZone control, you can add other individual WebPart controls, which work similar to HTML form pages.

- ◆ **AJAX Extensions.** This category (**New!**) provides controls for user interface elements—Timer, UpdatePanel, UpdateProgress, ScriptManager, and ScriptManagerProxy.

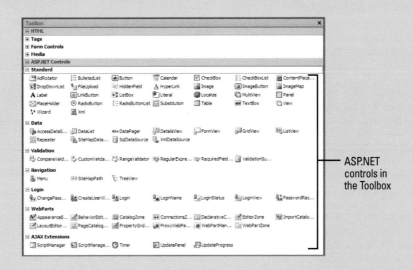

ASP.NET controls in the Toolbox

Inserting ASP.NET Controls

You can insert a ASP.NET controls into a page by using the ASP.NET Controls submenu on the Insert menu or dragging a control from the Toolbox (**New!**). The ASP.NET Controls submenu provides easy access to commonly used standard controls, while the Toolbox provides access to all the available controls broken down by category, which includes Standard, Data, Validation, Navigation, Login, WebParts, or AJAX Extensions (**New!**). After you insert an ASP.NET control, you may be prompted with a control menu requesting information or providing options specific to the control. Before you can work with ASP.NET controls, you need to install .NET Framework 2.0, 3.0, or 3.5 (recommended) at *www.microsoft.com*.

Insert a ASP.NET Controls from the Toolbox Task Pane

1. Open and display the ASP page you want to use.

2. Expand the **ASP.NET Controls** category in the Toolbox task pane.

3. Expand the category (**Standard, Data, Validation, Navigation, Login, WebParts,** or **AJAX Extensions**) in the Toolbox task pane with the control you want to insert.

4. Drag control icon to your Web page in Design view where you want to insert it.

   TROUBLE? *If the controls are missing in the Toolbox, you need to install .NET Framework 2.0, 3.0, or 3.5 (recommended), which is available at* www.microsoft.com.

5. If a control menu appears, click a link to execute the command, or an option to enable it. Link commands and options vary depending on the control.

6. If prompted, specify the options you want, and then click **OK**.

7. To change control properties, open the Tag Properties task pane, and then specify individual properties.

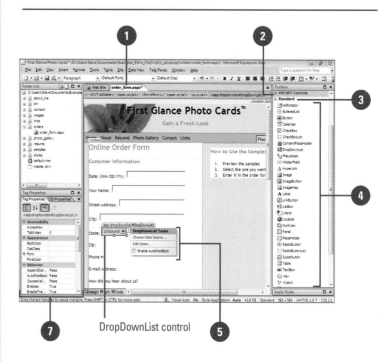

DropDownList control

Edit Items link on control menu

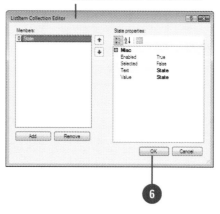

Insert Common ASP.NET Controls from the Insert Menu

1. Open and display the ASP page you want to use in Design view.

2. Click to place the insertion point where you want the control.

3. Click the **Insert** menu, point to **ASP.NET Controls**, and then select the code script you want:

   ◆ **Button.** Inserts a button to perform a command.

   ◆ **Checkbox.** Inserts a check box for users to turn on or off.

   ◆ **Checkbox List.** Inserts a check box as a parent control.

   ◆ **Dropdown List.** Inserts a dropdown list box to select an item from a list.

   ◆ **Image Button.** Inserts a button with an image to perform a command.

   ◆ **Label.** Inserts a text label.

   ◆ **Listbox.** Inserts a list box to select one or more items.

   ◆ **Radio Button.** Inserts an option button to select one or more items.

   ◆ **Radio Button List.** Inserts a radio button as a parent control.

   ◆ **Textbox.** Inserts a text box for users to type information.

4. If a control menu appears, click a link to execute the command, or an option to enable it. Link commands and options vary depending on the control.

5. If prompted, specify the options you want, and then click **OK**.

6. To change control properties, open the Tag Properties task pane, and then specify individual properties.

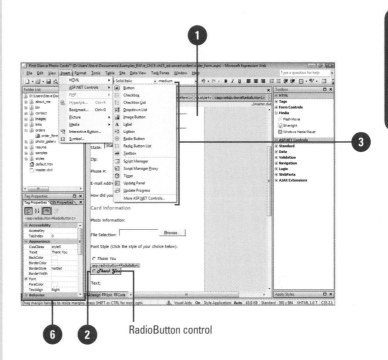

RadioButton control

For Your Information

Using Added ASP.NET Data Controls

ASP.NET Data controls allow you to retrieve and display data to create a data-driven Web site. When you install .NET Framework 3.5, you also get access to two additional ASP.NET Data controls (**New!**): DataPager and ListView. The DataPager control allows you to display data as a sequence of pages and displays navigation controls for the ListView control. The ListView control allows you to bind data items provided by the data source and display them. This control is useful because it allows users to edit, insert, and delete data, and to sort and display data as a sequence of pages.

Inserting ASP.NET AJAX Controls

ASP.NET AJAX controls (**New!**) provide more response to user actions through partial-page updates (for faster page refreshes and avoid page flicker) and status information without writing scripts. You can insert a ASP.NET AJAX controls into a page by dragging a control from the Toolbox. After you insert an ASP.NET AJAX control, you may be prompted to add a web.config file and turn turn on a visual aid to view a non-visual control. Before you can work with ASP.NET controls, you need to install .NET Framework 3.5 or ASP.NET AJAX 1.0 at *www.microsoft.com*.

Insert a ASP.NET AJAX Controls from the Toolbox Task Pane

1 Open and display the ASP page you want to use.

2 Expand the **ASP.NET Controls** category in the Toolbox task pane.

3 Expand the **AJAX Extensions** category in the Toolbox task pane.

4 Drag control icon to your Web page in Design view where you want to insert it.

◆ **Script Manager.** Manages a client script for AJAX.

◆ **Script Manager Proxy.** Allows content pages and user controls (nested or child elements) to add script and service references to pages, when the ScriptManager is defined in a parent element.

◆ **Timer.** Performs postbacks at defined intervals.

◆ **Update Panel.** Performs a partial-page update.

◆ **Update Progress.** Provides status information on updates.

5 If prompted to add or update a web.config file, click **Yes**, or if prompted to turn on a visual aid to view a non-visual control, click **Yes**.

6 To change control properties, open the Tag Properties task pane, and then specify individual properties.

web.config file ① ScriptManager control ②

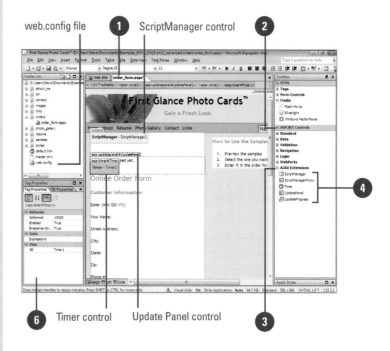

6 Timer control   Update Panel control ③

5

Using Custom ASP.NET Controls

If you don't find the controls you need from the ones provided by .NET Framework, you can use custom ASP.NET controls created by other developers (**New!**) or create your own custom controls by using visual design tool, such as Microsoft Visual Studio. You can view a list of custom ASP.NET controls on the Microsoft ASP.NET Web site at *www.asp.net.com* under Control Gallery in the Community area. When you place the custom ASP.NET control in the BIN folder of your Web site and reference the custom control, you can take advantage of the added functionality. You can preview custom controls and access the Common Tasks smart tag menu in Design view, edit properties, and use IntelliSense and syntax checking in Code view. The custom controls are not available in the Toolbox or on the Insert menu. Before you can work with ASP.NET controls, you need to install .NET Framework 3.5 at *www.microsoft.com*.

Use Custom ASP.NET Controls

1. Add the custom control assembly file (.dll) to the **bin** folder—create one if necessary—in the root folder of your Web site or install the custom control into the Global Assembly Cache (GAC) on both your computer and Web server.

2. Reference the custom control in an ASP.NET page or web.config file.

   ◆ **ASP.NET Page.** Display page in Code or Split view, and then add the reference code provided in the illustration.

   ◆ **web.config file.** Open or create a Web site web.config file, and then add the reference code provided in the illustration.

3. To add a custom ASP.NET control to a page, open and display the page in Code or Split view, place the insertion point in the body, and then type the following code or use the IntelliSense menu:

   `<TAG_PREFIX:CLASS_NAME runat=server" />`

   Replace TAG_PREFIX with the one used in the reference, and replace the CLASS_NAME with the one for the custom control.

2 Text file with code to copy into appropriate files

Copy to ASP.Net page

Copy to web.config file

Getting Started with PHP

PHP is short for PHP (Personal Homepage): Hypertext Preprocessor. PHP is a server-side, HTML embedded scripting language and interpreter used to create dynamic Web pages. A PHP script is embedded in an HTML Web page, and interpreted on the server before being sent to the user who requested the page. The user receives the interpreted PHP code as pure HTML code. PHP is a collection of modules that can be added on the server as needed to perform a large variety of specific tasks. One of the modules controls database access. Using PHP with MySQL database has become common enough that the MySQL interface is now part of core PHP instead of a plug-in module. PHP can also access most any SQL or ODBC database.

Three things make PHP popular. (1) It's easy to implement, learn, and use. (2) It's free. (3) It runs on almost any Web server on almost any platform currently available, including Windows, Linux and Mac servers. PHP is open source, and may be downloaded from *www.php.net*, and then installed and configured on your Web server.

Getting Started with PHP Code

PHP code is similar to the syntax for C, Perl, and Java, so if you are familiar with any of these scripting language, you have ahead start with PHP. PHP scripts have the extension .php. A PHP script begins with '<?php' and ends with '?>' with PHP code statements in between. When set within a page of HTML, the start and end indicators tell the computer where to differentiate between HTML and PHP. A semicolon at the end of a PHP statement signifies the completion of the line of code. As with HTML, whitespace is ignored between PHP statements. You can also press tab to indent your code and the PHP interpreter will ignore those spaces as well.

Working with Variables

A variable is a means of storing a value, such as text string "Hello!" or the integer value 10, and reusing it throughout your code. In PHP you define a variable with the following form: $variable_name = Value;

If you forget that dollar sign at the beginning, it will not work. Variable names are case-sensitive, so use the exact same capitalization when using a variable. There are a few rules that you need to follow when choosing a name for your PHP variables. (1) PHP variables must start with a letter or underscore "_". (2) PHP variables may only be comprised of alpha-numeric characters and underscores. a-z, A-Z, 0-9, or _ . (3) Variables with more than one word should be separated with underscores (for example, $my_variable) or capitalization (for example, $myVariable).

Adding Comments

Comments in PHP are similar to comments that are used in HTML. A single line comment starts with "//" and all text to the right is ignored, while a multiple line comment begins with " /* " and ends with " */ ".

Viewing an Example

The example sends an email from within a PHP page using the built in mail() function:

```php
<?php
// Your email address
$email = "you@example.com";
// The subject
$subject = 'Enter your subject here";
// The message
$message = Enter your message here";
mail ($email, $subject, $message, "From: $email");
// Display text
echo "The email has been sent.";
?>
```

Creating a PHP Page

With Expression Web, you can create a PHP page (**New!**) in the same you create an HTML page. A PHP page with a script uses the extension .php. The PHP script is embedded in an HTML Web page, and interpreted on the server before being sent to the user who requested the page. The PHP script is enclosed/embedded within special PHP tags (`<?php` and `?>`), which allows the author to jump between HTML and PHP. PHP runs reliably on almost any platform currently available, including Windows, Linux and Mac servers and clients; it can perform a variety of tasks using module controls, but its strength lies in its compatibility with many types of databases, including MySQL and other SQL or ODBC databases.

Create a PHP Page

1. Click the Web Site tab for the site in which you want a new page.

2. Click the **New** button list arrow on the Common toolbar, and then click **Page**.

   TIMESAVER *Click the New button list arrow, and then click PHP to create a PHP page.*

3. In the left pane, click **General**.

4. Click **PHP**.

5. Click **OK**.

   An untitled Web page appears.

6. Click the **Save** button on the Common toolbar, type a name for the page, and then click **Save**.

   When you have PHP inserted into your HTML and want a Web browser to interpret it correctly, then you must save the file with a .php extension, instead of the standard .html extension, and place the .php file on a PHP enabled (installed and configured) Web server.

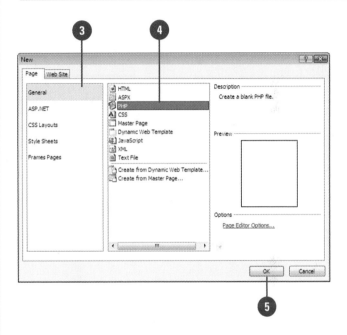

For Your Information

Previewing and Testing a PHP Page Locally

If you want to preview and test a PHP page locally (**New!**), you can use the Expression Development Server—just like ASP.NET pages—instead of having to install and configure Internet Information Server (IIS) or Apache. If you are using a database, such as MySQL, you need to install and configure it on your local computer. For information about installing MySQL, visit the MySQL Web site at *www.mysql.com*.

Working with PHP Code

A PHP script begins with '<?php' and ends with '?>'. The script that is interpreted on the server into HTML, before being sent to the client. The client will receive a pure HTML page. When set within a page of HTML, these indicators tell the computer where to differentiate between HTML and PHP. The semicolon signifies the end of a PHP statement. As with HTML, whitespace is ignored between PHP statements. You can also press tab to indent your code and the PHP interpreter will ignore those spaces as well. Comments in PHP are similar to comments that are used in HTML. To do a single line comment type "//" and all text to the right will be ignored by PHP interpreter, while the multiple line PHP comment begins with " /* " and ends with " */ ". You can use IntelliSense to help you enter PHP code correctly (**New!**).

Enter PHP Code Manually

1. Open and display the Web page you want to use.

2. Click the **Code** or **Split** button.

3. Click to place the insertion point where you want.

4. Type **<?php**, and then press Enter.

5. Type the PHP code statements you want followed by the Enter key. Be sure to end a PHP statement with a semicolon.

6. When you're done entering PHP code statements, press Enter, type **?>**, and then press Enter.

See Also

See "Getting Start with PHP" on page 319 for information on using PHP code.

See "Setting Code Formatting Options" on page 362 for information on changing the color of PHP code.

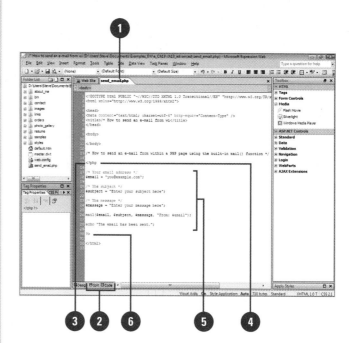

Use IntelliSense to Enter PHP Code

1. Open and display a PHP page you want to use.

2. Click the **Code** or **Split** button, and then click to place the insertion point between the PHP script block start and end tags (<? and ?>).

3. Click the **Edit** menu, point to **IntelliSense**, and then click **List Members** to insert a function, or type **$_** to insert a PHP variable.

4. Type part of the item name or move down the IntelliSense shortcut menu list, and then press either Tab or Enter for the selected item or double-click the item to insert it in the code.

5. To display a tooltip with PHP function parameters, press Shift+Ctrl+Spacebar.

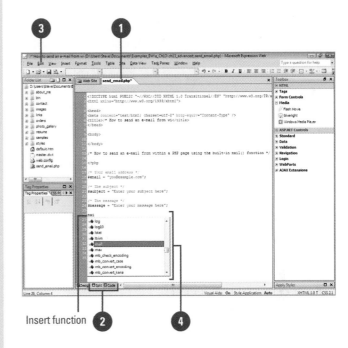

Insert function

Set PHP IntelliSense Options

1. Click the **Tools** menu, and then click **Page Editor Options**.

2. Click the **IntelliSense** tab.

3. Select the **PHP global variable completion** check box to have IntelliSense complete global variables.

4. Select the **PHP parameter information** check box to have IntelliSense provide parameter information.

5. Select the check boxes next to the PHP function categories you want to use with IntelliSense.

6. Click **OK**.

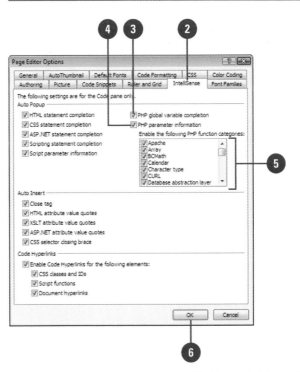

Inserting a PHP Script

A PHP script begins with '<?php' and ends with '?>'. Instead of manually typing the beginning and ending code before you type a PHP statement, you can quickly insert commonly used PHP code snippets that includes them into your page. You can insert a PHP code snippet by using the PHP submenu on the Insert menu (**New!**). When you insert a code snippet, the code appears all on one line. The code line starts with <?php followed by the PHP code statement, and then ends with ?> all separated by spaces. If you want, you can separate the three parts into individual lines of code.

Insert a PHP Script

① Open and display the Web page you want to use.

② Click the **Code** or **Split** button.

③ Click to place the insertion point where you want.

④ Click the **Insert** menu, point to **PHP**, and then select the code script you want:

- ◆ **Form Variable.** Use to collect information from a form when using the HTTP post method.

  <?php $_POST[]; ?>

- ◆ **URL Variable.** Use to collect information from a form when using the HTTP get method.

  <?php $_GET[]; ?>

- ◆ **Session Variable.** Use to save information about a user's session time at your site.

  <?php $_SESSION[]; ?>

- ◆ **Cookie Variable.** Use to retrieve a cookie value from a user's computer. A cookie is a file that is embedded in the user's computer by the server in order to identify it.

  <?php $_COOKIE[]; ?>

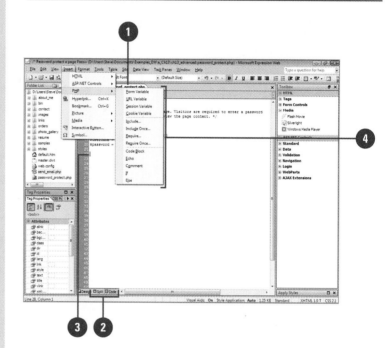

◆ **Include.** Use to insert a file and doesn't require a successful script. In the dialog box, select a file, and then click **Open**.

`<?php include(); ?>`

`<?php include_once(); ?>`

◆ **Require.** Use to insert a file and does require a successful script. In the dialog box, select a file, and then click **Open**.

`<?php require(); ?>`

`<?php require_once(); ?>`

◆ **Code Block.** Use to insert the beginning <?php and ending ?> PHP code.

`<?php ?>`

◆ **Echo.** Use to display HTML in your browser.

`<?php echo ?>`

◆ **Comment.** Use to insert a multiple-line comment.

`/* */`

◆ **If.** Use to check whether a condition is true.

`<?php if ?>`

◆ **Else.** Use as an option when an if statement is false.

`<?php else ?>`

5 If desired, you can separate the three parts into individual lines of code.

Did You Know?

You can show or hide PHP formatting marks in Design view. In Design view, click the View menu, point to Formatting Marks, and then click Show. Click the View menu, point to Formatting Marks, and then click Script Block.

Form Variable: $_POST[];

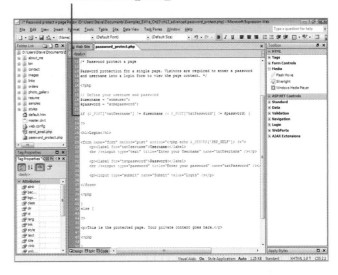

Creating an XML Page

XML is short for Extensible Markup Language. XML is designed specifically for Web pages. XML is a complementary yet stricter format to HTML. XML is ideal for producing extensive, highly-structured data from an application in a consistent manner. The difference between XML and HTML is subtle but profound: XML describes the content of a Web page, while HTML tags describe how the page looks. HTML tags assign certain characteristics to the text they surround. XML is ideal for data-intensive Web environments and, unlike HTML, supports customized tags for specific data. After you create an XML page with the customized, you can use the XML file in HTML and ASP.NET pages to create Data Views that integrate XML data.

Create an XML Page

1. Click the Web Site tab for the site in which you want a new page.

2. Click the **New** button list arrow on the Common toolbar, and then click **Page**.

3. In the left pane, click **General**.

4. Click **XML**.

5. Click **OK**.

   An untitled Web page appears.

6. Click the **Save** button on the Common toolbar, type a name for the page, and then click **Save**.

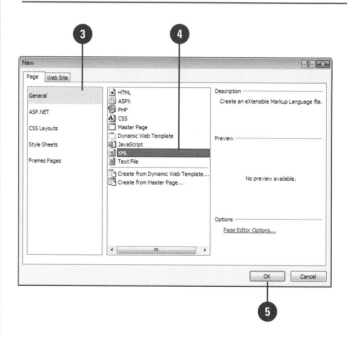

Did You Know?

You can change the XML encoding. Open the Web site with the XML page you want to change, right-click the XML page in the editor, and then click Encoding. To reload the file, click a different encoding, and then click Reload. To save the file, click the encoding you want, click Save As, and then save the file.

Creating a Data View ▶

A Data View retrieves data from a data source with XML and displays the data using XSLT (eXtensible Stylesheet Language Transformation) formatting. You can create Data Views to integrate XML data in HTML and ASP.NET pages by simply dragging an XML file onto your page. However, the code generated in HTML and ASP.NET is different. When you create a Data View in HTML, Expression Web adds an IFRAME element to your page and creates a JavaScript file to run the IFRAME element and an XSLT file to provide formatting. In ASP.NET, Expression Web adds an ASP XML control to your page, sets control properties, and creates an XSLT file. A Data View is a live, customizable view of an XML data source that you can sort, filter, or group.

Create a Data View

1. Open and display the HTML or ASP.NET page where you want to create a Data View in Design view.

2. To create a Data View with all XML data, drag the XML file onto your Web page from the Folder List task pane or the Data Source Source Library task pane.

3. To create a Data View with selected XML data, do the following:

    ◆ Click the **Data View** menu, and then click **Insert Data View**.

    ◆ In the Data Source Library task pane, select the XML data file, and then click **Show Data**.

    ◆ In the Data Source Details task pane, select the fields you want to insert in the Data View.

    ◆ Click **Insert Selected Fields as**, and then click **Single Item View** or **Multiple Item View** to insert the data.

    The data appears in a basic table layout, but you can change it later.

4. Place the insertion pointer in the table cells to edit the data; use the Delete submenu on the Table menu to remove elements.

5. Click the **Save** button on the Common toolbar, and then click **OK** to save the embedded file.

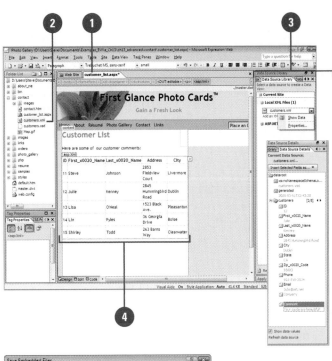

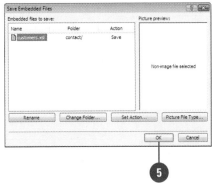

Working with Data in Data View

In a Data View, you can add, remove, or arrange columns, which displays data fields. After you display and position columns in Data View, you can sort and filter the data to display the information you want in the most effective way that works for you. A sort arranges all the data in a Data View by a field. You can sort by one or more fields in ascending (A to B or 1, 2, 3) or descending order (Z to A or 3, 2, 1). A filter displays data in a Data View by a field based on rules. A filter is built upon one or more expression rules, known as clauses, that get applied to the data. If the data meets the expression clauses, the data appears in Data View.

Modify the Columns in a Data View

1. Open and display the HTML or ASP.NET page with a Data View.

2. In Design view, select the Data View you want to change.

3. Click the **Data View** menu or **Data View Tasks** arrow, and then click **Edit Columns**.

4. To add a column, click the field you want to include, and then click **Add**.

5. To remove a column, click the field you want to delete, and then click **Remove**.

6. To arrange columns, click the field you want to move, and then click **Move Up** or **Move Down**.

7. Click **OK**.

Did You Know?

You can edit the data in Data View. In Expression Web, click in the xml table in Data View, and then edit the data. Editing changes in one field affect all cells. In the xml file or data source, click in the data fields, edit the data, and then export or save it.

Data View Tasks arrow

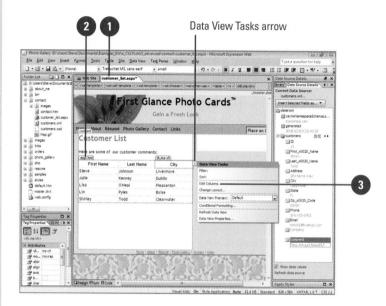

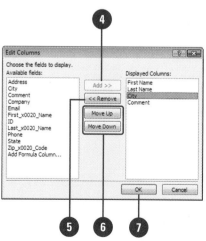

Sort Data in a Data View

1. Open and display the HTML or ASP.NET page with a Data View.

2. In Design view, select the Data View you want to change.

3. Click the **Data View** menu or **Data View Tasks** arrow, and then click **Sort**.

4. Click the field you want to sort on, and then click **Add**.

5. Click the **Ascending** or **Descending** option.

6. To sort on multiple fields, add more fields to the Sort Order list, and then click **Move Up** or **Move Down** to change the sort order.

7. Click **OK**.

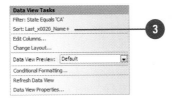

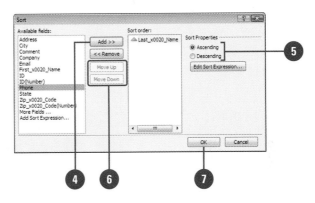

Filter Data in a Data View

1. Open and display the HTML or ASP.NET page with the Data View.

2. In Design view, select the Data View you want to change.

3. Click the **Data View** menu or **Data View Tasks** arrow, and then click **Filter**.

4. Click **Click here to add a new clause**.

5. Click the **Field Name**, **Comparison**, and **Value** boxes, and then specify the values or operator you want.

6. To add to a clause, click the **And/Or** box, click **And** or **Or**, and then repeat Steps 4 and 5.

7. To delete a clause, click the clause column arrow, and then press Delete.

8. Click **OK**.

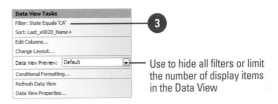

Use to hide all filters or limit the number of display items in the Data View

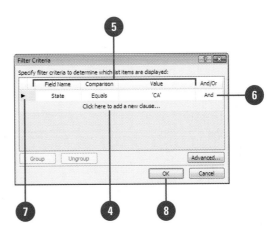

Formatting Data in a Data View

When you create a Data View, the data appears in a basic table layout. You can use formatting tools to manually change different aspects of the layout or apply one of the built-in layouts in Expression Web. If you use a built-in layout that displays fewer fields than your original Data View, those fields are removed from your Data View. In addition, any previous layout formatting is removed. If you want to manually format a Data View, you can change font formatting and color using tools on the toolbar, and apply styles and conditional formatting. When you change a data element in one field, the same data element change is applied to all the fields. As you format a Data View, Expression Web creates and modifies an external XSLT file.

Change the Layout of a Data View

1. Open and display the HTML or ASP.NET page with a Data View.

2. In Design view, select the Data View you want to change.

3. Click the **Data View** menu or **Data View Tasks** arrow, and then click **Change Layout**.

4. Select the layout style you want.

5. Click **OK**.

6. Click **Yes** or **No** to remove any previous custom formatting.

7. In Data View, edit or delete the data, and drag fields to add (from the Data Source Details task pane) or move them.

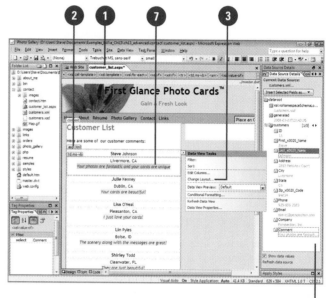

Fields in the Data Source Details task pane

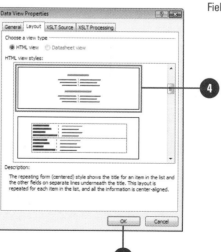

Did You Know?

You can manually format elements in Data View. In Design view, select the data in the Data View you want to format, and then click buttons on the Formatting toolbar to change font style, size, and color, and align text. You can also use the Apply Style task pane to apply formatting styles to data. When you change a data element in one field, the same data element change is applied to all the fields.

Apply Conditional Formatting to a Data View

1 Open and display the HTML or ASP.NET page with a Data View.

2 In Design view, select the Data View you want to format.

3 Click the **Data View** menu or **Data View Tasks** arrow, and then click **Conditional Formatting**.

4 In Data View, select any cell, except for the header cell, such as the HTML tag, data value, or range of text.

> **TIMESAVER** *Right-click inside a cell, point to Select, and then click Cell.*

5 Click **Create**, and then click **Apply Formatting**.

6 Click anywhere in the first row to add a new clause.

7 Click the **Field Name**, **Comparison**, and **Value** (and **More Fields**) arrows, and then specify the field, value, or comparison operator you want for the rules to apply the formatting.

8 Click **OK**.

9 Specify the formatting to apply when the conditions are met.

10 Click **OK**.

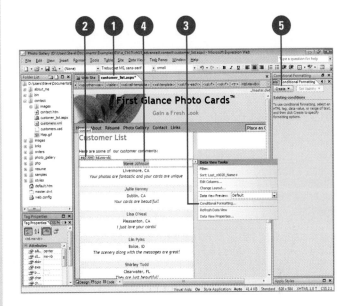

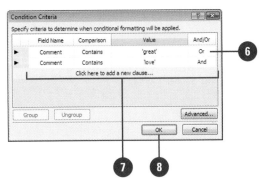

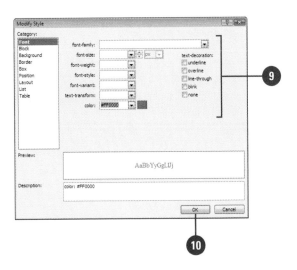

Did You Know?

You can change the data format type. In Design view, select the data in the Data View you want to format, click the Data View menu, point to Format Item as, and then click a formatting option: Text, Boolean, Number, Hyperlink, or Picture.

Checking XML Pages

When you create and work with an XML file, you need to make sure the XML code are written and formed correctly. The standards for XML tags and related attributes are stricter than those for HTML, so it's important that you check the file; otherwise, the file will not display correctly. For example, so much as a single missing tag or mis-formatted attributes makes the entire file unreadable.

Check for Well-Formed XML

1. Open the Web site with XML page you want to check.

2. Right-click the XML page in the editor, and then click **Verify well-formed XML**.

   If an error appears, the XML Validation dialog box appears, displaying a description of the error, and the line number of the error.

3. To display the error, click **Go To Error**.

4. Make the changes to fix the error.

5. Click the **Save** button on the Common toolbar to save the file; if prompted, click **Yes** to confirm the save.

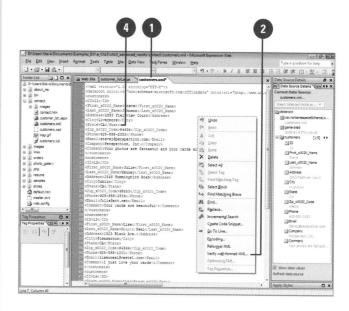

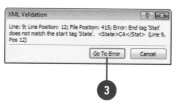

> ## Did You Know?
>
> **You can reformat XML for easier editing.** Open the Web site with the XML page you want to reformat, right-click the XML page in the editor, and then click Reformat XML.

Apply XML Formatting

1. Open the Web site and page you want to apply XML formatting.

2. Click the **Code** or **Split** button at the bottom of the window.

3. Right-click anywhere on the page, and then click **Apply XML Formatting Rules**.

   Expression Web scans the XML code for missing or incomplete tags.

See Also

See "Creating an XML Page" on page 326 for information on creating an XML page.

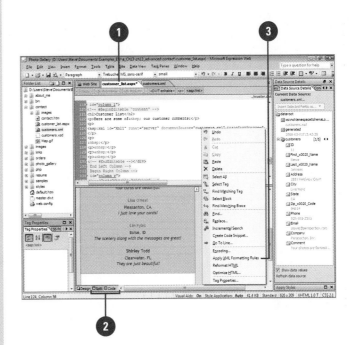

Adding RSS Feeds

An RSS (Really Simple Syndication) feed provides a way for Internet content publishers to make news, blogs, and other content available to subscribers in an standardized XML format. You can integrate RSS feeds in your Web pages. An RSS feed is an XML file that gets updated with new information. To add a local RSS feed to a Web page, add the XML file to the Data Source Library task pane, and then add the data from the XML file to your Web page, which creates a Data View.

Add RSS Feeds

1. Open the Web site and Web page you want to add a RSS feed.

2. If the XML file isn't in your Web site, do the following:

   ◆ Click the **Task Panes** menu, and then click **Data Source Library**.

   ◆ Under Local XML Files, click the **Add an XML file** link.

   ◆ Browse to and select the XML file, and then click **OK**.

3. Use either of the following to add the XML data to a page:

   ◆ **All Data.** Drag the XML file from the Data Source Library task pane into the RSS Web page in Design view.

   ◆ **Selected Data.** Place the cursor where you want to place the selected data in Design view, click the XML file, and then click **Show Data**. In the Data Source Details task pane, Ctrl+click to select the fields you want in the RSS Web page. Click **Insert Selected Fields as** and then click **Single Item View** to insert the RSS feed as a new Data View in the page.

See Also

See "Creating a Data View" on page 327 for information on using XML files to create a RSS feed in a Data View.

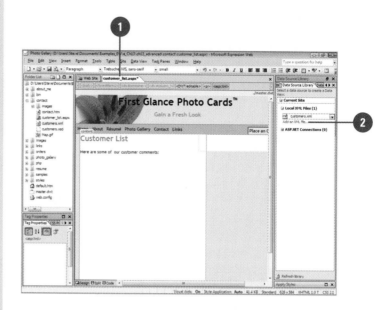

Use the Data Source Details task pane to insert selected data

Use XML file to insert all data

Publishing and Managing a Web Site

Introduction

Now that you know how to plan, build, and run a Microsoft Expression Web Web site, the only areas that remain are publishing and managing the Web site. Publishing a Web site is the process of copying all of the files that make up a Web site to a predetermined destination, while managing a Web site is the process of administering the day-to-day maintenance, which includes viewing reports and creating, assigning, and performing tasks.

You can publish copies of your Web site content files, and also copies of additional Expression Web files. However, it will require the server to display pages and perform Web functions. Using Remote Site view, you can publish an entire Web site or individual files. Expression Web can publish to any Web server running any version of the FrontPage Server Extensions (FPSE).

Expression Web also provides tools to help you make sure your Web site adheres to HTML and Accessibility industry standards. You can use Compatibility Reports to check the compatibility of your code to make sure your Web site works properly and complies to standards and rules, and you can use Accessibility Reports to check the compatibility of your Web site for the accessibility of users with disabilities.

What You'll Do

Generate Reports for a Web Site

Save or Copy a Web Site Report

Mark Site Files to Not Publish

Check for Accessibility

Check HTML Compatibility

Optimize HTML Before Publishing

Connect to a Remote Web Server

Publish a Web Site

Publish a Web Page

Update a Web Site

Change Web Site Settings

Generating Reports for a Web Site

Expression Web provides a collection of reports to help you manage your Web site. With Expression Web, you can generate reports on a wide variety of on-site activities, including a site summary, files, shared content, and problems. In the Files area, you can find out the age of all files, who is assigned to them, when they were last edited, and when they first appeared on your site. In the Problems area, you can produce reports on maintenance problems, such as large pages (big files download slowly) or pages containing broken hyperlinks. You can view any of the reports using Reports view. While you're viewing a report, you can sort information by category, filter information by category values, and edit individual entries.

View Reports for a Web Site

1. Click the **Site** menu, and then point to **Reports**.

2. Point to a submenu to display a list of reports.

   ◆ **Site Summary.** Displays an overview of your site's vital statistics, from number of files to number of hyperlinks.

   ◆ **Files.** Access reports: All Files, Recently Added Files, Recently Changed Files, Older Files, and Checkout Status.

   ◆ **Shared Content.** Access reports: Dynamic Web Templates, Master Pages, and Style Sheet Links.

   ◆ **Problems.** Access reports: Unlinked Files, Slow Pages, and Hyperlinks.

3. Click a report. The report opens.

4. To open other reports from within Reports view, click the list arrow at the left of the Reports View toolbar.

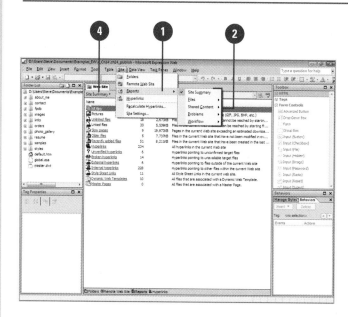

Work with Reports

① Click the **Site** menu, point to **Reports**, point to a submenu to display a list of reports, and then click a report.

② To sort choices in a report by the information in a column (Name, Title, etc.), click the column heading.

③ To filter a report by a specific column values, click the list arrow next to the column header, and then select a filter method.

◆ **All.** Removes a filter already in place.

◆ **Custom.** Opens the Custom AutoFilter dialog box, where you can apply a filter using two conditions.

④ To edit a field in a report, click the report line, click the field, and then edit the field or select an option from a list.

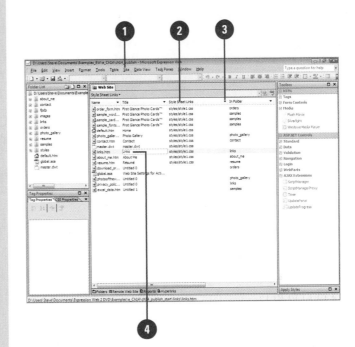

See Also

See "Customizing Reports View" on page 358 for information on changing the information gathered in Reports view.

Did You Know?

You can perform commands on the report files. Right-click a report entry, and then click a command, such as Open, Copy Report, Remove Filters, Publish Selected Files, Don't Publish, and Properties.

Saving or Copying a Web Site Report

After you create a site report, you can save or copy the data to HTML or into other Microsoft programs, such as Microsoft Office Word or Excel, which is helpful for sharing and saving the report information. You save a report as an HTML file in the same way you save a Web page. If you want to use report data in another program, you can quickly copy the report, switch to the other program, and then paste it.

Save a Web Site Report

1. Click the **Site** menu, point to **Reports**, point to a submenu to display a list of reports, and then select the report you want to save.

2. Modify the report to display the information you want.

3. Click the **File** menu, and then click **Save As**.

4. Navigate to the drive and folder location where you want to save the Web site report.

5. Type a name for the report file.

6. Click **Save**.

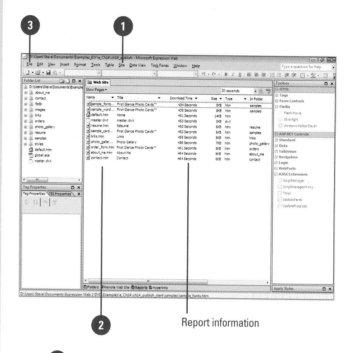

Report information

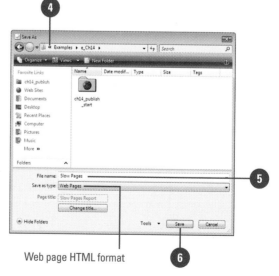

Web page HTML format

Copy a Web Site Report

1. Click the **Site** menu, point to **Reports**, point to a submenu to display a list of reports, and then select the report you want to save.

2. Modify the report to display the information you want.

3. Right-click anywhere in the report, and then click **Copy Report**.

4. Switch to the program where you want to copy the information.

5. Click to place the insertion point, and then click the **Paste** button on the toolbar or right-click the location, and then click **Paste**.

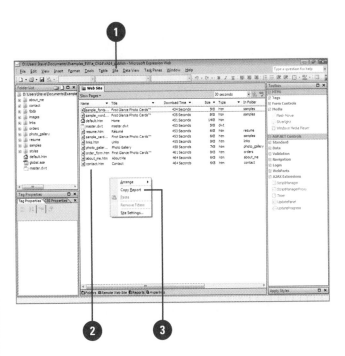

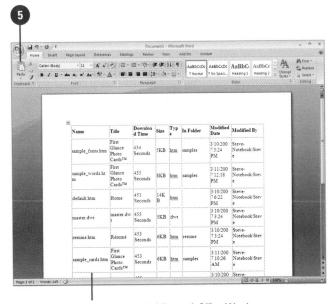

Pasted report in Microsoft Office Word

Marking Site Files to Not Publish

Before you publish your Web site, it's a good idea to check the publishing status of your site files. Some files may not be ready to publish on the Web. By default, all Web pages are marked "Publish," unless you change it. If a Web page is not ready, you can mark it "Don't Publish," which adds a red x to the file icon. You can use the All Files report to quickly review the marked files on your Web site and prevent you from accidentally publishing pages before they are ready.

Mark Site Files to Not Publish

1. Click the **Site** menu, point to **Reports**, point to **Files**, and then click **All Files** to display the files you want to mark.

2. Right-click the file you want to change, and then click **Don't Publish**.

3. To unmark a file to publish, right-click the file you want to change, and then click **Don't Publish** to deselect the check mark.

Don't Publish icon

Checking for Accessibility

Expression Web can help to check the compatibility of your Web site for the accessibility of users with disabilities. The Accessibility Checker checks your Web site to determine whether it meets industry-wide accessibility standards against WCAG and Section 508 requirements and provides a comprehensive report of the results. Priority 1 problems need to be corrected for a Web page to be compliant. Priority 2 problems should be fixed, but not essential. After you check for accessibility problems, the results appear in the Accessibility task pane, where you can review and fix any problems, and generate an HTML report.

Check for Accessibility

1 Click the **Tools** menu, and then click **Accessibility Reports**.

2 Click the option to specify which pages you want to search.

3 Select or clear the Check for check boxes you want to include or exclude.

4 Select or clear the Show check boxes you want to include or exclude.

◆ **Errors**. Shows priority 1 accessibility problems.

◆ **Warnings**. Shows possible accessibility problems.

◆ **Manual Checklist**. Lists the general requirements for the selected standards.

5 Click **Check**.

6 In the Accessibility task pane, right-click inside the pane, point to **Arrange**, and then select the arrangement type you want.

7 To correct a problem, double-click the entry to open the page, where you can correct the code.

8 To generate an HTML report, click the **Generate HTML Report** button.

9 When you're done, click the **Close** button in the task pane.

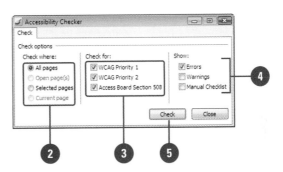

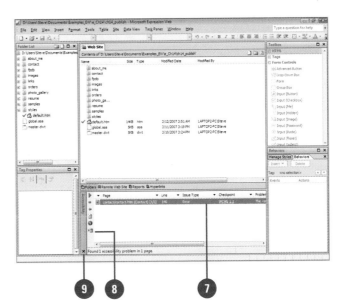

Checking HTML Compatibility

Expression Web can help to check the compatibility of your code to make sure your Web site works properly and complies to standards and rules. Expression Web uses the specified doctype declaration (such as XHTML 1.0 Transitional rules; the latest standard) to determine compatibility, which appears at the top of HTML pages. If a doctype doesn't exist, Expression Web uses a secondary schema, which is a set of rules that defines the elements and content used in an HTML document. In the Page Editor Options dialog box, you can select the Document Type Declaration and Secondary Schema standards you want. In Code view, invalid code appears with a red underline, while errors in code appear in yellow. When you point to it, a ScreenTip appears, informing you of the problem. After you create your site, you can check pages and CSS files—internal and external (**New!**)—for code errors and compatibility issues with the doctype and CSS schema you select. Results appear in the Compatibility task pane, where you can view and fix problems and generate an HTML compatibility report.

Select Compatibility Options

1. Click the **Tools** menu, and then click **Page Editor Options**.

    TIMESAVER *Double-click the doctype, schema, or CSS schema in the Status bar to open the Page Editor Options dialog box.*

2. Click the **Authoring** tab.

3. Click the **Document Type Declaration**, and then select the doctype you want; XHTML 1.0 Transitional is the current standard.

4. Click the **Secondary Schema** list arrow, and then select the schema you want.

5. Click **OK**.

> **Did You Know?**
>
> *You can view code errors in the Status bar.* The Status bar displays an icon when it finds incompatible code or a code error. The current Doctype and CSS version also appear on the Status bar.

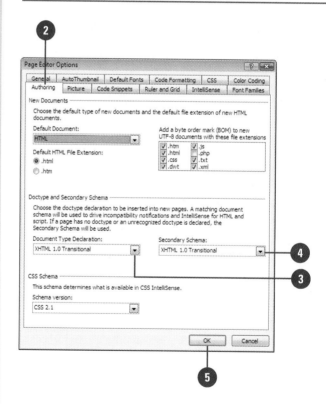

Search for Code Compatibility Problems

1 Click the **Tools** menu, and then click **Compatibility Reports**.

2 Click the option to specify which pages you want to search.

3 Click the **Check HTML/XHTML compatibility with** list arrow, and then select the schema you want to check incompatibility against.

4 Click the **Check CSS compatibility with** list arrow, and then select the CSS version you want to check internal and external (**New!**) CSS against.

5 If you have a doctype declaration on your pages, select the **Run check based on doctype declaration in page if available** check box.

6 Click **Check**.

The Compatibility task pane opens.

7 To correct a problem, double-click the entry to open the code page, where you can correct the code.

8 To sort or filter the results, use the following:

◆ **Sort the Results.** Click the name of the column in which you want to sort. To reverse a sorted list, click the name of the column again.

◆ **Filter the Results.** Click the down arrow next to the column heading, and then select the criterion to filter the results.

9 To generate an HTML compatibility report in Design view, click the **Generate HTML Report** button.

10 When you're done, click the **Close** button in the task pane.

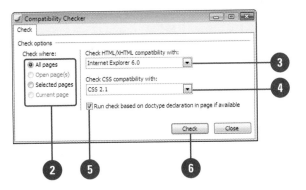

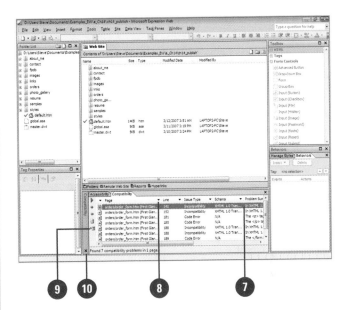

For Your Information

Viewing the Compatibility Task Pane

When you generate an HTML compatibility report, the Compatibility task pane provides the columns of information, which include Status, Page, Line, Issue Type, Schema, and Problem Summary. Status shows a file type icon and status. Page list the Web page with the issue. Line identifies the line in Code view with the issue. Issue Type is either Incompatibility or Code Error. Schema identifies the doctype or level of CSS that is incompatible. Problem Summary describes the issue.

Optimizing HTML Before Publishing

Sometimes Web developers leave things in Web pages, such as comments, whitespace, and other HTML attributes, which have no value to visitors. Expression Web allows you to optimize your HTML code when you publish a Web site or Web page or when you are working on a page in Design view. Optimizing HTML code makes the code easier to read and faster to download on the Web. Expression Web is more aggressive optimizing individual pages in Design view. If the changes cause problems you can undo the change.

Optimize Published HTML Code

1 Open the Web site you want to publish, click the **Site** menu, and then click **Remote Web Site**.

2 Click the **Remote Web Site Properties** button.

3 Click the **Optimize HTML** tab.

4 Select the **When publishing, optimize HTML by removing the following elements** check box.

5 Click the options you want. Some of the common ones include:

◆ **All HTML comments.** Select to remove all comments; selects all the comments check boxes.

◆ **HTML Whitespace.** Select either check box to remove leading or all whitespace.

6 Click **OK**.

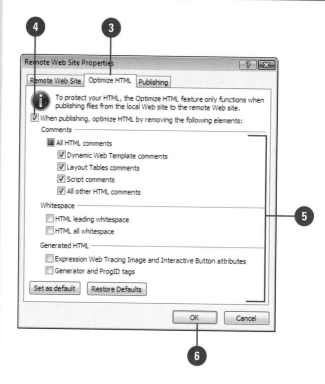

Optimize HTML Code in Design View

1. Open the Web page in which you want to optimize in Design view.

2. Click the **Tools** menu, and then click **Optimize HTML**.

3. Select the check boxes with the settings you want to optimize. Some of the common options include:

   ◆ **All HTML Comments.** Select to remove all comments; selects all the comments check boxes.

   ◆ **Merge Adjacent Tags.** Select to combine multiple tags into one.

   ◆ **Empty Tags.** Select to remove tags with no content.

   ◆ **Unused Styles.** Select to remove unused styles.

   ◆ **Word HTML.** Select to remove extra HTML elements from Microsoft Word.

4. Click **OK**.

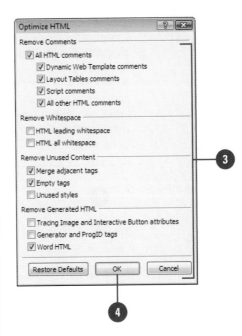

Connecting to a Remote Web Server

The Remote Site view allows you to compare the content of the current local Web site and a target remote Web site. Typically, the local Web site contains the development version of a site and the remote Web site on a Web server contains the "live" site on the Internet. Using Remote Site view, you can publish an entire Web site or individual files. If you display Remote Site view for a site you have not published, a blank window appears with the message *"Click the Remote Web Site Properties... to setup a remote site."* You can publish your files to a Web site with FrontPage Server Extensions, WebDAV (Distributed Authoring and Versioning), FTP (File Transfer Protocol), or Windows file system.

Specify the Remote Web Server Location

1. Open the Web site you want to publish, click the **Site** menu, and then click **Remote Web Site**.

2. Click the **Remote Web Site Properties** button.

3. Click the **Remote Web Site** tab.

4. Click the option with the remote Web server type in which you want to publish your files.

   ◆ **FrontPage Server Extensions.** The site is running FrontPage Server Extensions; use http://URL.

   ◆ **WebDAV.** The site supports WebDAV; use http://URL.

   ◆ **FTP.** The site supports FTP; use ftp://URL and the FTP directory path. Select or deselect the Use Passive FTP check box (**New!**). After you click OK (step 6), enter your user name and password, select the Remember my password check box (**New!**) to save login settings, and then click OK.

   ◆ **File System.** The site resides on a local or network drive; use C:\MyWeb or \\Server\MyWeb.

5. Type the remote Web site location or use **Browse** to select it.

6. Click **OK**.

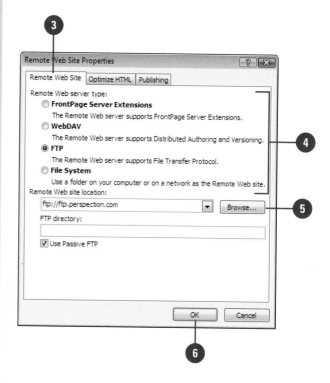

For Your Information

Working on and Publishing Web Sites

There are several ways to work on and publish a Web site. To work on your local computer and publish to the remote (final) production server, open the site on your computer and set your remote site to the production server site. To work on a remote staging server and publish to the remote production server, open the site directly from the remote staging server and set your remote site to the production server site. To work directly on the remote production server, open the site from the remote production server.

Change Publishing Properties

1. Open the Web site you want to publish, click the **Site** menu, and then click **Remote Web Site**.

2. Click the **Remote Web Site Properties** button.

3. Click the **Publishing** tab.

4. Click the publish options you want.

   ◆ **Changed pages only**

   ◆ **All pages, overwriting pages already on destination**

   ◆ **Include Subsites.** Select the check box to publish all Web sites contained within the main Web site.

5. Click the option you want to specify how Expression Web compares file in the two Web sites.

   ◆ **Determine changes by comparing source and destination sites**

   ◆ **Use source file timestamps to determine changes since last publish**

6. To keep a log of changes, select the **Log changes during publish** check box.

7. To display the log for the most recent publish operation, click **View Log file**.

8. Click **OK**.

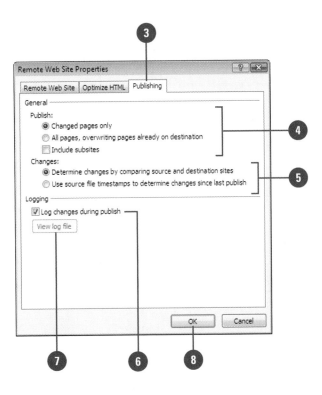

See Also

See "Customizing FTP Options" on page 359 for information on using the Use Passive FTP option.

For Your Information

Entering the Publishing Destination

When you publish your site to a folder on your local file system, you enter a location using the syntax *C:\\sitefolder*, where C is the drive letter. When you publish your site to a folder on a network server, you enter a location using the **Universal Naming Conventions (UNC)**. UNC is a convention that produces a machine-independent way to locate a file. The UNC name employs the syntax \\server\share\path\folder-name. When you publish your site to a folder on a Web server on the Web, you enter a Uniform Resource Locator (URL). A URL consists of three parts: the prefix http://, which indicates a Web address; a network identification, such as www for the World Wide Web; and a Web site name, or domain name, such as *perspection.com*.

Publishing a Web Site

Publishing a Web site refers to the process of copying all of the files that make up a Web site to a predetermined destination. In Expression Web, you typically publish your site for one of two reasons. The first reason is to launch the site on either a company intranet (a network limited to members of a specific group, usually a business) or on the World Wide Web. The second reason is to back up the site on either your computer or a network drive. Using the Expression Web Publish Web command you can publish all your Web files, only those that have been edited, or individual files. You can publish your Web files to a folder on your local or network drive, or on a Web server. When you publish a site, Expression Web maintains all the hyperlinks.

Publish a Web Site

1 Open the Web site you want to publish.

2 Click the **File** menu, and then click **Publish Site**.

3 If necessary, click the **Remote Web Site Properties** button to connect to a Web server.

4 Display the folder with the local Web site.

5 Display the folder with the remote Web site.

6 To view only specific files, click the **View** list arrow, and then select a view option: Folder Contents, Files to Publish, Files not to Publish, or Files in Conflict.

7 Click the **Local to remote** option.

8 Click **Publish Web Site**.

9 If a file conflict occurs, a dialog box appears, click **Ignore and Continue**, **Overwrite Remote Files**, or **Cancel**.

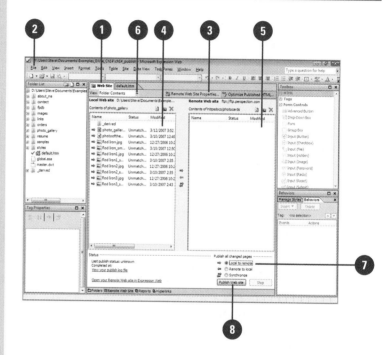

Publishing a Web Page

In addition to publishing an entire Web site, you can also publish individual files and folders. Instead of waiting for Expression Web to compare all the files to find the one or two you changed, you can quickly select the files and publish them. When you are working on a large Web site, publishing individual files gives you the control you need and saves times.

Publish a Web Page

1. Open the Web site you want to publish.

2. Click the **File** menu, and then click **Publish Site**.

3. Display the folder with the local Web site and select the Web page you want to publish.

4. Display the folder with the remote Web site.

5. Click the **Local to remote** option.

6. Click the **Right Arrow** (-->) button between the two Web sites.

7. If a file conflict occurs, a dialog box appears, click **Ignore and Continue**, **Overwrite Remote Files**, or **Cancel**.

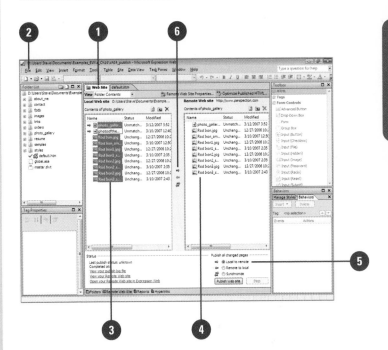

Did You Know?

You can publish an individual file in Folders view or Folder List. Right-click the file(s) you want to publish, and then click Publish Selected Files.

You can display certain files in the local Web site. In Remote Web Site view, click the View list arrow, and then click Folder Contents, Files to Publish, Files not to Publish, or Files in Conflict.

Updating a Web Site

Historically, a site that does not periodically update its material will not attract many repeat visitors. Housekeeping, therefore, is a crucial component of Web maintenance. You can opt to publish only those files that have been edited or altered in some way. Expression Web can compare the files in the working site on your local computer to the published files on the server, and determine if changes have been made on each file. If it detects a more recent version on your computer, that's what gets published. You can also choose which files you don't want to publish. For example, if a page is incomplete, not directly part of your Web site, or simply out-of-date, you can mark the file as Don't Publish. If you have multiple developers working on pages, the local and remote sites might become different. You can synchronize files from the remote site.

Set Options to Update a Web Site

① Open the Web site you want to update, and then modify the Web pages you want to update.

② Click the **File** menu, and then click **Publish**. An arrow appears next to files that need to be updated.

③ Click the **Remote Web Site Properties** button.

④ Click the **Publishing** tab.

⑤ Click the **Changed pages only** option.

⑥ Click **OK**.

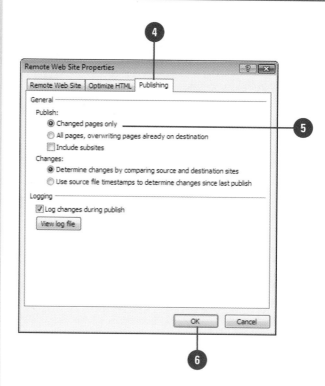

Update a Web Site

1. Open the Web site you want to update, and then modify the Web pages you want to update.

2. Click the **File** menu, and then click **Publish**. An arrow appears next to files that need to be updated.

3. To mark a file as don't publish, right-click the Web page you don't want to publish, and then click **Don't Publish**. A small stop sign icon appears next to the file.

4. Click the publishing option you want to use.

   ◆ **Local To Remote.** Copies changed files from the local to the remote site.

   ◆ **Remote To Local.** Copies changed files from the remote to the local site.

   ◆ **Synchronize.** Copies all remote files to local.

5. Click **Publish Web site**.

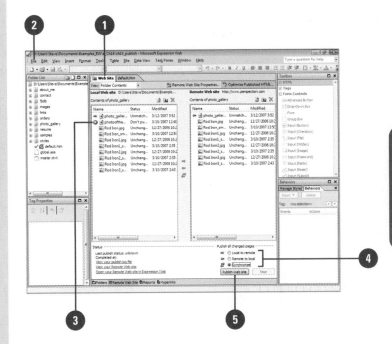

Changing Web Site Settings

Expression Web provides the Site Settings dialog box to specify options that affect an entire Web site. The dialog box contains five tabs including General, Preview, Advanced, and Language. The General tab allows you to change the Web site name, configure the use of metadata. Metadata is used by Dynamic Web Templates and Expression Web to maintain hyperlinks between pages, which is stored in hidden folders (that begin with _vti_). The Preview tab provides options to configure the way your Web site previews in a browser. The Microsoft Expression Development Server allows you to locally preview PHP and ASP.NET Web pages without having to install server software (**New!**). You can specify a PHP executable for previewing PHP pages for typical use or a specific Web site (**New!**). The Advanced tab specifies the script language used for form field validation, determines whether or not to show hidden files and folders, and allows for the deletion of temporary files. The Language tab specifies the language used for server messages and defines the encoding used for Web pages.

Change Web Site Settings

1. Click the **Site** menu, and then click **Site Settings**.

2. Click the **General** tab.

   ◆ Type a name for the Web site.

   ◆ To allow Expression Web to add hidden files to your site, select the **Manage the Web site using hidden metadata files** check box.

3. Click the **Preview** tab.

   ◆ If you want to preview PHP or ASP.NET Web pages on your local computer, click the **Preview using Web site URL** option, select the **Microsoft Expression Development Server** check box, and then click the **For only PHP and ASP.NET Web pages** or **For all Web pages** option.

   The For all Web pages option allows you to check non-PHP and ASP.NET pages too.

   Continue Next Page

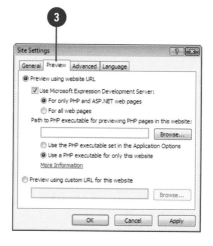

Expression Development Server provides PHP and ASP.NET support on your computer for development purposes; it gets installed with .NET Framework 3.5 or later.

General tab on the Application Options dialog box

Click Browse to select a PHP executable for typical use

◆ For PHP pages, click the **Use a PHP executable for only this website** option, and then click **Browse** to select a PHP executable to use; or click the **Use the PHP executable set in the Application Options** option, and then click **Browse** on the General tab of the Application Options dialog box to select a default PHP executable for typical use; click the **Tools** menu , and then click **Applications Options**.

4 Click the **Advanced** tab.

◆ Select the script language used for form field validation.

◆ To show hidden files and folders, such as the _vti folder with metadata.

IMPORTANT *You may also need to open the Folder Options dialog box in Windows and select the Show Hidden Files and Folders option. The default setting in Windows is to not show hidden files and folders.*

◆ To delete temporary files created by Expression Web, click **Delete Files**.

5 Click the **Language** tab.

◆ Select the language you want for server-side messages.

◆ Select the default page encoding (for character set compatibility) you want to use. The default for HTML encoding is Unicode (UTF-8).

6 Click **OK**.

Customizing Expression Web

Introduction

Once you've become familiar with Microsoft Expression Web and all the features it contains, you might want to customize the way you work with Expression Web. You can change the way Expression Web starts up and whether you want to check if Expression Web is the default editor for Web pages. You can also configure Expression Web to associate editors on your computer with a specific file type you want to use, which makes it easy to open and work with the files, or specify options to determine what information appears in reports.

You can set general options to specify when files are considered "Recent" or "Older", or the download time that qualifies a Web page for inclusion in the Slow Pages report. You can also set the connection speed, display row and column gridlines when viewing reports, and the maximum number of months shown in usage reports.

You can change the configuration of the menus and toolbars that you use. You can also create your own toolbar or menu for just the commands that you use when creating and formatting your pages.

Macros can simplify common repetitive tasks that you use regularly in Expression Web. Macros can even reside on a Expression Web toolbar for easy access. If a macro has a problem executing a task, Expression Web can help you debug, or fix the error in your macro.

If you need functionality not currently provided by Expression Web, you can install and load an add-in program, which provides add features to Expression Web. For example, you can install an add-in to use with Paypal, an e-commerce shopping cart. Add-ins are developed by Microsoft and third-party developers. You can search the Web to find Expression Web add-ins.

What You'll Do

Change General Options

Configure External Editors

Customize Reports View

Customize FTP Options

Set General Page Editor Options

Set Code Formatting Options

Change Code Snippet Options

Set Design View Formatting Options

Set Byte Order Mark Options

Customize the Menu Bar

Add and Remove Toolbar Buttons

Customize a Toolbar

Edit Toolbar Buttons and Menu Entries

Change Menu and Toolbar Options

Create Custom Colors

Understand How Macros Automate Your Work

Automate Your Work with Macros

Modify a Macro

Load and Unload Add-ins

Change Plug-in Properties

Changing General Options

You can customize several settings in the Expression Web work environment to suit the way you like to work. You can customize the way Expression Web starts up and whether it warns you about certain actions that you cannot undo. For example, one option automatically opens the last Web site you worked on when you start Expression Web. You can also set options to use your current Windows color scheme instead of the gray Expression Web 2 interface (**New!**) and show or hide the Status bar at the bottom of the Expression Web window.

Change General Options

1. Click the **Tools** menu, and then click **Application Options**.

2. Click the **General** tab.

3. Select the startup and general options you want. Some of the common options include:

   ◆ **Open last Web site automatically when Expression Web starts.** Opens the Web site you most recently worked on.

   ◆ **Check if Expression Web is the default editor for pages.** Verifies Expression Web is the standard editor for Web pages.

   ◆ **Use your current Windows color scheme.** Applies your Windows color scheme to the Expression Web application interface instead of the new gray color scheme (**New!**).

   The change takes effect when you restart Expression Web.

   ◆ **Show status bar.** Shows or hides the status bar.

4. To change proxy firewall settings for the Internet, click **Proxy Settings**.

5. Click **OK**.

6. If prompted, click **OK** to the dialog box for a color scheme change.

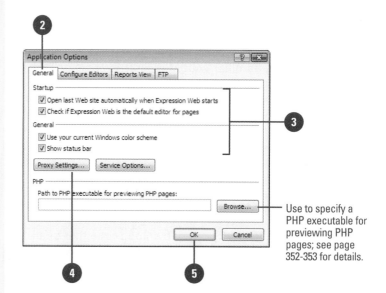

Use to specify a PHP executable for previewing PHP pages; see page 352-353 for details.

Configuring External Editors

You can configure Expression Web to associate any editor on your computer with any file type you want to use, which makes it easy to open and work with files. You can associate several editors with a file type. However, one of the editors is the default. Expression Web starts the default editor when you double-click the file in the Folder List, Folders view, and other file locations, or when you right-click the file and choose Open from the shortcut menu.

Configure External Editors

① Click the **Tools** menu, and then click **Application Options**.

② Click the **Configure Editors** tab.

③ To add a new extension, click the **New Extension** button, type the extension, select the editor you want to use, and then click **OK**.

④ To add a new editor, click the **New Editor** button, select the editor you want to use (if necessary, click **Browse** for more), and then click **OK**.

⑤ To add, rename, or remove an existing extension, select the extension, click the **Modify Extension** button, type the changes you want, and then click **OK**.

⑥ To set a default editor, select the extension, select the editor you want as the default, and then click **Make Default**.

⑦ Click **OK**.

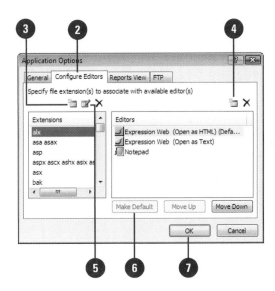

Customizing Reports View

You can customize the way information appears in Reports view by changing settings on the Reports View tab in the Applications Options dialog box. You can set general options to specify when files are considered "Recent" or "Older", or the download time that qualifies a Web page for inclusion in the "Slow Pages" report. You can also set the connection speed, display row and column gridlines when viewing reports, and the maximum number of months shown in usage reports.

Customize Reports View

1. Click the **Tools** menu, and then click **Application Options**.

2. Click the **Reports View** tab.

3. Select the general and usage options you want. Some of the common options include:

   ◆ **"Recent" files are less than** *X* **days old.** Determines which files appear in the Recently Added Files report.

   ◆ **"Older" files are more than** *X* **days old.** Determines which files appear in the Older Files report.

   ◆ **"Slow pages" take as least X seconds to download.** Determines whether a Web page appears in the Slow Pages report.

   ◆ **Number of months shown.** Determines the maximum number of months shown in usage reports.

4. To display a grid, select the **Display gridlines when viewing reports** check box.

5. To include a chart, select the **Include chart when usage report is saved** check box.

6. Click **OK**.

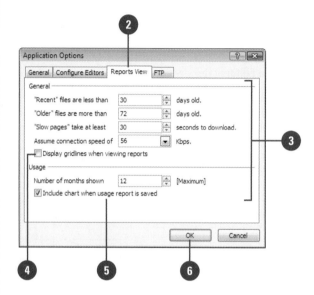

Customizing FTP Options

Expression Web allows you to customize FTP (File Transfer Protocol) transfer options for text files (ASCII). When you use FTP to transfer files, you can connect to another computer or server using passive or normal FTP (**New!**). Most network configurations work with either passive or normal FTP; however if one or the other doesn't work, you may need to try both settings. The passive FTP mode is more secure. When you transfer text files between a PC and Unix, click the FTP tab in the Application Options dialog box, and then specify the extensions you want to be treated as text files. You can add more extensions to the list; any extension not on the list is transferred as binary. If you no longer want an extension in the list, you can remove it.

Customize FTP Options

1. Click the **Tools** menu, and then click **Application Options**.

2. Click the **FTP** tab.

3. Select the **Use Passive FTP** check box to use passive FTP mode or deselect the check box to use normal FTP mode.

4. To add a new extension, type the extension, and then click **Add**.

5. Select the extension you want to remove, and then click **Remove**.

6. Click **OK**.

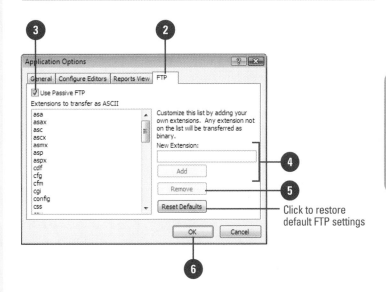

Click to restore default FTP settings

See Also

See "Connecting to a Remote Web Server" on page 346 for information on connecting to a server by using FTP.

For Your Information

Customizing ASP Options

If Expression Web allows you configure two settings applicable to Microsoft ASP.NET pages in your Web site. You can specify the folder that contains compiled versions of ASP.NET user controls available to the entire Web server and to the current Web site only. You can specify a folder or leave it blank to use the system default location. Click the Tools menu, click Application Options, click the ASP.NET tab, specify the default location for ASP.NET Control Assemblies, and then click OK. If Framework 3.5 is not installed correctly, the ASP.Net tab may not appear in the Application Options dialog box. Reinstall to show the tab.

Setting General Page Editor Options

Expression Web allows you to configure the way most features and functions work in a single location using the Page Editor Options dialog box. The Page Editor Options dialog box consists of 12 tabs that allows you set options in the following areas: General, Authoring, Auto-Thumbnail, Picture, Code Snippets, Ruler and Grid, IntelliSense, CSS, Code Formatting, Code Coloring, Default Fonts, and Font Families. The General tab provides varied options that don't fit in any of the other tabs.

Set General Page Editor Options

1. Click the **Tools** menu, and then click **Page Editor Options**.

2. Click the **General** tab.

3. Select the general and usage options you want. Some of the common options include:

   ◆ **Automatically enclose form fields within a form.** Happens on first field you insert.

   ◆ **Assign unique IDs to new tables.** Adds ID attribute to new tables; existing ones unchanged.

   ◆ **Make ID unique on paste.** Makes sure no duplicate IDs when you paste.

   ◆ **Use <strong> and <em> when using bold and italic toolbar buttons.** Uses updates tags for bold and italic; recommended.

   ◆ **Automatically switch keyboard to match language of surrounding text.** Use when you use different virtual keyboard layouts.

   ◆ **Prompt form accessibility properties when inserting images.** Prompts for accessibility information when you insert a picture.

4. Click **OK**.

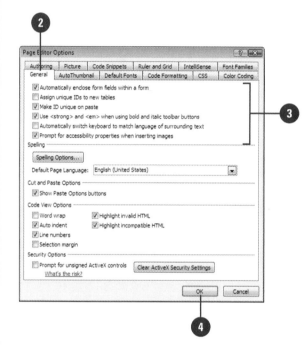

Change General Code Options

1. Click the **Tools** menu, and then click **Page Editor Options**.

2. Click the **General** tab.

3. Select the general code usage options you want. Some of the common options include:

   ◆ **Word wrap.** Select to automatically word wrap in Code view.

   ◆ **Auto indent.** Select to automatically indent based on the level and structure of the code.

   ◆ **Line numbers.** Select to display line numbers along the left side of Code view.

   ◆ **Selection margin.** Select to add a left margin in Code view to make selecting code easier.

   ◆ **Highlight invalid HTML.** Select to highlight invalid HTML code.

   ◆ **Highlight incompatible HTML.** Select to highlight incompatible HTML code with the current schema.

4. Click **OK**.

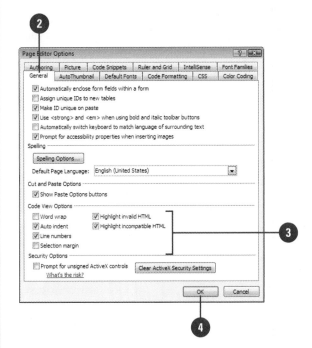

Setting Code Formatting Options

The Page Editor Options dialog box provides two tabs—Color Coding and Code Formatting—to make it easier to work with code. The Color Coding tab allows you to change the way individual elements appear in color while you work in Code or Design view. The Code Formatting tab provides options to format bookmarks, hyperlinks, and HTML, CSS, PHP (**New!**), and Script elements to suit your preferences and work habits. The settings at the top apply to all new code in Code view, while the CSS options at the bottom of the Code Formatting tab apply to existing and new CSS code.

Set Code Formatting Options

1. Click the **Tools** menu, and then click **Page Editor Options**.

2. Click the **Color Coding** tab.

3. Click the **Code view settings** option.

4. Select the element you want to change.

5. Use the Item foreground and Item background list arrows to select the colors you want.

6. Select or clear the **Font**, **Italic**, or **Underline** check boxes.

7. Repeat steps 4 through 6 for the elements you want to change.

8. Click **OK**.

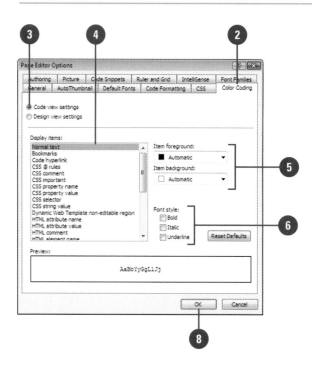

Did You Know?

You can change color coding for Design view elements too. On the Color Coding tab in the Page Editor Options dialog box, click the Design view settings option, select the element you want to change, use the Item foreground and Item background list arrows to select colors, select or clear Font style check boxes, repeat for the elements you want, and then click OK.

Set Code Formatting Options

1. Click the **Tools** menu, and then click **Page Editor Options**.

2. Click the **Code Formatting** tab.

3. Select the tab, indent, margin, and and other related settings you want at the top of the dialog box.

4. Select the tag you want to change, and then specify the line break and related options to the right you want.

5. Select the CSS element you want to change, and then specify the formatting options to the right you want.

6. Select the **Use shorthand properties when generating styles** check box to combine CSS properties in one element when needed to create complex CSS.

7. Click **OK**.

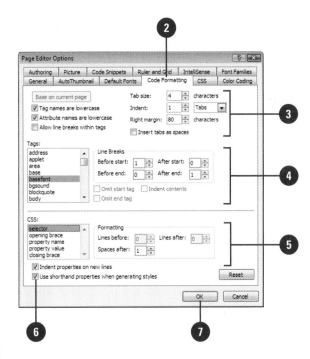

Changing Code Snippet Options

Code snippets allow you to reuse code while you work in Code view, which can save you time and cut down on errors. Expression Web comes installed with pre-existing snippets you can use. If you're not sure what is available, you can view a list of installed code snippets on the Code Snippets tab in the Page Editor Options dialog box, where you can also add, modify, or remove ones you no longer use. To insert a code snippet, switch to Code view, press Ctrl+Enter, and then select the code snippet you want from the dropdown list.

Change Code Snippet Options

1. Click the **Tools** menu, and then click **Page Editor Options**.

2. Click the **Code Snippets** tab.

3. Perform the options you want:

   ◆ **Add.** Click **Add**, type a unique keyword, description, the code you want to use as a snippet, and then click **OK**.

   ◆ **Modify.** Select the code snippet you want, click **Modify**, make the changes you want, and then click **OK**.

   ◆ **Remove.** Select the code snippet you want, and then click **Remove** to delete it.

4. Click **OK**.

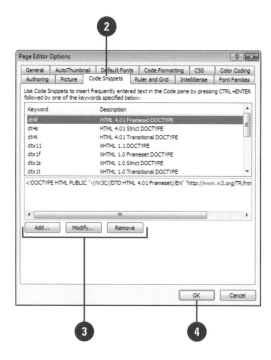

Did You Know?

You can reuse code snippets on other computers. When you add your code snippets, Expression Web stores them in an XML file called Snippets.xml located in the App\Roaming\Microsoft \Expression\Web Designer\Snippets folder, which you can move to other computers and reuse.

Setting Design View Formatting Options

The Color Coding tab on the Page Editor Options dialog box provides an option to make it easier to work with display elements in Design view. The Color Coding tab allows you to change the way individual elements appear in color while you work Design view. You can set foreground and background (when available) colors for a variety of display items, including Dynamic Web Template editable region, Layout site selection border, Layout positioning lines, Layout table border or cell, Master Page content region, and Web Part border. For some display items, such as Layout label, you can set font styles, including bold, italic and underline.

Set Design View Formatting Options

1. Click the **Tools** menu, and then click **Page Editor Options**.

2. Click the **Color Coding** tab.

3. Click the **Design view settings** option.

4. Select the element you want to change.

5. Use the Item foreground and Item background (if available) list arrows to select the colors you want.

6. Select or clear the **Font**, **Italic**, or **Underline** check boxes, if available.

7. Repeat steps 4 through 6 for the elements you want to change.

8. Click **OK**.

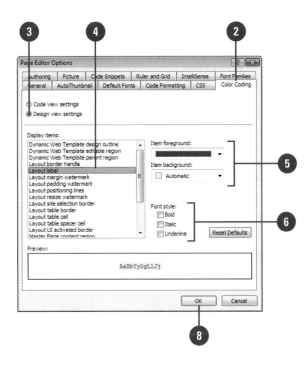

Setting Byte Order Mark Options

A Byte Order Mark (BOM) is a sequence of bytes embedded in a document that uses the Unicode encoding standard. The BOM helps make sure your documents are read correctly by some web browsers and servers. Expression Web allows you to add or remove a BOM in existing Web pages and documents as well as add a BOM to a new documents (**New!**). By default, Expression Web adds a BOM to new documents with extensions HTM, HTML, CSS, DWT, JS, TXT, or XML that are encoded as Unicode (UTF-8), unless you change it. Be aware that not all documents, such as PHP, or servers support BOM, so you should not add BOM to them, which add unwanted characters.

Add or Remove a BOM from an Existing Page or Document

1. Open the Web page or document you want to add or remove a BOM.

2. In Code view, right-click in the page, and then click **Encoding**.

   The Page Properties dialog box (for a Web page) or Text File Encoding dialog box (for a document) appears.

3. In the Page Properties dialog box, click the **Language** tab.

4. Select the **Include a byte order (BOM)** check box to add it to an existing page or document, or clear the check box to remove it.

   TROUBLE? *The BOM option is not available if the Save the document as or Save the current file as option is not set to Unicode (UTF-8).*

5. Click **OK**.

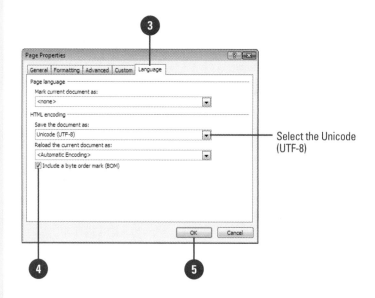

Select the Unicode (UTF-8)

Add or Remove a BOM to New Documents

1. Click the **Tools** menu, and then click **Page Editor Options**.

2. Click the **Authoring** tab.

3. Select the check boxes next to the extensions you want to add a BOM when you create new UTF-8 documents, or deselect the ones you don't want to have a BOM.

   ◆ **HTM** or **HTML.** A Web page.

   ◆ **CSS.** A Cascading Style Sheet document.

   ◆ **DWT.** A master page.

   ◆ **JS.** A JavaScript document.

   ◆ **PHP.** A PHP script page.

   ◆ **TXT.** A text document.

   ◆ **XML..** An XML page.

4. Click **OK**.

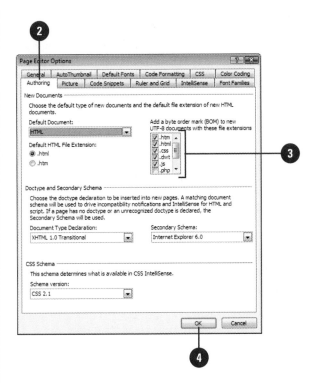

See Also

See "Changing Web Page Properties" on page 54 for information on the Unicode standard.

See "Working with Template Content" on page 26 for information on master pages.

Customizing the Menu Bar

You can customize the existing Expression Web menu bar by adding buttons, commands, and macros that you use frequently. Adding items to the menu bar is a great way to have easy access to features without adding more buttons or toolbars. The ability to drag features from different parts of the program window makes it easy to add items to the menu bar. Imagine, having a menu with all of your most commonly used formatting, sorting, or printing commands.

Customize the Menu Bar

① Click the **Tools** menu, and then click **Customize**.

② Click the **Commands** tab.

③ Select a category.

④ To add a command, drag the command to the appropriate place on the menu you want to modify. A solid horizontal line appears below the place where the new menu command will be placed.

⑤ To remove a command, drag the menu command you want to remove to an empty area in the workspace.

⑥ Click **Close**.

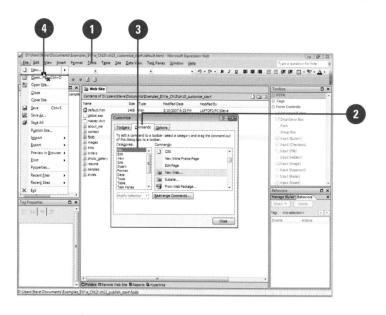

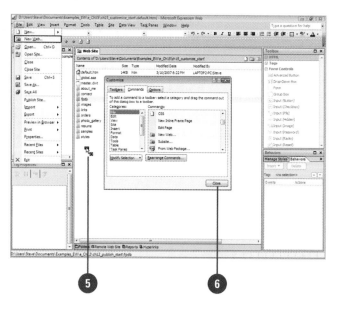

Did You Know?

You can assign an accelerator key to a menu. An accelerator key is the key you press to display a menu or run a menu command. For example, the accelerator key for the File menu is "F." To add an accelerator key to a menu item, type an ampersand (&) before the letter that will be the accelerator key. For example, enter the menu name "&New Menu" to create the menu entry New Menu with the accelerator key "N."

Create a New Menu

1. Click the **Tools** menu, click **Customize**, and then click the **Commands** tab.

2. Click **New Menu** in the Categories box.

3. Drag New Menu from the Commands list to an empty spot on the menu bar.

4. Click **Close**.

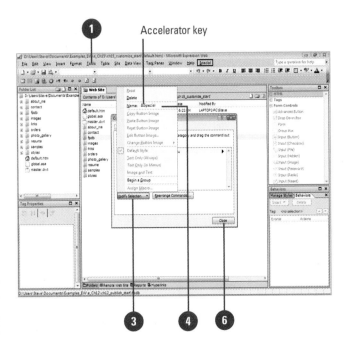

Name a New Menu

1. Click the **Tools** menu, and then click **Customize**.

2. Click **New Menu** on the menu bar.

3. Click **Modify Selection**.

4. Click the Name box on the menu, and then type a new name.

5. Press Enter.

6. Click **Close**.

> **Did You Know?**
>
> **You can copy a command to toolbars and menus.** Copy commands from other menus or toolbars to new menus and toolbars by pressing and holding Ctrl as you drag the new command.

Accelerator key

Adding and Removing Toolbar Buttons

Each toolbar initially appears in a default configuration, but many toolbars actually contain many more commands than are displayed. When monitors are set to low resolution, sometimes not all toolbar buttons are visible. You can modify Expression Web's toolbars so that they display only the buttons you want. For example, you can add buttons to a toolbar for commands you frequently use, or you can remove buttons from toolbars that have too many. You can also use the Add Or Remove command on the Toolbar Options menu to quickly show or hide buttons on a toolbar. If a button doesn't appear on the button list for a toolbar, you can add it. If you no longer need a button on the button list, you can remove it.

Show or Hide a Toolbar Button

1. Click the **Toolbar Options** list arrow on the toolbar.

2. Point to **Add or Remove Buttons**.

3. Click to select or clear the check box next to the button you want to show or hide.

4. Click outside the toolbar to deselect it.

Did You Know?

You can use the Customize dialog box to show and hide toolbars. Click the Tools menu, click Customize, click the Toolbars tab, select or clear the check box next to the toolbar name you want to show or hide, and then click Close.

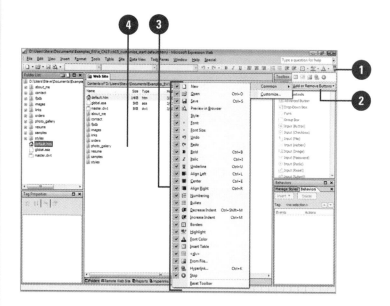

Add or Remove a Toolbar Button

1. Click the **Tools** menu, and then click **Customize**.

2. Click the **Commands** tab.

3. Click the category containing the toolbar button you want to add.

4. Drag a command from the Commands tab to the toolbar to add a button, or drag a button off a toolbar to a blank area to remove it.

5. Click **Close**.

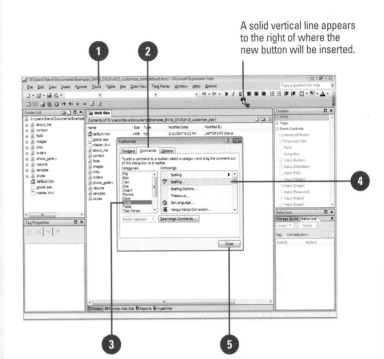

A solid vertical line appears to the right of where the new button will be inserted.

See Also

See "Changing Menu and Toolbar Options" on page 375 for information on changing general options for menus and toolbars.

Did You Know?

The Customize dialog box uses a special operating mode. When you use the Customize dialog box, menus and toolbars don't act in the normal way. The special mode allows you to drag-and-drop items on menus and toolbars.

Customizing a Toolbar

You can create your own toolbars to increase your efficiency. You might, for example, create a toolbar that contains formatting and other features that you use most often when you are performing a particular task, such as editing Web pages. This will give you a greater workspace, since you will not have to have all the various toolbars up at once. Using one toolbar will help you achieve this.

Create a Custom Toolbar

① Click the **Tools** menu, and then click **Customize**.

② Click the **Toolbars** tab.

③ Click **New**.

④ Type a name for the new toolbar.

⑤ Click **OK**.

⑥ Add buttons to the new toolbar by dragging commands found on the Commands tab.

⑦ Click **Close**.

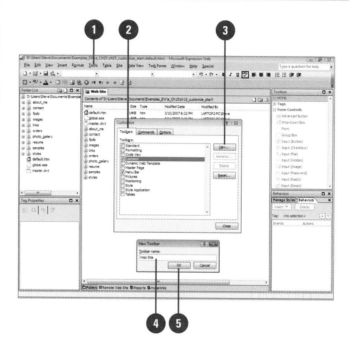

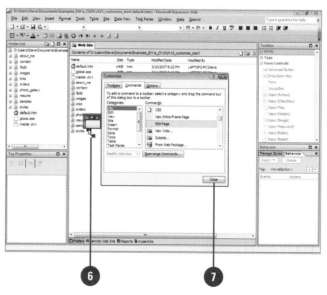

Delete a Custom Toolbar

1. Click the **Tools** menu, and then click **Customize**.

2. Click the **Toolbars** tab.

3. Click the toolbar name you want to delete.

4. Click **Delete**.

5. Click **Close**.

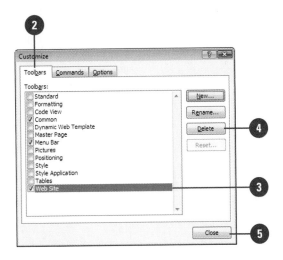

Rename a Custom Toolbar

1. Click the **Tools** menu, and then click **Customize**.

2. Click the **Toolbars** tab.

3. Click the toolbar name you want to rename.

4. Click **Rename**.

5. Type a name for the toolbar.

6. Click **OK**.

7. Click **Close**.

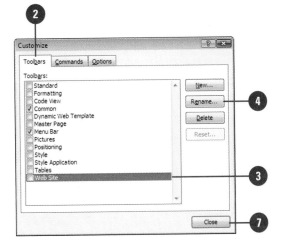

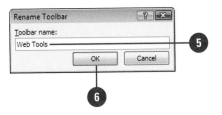

Editing Toolbar Buttons and Menu Entries

Expression Web includes tools that allow you to edit toolbar buttons and menu entries. You can specify whether the button or menu item will display text, an image, or both text and an image. If you choose to display an image, you can edit the image, copy it from another button or use one of Expression Web's predefined images. You can also use the Customize dialog box to makes these and other changes to your buttons and menus.

Edit a Button or Menu Entry

1 Click the **Tools** menu, and then click **Customize**.

2 Select the button on the toolbar or command on the menu you want to edit.

3 Click **Modify Selection**.

4 Choose the commands that will modify the selection in the way you prefer.

◆ Click **Copy Button Image** to copy the button image.

◆ Click **Paste Button Image** to paste the button image.

◆ Click **Reset Button Image** to reset the selected item to its default image.

◆ Click **Edit Button Image** to edit the button image.

◆ Click **Change Button Image** to select from a group of predefined images, as shown.

◆ Click **Image and Text** to paste a button image into the selected item.

◆ Click **Begin a Group** to begin a group of menu items, separated by horizontal lines.

5 Click **Close**.

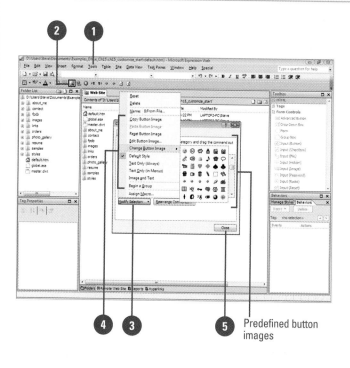

Predefined button images

Changing Menu and Toolbar Options

In addition to creating, adding, or removing menu command and toolbar buttons, you can also use the Customize dialog box to make global changes to menus and toolbars to personalize the Expression Web interface. The Options tab allows you to reset menu and toolbar changes, show the Standard and Formatting toolbars on one row to save space, and always show full menus so you don't have to wait or click the expand arrow. If you do not want to view ScreenTips, you can turn them off.

Change Menu and Toolbar Options

① Click the **Tools** menu, and then click **Customize**.

② Click **Options** tab.

③ Select the general options you want. Some of the common options include:

◆ **Show Standard and Formatting toolbars on two rows**. Displays the Standard and Formatting toolbars on two rows.

◆ **Always show full menus.** Displays the full contents of a menu as soon as you open the menu.

◆ **List font names in their font.** Displays fonts in the Font menu using the actual font.

◆ **Show ScreenTips on toolbars.** Displays descriptive text when you move the pointer over a toolbar button.

◆ **Show shortcut keys in ScreenTips.** Displays the shortcut key for a button along with the ScreenTip.

④ To reset personalized menus and toolbars to the default, click **Reset menu and toolbar usage data**.

⑤ Click **Close**.

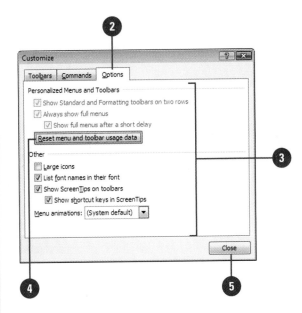

Creating Custom Colors

RGB (red, green, blue) is a set of color values that describe colors. RGB identifies a color by a set of hexadecimal numbers, an internal computer numbering scheme, that specify the amounts of red, green, and blue needed to create the color. RGB colors appear best over the Web (true color representation without dithers or substitutes) when you use only **browser safe colors**, which is a standard set of 216 color combinations. These RGB values are 0, 51, 102, 153, 204, or 255 in decimal or 00, 33, 66, 99, CC, or FF in hexadecimal. When you use the color dialog boxes, you use decimal values. In Code view, you use hexadecimal values. You can access and create colors using any Expression Web color menu. You can define up to 16 different colors, and then save them to a custom palette. The custom colors become available on all color menus.

Define a Custom Color Palette

① Open and display the Web page you want to use.

② Click any color list arrow (such as **Font Color** button list arrow) to open a color palette.

③ Click **More Colors** on the color palette.

④ Click **Custom**.

⑤ Click a blank box.

⑥ Select a color by entering a combination of numerical values, or selecting one of the basic colors in the main palette or a custom color in the color spectrum palette.

⑦ Click **Add to Custom Colors**.

⑧ When you're done, click **OK**.

⑨ Click **OK** again to close the More Colors dialog box.

⑩ Click **OK** to close the Page Properties dialog box.

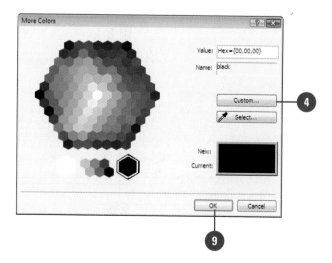

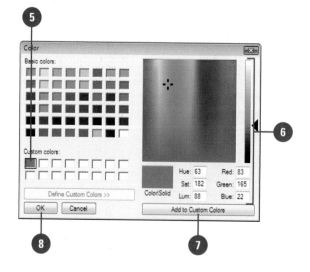

Remove a Custom Color

1. Open and display the Web page you want to use.

2. Click any color list arrow (such as **Font Color** button list arrow) to open a color palette.

3. Click **More Colors** on the color palette.

4. Click **Custom**.

5. Click the box with the color you want to remove.

6. Click the white color in the standard color palette.

7. Click **Add to Custom Colors**.

8. When you're done, click **OK**.

9. Click **OK** again to close the More Colors dialog box.

10. Click **OK** to close the Page Properties dialog box.

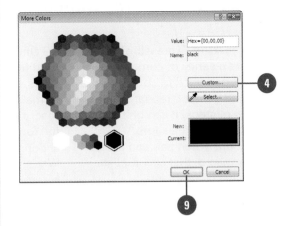

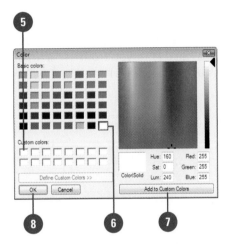

Understanding HSL Colors

Color	Description
Hue	The color itself; every color is identified by a number, determined by the number of colors available on your monitor.
Saturation	The intensity of the color. The higher the number, the more vivid the color.
Luminosity	The brightness of the color, or how close the color is to black or white. The larger the number, the lighter the color.

Understanding How Macros Automate Your Work

To complete many tasks in Expression Web, you need to execute a series of commands and actions. If you often need to complete the same task, you'll find yourself repeatedly taking the same series of steps. It can be tiresome to continually repeat the same commands and actions when you can create a mini-program, or macro, that accomplishes all of them with a single command.

When you create a macro, Expression Web stores the list of commands with any name you choose. You can store your macros in Microsoft Expression Web or All Open Projects. Storing your macros in Expression Web makes the macros available to you from any location in Expression Web, even when no project is open.

Once a macro is created, you can make modifications to it, add comments so other users will understand its purpose, and test it to make sure it runs correctly. You can run a macro by choosing the Macro command on the Tools menu, or by using a shortcut key or clicking a toolbar button you've assigned to it. When you click the Tools menu, point to Macro, and then click Macros. The Macro dialog box opens, where you can run, edit, test, or delete any Expression Web macro on your system, or create a new one.

If you have problems with a macro, you can step through the macro one command at a time, known as **debugging**. Once you identify any errors in the macro, you can edit it.

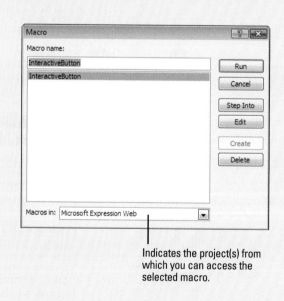

Indicates the project(s) from which you can access the selected macro.

You can create and edit a macro with the Microsoft Visual Basic Editor, which comes with Expression Web. Macro code is written in Microsoft Visual Basic, a programming language.

Each action listed in a macro either performs a step or states what attributes are turned on (true) or off (false). Quotation marks are used to indicate typed text, and the terms **Sub** and **End Sub** are used to indicate the beginning and ending of subroutines, respectively.

Because not everyone wants to read through codes to figure out what a macro does, comments are often included within the code. The comments don't affect the macro; they simply clarify its purpose or actions for a person viewing the code. Comments can be used to help you remember why you took the steps you did, or to help co-workers understand what is going on in the macro and how the macro should be used. A comment always begins with an apostrophe to distinguish it from a command code.

To learn more about macro code, check out Visual Basic titles on the Que Publishing Web site at *www.quepublishing.com*.

A comment describing the macro

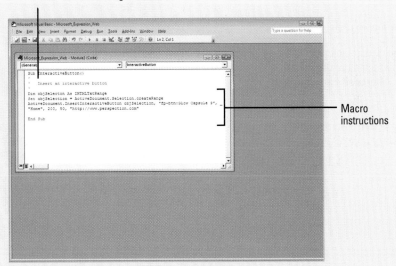

Macro instructions

Automating Your Work with Macros

Do you often redo many tasks that require the same, sometimes lengthy, series of steps? Rather than repeat the same actions, you can work faster by recording the entire series of keystrokes and commands in a custom command, or **macro**. A macro is a sequence of commands and entries that can be activated collectively by clicking a toolbar button, clicking a menu command, typing a key combination, or clicking the Run command in the Macros dialog box. Macros are a perfect way to speed up routine formatting, combine multiple commands, and automate complex tasks. Any time you want to repeat that series of actions, you can "play," or run, the macro.

Record a Macro

1. Click the **Tools** menu, point to **Macro**, and then click **Macros**.

    TIMESAVER *Press Alt+F8 to open the Macros dialog box.*

2. Type a name for the new macro.

3. Click **Create**.

    The Microsoft Visual Basic window opens, where you can create a macro.

4. Type your macro code.

5. When you're done, click the **File** menu, and then click **Close and Return to Microsoft Expression Web**.

    TIMESAVER *Press Alt+Q to close and return to Expression Web.*

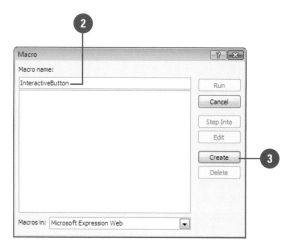

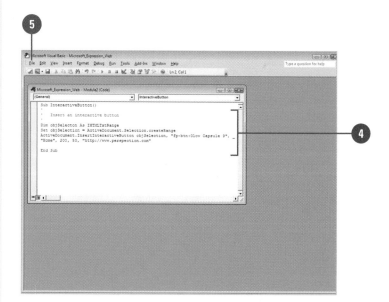

Run a Macro

1. Click the **Tools** menu, point to **Macro**, and then click **Macros**.

2. If necessary, click the **Macros In** list arrow, and then click the page that contains the macro you want to run.

3. Click the name of the macro you want to run.

4. Click **Run**.

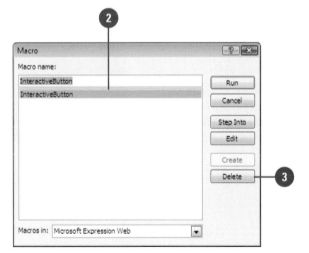

Interactive button

Delete a Macro

1. Click the **Tools** menu, point to **Macro**, and then click **Macros**.

2. Select the macro you want to remove.

3. Click **Delete**.

4. Click **Yes** to confirm the deletion.

Modifying a Macro

If a macro doesn't work exactly the way you want it to, you can fix the problem. Expression Web allows you to **debug**, or repair, an existing macro so that you can change only the actions that aren't working correctly. When beginning the process, Expression Web will step through each of the actions that you supplied when you created the macro. Look carefully for any mistakes, and then correct as necessary.

Debug a Macro Using Step Mode

1. Click the **Tools** menu, point to **Macro**, and then click **Macros**.

   TIMESAVER *Press Alt+F8 to open the Macros dialog box.*

2. Click the name of the macro you want to debug.

3. Click **Step Into**.

   The Microsoft Visual Basic window opens, where you can edit your macro.

   TIMESAVER *Press Alt+F11 to open the Visual Basic Editor program.*

4. Click the **Debug** menu, and then click **Step Into** to proceed through each action.

5. When you're done, click the **File** menu, and then click **Close and Return to Microsoft Expression Web**.

   TIMESAVER *Press Alt+Q to close and return to Expression Web.*

6. Click **OK** to stop the debugger.

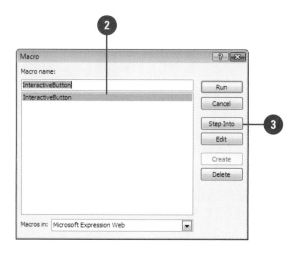

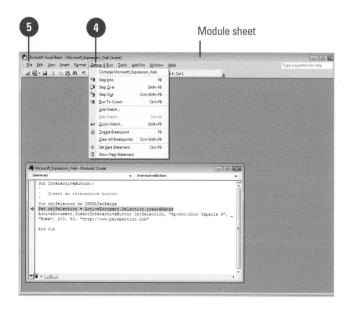

Module sheet

Loading and Unloading Add-ins

Add-ins are additional programs designed to run and add functionality within Expression Web. **Component Object Model (COM)** add-ins are designed to run in one or more programs and use the file name extension .dll or .exe. Some add-ins are installed when you run the Setup program, while others can be downloaded from Microsoft or purchased from third-party vendors. You can use the COM Add-Ins dialog box to add (load) or remove (unload) add-ins. When you load an add-in, the feature may add a command to a menu or toolbar. You can load one or more add-ins. If you no longer need an add-in, you should unload it to save memory and reduce the number of commands. When you unload an add-in, you also may need to restart Expression Web to remove an add-in command from a menu or toolbar.

Load or Unload a COM Add-in

1. Click the **Tools** menu, and then click **Add-Ins**.

2. Select the check box next to the add-in you want to load, or clear the check box you want to unload.

   TROUBLE? *If the add-in is not available in the list, click Add, locate and select the add-in you want, and then click OK.*

3. To remove the selected add-in, click **Remove**.

4. Click **OK**.

Did You Know?

You can get more information about COM online. Visit *www.microsoft.com/com.*

You can get add-ins from WebAssist; some are free. Visit *www.webassist.com,* and then search for Expression Web add-ins.

Changing Plug-in Properties

A plug-in is different than an add-in. A plug-in is a software module that integrates into Web browsers to offer a range of interactive and multi-media features. If you open a Web page with an object that uses a plug-in, such as an MPEG movie file, you can change plug-in properties in Expression Web. You can change the path to the data source, and object size and layout. You can also include a message for browsers without support for the plug-in.

Change Plug-in Properties

1. Open and display the Web page with the plug-in based object you want to change.

2. Double-click the plug-in based object.

3. Perform the options you want (options vary depending on the selected object):

   ◆ **Data Source.** Specify the path and file to the data source.

   ◆ **Message for browsers without plug-in support.** Enter the message you want a browser to display when it doesn't support the plug-in.

   ◆ **Size.** Specify the height, width, and weather to hide the plug-in.

   ◆ **Layout.** Specify options for alignment, border thickness, and horizontal and vertical spacing.

4. Click **OK**.

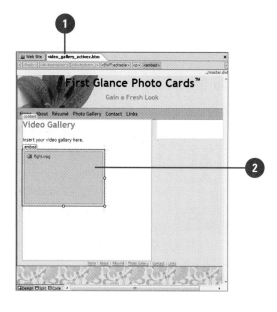

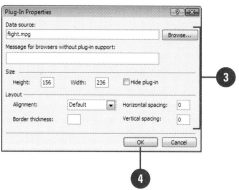

Working with Expression Studio

Introduction

Expression Web is part of the Microsoft Expression Studio, which includes Expression Design, Media, and Blend. **Expression Design** is a professional illustration and graphic design tool that lets you build compelling elements for both Web and desktop application user interfaces. **Expression Media** is an asset management tool to visually catalog and organize all your digital assets for effortless retrieval and presentation. **Expression Blend** is the professional design tool to create engaging, Web-connected, rich experiences for users on the Web. If you don't have the Expression Studio software, you can purchase and download it online at *www.microsoft.com/expression* or you can download trial versions of each program and take them for a test drive.

The Expression Studio programs work together to create graphics and organize media for use on the Web. In terms of a process, you can use Expression Design to create vector and bitmapped graphics for use in Expression Blend and Expression Web, and store and organize them along with other media in Expression Media.

Expression Blend and Expression Encoder allow you to create Silverlight media applications, which you can insert into Web pages with Expression Web and display in a Web browser with the Microsoft Silverlight cross-browser, cross-platform plug-in. Microsoft Silverlight is an exciting new technology that helps you design, develop, and deliver media-enabled experiences and rich interactive applications for the Web.

What You'll Do

Explore Expression Design

Get Started with Expression Design

Work with Expression Design

Explore Expression Media

Manage Media with Expression Media

Explore Expression Encoder

Use Expression Encoder

Explore Expression Blend

Work with Expression Blend

Add Interactivity with Expression Blend

Exploring Expression Design

Expression Design is a professional illustration and graphic design tool that lets you build compelling elements for both Web and desktop application user interfaces.

Expression Design provides extensive drawing tools that lets you create vector and bitmapped graphics for use in other programs, such as Expression Web, Expression Blend, or Microsoft Office. Vector graphics are comprised of anchor points connected to each other by lines and curves, called **vectors**. Because they are general descriptions of the coordinates of a shape, they are resolution-independent; that is they can be resized with-

out any loss to the quality of the graphic. Bitmapped graphics are made up of small, colored squares, called **pixels** that form a grid. Because of this, bitmaps are dependent on resolution (the number of pixels in the grid). Resizing up or down forces pixels to be created or removed to accommodate the new grid size, which can result in a loss of image quality.

Before you can create or edit a graphic in Expression Design, you need to open or create one, known as a document. With an open document, you can explore the user interface in Expression Design.

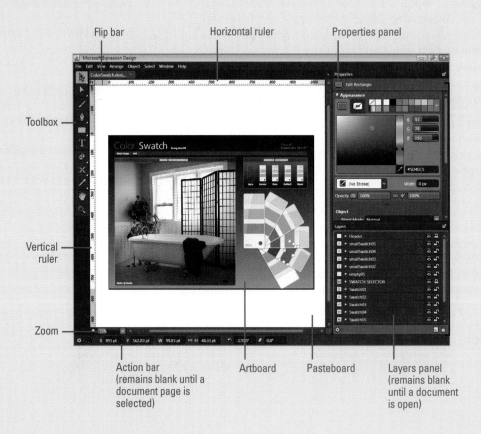

Flip bar   Horizontal ruler   Properties panel

Toolbox

Vertical ruler

Zoom

Action bar
(remains blank until a
document page is
selected)

Artboard   Pasteboard

Layers panel
(remains blank
until a document
is open)

Getting Started with Expression Design

You can either open an existing graphic or create one of your own. You can use the Open command on the File menu to browse and select the graphic you want to change. To create your own graphic, you open a new document and specify an artboard size and resolution. A blank new document window appears, where you can create your art work, known as the **artboard**. You can also use the area outside the artboard, known as the **pasteboard**, to work with graphic elements. Anything on the pasteboard, including overlapping elements, doesn't appear in the graphic.

Create a New Document in Expression Design

1. Click the **Start** button, point to **All Programs**, click **Microsoft Expression**, and then click **Expression Design**.

2. Click the **File** menu, and then click **New**.

3. Enter a name for the document.

4. Click the **Presets** list arrow, and then select an artboard size, or enter a width and height.

5. Enter a resolution value for the type of graphic you want to create (96 ppi is the standard for on-screen display; 72 ppi is standard for Web graphics; and 220 ppi is a minimum for print graphics).

6. Click **OK**.

   A frame appears, displaying the artboard.

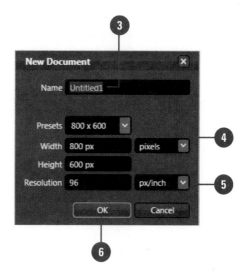

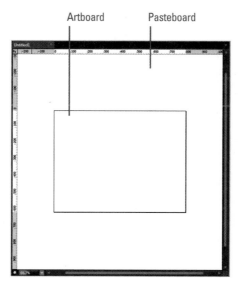

Artboard   Pasteboard

Did You Know?

You can open an existing graphic. Click the File menu, click Open, navigate to the graphic file you want, and then click Open.

You can open a variety of existing graphics. You can open the following file types: PSD, GIF, PNG, BMP, JPEG, WMPhoto, TIFF, ICO, and related extensions.

Working with Expression Design

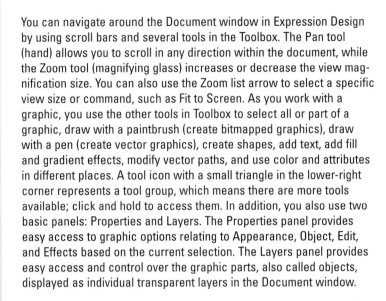

You can navigate around the Document window in Expression Design by using scroll bars and several tools in the Toolbox. The Pan tool (hand) allows you to scroll in any direction within the document, while the Zoom tool (magnifying glass) increases or decrease the view magnification size. You can also use the Zoom list arrow to select a specific view size or command, such as Fit to Screen. As you work with a graphic, you use the other tools in Toolbox to select all or part of a graphic, draw with a paintbrush (create bitmapped graphics), draw with a pen (create vector graphics), create shapes, add text, add fill and gradient effects, modify vector paths, and use color and attributes in different places. A tool icon with a small triangle in the lower-right corner represents a tool group, which means there are more tools available; click and hold to access them. In addition, you also use two basic panels: Properties and Layers. The Properties panel provides easy access to graphic options relating to Appearance, Object, Edit, and Effects based on the current selection. The Layers panel provides easy access and control over the graphic parts, also called objects, displayed as individual transparent layers in the Document window.

Work with Expression Design

1 Click the **Start** button, point to **All Programs**, click **Microsoft Expression**, and then click **Expression Design**.

2 Click the **File** menu, click **New**, use the default settings and then click **OK**.

3 Click the **Window** menu, and then click **Layer** to hide the panel, so you can view the Properties panel.

4 Click and hold the **Rectangle** tool in the Toolbox, and then click the **Polygon** tool.

5 Change the **Points** slider to 5 in the Create Polygon category of the Properties panel.

6 Change the **Inner Depth** slider to 50%.

7 Change the **Twirl Angle** slider to 10%.

8 In the artboard, drag to draw a star shape.

When you release the mouse, the drawing appears in the artboard.

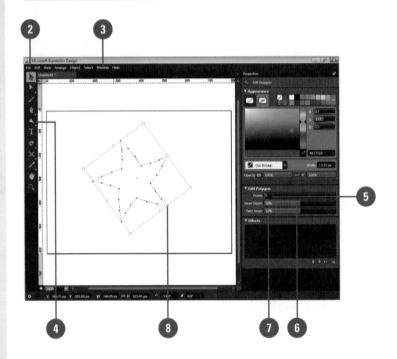

9 Click the **Selection** tool in the Toolbox.

10 Click the edge (the stroke or path) or a filled area of the object to select it.

11 With the object selected, you can perform any of the following:

- ◆ **Move.** Drag the edge of the object.

- ◆ **Resize.** Drag one of the corner resize handles. Hold down the Shift key to maintain proportion.

- ◆ **Rotate.** Point outside one of the corner resize handles to display a curved double arrow cursor, and the drag.

12 Click the **Fill** icon in the Appearance panel.

13 Click a color box or a point in the color spectrum. In the color spectrum, drag the black arrows to change the color range.

14 To fill the object with a gradient (fade from one color to another), image or none, click the option you want (next to the color boxes).

15 Click the **Stroke** icon in the Appearance panel, and then adjust the brush stroke and width:

- ◆ **Brush Stroke.** Click the **Brush Stroke** list arrow, and then select the stroke you want to apply from the gallery.

- ◆ **Brush Width.** Change the **Width** slider.

17 In the Object panel, specify options to apply color blending mode effects and fill rules to objects and joint, caps, and dashes to strokes.

18 Click the **File** menu, click **Save**, specify a name and location, and then click **Save**.

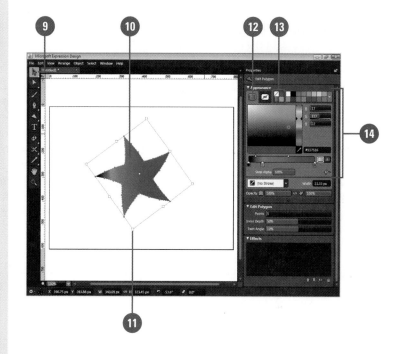

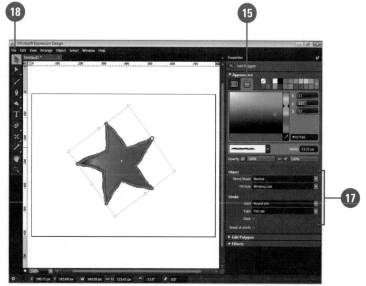

Exploring Expression Media

Expression Media is a professional asset management tool to visually catalog and organize all your digital assets—media items including graphics, camera RAW, videos, animations, sounds, desktop publishing, fonts, and text documents—for effortless retrieval and presentation. Before you can use Expression Media, you need to install Apple QuickTime 7.1.5 or later on your computer, which you can download for free at *www.apple.com/quicktime/download/*.

After you start Expression Media for the first time, a Welcome Screen appears (which you can access later on the Help menu),

requesting to creating a catalog with media from your Pictures folder or from a folder you choose. A **catalog** is a way to reference files on your computer or other storage device without moving them. You can select an option to import media now, or you can use the Import Items submenu on the File menu to import media from a variety of sources—including Files/Folders, Catalog File, Disc/Camera, or URL—later.

After you import your media, you can view your assets in several ways: Thumbnail, List, Media, and Light Table. Simply, use the View tabs or the toolbar for Light Table.

Toolbar View tabs Media information Search box

Panel Rotate and Zoom buttons Media window Status bar

Thumbnail view

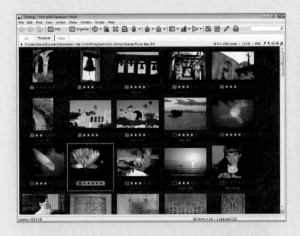

Media view

List view

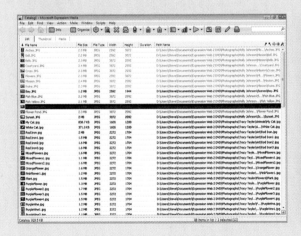

Light Table view

Managing Media with Expression Media

With Expression Media, you can organize, view, and sort your assets several different way depending your needs. You can assign and view your assets by color label, rating (1 to 5 stars), date, file type, event, author, or keyword. A **keyword** is a custom information label that a program or you create and attach to assets to make them easier to locate. For example, you can create a custom keyword called *Flower* and attach it to every media item that includes a flower. You can use buttons the toolbar at the top of the window and the Organize panel—accessible with the Organize button on the toolbar—to quickly and easily assign and view your assets.

Work with Assets in Expression Media

1. Click the **Start** button, point to **All Programs**, click **Microsoft Expression**, and then click **Expression Media**.

2. Open a catalog or import assets:

   ◆ **Open Catalog.** Click the **File** menu, and then click **Open Catalog**.

   ◆ **Import Assets.** Click the **File** menu, point to **Import Items**, and then select an import command.

3. To remove assets from your catalog and move it to the Recycle Bin, select the items, click the **Move to Recycle Bin** button on the toolbar, and then click **Move to Recycle Bin**.

4. Click the **Organize** button on the toolbar.

5. To add a keyword, click the **Add Term** button at the top of the Organize panel, click the **Field** list arrow, click **Keywords**, type a keyword, and then click **OK**.

6. Select the assets you want to assign with viewing attributes.

7. To assign attributes to the selected assets, drag the assets onto the attribute, such as a color label or keyword, in the Organize panel.

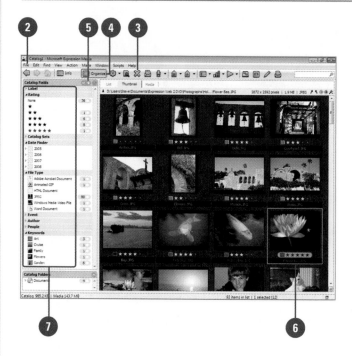

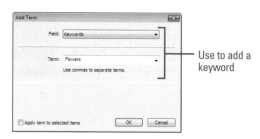

Use to add a keyword

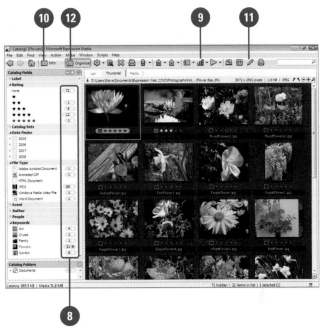

8 To quickly view only the assets in a viewing attribute, click the circle to the right of the attribute name next to the number of items in the Organize panel.

◆ To display all the assets, click the **Show All Items** on the toolbar.

9 To sort the assets in the Media window, click the **Sort** button on the toolbar, and then select a sort command; click Default to display the typical sort.

10 To set or change individual attributes, select the assets you want, click the **Info** button on the toolbar, and then add or change the information you want in an attribute. In some cases, you need to right-click an attribute to add, change, or delete it.

11 To edit an image, select the image, click the **Image Editor** button on the toolbar, click a filter option, click **Undo**, **Revert**, or **Save**. When you're done, click the **Close** button.

◆ To edit an image in another program, right-click the asset, point to **Open With**, and then select a program.

12 To work with slide shows, select the photos you want to use, and then use any of the following:

◆ **Options.** Click the **Make** menu, click **Slide Show Options**, set options, and then click **OK**.

◆ **Run.** Click the **Run Slide Show** button on the toolbar.

◆ **Save as QuickTime.** Click the **Make** menu, click **Save Slide Show as Movie**, set options, click **Make**, type a name, and then click **Save**.

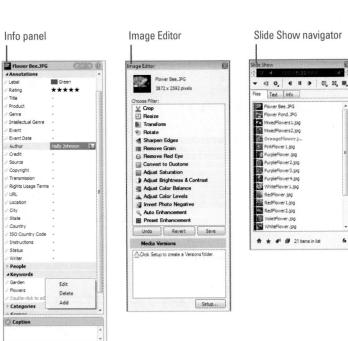

Info panel   Image Editor   Slide Show navigator

Exploring Expression Encoder

Microsoft Expression Encoder is a stand-alone (**New!**) video encoding—a process to compress/optimize for maximum quality—and live broadcasting program that helps you prepare and save video clips to the Web for playback using Microsoft Silverlight or Windows Media Player.

The Expression Encoder window provides four areas to work in: Viewer pane, Timeline and transport controls, Media Content panel, and Settings/Metadata/Output panels. The Viewer pane displays video images and allows you to zoom in and out. The timeline and transport controls allows you to manually control playback, add a leading or trailer video, view and adjust markers, and trim the video points. The Media Content panel lists imported videos along with the Video information bar, displays an activity log, and encodes your video to create a Silverlight application. The Settings panel provides options to modify encoding and video profiles, import and modify overlay images, and attach leaders and trailers. The Metadata panel provides options to add metadata information, import and edit scripts and markers. The Output panel provides options to create a Silverlight or Windows Media output file.

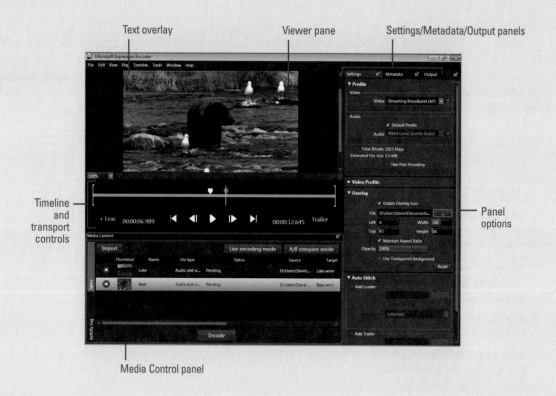

Text overlay

Viewer pane

Settings/Metadata/Output panels

Timeline and transport controls

Panel options

Media Control panel

Working with Expression Encoder

You start working with Expression Encoder (**New!**) by creating an encoding session, called a **job**. A job is a collection of one or more videos or audios that you can modify—add markers, trim, add overlays, or attach a leader or trailer—and save as a file to create the output you want. A job file consists of an XML description of the job settings and references to the imported source media. After you complete your job changes, you need to set encoding options, known as **profiles**, for each video in the job. You can create your own profile (PRX), or use a default profile provided by Expression Encoder. When your profiles are all set, you can encode your job with one of the built-in Silverlight templates (created in Expression Blend), which provide graphically rich skins and interactivity, or as a high-quality Windows Media video (WMV) file. As an additional option, you can also encode live media that you can stream over the Web using Live Encoding mode.

Use Expression Encoder

1. Click the **Start** button, point to **All Programs**, click **Microsoft Expression**, and then click **Expression Encoder**.

2. Click the **Import** button in the Media Content panel to start a new job file or click the **File** menu, and then click **Open Job** to use an existing job file.

3. Click the **Settings** tab, select an encoding and video profile, and then select an overlay file and add a leader or trailer (both optional).

4. Click the **Metadata** tab, and then enter metadata information and make any adjustments to markers.

5. To encode with Silverlight, click the **Output** tab, click the **Template** list arrow, select a template, and then select any other job output options; skip this step to encode as a WMV file.

6. Click the **Encode** button in the Media Content panel for all items, or right-click a video, and then click **Encode Selected Item**.

7. Click the **File** menu, and then click **Save**. For a new job file, specify a name, and then click **Save**.

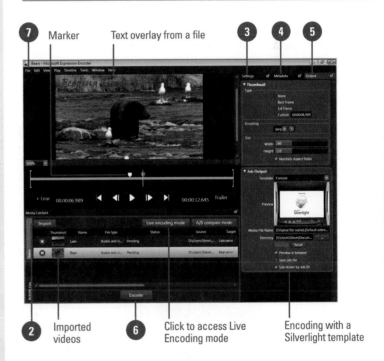

Marker   Text overlay from a file

Imported videos

Click to access Live Encoding mode

Encoding with a Silverlight template

Exploring Expression Blend

Expression Blend is a professional design tool to create engaging, interactive, Web-connected user experiences. With Expression Blend 2 (New!), you can create or modify a Windows Presentation Foundation (WPF) or Silverlight .NET based media application. You can insert a Silverlight application into a Web page with Expression Web and display it in a Web browser with the Microsoft Silverlight cross-browser, cross-platform plug-in.

When you create an application, known as a **project**, in Expression Blend, the program generates XAML code (in the background), which is a declarative markup language used by the Silverlight browser plug-in. XAML is similar to HTML, yet more powerful and extensible.

Expression Blend uses three views: Design, XAML, and Split. Design view, also known as the **artboard**, is where you visually create your project. XAML view is where Blend generates XAML code based on what you create in Design view. If you have some experience with XAML code, you can make

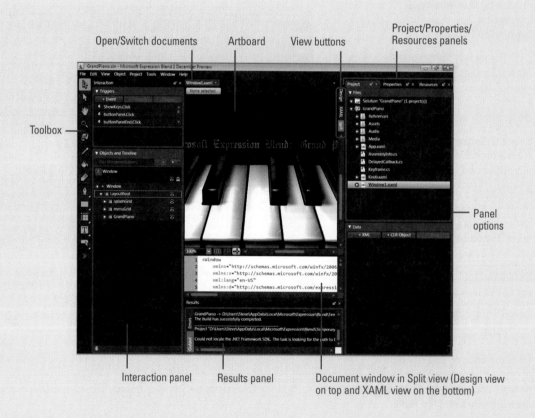

Open/Switch documents Artboard View buttons Project/Properties/Resources panels

Toolbox

Panel options

Interaction panel Results panel Document window in Split view (Design view on top and XAML view on the bottom)

adjustment directly in XAML view. Split view displays a split screen with Design view at the top and XAML view at the bottom.

When you create a new project in Expression Blend, the program creates a main canvas, also known as a page in Design view, in XAML, which is designed to contain position shapes and controls. Every object you create is positioned within the main canvas, including other canvas objects. The main canvas and other canvas objects have individual properties, which you can change using the Properties panel and the Object and Timeline Inspector within the Interaction panel.

After you finish creating your project in Expression Blend, you can test it to see how it works. As you test your project, you can use the Results panel—available using the Window menu—to see if there are any errors that you need to debug and fix. If you like what you see, you can build it for insertion in a Web page using Expression Web.

Project Solution

Working with Expression Blend

You can start working with Expression Blend 2 (**New!**) by opening an existing project or creating a new one. You use the tools in Toolbox to select an object, draw with a paintbrush (create bitmapped graphics), draw with a pen (create vector graphics), create shapes, add text, add fill and gradient effects, and use color and other attributes in different places. A tool icon with a small triangle in the lower-right corner represents a tool group, which means there are more tools available; click and hold to access them. After you create an object, you can use the Properties panel to modify it.

Create a New Silverlight Project with Expression Blend

1. Click the **Start** button, point to **All Programs**, click **Microsoft Expression**, click **Expression Design 2**, and then click **Close** to the Welcome Screen, if necessary.

2. Click the **File** menu, and then click **New Project**.

3. Click the **Silverlight 1.0 Site** icon, and then specify a name and location.

4. Click **OK**.

   A new blank project appears within the Document window.

5. Click **Page** in the Objects and Timeline pane.

6. Click the **Properties** tab.

7. Click the **Solid Color Brush** tab, and then select a color from the color spectrum to change the background.

   TIMESAVER If you can't find a property in the Properties panel, you can use the Search box at the top to help you locate it.

See Also

See "Working with Silverlight Media" on page 162 for information on Microsoft Silverlight.

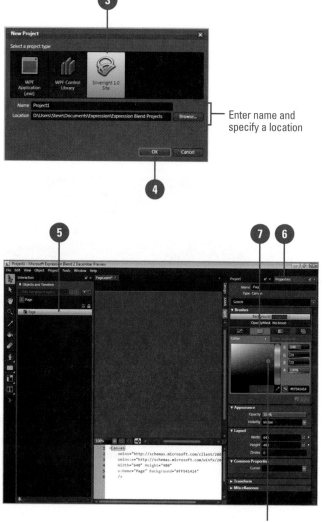

Enter name and specify a location

Select a color in the color spectrum

8 Click the **Rectangle** tool in the Toolbox.

A [Rectangle] object appears in the Objects and Timeline pane.

9 Drag a rectangle in the artboard to the size you want, and then drag a control point to round the corners.

The rectangle is selected, along with the Fill button in the Brushes pane.

10 Click the **Gradient Brush** tab.

A blank to white gradient appears.

11 Click the **Stroke** button in the Brushes pane.

12 Change the **StrokeThickness** to make the rectangle edge thicker.

13 Click the **TextBlock** tool in the Toolbox, and then drag a text box in the artboard.

A [TextBlock] appears in the Objects and Timeline pane.

14 Click the **Selection** tool in the Toolbox, double-click the text in the textblock to select the text, change the font size, color, and style in the Text pane, and then type a name to change the text.

15 Hold down Ctrl, and the click the [Rectangle] and [TextBlock] items in the Objects and Timeline pane.

16 Click the **Object** menu, point to **Group Into**, and then click **Canvas**.

The objects appear under a new canvas.

17 Click the **Project** menu, and then click **Test Site** or press F5 to open the project in your browser.

18 Click the **File** menu, click **Save**, click the **File** menu, and then click **Close Site**.

Control point   Fill button

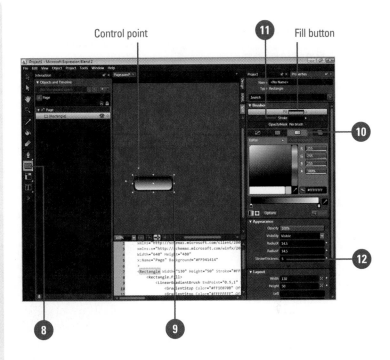

Text font color

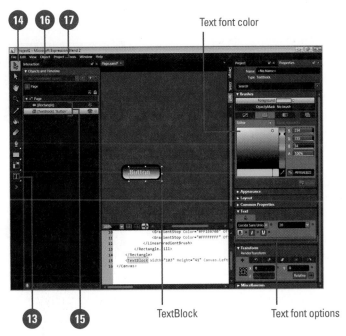

TextBlock   Text font options

Adding Interactivity with Expression Blend

After you create the user interface with Expression Blend 2 (**New!**) for your application, including buttons, menus, etc., you need to add interactivity and functionality, known as an event listener, or handler, to the individual objects to make them work. You attach an event handler to an object by adding XAML code to the canvas object. For example, when you attach the MouseEnter and MouseLeave events to a button object, the corresponding functions get executed when the mouse pointer enters or leaves the button object. You define these functions in the JavaScript file (for Silverlight 1.0), which you can access from the Project tab.

Add Interactivity with Expression Blend

1 In Expression Blend 2, click the **File** menu, point to **Open**, and then click **Site** to open the project you want to change.

2 To rename an object, click the object in the Object and Timeline pane to highlight it, type the name you want, and then press Enter.

3 Click the **XAML** or **Split** view button to display XAML code.

4 In XAML code view, enter the following event code as shown in the illustration:

```
<Canvas x:Name="Button"
MouseEnter="ButtonMouseEnter"
MouseLeave="ButtonMouseLeave"
.... >
```

◆ To display more of XAML view, click the **Window** menu, and then click each panel to hide them. After you finish, display them again.

5 Click the **Project** tab.

6 Double-click the **Page.xaml.js** file in the Files pane to open it.

7 Type the JavaScript code as shown in the illustration.

8 Click the **File** menu, click **Save**, click the **File** menu, and then click **Close Site**.

Panels hidden using Window menu

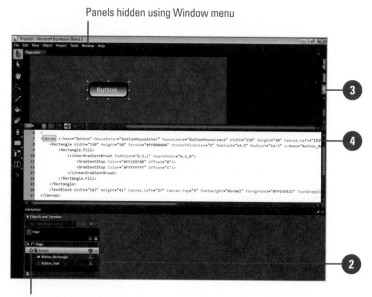

Grouped and expanded

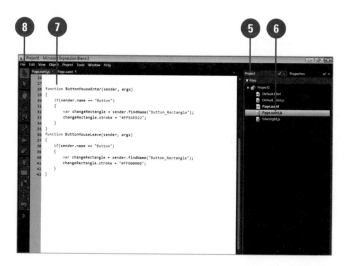

New! Features

Microsoft Expression Web 2

Microsoft Expression Web 2 means superior results faster with new features and enhancements that help you create and manage your images more easily and efficiently. The new and improved features help graphic web designers and photographers create the highest quality images with the control, flexibility, and capabilities that you expect from the professional standards in desktop digital imaging.

Only New Features

If you're already familiar with Expression Web you can access and download all the tasks in this book with Microsoft Expression Web 2 New Features to help make your transition to the new version simple and smooth. The Expression Web 2 New Features as well as other Microsoft Expression Web to Expression Web 2 transition helpers are available on the web at *www.perspection.com.*

What's New

If you're searching for what's new in Expression Web 2, just look for the icon: New!. The new icon appears in the table of contents and throughout this book so you can quickly and easily identify a new or improved feature in Expression Web 2. The following is a brief description of each new feature and it's location in this book.

Expression Web 2

- **.NET Framework 3.5 (p. 2, 317)** Install .NET Framework 3.5 (updated version) available for download at— *www.microsoft.com*—to work with ASP.NET AJAX and DataPager and ListView ASP.NET controls.

- **Program window color scheme (p. 5)** View an updated gray color scheme for the program window that complements the look of other Microsoft Expression Studio programs.

- **Change window color scheme (p. 5, 356-357)** Apply your Windows color scheme to the Expression Web application interface instead of the new gray color scheme.

- **HTML file extension (p. 44-45)** Set a preference for the default HTML file extension to .html or htm.

- **Byte Order Mark (p. 44-45, 54-55, 364-365)** Byte order mark (BOM) encoding options that you can set according to file extension, and that work across all of your Web sites.

- **Create PHP pages (p. 75, 321-325)** Create PHP pages, insert PHP code snippets, using PHP includes, and use IntelliSense to auto complete PHP code.

- **Import Photoshop files (p. 120-121)** Import a Photoshop PSD file into a page and selecting which Photoshop layers to include and which to exclude from the optimized image. Start Adobe Photoshop directly from Expression Web to edit the original PSD file and then update it back in your Web site.

- **Insert Flash and Windows Media (p. 154-161, 164-167)** Insert Adobe Flash SWF movies and Windows Media files, and play other ActiveX controls.

- **Insert Silverlight applications (p. 162-163)** Inserting a Silverlight web application into a page. All you need to start is the XAML file, JavaScript files, and web page created by your Silverlight authoring program, such as the Microsoft Expression Blend 2.

- **CSS overflow (p. 292)** Display the CSS overflow property in Design view. Use the CSS overflow property to when the content is too large to fit in the containing element.

- **ASP.NET configuration file (p. 314)** Create an ASP.NET file used to configure .NET 2.0 or 3.5 web application settings in the New dialog box for ASP.NET pages.

- **Insert ASP.NET AJAX controls (p. 315-318)** Insert ASP.NET AJAX controls, which provide more response to user actions through partial-page updates (for faster page refreshes) and status information without writing scripts. Use the following controls: UpdatePanel, Timer, UpdateProgress, ScriptManager, and ScriptManagerProxy.

- **ASP.NET Data controls (p. 317)** Use two new ASP.NET Data controls: DataPager and ListView. The DataPager control allows you to display data as a sequence of pages and displays navigation controls for the ListView control. The ListView control allows you to bind data items provided by the data source and display them.

- **Custom ASP.NET controls (p. 319)** Use for ASP.NET custom controls created by other developers in a Web site's "\bin" folder.

- **Preview PHP locally (p. 321, 352-353)** Conveniently preview your PHP pages locally in the Expression Development Server without the need to configure IIS or Apache on Windows (similar to previewing ASP.NET pages).

- **PHP code formatting (p. 360-361)** Use color coding in Code view, formatting marks in Design view, and visual aids to help identify different components in PHP code.

- **CSS file-checking (p. 342-343)** Check internal and external CSS files for compatibility against a specified schema.

- **FTP publishing mode (p. 346-347, 359)**   Use the ability to set Passive or Active FTP modes in order to connect to a remote Web server.

- **Save FTP settings (p. 346-347)**   Set the option to save FTP username and password for easier connections to a remote Web server.

- **Microsoft Expression Encoder (p. 394-396)**   Expression Encoder is a stand-alone video encoding—a process to compress/optimize for maximum quality—and live broadcasting program that helps you prepare and save video clips to the Web for playback using Microsoft Silverlight or Windows Media Player.

- **Microsoft Expression Blend 2 (p. 397-400)**   Expression Blend 2 is an expanded version of the design tool that creates engaging, interactive, Web-connected user experiences as a Silverlight .NET based media application or Windows Presentation Foundation (WPF).

What Happened To . . .

- **Workgroup Properties**   Selecting workgroup properties are no longer part of the product. The Workgroup tab in file Properties and Page Properties dialog boxes are no longer available.

- **Workflow Reports**   Viewing and assigning workflow task assignments are no longer part of the product. The Workflow submenu under the Reports submenu on the Site menu is no longer available.

- **Document Check-In and Check-Out**   Selecting document check-in and check-out properties are no longer part of the product. The check-in and check-out options on the General tab in the Site Settings dialog box, and the Check Check Out and Check In commands on the Edit menu are no longer available.

- **Microsoft Script Editor**   Microsoft Script Editor is no longer part of the product. The Microsoft Script Editor command under the Macro submenu on the Tools menu and the Microsoft Script Editor button on the Code View toolbar are no longer available.

- **VJ# Programming Language**   The VJ# (Visual Java++) programming language option for the ASP.NET page in the New dialog box is no longer part of the product. The available programming languages for ASP.NET pages includes C# (C++) and VB (Visual Basic).

- **Database Connections**   The Database tab in the Site Settings dialog box, which configured database connections for use with older ASP pages (not ASP.NET) related to compatibility with FrontPage Database Results, is no longer part of the product.

Keyboard Shortcuts

Microsoft Expression Web 2

If a command on a menu includes a keyboard reference, known as a keyboard shortcut, to the right of the command name, you can perform the action by pressing and holding the first key, and then pressing the second key to perform the command quickly. In some cases, a keyboard shortcut uses three keys. Simply press and hold the first two keys, and then press the third key. Keyboard shortcuts provide an alternative to using the mouse and make it easy to perform repetitive commands.

Expression Web 2 Keyboard Shortcuts

Command	Shortcut
Manage Web Pages	
Run accessibility checker	F8
Create new Web page	CTRL+N
Open	CTRL+O
Close	CTRL+F4
Save	CTRL+S
Print	CTRL+P
Refresh Web page; Folder List	F5
Switch between open Web pages	CTRL+TAB
Preview Web page in Web browser	CTRL+SHIFT+B
Quit Microsoft Expression Web Designer	ALT+F4
Display nonprinting characters	CTRL+SHIFT+8
Display HTML tags in Design view	CTRL+/
Find text or HTML on a Web page	CTRL+F
Replace text or HTML on a Web page	CTRL+H
Check spelling	F7
Thesaurus	SHIFT+F7

Keyboard Shortcuts *(continued)*

Command	Shortcut
Cancel	ESC
Undo	CTRL+Z or SHIFT+ALT+BACKSPACE
Redo or repeat	CTRL+Y or SHIFT+ALT+BACKSPACE
Delete	DELETE
Move up one level	BACKSPACE
Views	
Preview	F12
Move between Code, Design and Split	CTRL+PAGE DOWN or CTRL+PAGE UP
Move between Code and Design panes in Split view	ALT+PAGE DOWN or ALT+PAGE UP
Show or hide Folder list	ALT+F1
Move through hyperlink nodes in Hyperlinks view	UP, DOWN, LEFT or RIGHT ARROW
Expand current node and move to right	SHIFT+RIGHT ARROW
Expand current node and move to left	SHIFT+LEFT ARROW
Coding	
Quick tag editor	CTRL+Q
Insert temporary bookmark	CTRL+F2
Next temporary bookmark	F2
Previous temporary bookmark	SHIFT+F2
Go to line	CTRL+G
AutoComplete	CTRL+L
Insert coding snippet	CTRL+ENTER
Insert end tag	CTRL+>
Insert start tag	CTRL+<
Insert HTML comment	CTRL+/
Complete word	CTRL+SPACEBAR
Increase indent	TAB
Decrease indent	SHIFT+TAB
Select tag	CTRL+:
Find matching tag	CTRL+;

Keyboard Shortcuts *(continued)*

Command	Shortcut
Select block	CTRL+'
Find matching brace	CTRL+]
Insert start tag	CTRL+,
Insert end tag	CTRL+.
Follow code hyperlink	CTRL+[
Previous code hyperlink	ALT+LEFT ARROW
Next code hyperlink	ALT+RIGHT ARROW
Format text and paragraphs	
Change font	CTRL+SHIFT+F
Change font size	CTRL+SHIFT+P
Bold	CTRL+B
Underline	CTRL+U
Italic	CTRL+I
In More Colors, activate color picker NOTE: SHIFT+TAB should activate, in order: Cancel, OK, Select, Custom Value, and then the color picker	SHIFT+TAB
Use color picker	LEFT, RIGHT, BACK or FORWARD ARROW KEY
Superscript	CTRL+PLUS SIGN
Subscript	CTRL+MINUS SIGN
Copy formatting	CTRL+SHIFT+C
Paste formatting	CTRL+SHIFT+V
Remove manual formatting	CTRL+SHIFT+Z or CTRL+SPACEBAR
Center	CTRL+E
Left align	CTRL+L
Right align	CTRL+R
Left indent	CTRL+M
Right indent	CTRL+SHIFT+M
Apply style	CTRL+SHIFT+S
Apply normal style	CTRL+SHIFT+N
Apply Heading 1 style	CTRL+ALT+1
Apply Heading 2 style	CTRL+ALT+2

Keyboard Shortcuts *(continued)*

Command	Shortcut
Apply Heading 3 style	CTRL+ALT+3
Apply Heading 4 style	CTRL+ALT+4
Apply Heading 5 style	CTRL+ALT+5
Apply Heading 6 style	CTRL+ALT+6
Apply List style	CTRL+SHIFT+L
Edit and move text and graphics	
Delete one character to left	BACKSPACE
Delete one character to right	DELETE
Delete one word to left	CTRL+BACKSPACE
Delete one word to right	CTRL+DELETE
Copy text or graphics	CTRL+C or CTRL+INSERT
Paste Clipboard contents	CTRL+V or SHIFT+INSERT
Insert line break	SHIFT+ENTER
Insert nonbreaking space	CTRL+SHIFT+SPACEBAR
Select text and graphics	
Move one character to right	SHIFT+RIGHT ARROW
Move one character to left	SHIFT+LEFT ARROW
Go to end of word	CTRL+SHIFT+RIGHT ARROW
Go to beginning of word	CTRL+SHIFT+LEFT ARROW
Go to end of line	SHIFT+END
Go to beginning of line	SHIFT+HOME
Move one line up	SHIFT+UP ARROW
Move one line down	SHIFT+DOWN ARROW
Go to end of paragraph	CTRL+SHIFT+DOWN ARROW
Go to beginning of paragraph	CTRL+SHIFT+UP ARROW
Move one screen down	SHIFT+PAGE DOWN
Move one screen up	SHIFT+PAGE UP
Select entire page	CTRL+A
Display properties of selection	ALT+ENTER
Work with tables, graphics and hyperlinks	
Insert table	SHIFT+CTRL+ALT+T
Select next table cell's content	SHIFT+TAB

Keyboard Shortcuts *(continued)*

Command	Shortcut
Select preceding table cell's content	SHIFT+TAB
Extend a selection to adjacent cells in a row	Hold SHIFT and press LEFT or RIGHT ARROW repeatedly
Select a column from top or bottom	Hold SHIFT and press UP or DOWN ARROW repeatedly
With graphic selected, create auto thumbnail	CTRL+T
Create hyperlink on Web page	CTRL+K
Help task pane	
Display Help task pane	F1
Switch between Help task pane and active application	F6
Select next item	TAB
Select previous item	SHIFT+TAB
Perform action for selected item	ENTER
In Table of Contents, select next and previous item	DOWN ARROW or UP ARROW
In Table of Contents, expand and collapse selected item	RIGHT ARROW or LEFT ARROW
Move to previous task pane	ALT+LEFT ARROW
Move to next task pane	ALT+RIGHT ARROW
Open menu of pane options	CTRL+SPACEBAR
Close and reopen current task pane	CTRL+F1
Expand a +/_ list	RIGHT ARROW
Collapse a +/_ list	LEFT ARROW
Help window	
Select next hidden text or hyperlink, or Show All or Hide All	TAB
Perform action for selected Show All, Hide All, hidden text or hyperlink	ENTER
Move to previous Help topic	ALT+LEFT ARROW
Move to next Help topic	ALT+RIGHT ARROW
Print current Help topic	CTRL+P
Scroll small amounts up and down	UP ARROW or DOWN ARROW
Scroll larger amounts up and down	PAGE UP or PAGE DOWN
Connect or separate Help window from application	ALT+U
Display menu of commands in active Help window	SHIFT+F10

Index

F

feedback forms, 257

fields. *See* forms

File command, 115

file formats. *See also* specific types

different format, saving Web page in, 74

supported formats, list of, 75

files. *See* file formats; folders and files

Fill Color button, 238

Fill Down command, 223

Fill Right command, 223

Find and Replace dialog box, 102-105

Find task pane, 102-105

finding/replacing

code, 102-103

HTML tags, 104-105

query, saving search as, 105

text, 102-103

FireFox, Mozilla

version checking, 204

work with Silverlight, 162

fixed positioning, 305

fixed-width fonts, 114

Flash. *See* Adobe

flipping graphics, 133

floating properties, 305

Folder list, 10. *See also* importing/exporting

graphics, inserting, 120-121

opening Web page with, 47

publishing individual files in, 349

Folder List task pane, 8

folders and files, 10. *See also* file formats; forms; templates;

copying files, 12

deleting files, 12

determining contents of, 10

graphics from files, inserting, 120

hidden files, tracking, 24

hyperlinks to files, creating, 174-175

importing Web content from, 34

metadata, tracking with, 24

moving files, 12

new folders, creating, 51

renaming

files, 12

Web folder, 40

text from file, inserting, 115

Folders view, 14

opening Web pages in, 46

publishing individual files in, 349

Font dialog box, 99

Font menu, 375

fonts

Change Property behavior, 206

changing, 98-99

colors

more colors, adding, 101

selecting, 98

default fonts, changing, 114

displaying fonts in Font menu, 375

effects, adding, 100

for interactive buttons, 190

for Jump Menu, 199

size, changing, 98-99

Footer template, 243-244

footers. *See* headers and footers

Footnotes template, 243-244

Form Controls, 258

form handlers

overview, 282-283

saving results to, 278-279

formatting. *See also* CSS (Cascading Style Sheets)

bulleted/numbered lists, 92

graphics formats, changing, 148-149

setting Design View options, 365

showing/hiding marks, 82

tables, 236-237

text, 98-99

Web page formatting, setting, 54

XML formatting, applying, 332-333

forms, 257. *See also* registration forms

advanced buttons in forms, 261, 270-271

buttons, inserting, 270-271

check boxes in, 261, 269

confirmation page, custom, 275

creating, 258-259

custom form handler, results to, 278-279

customizing options, 360

database, saving results to, 280-281

deleting forms or fields, 259

discussion form handler, creating, 279

drop-down boxes in, 261, 266

e-mail, sending results as, 276-277

fields

Safari®
BOOKS ONLINE
ENABLED

THIS BOOK IS SAFARI ENABLED

INCLUDES FREE 45-DAY ACCESS TO THE ONLINE EDITION

The Safari® Enabled icon on the cover of your favorite technology book means the book is available through Safari Bookshelf. When you buy this book, you get free access to the online edition for 45 days.

Safari Bookshelf is an electronic reference library that lets you easily search thousands of technical books, find code samples, download chapters, and access technical information whenever and wherever you need it.

TO GAIN 45-DAY SAFARI ENABLED ACCESS TO THIS BOOK:

- Go to **informit.com/safarienabled**

- Complete the brief registration form

- Enter the coupon code found in the front of this book on the "Copyright" page